ON THE MOVE

ON THE MOVE

Changing Mechanisms of Mexico-U.S. Migration

Filiz Garip

PRINCETON UNIVERSITY PRESS

Princeton and Oxford

Published by Princeton University Press, 41 William Street, Princeton, New Jersey 08540
In the United Kingdom: Princeton University Press, 6 Oxford Street, Woodstock, Oxfordshire
   OX20 1TR

press.princeton.edu

Cover photograph courtesy of Patricia Martín

First paperback printing, 2019
Paperback ISBN 978-0-691-19188-1
Cloth ISBN 978-0-691-16106-8

British Library Cataloging-in-Publication Data is available

This book has been composed in Janson Text LT Std

Printed on acid-free paper. ∞

Printed in the United States of America

To Rukiye, Remzi,
Aylin, and Mert

Contents

———

List of Illustrations

List of Tables

Acknowledgments

I could not have written this book without the help and support of my family, friends, and colleagues. The initial idea for the book came out of a conversation with my husband, Mert, over our kitchen table. We were talking about statistics (of all the topics out there) and how the specific applications varied across fields. Mert explained to me how classification tools were the key in his field of electrical engineering. And it was then that I thought it would be interesting to see if one could use these tools to identify different groups among migrants.

Mert not only gave me the initial insight, but also fully supported me through all the ups and downs of the project. For two years, he worked hard to create extra time for me, taking our children, Leyla and Deniz, on various excursions so that I could write freely for a few more hours on the weekends. During the last six months of writing, the most painful period by far, he sat across from me at the Gutman library every day. It is thanks to his presence that I could concentrate and continue to write despite my desperation at times.

For nearly four years, this book occupied a large space not just in my life, but also in the lives of my parents, Remzi and Rukiye, my sister, Aylin, my parents-in-law, Mustafa and Maggie, and my brother-in-law, Metin. They never tired of hearing my ramblings about the various analyses I was trying to complete or the paragraphs I was trying to work out. I am grateful to them for listening and not saying "enough already." I am also thankful to my dear friend Teresa Gelardo for setting strict deadlines for me and sending not-so-gentle reminders.

The data for the project come from the decades of work done by the Mexican Migration Project (MMP) team led by Doug Massey and Jorge Durand. It is to this team that I turned when I needed to collect qualitative data in Mexico. Doug and Jorge were incredibly generous in helping me gather a fantastic research team in Mexico, select communities for fieldwork, and figure out all the logistics. Helen Marrow and Jackie Hagan provided several ideas that shaped the data collection strategy. My research team included Anabel Flores, Bárbara Gómez, Yonathan Lizalde, Gabriela López, Leonardo Trujillo, and Karina Velasco—all members of the MMP family. Karina Sayrols, Marcela Casillas, and Paola Mora later helped with the translations. I am thankful to all of them for their hard work, but especially to Karina (santa de los perros) who masterfully organized our days, kept us to our schedule, and even cooked chicken soup for me when I got sick. I am also grateful to Gabriela, who turned out to be a natural at interviewing people, and continued to collect data for us even after the initial fieldwork ended. My dear friend, and brilliant artist, Patricia Martín-Sánchez, was my right hand during fieldwork, translating all conversations from Spanish to English, and shooting the stunning photographs that grace the pages of the book. She was also there long before the fieldwork started, reading and translating the Mexican literature on migration and acting as a sounding board for my preliminary ideas.

Doug Massey, who was an advisor on my dissertation, has given me unconditional support from the first day that he heard about this project. When a paper from the project was rejected by a journal, and when I was ready to give up on the idea, Doug told me the paper was good and that I should continue to work on it. I trusted his judgment more than I trusted mine. And I continued to work on it. Mary Waters, my dear colleague at Harvard, also played a similarly crucial role, giving me support, encouragement, and much needed feedback through the years. She also had the great idea of organizing a book conference where I would invite experts in the field to come to Harvard and to read my manuscript. It was hard to believe that people would agree to do that, but they did. Frank Bean, Katharine Donato, David FitzGerald, Peggy Levitt, and Roger Waldinger traveled from all over the country to Cambridge in the dead of winter to lend me their wisdom. The book improved immensely thanks to their feedback and also to feedback from Asad L. Asad and Mao-Mei Liu, who were in attendance as well. I can never pay back their generosity, but I promise to at least try to pay forward to the next generation of scholars.

I shared earlier versions of this book with many colleagues. My former advisors from Princeton, Sara Curran, Paul DiMaggio, and Viviana Zelizer, were among the first to see the book proposal. Their immediate and glowing response gave me much-needed confidence. My editors at Princeton University Press, Eric Schwartz and Meagan Levinson, and editors of the Analytical Sociology series, Peter Bearman and Peter Hedström, also believed in the project, which helped me go on.

I presented versions of this book at seminars at Barnard, Brown, Columbia, Cornell, Duke, Max Planck Institute, Michigan, MIT, Oxford, Princeton, Stanford, University of Washington, UMass–Amherst, UCLA,

Project team in Mexico (from left to right): Bárbara, Patricia,
Gabriela, Karina, Filiz, Leo, Anabel, and Yonathan
PHOTO BY Patricia Martín

UCSD, and Yale. The comments and suggestions at these seminars were important in pushing the ideas forward.

Many conversations with my colleagues at Harvard—Mary Brinton, David Carrasco, Matt Desmond, Frank Dobbin, Kathy Edin, Maggie Frye, Sandy Jencks, Gary King, Michèle Lamont, Stanley Lieberson, Peter Marsden, Devah Pager, Orlando Patterson, Rob Sampson, Judy Singer, Jocelyn Viterna, Bill Wilson, Chris Winship, Marty Whyte, and Bruce Western— helped me tease out my ideas and see the project from new angles. Intense writing sessions with my colleague (and one of my favorite writers) Mario Small improved the ideas and exposition immensely. Contributions by the students, Asad L. Asad and Yvette Ramirez in particular, allowed me to complete (and make sense of) the analysis of the qualitative data. Funding from the Weatherhead Center for International Affairs (for much-needed leave time that allowed me to focus fully on research, for fieldwork in Mexico, and for the book conference) and the David Rockefeller Center for Latin American Studies (for fieldwork and the book conference) enabled me to bring the project to fruition. Help from Jeff Blossom at the Center for Geographic Analysis was important in producing the spatial analysis in the book. The office space provided by Kathy Edin and Bruce Western at the Malcolm Wiener Center for Social Policy helped me avoid distractions and concentrate on the book during my sabbatical year. Barbara Whalen was most gracious as a host during my time there. I especially thank her for helping me get an appointment with Felipe Calderón, the former president of Mexico, during his stay at the Harvard Kennedy School. And I am most grateful to the president for making the time to meet with me.

I never thought I could write a book. The fact that I did is a testament to a large community of scholars, friends, and family members that stood behind me. I am eternally grateful to them and to the readers, who will surely bring their own wisdom to interpret, confirm, or challenge the story I present.

ON THE MOVE

INTRODUCTION

Goodbye, my beloved country, now I am going away;
I go to the United States, where I intend to work.
...
I go sad and heavy-hearted to suffer and endure;
My mother Guadalupe, grant my safe return.
—*Lyrics from a Mexican song of farewell*

The Basilica of San Juan de los Lagos is the main attraction in San Juan, a small town situated in a shallow valley surrounded the rolling hills of the Los Altos region of Jalisco in western Mexico. Its pink sandstone façade greets millions of pilgrims every year who come to visit a small image of the Virgin Mary, known as the Virgin of San Juan. According to the legend, the Virgin cured a little girl who fell gravely ill in 1623, and since then, has been venerated for cases involving life-threatening danger.

In a special chamber of the Basilica, there are thousands of votive objects left by pilgrims to offer thanks to the Virgin. Among those objects, one finds many *retablos*, colorful paintings on sheets of tin. Each *retablo* tells the story of a miracle, a dangerous event from which the pilgrim was delivered by divine intervention.

One of these paintings shows a river running wild and two men drifting in it. There is a stone bridge in the distance but no one on it. One of the men is waving his hands desperately in a plea for help and the other is swimming toward him. A brief text describes the scene. It is May 28, 1929, and the river is the Rio Grande near El Paso, Texas. The drowning man is Domingo Segura, a Mexican migrant trying to enter the United States. His friend pulls him out of the water in a narrow escape from death. This painting is Domingo's demonstration of thanks to the Virgin, his favorite icon.

Another painting shows four men in a desert under a searing sun. There are snow-capped peaks in the distance. One man is sitting down, apparently exhausted, and another next to him is standing with a blank stare fixed on the ground. Both are holding empty water jugs. On their left, two other men are looking at the sky, praying to an apparition of the Virgin. The text tells us that it is June 5, 1986, and the four men are migrants on their way to the United States. They run out of water in the middle of the desert, and although on the brink of dehydration, they manage to reach their final destination. One of the migrants, Braulio Barrientos, commissions the painting in gratitude to the Virgin.

Not all migrants are as lucky as Domingo or Braulio. About 500 migrants die every year by drowning, exposure to heat, or other causes while attempting to cross the border without documents. Yet, the Mexican-born population in the country stood at a staggering 12 million in 2011, about half of whom were thought to be undocumented. Who are these migrants? What brings them to the United States in such great numbers?

There is no single answer to these questions. Both Mexico and the United States are dynamic societies that have changed profoundly over time, as have the migrants moving between them. Consider the following figures. In the 1970s, about 72% of Mexicans crossing the border were men. By the early 1990s, the share of men had dropped to 64%. Although the migrant flow seemed destined to reach gender parity, the share of men quickly climbed back to 70% in the late 1990s.

The migrant stream changed in its geographic origins as well. In the 1970s, more than half of migrants came from just five states in central-western Mexico: Guanajuato, Jalisco, Michoacán, San Luis Potosí, and Zacatecas. In the mid-1990s, the share of migrants from these traditional migrant-sending regions dropped to less than a third. Migrants from interior urban areas, like Mexico City, or border cities, like Tijuana, began to join the persistent stream from rural communities in the central west.

Over time, the migrant flow became more diverse not only in its origins, but also in its destinations and settlement patterns in the United States. The once popular destinations of California, Texas, and Illinois began to give way to new places like Arizona, North Carolina, and Pennsylvania. Mexican migrants also began to shift from a sojourner to a settler strategy. In a nationally representative survey of Mexico, the share of migrants who identified the United States as their primary place of residence doubled, from 20% in the 1970s to almost 40% in 1990.

THE QUESTION

This book is about Mexico-U.S. migration flows between 1965 and 2010. I seek to characterize and explain the diversity in the Mexican migrant stream, which, in this period, changed remarkably not only in its composition and origins in Mexico, but also in its destinations and settlement patterns in the United States.

Much has been written on this topic and in multiple disciplines. But, in the vast outpouring of texts, a few key ideas emerge. Most social scientists have tried to explain who migrates in one of three ways: by reference to individual desires to maximize income, to family strategies to diversify risks to income, and to social ties to migrants already in destination.

In the early 1970s, the first of these ideas was prominent. Economists viewed migration just as they did any other behavior: as a choice by rational actors seeking to maximize utility. Migration decisions, from this perspective, were nothing but an optimization problem. Some of the inspiration at the time came from the attention given in the field to "human capital," that is, individual skills and knowledge. Migration was a way for individuals to obtain better return on their human capital. Individuals did that by evaluating their skills—or, more specifically, what those skills were worth in their own country as compared to another. Individuals also considered the potential costs of migrating, which could include anything from the psychological costs of family separation to the financial costs of completing the trip. Migrants were those individuals for whom the benefits exceeded the costs, or, those who were able to maximize their expected income by migrating. This simple model stripped migration to its bare essentials and predicted the direction of migration flows on a regional scale. Given the vast differences in wages between the two societies, for example, it was no surprise that many Mexicans chose to migrate to the United States.

By the early 1980s, sociologists and anthropologists had amassed considerable evidence questioning this individualistic model of migration. Case studies revealed how the family was the key unit in which migration decisions were discussed, contested, and finalized. These ideas began to find traction in economics. The inspiration for their mathematical formulation, however, came from an unlikely place: the risk diversification models in finance. The family, as a decision-making unit, was categorically different from the individual as it had multiple members. It could place its eggs in different baskets, so to speak. Similar to an investor buying different types of assets, a family could allocate its members in different sectors of the economy to diversify potential risks to its earnings. This strategy was critical to family survival in developing countries, such as Mexico, where the risks were abundant, but the formal market mechanisms to manage them were still insufficient. The risk diversification model began to catch on in the late 1980s, its empirical predictions confirmed in many empirical studies. But this model hardly replaced the existing income maximization paradigm, which has retained its strong foothold to this day.

Both economic models left out the social ties that connected migrants to those they left behind. Anthropologists, sociologists, and geographers had long written about "chain migration," a process by which a migrant pulls other migrants to his or her destination, and those migrants in turn pull other migrants, and so on. Sociologists began to delve into the potential mechanisms underlying this process. Some argued that social ties provide useful resources, like information about crossing a border or help in finding a job in destinations that made migration easier for others. Others suggested that social ties eventually become purveyors of norms that dictate migration as a rite of passage for young adults. These ideas culminated in the more general cumulative causation model that viewed past migration as the main catalyst for future moves. This model was inspired by economist Gunnar Myrdal's similar ideas on development, specifically, that development begets more development. In this model, past migration not only created an expanding web of social ties to migrants in destination, but it also shifted distributions of income, wealth, and skills in the place of origin. These changes, in turn, created additional pressures for migration.

Other explanations have also been put forth to explain migration flows on a grander scale. Some argued that migration resulted from a dual labor market structure in advanced capitalist societies, where natives filled the high-paying jobs in the capital-intensive sector and left low-paying, labor-intensive work to immigrants. Others saw migration as an inevitable consequence of a world system, where capitalism expanded from the more advanced "core" countries, like the United States, to developing "periphery" nations, causing disruptions in the latter. These disruptions typically undermined local institutions, like the agricultural sector, and created incentives for more migration.

One could ask which of these ideas is most applicable to the Mexico—U.S. migration; indeed, many studies have done just that by pitting different models against one another. But that is not my goal here. Instead, I view all explanations as equally plausible, and ask *when* and *for whom* each one might be most relevant.

THE ARGUMENT

Mexican migrants to the United States are a diverse population. But this diversity gets lost in scholarly work and in the popular press. All too often, our attention is grabbed by how many Mexicans enter the country each year, or by how well they fare along group-level characteristics like education from year to year. But, looking more closely, one can see quite a bit of variation in the migrant population: there are men and women, adults and children, those with no education and those with higher degrees, and those from tiny rural villages and those from bustling cities. How do we make sense of this diversity? First, we need to make it the focus of our inquiry.

As social scientists, we search for general patterns and trends. We often identify these patterns by taking a typical case and generalizing its attributes to the entire population. This strategy works well in the hard sciences, where the average case provides an accurate representation of its kind. If we take an iron rod, for example, and measure its ultimate strength—the load it can bear before breaking—we will know the strength of any other iron rod of similar specifications. But if we take a migrant, even the most typical migrant, and look at the conditions under which he or she decided to migrate, those conditions can be a lot different for other migrants in the population.

This inherent variability makes it difficult to arrive at universal explanations for migration behavior. Most social scientists today find it futile to search for such explanations, but many empirical studies still present just that. There are two root causes for this apparent disconnection. First, we rely on methods that are good at describing the average case but not at characterizing the variation across cases. I mean here the methods for analyzing large-scale survey data. Second, we evaluate competing theories based on their predictive power, or their ability to explain events (if only in retrospect). This reflects a specific epistemological orientation, one that is adapted from classical physics, and one that presumes simple cause-effect relationships that can be revealed in an experimental setting. This presumption rarely holds in the social sciences, where the cause-effect chains tend to be complex, and the data are only partial. Our choice of methods and epistemology together leads us to an analytic approach where we first characterize the average case, and then select among theories based on how well they can account for that case. We are pluralistic when it comes to embracing different theories but monistic when testing those theories with data.

Let us consider the seemingly simple question of who migrates. We often take large-scale survey data from a setting, compare migrants to non-migrants, and note the apparent differences. For example, an average migrant may be less educated than an average non-migrant or more likely to have family ties to other migrants. We then connect these patterns to theories of migration. Many studies have linked the former pattern to the income maximization thesis and the latter to the cumulative causation idea. The logic runs as follows. Individuals with low education have little access to lucrative jobs in their local labor market, and they enjoy a higher premium to migrating internationally than their more educated peers do. Individuals in an origin place with migrant family members in destination places often find it easier to migrate for work, or more appealing to do so in order to reunite with family members. When seeing an average migrant who is both less educated than typical non-migrants and more connected to former migrants in our data, then, we would claim that both wage differences and social ties matter for migration behavior, and more importantly, that they matter for *all migrants* in the same way.

But one can imagine migrants with different characteristics and different motivations for moving to the United States. It is perfectly plausible that some individuals migrate mostly to earn more, while others migrate primarily to join their family or friends. It is possible that wage differences matter more for some groups of migrants, and social ties are more important to the mobility of others. When we look at an average migrant only, we dismiss such heterogeneity a priori.

This is the first, and central, thesis of the book: Mexicans may be on the move to the United States for a variety of reasons. The reasons underlying migration may depend on personal circumstances, as well as the larger economic, social, and political climates in both Mexico and the United States. Consider how the two countries changed over just a few decades. In 1965, the minimum hourly wage in Mexico stood at 32 cents (in 2010 U.S. dollars), and its ratio to average wage in the United States at 1 to 56. In 1990, the Mexican minimum wage had climbed to 67 cents, and its ratio to U.S. wage receded to 1 to 25. The wage increased in this period both in absolute and relative terms but not in a linear fashion. In the 1980s, the Mexican economy fluctuated extensively—and the wages with it—after the peso devaluations in 1976 and 1982. The inflation rate remained higher than 50% for most of the decade. The economy stabilized in the early 1990s but ended up plummeting to a crippling low with the peso devaluation in 1994.

In the same period, the United States also experienced major shifts, most significantly in its outlook on immigration. Its policy changed dramatically from actively recruiting short-term Mexican laborers in the 1960s to guarding its border with thermal imaging systems and aerial surveillance in the 1990s. This drastic shift occurred despite a prolonged growth in the U.S. economy, around 2% per year. Agriculture, a major sector for immigrant workers, contributed less to that growth over time, but that decline was more than offset by the drastic increases in the contributions from construction, another important line of work for immigrants. These changes surely affected who migrates from Mexico to the United States, and with what purpose.

This leads to the second thesis of this book: The different reasons underlying migration depend on individual interests, but these interests are shaped by the structural or cultural contexts these individuals inhabit, or seek to inhabit, by migrating. More generally, interests are inherent not just in individuals, but also in the context.

This is to say that different structural or cultural circumstances can mobilize different groups of migrants. These circumstances receive different degrees of emphasis from migration theories. While the income maximization thesis puts wage and employment differentials between the origin and destination contexts at the forefront, the cumulative causation idea underscores how social structure and cultural understandings encourage migration.

This brings us to the third, and final, thesis of this book: Different theories may be more or less relevant to explain migration behavior to the extent that the conditions they deem essential to the process are at work in a given place or period or for a specific group of individuals. The income maximization hypothesis may be more likely to be confirmed when wage differentials are high, and the cumulative causation argument may be most plausible when there is a critical mass of migrants from a region to act as social or cultural facilitators for future flows. In other words, there may be regional variation in the usefulness of each explanation as well as a temporal order.

ANALYTICS

This book follows an analytic strategy to describe such heterogeneity at work. It also seeks new ways of connecting evidence to theory, recognizing the former as only partial and the latter as conditional. In what follows, I briefly sketch the decisions that make up the skeleton of the book's analytical approach.

The argument, in its most general form, is that individuals may reach the same outcome, migration in our case, through different pathways. These pathways may be specific to the context, and may reflect the mechanisms identified in different theories.

How do we identify these pathways empirically? The book relies on multiple sources of data and multiple types of analysis. It begins by characterizing the diversity in the Mexican migrant population with data from the Mexican Migration Project (MMP), a binational data collection effort that has surveyed more than 145,000 individuals in 143 communities in Mexico between 1982 and 2013 and followed up with some of the migrants in the United States. The data include retrospective life, family, and community histories, and thus, contain extensive information on individuals crossing the border from 1965 and 2010. The data come mainly from migrant-heavy regions of Mexico, and though not representative of the population at large, provide an accurate profile of Mexican migrants to the United States.

The analysis starts by focusing on migrants alone, that is, 19,243 individuals who have made at least one trip to the United States in the study period. I re-construct the characteristics of each migrant during his or her first U.S. trip, that is, before U.S. migration can change the socioeconomic status of that migrant. I then search for different groups among migrants with cluster analysis. This computer-assisted method allows me to classify thousands of individuals across several dimensions, including personal, family, and community attributes.

I assume that individuals with similar configurations of attributes are likely to face similar opportunities or constraints. This assumption is often made implicitly, for example, when researchers study an outcome separately among men or women, high school or college graduates, people living in good or bad neighborhoods, and so on. The innovation here is this: I am not just looking at one attribute, like gender or education, to define a group, but I am also considering configurations of multiple attributes at the same time.

Once I identify different groups of migrants, I look at the contextual conditions that set apart each group from other migrant groups as well as from non-migrants. I use a wide array of macro-level indicators that capture the economic, demographic, social, and political circumstances in both Mexico and the United States over a period of nearly five decades. Using this historical information, I identify the specific conditions under which each migrant group proliferates. I then evaluate the emergent patterns—the apparent associations between attributes of migrants and their contexts—in light of different migration theories. My goal is to determine whether different theories are relevant for different groups of migrants, and if so, under what circumstances.

Finally, I look at the root of these observed associations with qualitative data from in-depth interviews conducted with 139 migrants, migrant-family members, and non-migrants in Mexico in 2011 and 2012. How do individuals and families think about migration? How do different individuals respond to different kinds of economic, social, or cultural stimuli related to migration? I analyze at close range the motivations migrants state for their decision to migrate (and the reasons non-migrants list for their decision not to). In so doing, I seek to uncover the mechanisms that give rise to the diversity in the migration process.

ROAD MAP

For ease of reading, I refrain from using citations or superscripts in the text; instead, I provide the references and extended descriptions at the end of the book. Throughout the book, I use "origin" as a shorthand to refer to the community or location a person is migrating from, and "destination" to refer to the place the migrant is headed to.

In chapter 1, I provide an overview of the migration field, and a brief review of Mexico-U.S. migration flows up to 1965, the year the analysis here begins. I then describe the data and methods that led me to discover four groups among first-time migrants from Mexico to the United States between 1965 and 2010. Each migrant group, I show, emerges in a specific time period. In the four chapters that follow, I take each migrant group in turn and describe the economic, social, and political circumstances related to its rise and fall. Because each group becomes prevalent in a particular era, by moving through the four groups in the four chapters, I also move through time and provide a roughly chronological account of the migration context between Mexico and the United States. In each chapter, I include individual stories of migrants, relying on their accounts to identify some general patterns about how individuals and families think about migration under different circumstances, and how they might be inspired or influenced by others around them.

I begin by orienting the reader to who the Mexican migrants are, and illuminating how their characteristics have changed, over the 45-year period from 1965 to 2010.

Chapter 1

WHY DO PEOPLE MIGRATE?

Identifying Diverse Mechanisms of Migration

FIGURE 1.1. Mexican migrants waiting to cross the U.S. border
PHOTO BY Patricia Martín

THREE STORIES

"I STUDIED hydraulic engineering," Jorge tells us. He finds little use for his degree these days in Buenavista, his small village in western Mexico. He has worked many jobs in his life: collecting cotton, driving a truck, fixing cars, and supervising a farm field. He is 38 now and feels too old to change careers one more time. "She tells me I am already an oldie," he jokes while pointing to his mother-in-law, who smiles in innocent agreement. Jorge already owns a house, one that is connected to his mother-in-law's through a large courtyard. He is now planning to open an auto repair shop in his village. "I have learned many crafts, like car painting and car repair . . . which is what we are going to do here," he says, "with God's help."

Mateo lives in the same village as Jorge but seems much less certain about what he wants to do in life. At age 20, he is already married with a toddler son. They all live with his father, Álvaro, who is a fisherman and the head of the Buenavista village. Álvaro talks about how Mateo's path has zigzagged until now. "He really wanted to study. . . . He was just beginning high school. He sent an application to the university in Guadalajara [for the technical high school program]. He wasn't admitted. . . . He doesn't have a diploma. . . . He liked construction work, but that did not work out either." Álvaro tried to encourage Mateo to learn different skills. "When he was little, I got him used to [working outdoors]. Maybe he is not a working professional, but he knows a lot about the fields." These skills helped Mateo land his current job: planting pine trees in the mountains.

Teresa is from San Marco, a town about 100 miles northeast of Buenavista with remarkable industrial activity and concomitant air pollution. She is the second of seven children in her family, tightly spaced between an older brother and five younger sisters. She finished middle school, and shortly thereafter, met her husband-to-be, Tomás, who was visiting the town. "She had a crush," her father remembers, which seemed certain to remain just that until Teresa decided to go where Tomás is. She is now 40, a happily married homemaker with two children.

Jorge, Mateo, and Teresa have little in common except that they were all migrants in the United States at some point in their lives. Jorge got into a fight with his parents over whether he should work or study, and, rather than seek resolution, chose to migrate to the United States with his uncle. He was 14 years old. Mateo was searching for work in his town when a recruiter approached him with an offer for a short-term work visa to go to Oregon. He borrowed money from his father for the trip, left his wife and son to his father's care, and took off. Teresa wanted to be with Tomás, a migrant in the United States, and left with some relatives headed there at the earliest opportunity.

"EVERY PERSON IS A DIFFERENT WORLD. THEY THINK DIFFERENTLY."

This is how a former migrant responded when we asked him, "Why do people migrate?" It is a simple but profound point, one that often gets sidelined in the ongoing debates on migration: Migrants in the United States are a diverse population. We can characterize this diversity in a number of ways. We can, for one, think of different generations of migrants. Given more than a century of migrant flows, there are now multiple generations of Mexicans living in the United States: those who were born in Mexico (first generation), those whose parents were born there (second), those whose grandparents (third) or great-grandparents (fourth) were of Mexican origin, and so on. The migrant experience varies across generations. The first generation often struggles to find work, to learn the language, to adjust to a new culture, and to obtain legal status. By the second generation, many of these issues get resolved, but some continue to leave an imprint. Many children of migrants are U.S. citizens by birth, for example but still work to mold a multicultural identity or to overcome their families' socioeconomic disadvantage.

We can also think of different cohorts of migrants, that is, groups entering the United States in particular historical periods, within each generation. The migrant experience varies across these cohorts too. Consider the first-generation Mexicans in the United States. The migrant cohort of the 1960s included mostly farmworkers (many on short-term work visas under the Bracero program, a temporary labor agreement between Mexico and the United States that ended in 1964). This cohort left a poor Mexico, whose gross domestic product (GDP) hovered around US$3,400 per capita (in constant 2005 values), and arrived to a relatively welcoming United States, where migrants were in heavy demand due to the labor shortages after World War II. The migrant cohort of the 1980s, many of them undocumented workers, faced dramatically different conditions. This cohort departed from a richer—though more volatile—Mexican economy, where the GDP reached US$7,200 (in 2005 values) per capita at one point, only to drop to about US$6,300 after the financial crisis in 1982. The cohort also encountered more restrictions to entry with increasing enforcement on the border. Migrant cohorts of the 1960s and 1980s, then, varied not only in composition, but also in the contexts of origin and reception.

We can, finally, think of different groups of migrants within each cohort (or across cohorts) for whom the circumstances surrounding migration vary. I mean mostly personal circumstances here. The three stories attest to this more elusive type of variability. The reasons Jorge describes for his move to the United States—a desire to study, a fight with his parents on this topic, and an opportunity to migrate with his uncle—seem quite different from those that pushed Mateo across the border—an unfruitful job search in his community, an unexpected job offer from a recruiter for a U.S. company, and encouragement from his parents. We can rationalize both moves as paths to economic opportunities in the United States, but Teresa's story complicates this simple logic. It suggests that migration may have a relational component—one that is borne out of a couple's desire to live together in this case—as well as an economic motif.

FOREST OR THE TREES? CAPTURING THE DIFFERENT REASONS FOR MIGRATION

It is, of course, not possible to account for each and every migrant story. Nor is it desirable. I do not want to lose sight of the forest for the trees. But, I also do not want to see only the forest and miss the trees. What I seek are common patterns that characterize the experience of many migrants, and also reveal the diversity in those experiences. To identify these patterns, I ask three questions in sequence: Who migrates, when, and why?

WHO MIGRATES?

Our first question is deceivingly simple: Who are the Mexican migrants who come to the United States? As human beings, we are drawn to making generalizations to make sense of our world. These generalizations are often organized around simple social categories (e.g., men and women, migrants and natives, us versus them). We seem to be hardwired to single out certain attributes, such as gender and race, in creating social categories and reaching social judgments. When it comes to migrants in the United States, it is perhaps not surprising that we use ethnic or national origin to place migrants into categories (e.g., Asians and Hispanics, Mexicans and Central Americans). It is surprising, however, to see similar categories, and broad generalizations on each category, prevail in scholarly work.

Many academic studies tell us about the average Mexican migrant: a young married man who has few years of schooling and some family ties to migrants who preceded them, earns low income, and comes from a poor rural community with few employment opportunities. Others show how the attributes of the average migrant have changed over time. The average Mexican migrant, one study shows, had nearly eight years of schooling as of 1990, up from six years in 1970.

These general patterns are important; they keep the pulse of the migrant flow. But the patterns also hide tremendous variation within the migrant population. The average migrant today may be more educated than one three decades ago, but that migrant still has many peers who are much less, or much more, educated. How similar is the migration experience for these individuals?

To answer such questions, scholars have investigated migration behavior separately for different groups of individuals, for example, among men and women, rural and urban residents, the more and less educated, and so on. One limiting factor is that studies typically considered a single dimension of social life, such as gender, community, or socioeconomic background, to differentiate migrants and their experience. But these dimensions often work in conjunction to produce different outcomes for different groups of individuals.

Take the case of gender. A woman may face more constraints to moving in a small community, where family and friends more easily enforce traditional gender roles, than one in a large city. Or take education. A man with no education from a rural area may have less incentive to migrate than a similar man from an industrial town, where job opportunities require formal education. These examples suggest how social categories, like those based on gender or education, may differentially influence one's migration propensity in different contexts.

This idea is not new, at least not in theory. Migration scholars have long noted "the situational and relational character" of social categories, like gender, race, and class. Giving the idea perhaps its most elaborate theoretical treatment, gender scholars have similarly written on *intersectionality*, "the relationships among multiple dimensions" of social life.

These theoretical points chart a distinct approach in empirical work: We need to focus not just on single attributes, like gender or education, but on configurations of multiple attributes to understand the heterogeneity in human experiences. But—and herein lies the main problem—how do we identify and study those configurations?

Migration scholars have deemed this task "difficult without recourse to qualitative methods." These methods allow researchers to become immersed in a setting—through in-depth interviews, participant observation, or a historical case study—and to reveal the complexities of social life there. We can see the payoff to this approach in numerous examples in migration research. It is through ethnographies, for example, that we learn how gender relations not only assign differential roles to men and women when it comes to migration, but also lead to differential access to key resources like migrant networks. We also see how gender relations vary by social class, or across rural or urban settings, and how these relations themselves get transformed through migration experience.

Similar insights emerge from quantitative data and methods as well. Scholars have used quantitative methods—analyzing large-scale social surveys, for example—to demonstrate the interactions between different personal and contextual attributes that lead to distinct migrant experiences. Massey, Goldring, and Durand, for example, show that personal attributes, such as gender, education, or family wealth, matter less for migration behavior as migration becomes more prevalent in a community. Women, the less educated, and the less wealthy—groups that are less inclined to migrate initially—become more likely to do so when they can rally support from others in their community who have already migrated.

Both qualitative and quantitative approaches, in other words, can be effective in showing how personal and contextual attributes jointly determine migration outcomes. Both approaches, however, can be equally limiting in *how many* attributes they allow us to consider. This is because each new attribute increases the complexity of the analysis exponentially. Consider a simple example. We want to study the heterogeneity in migration behavior across two binary attributes: sex (man or woman) and age (young or old). In combination, the two attributes yield four possible categories. It is easy to keep these categories in mind, and also to track any comparative evaluations of each category. Now, add three other binary attributes: education (none or some), wealth (poor or rich), and neighborhood (good or bad). If we cross-classify all five attributes, we get $2^5=32$ possible categories. It is hard for us to make sense of the patterns across all 32 categories even if we were able to identify such patterns with data analysis.

There is an easy way around this problem, however. Not all possible combinations are equally prevalent in the data. This is because many attributes are highly correlated with one another. For example, wealthier individuals tend to be more educated than their poor counterparts; they also often live in better neighborhoods. In real life, in other words, individuals tend to cluster around a few distinct configurations.

Our task, then, is not to consider all possible configurations of attributes, but to discover those most prevalent in the data. Cluster analysis methods, developed in statistics and computer science, allow us to do just that: discover groups of cases with similar configurations of attributes in data. These methods allow groupings to emerge from data without imposing any initial structure. The methods are used widely in fields as diverse as biology, physics, and computer science to produce effective descriptions of typically large and complex data. The methods, however, have been less popular in social science. (Appendix A provides a brief history to illuminate possible reasons for this state of affairs.)

Many social scientists have used cluster analysis and related methods, such as latent class analysis, to characterize the variability in outcomes or in potential determinants of a particular outcome. My approach here resembles that of Andrew Abbott and Charles Ragin, two prominent sociologists who have independently applied methods similar in their philosophy: the former to categorize sequences of events, such as career changes, and the latter to identify configurations of causal conditions for historical outcomes. In recent work, political scientists, Justin Grimmer and Gary King, have underlined the use of cluster analysis as a tool for *conceptualization*. This is how the method is understood and used here.

I seek to identify distinct configurations of personal, family, and community attributes that characterize different migrant types in Mexico-U.S. flows. This approach is often considered to be "data-driven" or "inductive" because it employs the data to identify a categorization scheme—a model through which we can understand those data. Like models in general, I do not evaluate a categorization scheme as "true" or "false," but instead ask: Is it useful? Does it allow us to describe the migrant population parsimoniously, while recognizing its heterogeneity? Does it reveal patterns that can be validated externally? These questions shape the analytic strategy that follows.

When do people migrate?

Cluster analysis, in this study, classifies migrants into distinct groups on the basis of their personal, family, and community characteristics. The method allows me to discover different configurations of migrants, and potentially, the different logics guiding their migration decisions.

I will explain this with an example. Say I use cluster analysis and discover two migrant groups in the data: One group includes mostly young uneducated men who are farmworkers in rural areas, and the other includes young professionals with advanced degrees in cities. This dichotomy reveals different configurations among migrants, but does it tell us anything about the logic underlying their migration? To see that, I can look at the conditions under which each group proliferates. Now, say, I observe the first group when there is a drought that reduces farm production, and the second when there is an economic crisis that leads to higher unemployment among professionals. This observation suggests that two groups may be reacting to different conditions when they migrate. In this case, the specific categorization scheme not only shows the different groups among migrants, but also suggests the different reasons that motivate migration behavior of each group.

Let me now retrace my steps and lay bare the reasoning here. The main premise is that individuals might reach the same outcome through different causal pathways. Different individuals, in other words, might decide to migrate for entirely different reasons. Here, I propose a distinct strategy to discover those reasons; it involves first fixing the outcome, migration in this case. This means that I focus only on migrants and identify the different groups among them. But studying migrants alone can be misleading; it can blind us to larger changes in a population. Consider a simple example. Say I compare two groups of migrants from Mexico—those entering the United States in the 1950s to those crossing the border in the 1980s—and find that the former are less educated than the latter. Does this mean that the drivers of migration are changing in Mexico, pushing the more educated out? Or does it mean that the levels of education are rising in the country? The only way to know is to compare migrants of each cohort to the non-migrants of that cohort. Here I do exactly that, but after I have discovered different groups of migrants with cluster analysis.

The second step in my analysis is to characterize the different conditions under which each migrant group proliferates. How is the emergence of each group related to economic, political, and demographic trends in the sending and receiving countries? Asking this question gives me a way to externally validate the migrant groups, that is, confirm their distinct character outside the data that led to their emergence in the first place.

The third step is to consider the observed patterns in light of existing explanations of migration. Social scientists have put forth various theories about who migrates and when. Each theory identifies a different set of contextual conditions that mobilizes a different group of individuals. In neoclassical economics, for example, higher wages in destination propel the migration of individuals who expect to earn more there. In new economics of migration, the uncertainty in the origin economy leads to migration from households that face risks to domestic earnings. In cumulative causation theory, the growing web of social ties between origin and destination fosters the migration of individuals who are connected to prior migrants. (Appendix B provides a general discussion of these and other migration theories.)

Each theory, in other words, suggests a different causal pathway for migration, and these pathways are not mutually exclusive. Individuals who migrate to increase earnings can co-exist alongside those who move to manage risks or those who join family and friends in destination. This idea is intuitive, and indeed, voiced in multiple agenda-setting books and articles, but it is also incredibly hard to capture in data.

Consider Massey and Espinosa's study, perhaps the best attempt to consider multiple theories to understand the migration from Mexico to the United States. The authors first identify variables that capture predictions of different migration theories. The inflation rate in Mexico, for example, measures the level of economic uncertainty, a catalyst for migration in new economics theory. Likewise, the prevalence of migration in an origin community signifies the density of connections to prior migrants, an important factor leading to migration according to cumulative causation theory. Using a regression model, and 41 such variables, the authors then evaluate which variables best predict who migrates in representative survey data from 25 Mexican communities over 25 years. They find strong support for the new economics and cumulative causation theories, and only weak and ambiguous support for the neoclassical perspective.

Their strategy, then, can be summarized as follows: Reduce each theory to a few variables, include variables on multiple theories in the same regression model, and then observe which ones better predict who migrates.

The variables that explain the most variance win and so do the theories they represent. By its very design, this empirical strategy sets up different theories against each other. It presumes that these theories provide competing—rather than complementary—accounts of migration.

This empirical strategy also implies that each theory applies universally to all individuals and over time. In reality, the theories are only conditional statements that identify specific conditions that affect specific groups of individuals. Consider the new economics theory. It suggests that the uncertainty in the origin economy increases the migration propensity from households facing risks to their earnings or assets. But, in Massey and Espinosa's study, the uncertainty—measured by the Mexican inflation rate—increases the migration probability for everybody.

This approach is, of course, entirely consistent with what Ernst Mayr has called *typological thinking*, that is, the view that social scientists should focus on average cases and identify generalizable patterns. (See appendix A for a detailed discussion.) Implicit in this view, sociologists Lieberson and Lynn argue, is an incorrect model for social science, one that is based on classical physics, and one that presumes the existence of law-like relationships that apply in a wide range of settings. This model, the authors argue, does not work in social science, where theories are often incomplete and data often observational.

Similar concerns might have led Massey and Taylor to ultimately critique their earlier work on migration for not being able to "state with any precision which theories were most important empirically in accounting for variations in the number, rate, and characteristics of immigrants over time and whether and why different theories may prove more or less efficacious in accounting for immigration patterns in different times and places." The authors identified the major challenge for migration research to be "test[ing] various theoretical explanations comparatively . . . to determine which ones prevail under what circumstances and why."

The main message here is that different explanations for migration might apply to different groups of individuals or different contexts or periods. But the problem still remains: How can we tell which explanations work for whom? One strategy is to test theories in different subsamples, for example, separately for men and women, or across different time periods, but one quickly runs into the usual limitations. The models become too complex, and the samples too small, once we combine different dimensions of social life (for example, jointly consider gender, education, and community of origin).

The analysis in this book attempts to circumvent these limitations by using a data-driven approach to identify different groups in data based on multiple personal, family, and community attributes. These groups, I assume, are likely to face different opportunity structures in Mexico and the

United States. I then put this assumption to the test by modeling the conditions under which each group proliferates. I seek to understand whether different migrant groups are responding to different economic, social, or political conditions in the two countries. Finally, I try to see if the observed associations between the larger conditions and the migrant groups resemble those suggested in different explanations of migration.

This approach provides an unconventional way of matching evidence to theory. It does not involve "testing" different theories, but instead piecing together evidence to suggest their plausibility under different circumstances and for different groups of individuals. It is in fact similar to Ragin's case-oriented approach and Abbott's colligation process, where one tries to link together facts in a different way to make a discovery. The common theme among our approaches is using evidence not to determine how a given factor works across all cases, but instead to understand how different combinations of factors differentiate each case. This approach, Lieberson and Lynn tell us, also resembles how biologists study complex processes like evolution.

WHY DO PEOPLE MIGRATE?

I begin my analysis with a simple question: Who migrates? I search for different groups among Mexico-U.S. migrants, those that have distinct configurations of personal, family, and community attributes. I then ask: When does each group migrate? I seek to identify the different conditions that might have mobilized different groups. With my final question, I dig deeper into this potential connection between who migrates and when: Why do I observe (if I actually do observe them) different groups under different conditions?

Let me return to the preceding example. Say I find two migrant groups— one of young, uneducated men from rural areas and the other of young, educated professional men from cities. I observe the first when there is a drought that reduces agricultural production, and the other when there is an economic crisis that leads to unemployment. Why could that be?

In social science, we refrain from asking the "why" question because it is incredibly difficult to answer. The question forces us to tell a causal story, one that is impossible to tell without discarding all the potential alternative stories. And we cannot do that with observational data. The best we can offer in most cases is a plausible story. And that story often comes from existing theory.

Consider the previous example. We can say that both groups are migrating under conditions of economic duress, one created by a drought and the other by an economic crisis. We can go further and claim their migration is economically motivated. Such claims are common in quantitative work. We often take a certain relationship, such as one between migration behavior and economic conditions, and suggest a plausible mechanism that produces it. Our data do not always allow us to distinguish between alternative mechanisms.

There is an increasingly prominent view in sociology that our explanations should identify the mechanisms, or the generative processes, that bring about social facts. In solidarity with this view, in this book, I supplement the quantitative analysis with qualitative data to better understand the mechanisms that generate the patterns I observe with statistical analysis.

I rely on the first-hand accounts of 139 migrants and non-migrants in Mexico to link the patterns from my statistical analysis to the particular reasoning underlying individual or family migration decisions. In the summers of 2011 and 2012, with a team of six local students from the University of Guadalajara, I visited four migrant-sending communities in the state of Jalisco. We tried to find migrants from different time periods and, whenever migrants were absent, we talked to family members who could report on them and also explain their own experience of being related to a migrant. We talked to different family members (parents, wives, siblings, and children) to get a variety of perspectives. We also spoke with individuals who had never migrated, nor had anyone in their immediate family done so. We asked each person to tell us about his or her life history first. We elicited information on major life events like marriage or birth of a child and then asked about migration decision in relation to those events. Instead of asking directly about migration motivations, we obtained detailed accounts of the circumstances surrounding the person before migration. In so doing, we tried to circumvent potential recall bias and avoid post-factum interpretations, which can be colored by events subsequent to migration. (For example, if a migrant ends up buying a house after migrating, he might say that he migrated for that purpose, when in fact he did not have that goal at all at the time of his first trip.) We coded the interviews systematically for emergent themes while also analyzing each interview in its entirety. Appendix C provides a detailed account of the interview and analysis procedures.

In the remainder of this chapter, I first provide a brief history of Mexico—U.S. migration, pointing to critical junctures until 1965 (the year my analysis begins) and to major trends thereafter. (Subsequent chapters will provide a detailed account of the migration context from 1965 to 2010.) I then describe the quantitative data and analysis, and present the answer to the first question: Who are the Mexican migrants entering the United States in this period?

FIGURE 1.2. Map of Mexico with state names
MAP BY Jeff Blossom, Center for Geographic Analysis, Harvard University

MEXICO-U.S. MIGRATION: A VERY BRIEF HISTORY

Migration between Mexico and the United States in the last century is the most prolonged movement of people in American history; it is also the largest international flow in the world. Understanding this flow is crucial to any student of migration, as it reveals insights that are applicable to other migrant streams in the world. But migration from Mexico to the United States is also unique in many ways. Mexico and the United States are not just two countries with vast economic differentials—like many other sending-receiving country pairings in the world—but they are also two countries connected by a 2,000-mile land border (see the map in figure 1.2) and a long history of movement in-between.

Mexico-U.S. migration goes far back in time. People have been leaving the interior of Mexico to travel north to what is now the American Southwest for almost four centuries. First, it was the settlers for the Spanish crown who migrated to the northern borderlands, and after 1821, those for the new Republic of Mexico. The border itself moved in 1848, when the treaty ending the Mexican-American War ceded Mexico's northern provinces including Texas, Arizona, New Mexico, as well as parts of Utah and California, to the United States. Some 50,000 Mexicans became U.S. migrants without ever leaving their homes.

In the 1890s, employers from the United States started recruiting Mexican laborers to work on the railroads, mines, farm fields, and factories. At the turn of the century, about 60,000 Mexicans entered the United States annually, but the majority returned to Mexico during winter, and as such, their numbers did not reach considerable levels in the population. But this state of affairs was to change in the new century.

Historian Albert Camarillo identifies four critical periods in the history of Mexico-U.S. migration in the twentieth century. The first period is the *Great Migration* in the 1910s and 1920s. The year 1910 marks the beginning of the Mexican Revolution, which led to an armed struggle in the country followed by decades of political and economic instability. In the next 20 years, Camarillo reports, 1.5 million Mexicans crossed the border to the United States to escape the economic disruption and political turmoil in their country. However, most of these migrants ultimately returned to Mexico; indeed, the Mexican-born population in the United States increased only by about a half-million during that period, from 103,000 in 1910 to 641,000 in 1930 (see figure 1.3). The *Great Migration* came to an end with the Great Depression in the United States. The stock market crash in 1929, and the mass unemployment that followed resulted in a backlash against all immigrants, including mass deportations that affected Mexican nationals. In 1940, the Mexican-born population in the United States had dropped to 377,000, nearly half its 1930 level (figure 1.3).

The second critical period in Mexico-U.S migration is the *Bracero era* between 1942 and 1964, when the United States entered into a labor agreement with Mexico. Labor shortages had reached dramatic levels in the United States due to the military draft for World War II in 1941 and the Korean War in 1950. These shortages were especially severe in the agricultural sector. Estimates suggest a loss of 2.8 million farmworkers between 1939 and 1943 (because of the draft as well as the growing manufacturing sector), and a shortage of about 8 million farmworkers in 1951. The labor agreement—known as the Bracero program (referring to those working with their arms, or *brazos*)—brought about 4.6 million Mexicans to the United States for short-term work.

Even the Bracero program could not keep up with the labor demand in the United States. Many Mexicans crossed the border without documents in the 1950s to take up the work in the fields, and to escape the poverty and lack of employment in their own country. Camarillo defines this decade, which overlaps with the Bracero era, as that of *Los Mojados*. (*Mojado*, a term used by im-

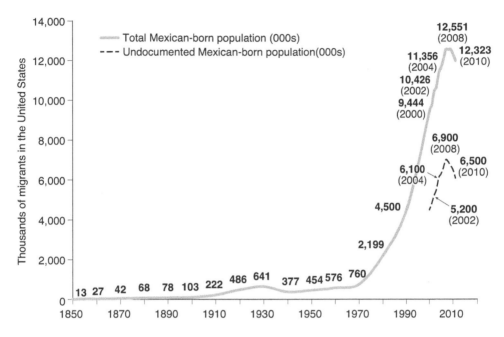

FIGURE 1.3. The Mexican-born population (total and undocumented) in the United States over time

migrants themselves, means "wet one," which refers to unauthorized migrants who cross into the United States through the Rio Grande river. Its counterpart in English, "wetback," is used in a derogatory sense in the United States.)

The number of undocumented immigrants apprehended at the border swelled from just under 70,000 in 1945 to nearly 900,000 in 1950. In response, the U.S. Immigration and Naturalization Services (INS) launched the so-called Operation Wetback in 1954. The campaign not only deported 2 million undocumented Mexicans, but also increased the number of Bracero visas for legal entries. Between 1955 and 1960, the annual number of Bracero workers ranged between 400,000 and 450,000, more than double the annual number from the preceding decade. The INS was instrumental in turning many undocumented migrants into Bracero workers, as Calavita reports, by first raiding the fields to capture the undocumented migrants, then transporting them across the border, only to process them back into the country as legal *braceros* and to return them to the very fields in which they had been captured.

The fourth, and final, period in the Mexico-U.S. flow is what Camarillo calls the *Second Great Migration*. This period begins at the end of the Bracero era in 1965 and continues to the present day. It is in this period that the Mexican-born population in the United States rose from less than one million to more than 12 million (figure 1.3). And it is this period on which this book focuses. Who were these migrants? What brought them to the United States? Let us now look at the data source that will help answer these questions.

DATA

Data on migration are not easy to come by. Migrants, by definition, are a mobile population. National surveys in the United States, like the Census, record the migrants already here, but not those who have returned to Mexico, or those who choose not to participate in the survey due to their vulnerable status. National surveys in Mexico capture migrants who have returned, or those on whom the left-behind family members can report, but not those who have moved their entire families to the United States.

The majority of the findings on Mexico-U.S. migration are based on data from two specialized surveys: the Mexican National Survey of Population Dynamics (ENADID) and the Mexican Migration Project (MMP). The former is a representative national sample, but contains information on only labor migrants, and starts in 1992. The latter is from specific Mexican communities, but covers all migrants, including those who have moved to the United States to join family members. The latter starts earlier, in 1982, and goes farther back in time through retrospective life histories.

The inclusion of all migrants—not just labor-force participants—and the longer time horizon make the MMP data more advantageous to study patterns in the Mexico-U.S. migrant stream, including its diversity and how it has changed over time. The MMP data are not strictly representative of the Mexican population. Indeed, the data are purposefully sampled from migrant-heavy regions in Mexico. Moreover, the data are mostly collected in Mexico, and as such, capture migrants who maintain ties to that country, and likely miss those who have moved with their entire families to the United States. The data cover different types of communities in different periods, but the share from urban communities roughly equals that from rural ones for most years.

Despite its potential shortcomings, research finds that the MMP data set yields an accurate profile of Mexican migrants to the United States, and this profile is largely consistent with that observed in the ENADID data. Here, whenever possible, I compare patterns from the MMP data to those obtained from other data sets to ensure that my results are not an artifact of the particularities of the survey at hand.

The MMP data come from 143 communities (at the time of this analysis) located in major migrant-sending areas in 24 Mexican states. Each community was surveyed once between 1982 and 2013, during December and January, when the U.S. migrants are mostly likely to visit their families in

Mexico. In each community, individuals (or informants for absent individuals) from about 200 randomly selected households were asked to provide demographic and economic information, and to state the timing of their first and last trip to the United States. Household heads were additionally asked to report the trips in between. These data were supplemented with information from a non-random sample of migrants identified through snowball sampling in the United States (about 10% of the sample). The data contain information on 145,276 individuals, of whom 19,243 have migrated to the United States sometime between 1965 and 2010.

Because more detailed information is available for household heads, most studies of the MMP have restricted attention to this subpopulation. To provide a more representative portrait of migrants, I include all household members. In the first set of analyses, I seek to identify the different configurations of attributes that characterize a sample of migrants on their first trip to the United States. I do not consider subsequent trips, the details of which are only recorded for the household heads and a subset of the spouses of the household heads, to avoid a complication that has haunted prior work on migration. This complication arises from the fact that many attributes related to migration behavior are also changed by it. Over successive trips, migrants gradually gain more experience, establish stronger ties to destination, and become wealthier. Their attributes change, not as a result of the changing selectivity of the stream, but due to the changes caused by prior migration trips. Focusing on first-time migrants allows me to observe migrants' attributes independently from this reciprocal relationship.

A concern with the MMP data is the retrospective nature of the information on migrants. Let's take a household surveyed in 1990, where the daughter has migrated to the United States for the first time in 1980. Her attributes, like age and education, were recorded in 1990, but could be projected linearly to 1980. The economic status of her household could be reconstructed using the data on the timing of asset purchases. The characteristics of her community could be traced back using the retrospective community history. All these plausible steps rely on one crucial assumption: that the daughter in question was living in the same household and community in 1980. While this assumption is viable for most cases, the study cannot account for the cases for which it is not.

METHODS: CLUSTER ANALYSIS

I use cluster analysis to discover groups of migrants with similar attributes in the MMP data. This method discovers categories based on several attributes, and then assigns individuals to those categories. Clustering or classifying cases can be fairly easy, if one considers a few attributes, that is. The human mind works through classification and inductive generalization rather than deductive logic. This means that we search for categories everywhere we look. But we cannot always create the most useful categorization schemes because we are limited by our working memories and computational abilities. Cluster analysis methods, Grimmer and King argue, resolve this ultimate "paradox, that human beings are unable to use optimally what may be human kind's most important methodological innovation."

The first step in cluster analysis involves selecting the attributes for partitioning the data. One can either examine the data or rely on theories to identify salient attributes. Here, I exploit the vast empirical work on the MMP and use several attributes that have been shown to shape migration behavior between Mexico and the United States.

The attributes, listed in table 1.1, include individuals' demographic characteristics (sex, age, and years of education), household wealth (properties, land, and businesses owned), prior migration experience (whether they migrated in Mexico, number of U.S. migrants and residents in household, and proportion of individuals who have ever migrated in their community), community characteristics (proportion working in agriculture, proportion earning less than the minimum wage, and whether the community is in an urban area with a population of 10,000 or more) and regional indicators (central-west, border, central, central-south, and southeast).

The attributes do not include other potentially important characteristics, like marital status or number of children, which are measured consistently over time only for a portion of the data (household heads). But such characteristics are often correlated with attributes included here (e.g., marital status is correlated with age), and thus, the resulting groupings end up being separated along the excluded characteristics, as I will shortly show.

The average values for the attributes in table 1.1 differ significantly ($p<0.05$, two-tailed t-test) for migrants and non-migrants. Migrants are individuals who have migrated to the United States at least once, and non-migrants are those who have never migrated. For the sake of comparison, both groups are observed on the survey year in each community. (In subsequent cluster analysis, migrants are observed on the year of their first U.S. trip.)

Compared to non-migrants, migrants are more likely to be older and male, and to have higher levels of education. They live in wealthier households with ties to U.S. migrants, and in poor communities that contain a higher proportion of agricultural workers and individuals earning less than the minimum wage. Migrants are more likely to originate from the central-western states in Mexico than are non-migrants.

Similar to the evidence in prior work, the significant differences between migrants and non-migrants observed here establish the relevance of

TABLE 1.1. SAMPLE CHARACTERISTICS FOR MIGRANTS AND NON-MIGRANTS IN 143 MEXICAN COMMUNITIES IN THE MMP DATA[a]

VARIABLE		MIGRANTS	NON-MIGRANTS
Demographic characteristics			
	Male	0.73	0.45
	Age	34.67	27.62
	Years of education	6.93	6.13
Household wealth			
	Number of rooms in properties	4.20	3.59
	Log of land value (US$ in 2010)	2.98	2.11
	Number of businesses	0.41	0.37
Migration experience			
	Migrated in Mexico	0.22	0.16
	Number of U.S. legal residents in household	0.51	0.13
	Number of U.S. migrants (non-residents) in household	6.26	6.83
	Proportion ever migrated in community	0.22	0.15
Community characteristics			
	Proportion in agriculture in community	0.28	0.24
	Proportion earning less than minimum wage in community	0.38	0.35
	Community in an urban area	2.76	2.48

continued

TABLE 1.1. *Continued*

VARIABLE		MIGRANTS	NON-MIGRANTS
Region			
	Central-west	0.71	0.58
	Border	0.07	0.11
	Central	0.02	0.03
	Central-south	0.13	0.19
	Southeast	0.06	0.10
N (persons)		19,243	126,033

[a] Migrants are individuals who first migrated sometime between 1965 and 2010 and who are between the ages of 15 and 65. Non-migrants are individuals who have never migrated prior to the survey year. Both groups are observed on the survey year. Means for migrants and non-migrants differ significantly (p<0.05, two-tailed test) for all variables.

the selected attributes for migration. Also relevant for migration, but not included in cluster analysis, are indicators that capture important economic or policy events, like the soaring Mexican inflation or interest rates in the 1980s or the passage of a new immigration legislation in the United States in 1986. These events introduce external shocks to the migration system, and typically shift the magnitude or composition of the migrant stream. Hence, they provide a perfect opportunity to externally validate the migrant clusters, which, if substantively valid, should display a temporal pattern reflecting these shifts. I will explore this connection in later analyses.

The selected attributes in this study are measured on different scales. About half are binary (e.g., sex, regional indicators), a few are counts (e.g., number of properties or years of education), and the rest are continuous. Clustering methods are typically sensitive to the scaling of attributes, which determines the importance assigned to a particular attribute. To avoid an arbitrary weighting of attributes, I dichotomized each non-binary attribute such that the values above the median are converted to 1 and those below it to 0.

I used the popular K-means method, a classical clustering algorithm that makes no assumptions about the data structure and thus has been applied to a diverse set of problems. The K-means method relies on a set of attributes to divide the data into a given number of groups (or "clusters") so that the cases in a group are as much alike as possible. The output is typically a cluster membership for each case and a centroid for each cluster that represents the mean (or average) of the cases in that cluster.

In appendix D, I describe the several steps involved in the method. I also present results from several cluster validation procedures, which are necessary for deciding on the number of clusters in the data. These procedures suggest that there are four distinct groups among first-time migrants in the MMP data between 1965 and 2010. What follows is a description of the characteristics of each group.

RESULTS
WHO ARE THE MIGRANTS?

The four columns in table 1.2 present the mean values of the attributes used in the cluster analysis for each of the four clusters. The last two rows show the number and proportion of migrants in each cluster, which appear to be relatively uniform. The attributes are measured on migrants' first trips to the United States. For each attribute, the highest cluster mean is shown in boldface and differs significantly ($p < 0.05$, two-tailed t-test) from the value closest to it in all cases but one (community with high number of low earners).

The first cluster contains the highest percentage of men (84%) and migrants with less than a primary school degree (60%) across all clusters. The group also includes the lowest share of wealthy migrants overall. Only 26% of migrants in this group own a property, 16% own some land, and 7% own a business. About a fifth have migrated in Mexico. A small share have family ties to U.S. migrants (20%) or residents (5%). A larger share (25%), but still small compared to other clusters, live in communities with high migration prevalence. 80% of migrants in this group live in rural communities with high agricultural employment, and a similarly high share (74%) live in communities where a high proportion of individuals earn less than the minimum wage.

A characteristic (or an ideal-typical) migrant in this cluster is a man in his twenties who has no education and, hence, no access to lucrative jobs in the local labor market. He lacks income-generating assets, like land or a business, and lives in a poor rural community with limited opportunities.

The second cluster consists of the youngest, and some of the wealthiest, migrants in the sample. 71% of these migrants are in their teens. 75% of these migrants live in a household that owns a property, 35% live in a household with land, and 17% live in a household with a business. Most of them have family ties to prior U.S. migrants (77%) and live in communities with high migration prevalence (77%). The majority are men (81%). About two-thirds of these migrants have primary education or less. 75% live in communities where a high proportion of individuals earn less than the minimum wage, and 88% come from the central-western states in Mexico.

A representative migrant in the second cluster is a young man with only primary education. He lives in a poor community, where the assets of his

TABLE 1.2. MIGRANT CHARACTERISTICS (INCLUDED IN CLUSTER ANALYSIS) BY CLUSTER MEMBERSHIP IN 143 MEXICAN COMMUNITIES[a]

VARIABLE		CLUSTER			
		1	2	3	4
Demographic characteristics					
Male		**0.84**	0.81	0.36	0.81
Age:	15–19	0.22	**0.71**	0.06	0.28
	20–24	0.36	0.21	0.24	**0.40**
	25–34	0.28	0.06	**0.47**	0.24
	35 or older	0.14	0.02	**0.24**	0.09
Education:	Less than primary school	**0.60**	0.16	0.26	0.04
	Primary school	0.28	**0.51**	0.45	0.22
	Middle school	0.08	0.26	0.17	**0.49**
	High school or more	0.04	0.07	0.12	**0.25**
Household wealth					
Own properties		0.26	0.75	**0.80**	0.64
Own land		0.16	**0.35**	0.30	0.18
Own business		0.07	0.17	**0.18**	0.16
Migration experience					
Migrated in Mexico?		**0.19**	0.02	0.04	0.10
Any U.S. legal residents in household		0.05	0.15	**0.20**	0.07
Any U.S. migrants (non-residents) in household		0.20	0.77	**0.83**	0.35
Community with high migration prevalence		0.25	0.77	**0.80**	0.24
Community characteristics					
Community with high agriculture employment		**0.80**	0.71	0.24	0.16
Community with high number of low earners		0.74	**0.75**	0.26	0.18
Community in an urban area		0.30	0.24	0.38	**0.68**
Region					
Central-west		0.80	**0.88**	0.82	0.35
Border		0.05	0.03	0.04	**0.18**
Central		0.01	0.00	0.01	**0.07**
Central-south		0.09	0.06	0.09	**0.29**
Southeast		0.06	0.03	0.03	**0.10**
N	(persons)	5,121	5,214	3,916	4,992
	(% of total number of migrants)	27	27	20	26

[a]All variables are binary. The highest mean value for each variable is shown in boldface, and differs significantly from the value closest to it ($p<0.05$, two-tailed test) in all cases but one (community with high number of low earners).

household—a property and either a piece of land or a business—place him in the middle or upper wealth category.

The third cluster is distinct in that it includes mostly female migrants (64%) who are well-connected to other migrants. 83% have family ties to U.S. migrants, 20% are connected to U.S. residents, and 80% live in communities with high migration prevalence. Most of these migrants are in their late twenties and thirties (71%)—the oldest group in the sample—and have a primary school degree or less. Many of them own assets. About four in five own a property, one in three owns some land, and one in five owns a business. Compared to the first two clusters, a lower share of them (26%) live in poor communities, but a higher share (38%) are located in metropolitan areas.

A typical migrant in this group is a woman. At least one member of her household, likely her father or husband, is a current or prior U.S. migrant.

The fourth cluster contains the highest percentage of educated migrants: One in two in this group has a middle school degree and one in four a high school degree or more. Migrants in this group overwhelmingly live in urban areas (68%). Most of them are male (81%). Sixty-four percent of migrants in this cluster own a property (home or other dwelling), 18% own some land, and 16% own a business. Almost half of these migrants have family ties to U.S. migrants, and about a fourth live in communities with high migration prevalence. Only a small share of them live in communities with high agriculture (16%) or a high share of low-wage earners (18%). Migrants in this group are the least likely to come from the traditional migrant-sending regions in the central-west across all groups, and most likely to come from the other regions like the central-south or the border.

The representative migrant in this cluster is a man who has some secondary education and lives in an urban community. Given his education and place of residence, this migrant has access to more and better job opportunities than a typical migrant in the other clusters. He owns a property, which provides him with economic security, but lacks risky assets like land or business. He does not have any prior migrants in his family, and does not live in a traditionally migrant-sending community.

For each cluster, table 1.3 presents the mean values of some additional attributes that are not used in the cluster analysis because of their limited availability in the data. The attributes include indicators of individuals' relationship to the household head (measured only on the year of the survey, and not on the year of first migration) as well as individuals' marital status and number of children (measured mostly for household heads).

The four clusters differ in some of these additional attributes too. The first cluster, for example, includes the highest share of heads (61%) on the survey year, while the second cluster consists mostly of sons (29% are the eldest son; 42% are younger sons). Interestingly, about a fifth of the sons (and also of

TABLE 1.3. MIGRANT CHARACTERISTICS (NOT INCLUDED IN CLUSTER ANALYSIS) BY CLUSTER MEMBERSHIP IN 143 MEXICAN COMMUNITIES

VARIABLE	CLUSTER			
	1	2	3	4
Relationship to head[a]				
Head	0.61	0.09	0.10	0.33
Spouse	0.08	0.04	0.17	0.05
Eldest son	0.15	0.29	0.13	0.31
Younger son	0.08	0.42	0.15	0.18
Eldest daughter	0.05	0.08	0.26	0.09
Younger daughter	0.01	0.07	0.17	0.03
Family characteristics during first trip				
Married or consensual union[b]	0.74	0.29	0.70	0.53
Any children?[c]	0.50	0.24	0.91	0.55
Migration experience on first trip				
Undocumented on first trip?	0.87	0.86	0.76	0.75
Duration of first trip (median)	12	24	24	36
Total number of trips	3.12	2.55	1.57	1.59
Occupation on first trip				
Unemployed	0.08	0.09	0.31	0.10
Agriculture	0.33	0.27	0.13	0.10
Manufacturing	0.33	0.33	0.27	0.45
Service	0.21	0.24	0.22	0.27
Destination				
California	0.58	0.60	0.58	0.44
Texas	0.14	0.11	0.09	0.11
Illinois	0.10	0.08	0.10	0.11
Other	0.19	0.21	0.23	0.33
Year of first migration (median)	1979	1986	1991	1992
Year of survey (median)	1995	1994	1995	2001
N (persons)	5,121	5,214	3,916	4,992
N[b]	2,723	1,088	1,602	3,362
N[c]	3,140	468	404	1,627

[a]Relationship to head is measured on the survey year. A respondent might have a different status in the household at the time of first migration.
[b]Marital status on first U.S. trip is recorded for household heads only in communities 1–71, and for everyone in communities 72 to 143.
[c]Number of children is available for household heads only.

the daughters) in cluster 2 have a father who is a cluster 1 migrant (separate calculation not shown on the table). Migrants in the first, third, and fourth clusters (at least those for whom I have this information) tend to be married and with children on the first U.S. trip, while those in the second cluster are mostly single. These differences reflect in part the age gap between groups; the latter group is much younger, on average, compared to the former ones.

Table 1.3 also lists indicators of migrants' experiences on the first trip to the United States. A majority of migrants in all four groups are undocumented (at least 75%). Migrants in the first cluster have the shortest median trip duration (12 months), and those in the fourth cluster have the longest (36 months). Those in the first cluster tend to make more than three trips, on average, while those in the third and fourth clusters make between one and two trips. The first cluster, then, makes many trips of short duration, while the other clusters take few trips of long duration. The four migrant groups are largely similar in their distribution across occupations and destinations but still display slight variations. The fourth cluster, for example, is more likely than the other groups to work in manufacturing, and to end up in a state outside the traditional receiving states of California, Texas, and Illinois. The third cluster is more likely than the other groups to be unemployed; nearly a third of the group does not work on the first trip compared to a tenth or less in the other groups.

When does each cluster migrate?

I identified the four migrant types based on migrants' individual, household, and community characteristics on their first trip to the United States. In this process, I included migrants observed at different points into a single cluster analysis and deliberately excluded indicators for economic, demographic, or policy trends that capture the Mexico-U.S. migration context. Despite the exclusion of these trends, I still obtained results that show a strong temporal pattern. Table 1.3 already revealed this pattern; the median year of first migration is 1979 for the first cluster, 1986 for the second, 1991 for the third, and 1992 for the fourth.

The four panels in figure 1.4 provide a more revealing visualization. Each panel displays the number of migrants in each migrant cluster over time. I divide the number of migrants in each year by the sample size in that year and show migrant numbers per 1,000 of population. This strategy allows me to account for the changing sample size over time. Figure E.1 in appendix E offers an alternative view; it shows the number of migrants in each cluster as a share of the total number of migrants in a given year. The patterns in the two figures are largely similar.

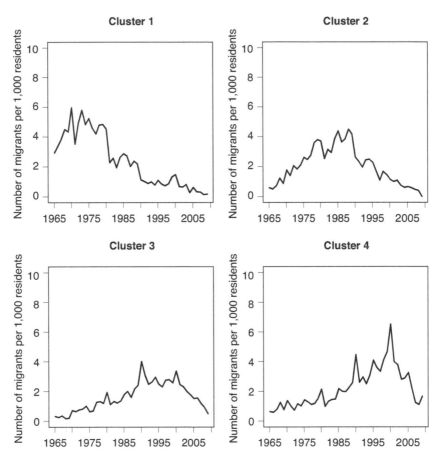

FIGURE 1.4. Trends in the number of migrants per 1,000
residents across the four clusters

Cluster 1, shown in the upper-left panel, contains the highest number
of migrants in the 1970s but declines consistently in size over time. The
group goes from containing six migrants per 1,000 residents in the 1970s
to including less than two migrants in the 1990s. The group also declines
in its share among all first-time migrants in the same period, from almost
70% in the 1970s to 10% in the 1990s. (See figure E.1.)

Cluster 2, shown in the upper-right panel, increases in size through the
1970s and reaches its highest level in the mid-1980s. Accounting for about
40% of first-time migrants at that time, this group shrinks relative to other
groups through the 1990s, and contains less than one-fifth of migrants in
2005.

Cluster 3, displayed in the lower-left panel, shows constant presence in the first half of the study period, increasing slowly in size to about two migrants per 1,000 in the 1980s. In the early 1990s, this group suddenly doubles in size and contains about four migrants per 1,000. Although accounting for less than one-fifth of migrants in earlier years, cluster 4 rises to majority status among the migrant groups in the early 1990s and makes up more than half of all migrants in 2005. (See figure E.1.)

The figure displays a striking temporal order in which each migrant type prevails in a different period. The first cluster characterizes the 1970s, and the second predominates the 1980s. The third cluster gains prominence in the early 1990s, and lags closely behind the fourth cluster, the majority group.

ARE THE DIFFERENCES BETWEEN MIGRANT CLUSTERS AN ARTIFACT OF TEMPORAL TRENDS?

The temporal ordering of each migrant group raises questions about the interpretation of group differences in table 1.2. If each group is prevalent in a different period, then the differences between groups in attributes like education or urban origin may not signal inherent divisions, as I assumed, but instead reflect general trends in Mexico, like rising education levels or increasing urbanization. Put differently, a migrant in cluster 4 may have higher education than one in cluster 1, not because he represents a different migrant type, but because he is observed at a later period when the education levels are generally higher in Mexico.

I investigated this possibility with a statistical model that compared the determinants of migration behavior in the overall sample, as well as in select samples that included non-migrants and each migrant cluster separately. This model allowed me to distinguish between two trends in data: the changes in the characteristics of the Mexican population, on the one hand, and the changes in the characteristics of Mexico-U.S. migrants, on the other. I explain the logic behind this model, and provide the estimates from it, in appendix F.

The results from this model largely confirm earlier descriptions of the migrant groups. That is, the characteristics that set a migrant group apart from the other migrant groups also set that group apart from the non-migrants. Cluster 1 migrants, for example, are not just the least educated and poorest among the first-time migrants, as table 1.2 showed, but they are also significantly less educated and poorer than the overall Mexican population. Similarly, cluster 2 migrants are not just significantly wealthier compared to other migrant groups, but also to Mexicans who have never migrated to the United States. In other words, not only is the Mexican population as

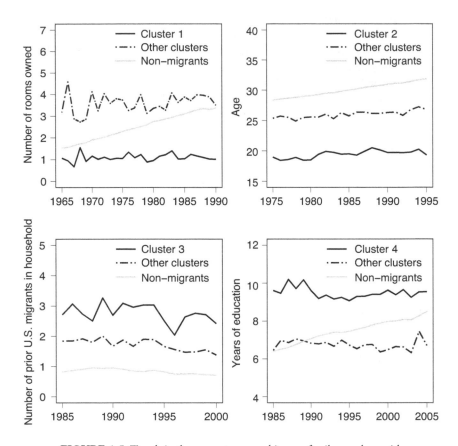

FIGURE 1.5. Trends in the property ownership, age, family members with
U.S. migration experience, and years of education among migrants in different
clusters and non-migrants in selected years in the MMP data

a whole changing over time, but so are the U.S.-bound migrants being selected from that pool.

Figure 1.5 presents some of the patterns with descriptive plots. Each
panel displays the time period for which the data contain at least 100 migrants in the cluster of interest in each year (that is, a sufficiently large
sample to draw statistically meaningful comparisons). The top-left panel
shows the average number of rooms owned by migrants in cluster 1 (solid
black line), migrants in other clusters (dashed black line), and non-migrants
(grey line) over time from 1965 through 1990. Property ownership has
been increasing among non-migrants in the MMP data, from an average of
1.5 rooms in 1965 to more than 3 rooms in 1990. The trends for migrants,
however, have remained stagnant. An average migrant in cluster 1 owned

a single room through the study period, while an average migrant in the other clusters owned almost 4 rooms. Migrants in cluster 1 were significantly poorer (at the 95% confidence level) than both non-migrants and migrants in the other clusters in each year between 1965 and 1990.

The top-right panel shows that cluster 2 migrants (solid black line) were at least five years younger, on average, than migrants in the other clusters (dashed black line), a difference that is statistically significant (at the 95% level) in all years between 1975 and 1995. While non-migrants (grey line) seem to be getting older, on average, this is an artifact of the retrospective nature of our data; meanwhile, first-time migrants in both groups retain the same age profile over time.

The bottom-left panel confirms that cluster 3 migrants are more likely to be connected to former migrants through family relations compared to the other clusters. And this is not just because this cluster peaks in a later period in our data. The difference between clusters stands—and actually seems quite fixed—even when the clusters are compared within the same period. Migrants in the third cluster (solid black line) have more former U.S. migrants in their households, on average, compared to migrants in the other clusters (grey line). The difference is statistically significant (at the 95% level) in all years from 1985 to 2000.

Finally, the bottom-right panel shows the average years of education among migrants in cluster 4 (solid black line), migrants in other clusters (dashed black line), and non-migrants (grey line) from 1985 through 2005. Cluster 4 migrants have at least three more years of education compared to migrants in the other clusters, a difference that remains statistically significant (at the 95% level) in all years from 1985 to 2005. Cluster 4 migrants also have significantly more years of schooling compared to non-migrants in each year. Non-migrants (grey line) are becoming more educated over time, on average, a result of the secular upward trend in education levels in Mexico; nevertheless, migrants in both groups retain stable education profiles over time. Migrants in cluster 4 are consistently positively selected on education, while those in the other clusters tend to be negatively selected, especially after 1990.

CONCLUSION

There are different reasons why Mexican migrants come to the United States. But these reasons are often overlooked in studies that focus on an average migrant and attempt to provide an all-encompassing explanation for migration behavior. Here I took a different approach. I first characterized the heterogeneity among migrants with cluster analysis. Using the

Mexican Migration Project data from 19,243 first-time migrants between 1965 and 2010, I found four clusters of migrants with distinct configurations of characteristics. Each cluster concentrated in a particular period, and its distinguishing characteristics did not merely reflect the changes in the Mexican population over time, but rather the changes in the selectivity of U.S.-bound migrants.

The first cluster—mostly uneducated and poor men from rural communities—was the majority in the 1970s but dropped to a small minority by the 1990s. The second cluster—many of them teenage boys from relatively better-off families—peaked in the 1980s, becoming the majority group at that time, but declined consistently in size thereafter. The third cluster—mostly women with family ties to former migrants—was increasing slowly in size until it experienced a sudden spike in the early 1990s. And the fourth cluster—mostly educated men from urban areas—grew persistently over time, grabbing the majority status among all first-time migrants in the early 1990s.

What explains the rise and fall of each group? What reasons motivate each group to move to the United States? In the following four chapters, I will seek an answer to these questions, focusing on one group at a time.

Chapter 2

"GO WORK OVER THERE AND COME DO SOMETHING HERE"

Circular Migrants

FIGURE 2.1. A return migrant in his convenience store opened
with savings from the United States
PHOTO BY Patricia Martín

JORGE'S STORY

On a hot day in August, almost halfway into our fieldwork in Jalisco, the research team and I are comfortably perched on the chairs scattered around Doña Rosa's courtyard. Doña Rosa is a woman in her late sixties. She seems quite at ease despite the three strangers in her house. She is busy embroidering a tablecloth while her grandchildren run around playing hide-and-seek. Lifting her gaze momentarily from her work, she tells her daughter, Alicia, to offer us their homemade salsa and tortillas. She then returns her attention to the delicate flower pattern in her hands and continues to recount her story.

Doña Rosa lives in Buenavista, a small town of about 200 households. The town is poor: One out of three houses still has dirt floors; only one in two contains any modern appliances, like a refrigerator or a washing machine. Half of the houses are "overcrowded," according to official statistics. Four out of five residents age 15 or older lack a basic education.

Many households in Buenavista depend on the communal plots of land (*ejido*) for subsistence. Doña Rosa's husband, Alfonso, is also an *ejidatario*, a farmer working the communal land. Every year, all *ejidatarios* in town come together to work the land; they remove the weeds, fumigate and fertilize, and plant the corn by hand. They use simple tools, like a hoe, or sometimes rent a tractor, and split the modest harvest evenly. Alfonso's share barely covers his family's subsistence needs. Too old to hold a regular job, Alfonso makes ends meet by collecting paper from the dumpster and selling it. He earns about US$50 a week.

Neither Doña Rosa nor Alfonso has ever been to the United States. Yet, like so many others in Buenavista, their lives are intricately connected to migrants there. All four of their children—two daughters and two sons—have migrated to the United States at some point in their lives. Today, Doña Rosa talks mostly about Angela, the only one still there. Soon, Angela's husband, Jorge, joins the conversation.

An athletic man in his thirties, Jorge is clad in American-brand apparel—faded jeans, white sneakers, and a baseball cap. He now lives in Mexico but not by choice. Two years ago, he was deported from the United States after living there on and off for about twenty-two years. He has been separated from his wife ever since.

Jorge first migrated to the United States in his teens. He lived in a small rural town then, not that different from Buenavista. "I wanted to be a doctor," he remembers. "I wanted to study, to get my degree, but there wasn't enough money." Jorge's father asked him to quit school and start working to help the family. "That is when I said I was leaving for the United States," Jorge told us. "That is how it started."

Jorge's uncle was a former migrant and agreed to take him along. The two of them crossed to Texas with the help of a *coyote* (smuggler). Soon, Jorge made new friends and left with them for California. "We arrived at this suburb," he recalls in vivid detail. "You should have seen these beautiful houses with beautiful green fields. I said to myself: 'Am I really going to live here?' No. Crossing the hill, we stayed in cardboard houses with a single mattress on the ground. We would pick up some sticks [to start a fire] so we could make our meals. We would take a shower under a hose. . . . We were lucky because at least we knew where we were staying the next day."

Jorge worked in cotton harvesting first. "That one is a job," he recalls, "Oh, boy. They pay you by the day. . . . It was about fifty-five dollars at that time. You have to put your fingers inside, grab the cotton, and pick it. It stings. Your fingers bleed."

After a few years in California, Jorge decided to move to Oregon to search for new opportunities. Many migrants there were working in planting pines. "It was very hard work," Jorge comments, "because sometimes you have to work on a mountain, almost ninety degrees up, and your job [is to plant] about a thousand pines a day."

The jobs were difficult, but Jorge never considered going back to Mexico, at least not at first. The difference in pay was too great to forego: "What I earn in one week in Mexico," Jorge explains to us, "I earn in one day's job in the United States."

But then Jorge met his wife-to-be, Angela, in Oregon and began thinking about having his own family. He could no longer stay in the apartment he rented with several other migrants in order to save money. He would have to get a new place just for himself and Angela, and they would have to pay for all their expenses, including food, water, and electricity, themselves. Suddenly, Jorge realized, it would be impossible to save enough for a comfortable future in the United States.

Angela had a house-cleaning business at the time. And, unlike Jorge, who had not contacted his father for more than a decade, Angela doted on her parents in Mexico. She convinced Jorge that it was important to have connections back home. It was also logical to invest in Mexico, where U.S. dollars were worth more. They decided the best strategy was "to work really hard, send money here [to Mexico], and to be able to live nicely afterwards."

Jorge and Angela kept sending money to Buenavista, where Angela's parents invested it for them. They ended up buying a house and some land there. Jorge's deportation was an unexpected obstacle along the way.

During our conversation, Jorge seems hopeful about the future. "I want to go back," he says, "[but] my intention is not to stay [in the U.S.]. I have about thirty-five thousand dollars in tools over there. . . . I need to pick them up." These tools are crucial for Jorge to set up his auto repair shop in Buenavista. He can then bring his wife and daughter back to Mexico as well. "That's the thing about an immigrant," he says. "You go work over there and come and do something here."

"THAT'S THE MAJOR ILLUSION, TO BUILD A HOUSE."

Many migrants, like Jorge and Angela, work in the United States in order to save money for a home, a business, or some other target. Migrants in the first cluster also followed this strategy, or a particular version of it.

Recall that our analysis in the preceding chapter uncovered four distinct clusters in a representative pool of first-time Mexican migrants to the United States from 1965 to 2010. Migrants in the first group were almost exclusively men, a majority of whom lacked formal education, and the majority coming from landless households in poor villages in the central-west of the country.

The modal pattern for migrants in this group was to make frequent trips, to send regular remittances to Mexico or to bring back savings, and eventually to return to origin, typically after buying a house or a piece of land. An average migrant in this group made significantly more trips compared to one in the other three groups (3.1 vs. 1.9 trips, p<0.05), and stayed in the United States for a shorter duration on the first trip (median 12 vs. 30 months). I call this group the *circular migrants* to highlight this distinctive pattern.

Circular migrants, for a long time, made up the majority among all first-time migrants in our data. In 1965, two in three migrants fell into this group. This number declined over time, to one in three migrants in 1980 and to one in ten in 2010.

A particular logic, as I will argue below, underlies the mobility of circular migrants: one that made sense given the large wage differentials between Mexico and the United States, and the possibility of crossing the border without documents; one that was viable due to social networks already spanning across the two countries; and one that followed from the cultural expectations of men to be the sole providers for their families. And a particular combination of economic, political, social, and cultural conditions in Mexico and the United States allowed for this logic to dominate the migrant stream in the 1960s and 1970s and to decline thereafter.

This decline, as we will see below, resulted from a shift in the prevailing conditions in Mexico and the United States that made circulating harder and migrating more costly to families. I provide a brief review of the various conditions in Mexico and the United States from the 1940s through the 1970s that set the stage for migration between the countries. The review highlights the conditions that are especially pertinent to circular migrants and is not meant to be a comprehensive account. Indeed, in subsequent chapters, I introduce events or processes from the same period that are more relevant to understanding the movement of the other three migrant groups in the data.

MEXICO 1940–1980
A RISE IN MANUFACTURING AND A DECLINE IN AGRICULTURE

Between 1940 and 1970, Mexico's economy was growing at an impressive rate of 6.2% per year. Much of this growth came from manufacturing, where production increased at an annual rate of 8%. Production in agriculture also grew around 8% per year in the 1940s, but the rate of growth dropped to 4% in the 1950s and 1960s and to less than 1% in the 1970s.

The state's development strategy of import-substituting industrialization in this period helped fuel the shift from agriculture to manufacturing. In 1947, Mexico began to impose restrictions on imports to protect domestic industries. Through the 1950s and 1960s, the government continued to expand the scope of these controls to stimulate any new industry that substituted imports. The manufacturing sector was the main beneficiary here. The effective protection rate, a measure of how much extra domestic producers can charge and still compete with imported goods, remained above 37% for manufacturing in both 1960 and 1970, while it dropped from just 3% in 1960 to -1.4% in 1970 for agriculture.

The Mexican government continued to support agriculture to some degree through input subsidies and guaranteed prices on stable crops. But the share of public investment in agriculture kept declining, from 17% in the 1940s to 11% in the 1960s, as did the share of credit given to the sector (from 15% of the total in 1960 to 9% in 1970). The agricultural sector went from employing almost 60% of the Mexican labor force in 1950 to containing less than 35% of the working population in 1975.

The sectorial differences became starker over time. In 1976, for the first time in Mexico's history, the average wage in the manufacturing sector was sufficient for a single earner to purchase a market basket of goods required to meet an urban family's basic needs in Mexico. This was by no means the case for agricultural workers or the average *ejidatario*. The social security system also favored those working in the manufacturing sector and, as a result, extended higher coverage to urban rather than rural areas. As of 1977, the agricultural sector contained only 29% of the working population but 79% of households earning less than minimum wage.

RURAL POVERTY CONCENTRATED IN THE CENTRAL AND SOUTHERN REGIONS

The benefits of economic growth in Mexico were unevenly distributed, not just across sectors, but also in the population. In 1968, the poorest 40% of Mexicans accrued less than 11% of the total income, while the richest 10% received almost four times that amount. Social tensions started to become visible in rural and urban guerilla activity through the 1960s and 1970s, as well as in the student movement of 1968, which ended in its bloody repression in President Díaz Ordaz's term (1964–1970).

President Luis Echeverría took office in 1970 with a proposal for "shared development" to alleviate inequality and to address the sluggish growth in agriculture. During his six-year term, public investments in agriculture increased from 11% of the total to nearly 16%. New programs extended credit and technical support to rural communities in the development of infrastructure projects. These initiatives, however, did not benefit all farmers equally.

New investments in irrigation and roads were directed to the commercial private farms in the north and northwestern regions, which produced most of Mexico's fruits and vegetables destined for export, and did not reach the smallholder or subsistence farmers in the central and southern states who continued to use traditional cultivation methods and produced for the domestic market. The latter group included many *ejidatarios*, or farmers working the communal plots.

Poverty in Mexico from 1940 to 1970 remained mostly a rural problem concentrated in the agricultural sector and in the center and south of the country. The central and southern states housed a majority of the poor in the country, estimated to be around 15.7 million people in 1977.

RAPID POPULATION GROWTH

The transformation of the Mexican economy occurred at a time of rapid population growth. The population more than doubled in 30 years, from 20 million in 1940 to 48 million in 1970. This growth put pressure on the communal lands, which quickly became insufficient in providing subsistence—let alone cash income—to larger families and communities.

In 1970, the fertility rate in Mexico was still very high, about 6.7 births per woman. This rate gradually dropped to 4.7 in 1980, 3.4 in 1990, 2.7 in 2000, and 2.3 in 2010. The large birth cohorts of the 1960s and 1970s, however, led to large worker cohorts entering the labor market in the 1980s and 1990s. The economic growth in this period was not nearly enough to accommodate the large numbers of young adults joining the workforce. The combination of strong growth in the labor supply and weak growth in the labor demand in Mexico, economists Gordon Hanson and Craig McIntosh argue, created additional pressures to emigrate to the United States. Indeed, the authors estimate that the variation in Mexican labor supply from 1977 to 1997 (a legacy of the birth rates between 1960 and 1984) can explain two-fifths of Mexican migrant flow to the United States in that period.

THE UNITED STATES, 1940–1980
THE END OF THE BRACERO ERA

Between 1942 and 1964, the United States entered into a labor agreement with Mexico known as the Bracero program. The program started as a temporary measure to meet the United States' labor demand in agriculture during World War II. Some 10 million men were conscripted into the military, leaving few able hands to work in the fields. During the war, from 1942 to 1945, the program brought nearly 170,000 Mexican workers (*braceros*) to the United States.

The labor shortages in agriculture did not end with the war. The dramatic increase in industrial production continued to pull American workers away from agriculture. Congress, under pressure from agricultural growers, extended the Bracero program on an annual basis through the 1940s. In 1951, Congress passed a law to give the program a permanent statutory basis. At that time, the number of Bracero visas doubled to around 200,000 per year.

Initially, the Bracero contracts were quite favorable to workers, requiring employers to guarantee work for at least three-fourths of the contract period, to pay the prevailing wages in their area, and to offer free housing and meals at a reasonable cost. The contracts could be enforced with help from the Mexican consuls in the United States. These terms changed in the early 1950s, when the Eisenhower administration stopped the oversight by the consuls and made the contracts more grower-friendly.

During the program's 22-year tenure, some 4.6 million *braceros* traveled from Mexican recruitment centers to the U.S. reception centers near the border. Even this large number, however, fell short of the labor demand in the fields. The growers continued to recruit undocumented Mexicans on the side, facing no liability for doing so under the Texas Proviso, an immigration law that prohibited the prosecution of employers for hiring undocumented workers.

Undocumented immigrant flows increased after 1950, when the war in Korea led to a reinstatement of the draft in the United States. From 1945 to 1950, the apprehensions on the border jumped from 69,000 to 883,000. In 1954, the Immigration and Naturalization Services (INS) responded with "Operation Wetback," deporting about 2 million undocumented Mexican workers. The campaign also doubled the number of Bracero contracts to around 400,000 per year.

By 1960, however, the support for the Bracero program began to fade. In a period of expanding civil rights in the United States, the program stood out as a discriminatory system that exploited workers, both Mexican and American. A coalition of advocates pressed for its elimination. Resistance from agricultural growers also weakened in this period, perhaps due

to their desire to avoid the Bracero program's costly bureaucratic procedures when undocumented immigrants were available to work in the fields.
The program dwindled at first, with the number of visas granted dropping
by more than half (from 438,000 in 1959 to 178,000 in 1964), until the
Kennedy administration brought it to a full stop in 1964.

NEW QUOTAS ON VISAS TO MEXICANS

The end of the Bracero program marked the dawn of a new immigration
era, one that would be dominated by undocumented flows from Mexico to
the United States. The Immigration and Naturalization Act in 1965 solidified this pattern.

The act abolished quotas for immigrants based on national origins, and
instead established a neutral system that allocated visas among countries
more or less uniformly. Countries in the Eastern Hemisphere (Europe,
Africa, the Middle East, Asia, and the Pacific) were each granted up to
20,000 visas annually, and were subject to a hemispheric cap of 170,000
visas annually. The visas were to be allocated according to a preference
system that ranked family members the highest, followed by those fulfill-
ing occupational needs of the United States, and then those qualifying for
humanitarian considerations. There was no numerical limitation for immediate family members of U.S. citizens (spouses, parents, and unmarried
children).

Countries in the Western Hemisphere (Latin America, the Caribbean,
and Canada) were not given a per-country limit, but starting in 1968, faced
a hemispheric quota of 120,000 visas per year. This ceiling represents the
first attempt by the United States to numerically restrict the number of
immigrants from Mexico.

These restrictions on legal entry, combined with persistent demand for
migrant workers in agriculture, left Mexican migrants no choice but to cross
the border without documents. During this period, migrants did so without
much difficulty given the relatively low level of border enforcement.

SUMMARY AND IMPLICATIONS FOR THE MEXICO-U.S.
MIGRANT FLOWS IN 1965–1980

From the 1940s onward, Mexico experienced a great transformation from
an agrarian society to a semi-industrial one. The decline in agricultural
subsidies hurt small producers. The rapid growth in population not only
increased the labor supply to higher levels than the labor demand, but also
diminished the capacity of communal lands (*ejidos*) to provide subsistence.

Poverty remained concentrated in rural areas in the central and southern parts of the country.

Two events in the United States in the 1960s—the end of the Bracero era in 1964 and the new Immigration and Naturalization Act in 1965—helped shape migrant flows from Mexico.

The circular migrants, the majority group among first-time migrants in our data from 1965 to 1980, left their poor rural communities in Mexico to take up jobs in the fields of California and Texas, which were in great supply after the Bracero program. Nearly 40% of circular migrants from 1965 to 1975 (and about 30% thereafter), for example, worked in agriculture, and 76% went to either California or Texas. Many of these migrants circulated partly because agricultural work was seasonal. Due to lack of work permits or visas, most circular migrants crossed the border without documents, but also without much difficulty given the relatively weak U.S. border enforcement.

CIRCULAR MIGRANTS: ESCAPING POVERTY, SEEKING HIGHER WAGES?

Particular conditions in Mexico (the decline in agriculture, the rise in population, and the concentration of poverty in the rural center and south) and the United States (the end of the migrant guest worker program, the residual demand for agricultural workers, and the weak border enforcement) seem to have made the flow of a particular migrant group—workers from rural areas of Mexico—inevitable. Although these migrants faced substantial constraints in their own country, considerable opportunities in the agricultural sector awaited them in the United States. This group was certain to gain from migrating, one can argue, especially given the few restrictions imposed on undocumented border crossing at the time.

"ONE GOES WHERE THE MONEY IS."

Alejandro, a former migrant from Buenavista, captures in a few words how most people, including scholars, think about migration: as a matter of economic differentials between countries. This idea forms the backbone of migration theory in neoclassical economics. Regional differences in wages or employment mobilize individuals, especially those who expect to earn more in destination compared to origin after factoring in the potential costs of migrating. In this theory, migrants are "income maximizers," rational agents seeking higher returns on their skills and knowledge.

Certain patterns we observe for circular migrants in our data are consistent with predictions from the neoclassical theory. These patterns emerge in an analysis detailed in appendix G, which relates the number of circular migrants over time to various macro-level indicators with a statistical model. The indicators—suggested by an extensive theoretical and empirical literature on migration also summarized in the appendix—track major economic, policy, and demographic trends in Mexico and the United States that might influence the migration rates between the two. This analysis cannot identify causal relationships in a statistical sense, but it does suggest strong correlations. I present these correlations with simple descriptive plots here, reserving the tables with full analysis results for the appendix.

Figure 2.2 shows the trend in the number of circular migrants (solid line with values on the left y-axis) along with three concurrent trends (dashed line with values on the right y-axis across the three panels) in the Mexico-U.S. context. In the 1970s, six out of 1,000 people joined this migrant stream annually. This number dropped to about three in 1,000 in the 1980s and to one in 1,000 in the 1990s. This downward trend ran almost perfectly counter to the trends in two series in the top panels—the Mexican GDP per capita (top) and the U.S. Border Patrol Enforcement budget (middle) both of which rose steeply through the observed period. The GDP per capita more than doubled in real terms in Mexico from 1965 to 2010, while the budget dedicated to border control grew exponentially in the United States. It is reasonable to assert that both trends might have deterrent effects on migration: the former by expanding the economic opportunities available in Mexico, and the latter, by making it more difficult to cross the border without documents over time.

The bottom panel plot suggests another plausible deterrent for circular migration: the declining real wages in the United States. The hourly wage paid to production workers was high, around US$20 in 1970 (adjusted to 2010 values). The wage fluctuated with the business cycle in the United States. It dropped significantly during each recession, in 1974–1975, 1981–1982, 1990–1992, and 2007–2008. By the late 1990s, the hourly wage had dipped to its lowest value of US$16 per hour but rose thereafter to approach US$19 per hour in 2010. (The wages for farmworkers in this period—for which the data are less complete—follow a similar pattern.)

The trend in the hourly wage nearly perfectly matches the trend in circular migration until 2000. Almost every spike in the wage rate (such as in years 1972, 1977, and 1983) is followed by a corresponding spike in the rate of circular migrants, typically within a year or two (such as in years 1973, 1978–1979, and 1984–1986). The two lines diverge after 2000, however. The increase in the U.S. wage rate no longer ignites an increase in the number of circular migrants, possibly owing to other conditions such as the

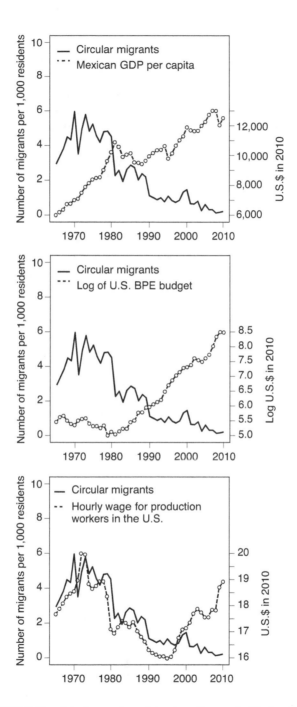

FIGURE 2.2. Trends in the number of circular migrants, the Mexican GDP per capita, the logarithm of U.S. Border Patrol Enforcement budget, and the U.S. average wage for production workers, 1965–2010

improving economy in Mexico and the mounting efforts to control the border in the United States.

These patterns (confirmed with the results from the regression model in appendix G) suggest that circular migrants do respond to changes in the Mexican GDP per capita, the budget allocated to U.S. border control, and the U.S. wages to low-skill workers—three parameters shaping the expected costs and benefits of migrating—in ways that are predicted by the neoclassical economics theory. More migrants circulate when the Mexican economy is doing poorly and when the U.S. border is easier to cross; fewer do so when the U.S. wages are in decline.

Circular migrants—or their individual attributes, to be more precise— confirm another pattern consistent with the neoclassical model. These migrants are selected from among the least educated in our data, a group that enjoys few alternatives in the internal labor market in Mexico.

"HERE ONE NEEDS A COLLEGE DEGREE . . . TO HAVE ENOUGH MONEY."

This was Father Fernando's response to our question, "Why do people from Buenavista migrate to the United States, and not to Guadalajara or Mexico City?" He elaborated that the better-paying jobs in the cities, those that would allow one to "build a house or to renovate it," would require advanced education, which most residents of Buenavista lacked.

In fact, many individuals from the rural-central and southern regions of Mexico did resort to internal, rather than U.S.-bound, migration. Between 1965 and 1980, at least one in five households in the MMP data had an internal migrant. About half of these households were located in a rural area where a majority of the labor force worked in agriculture; about 60% lived in a poor community where earning less than the minimum wage was the norm. Most households with internal migrants had either no land (91%) or a small plot of less than 10 acres (4%) sufficient only for subsistence farming.

Internal migration provided a potential way out of poverty, but as Father Fernando correctly inferred, the greatest returns accrued to more educated individuals. Consider two groups of individuals in the MMP data between 1965 and 1980: internal migrants with a middle school degree or higher (25% of the total) and those with less than a primary school degree (49%). The former group worked mostly in professional, service, or administrative jobs (65% of the group), some in the growing cities of Guadalajara and Mexico City (at least 19% of the group) and some (21%) in the border region, where new plants were opening as part of Mexico's Border Industrialization Program. Individuals in this more educated group enjoyed average earnings of almost US$1,600 per month (in 2010 values). The latter, less educated group, by contrast, worked mainly in manufacturing and agriculture (65% of the group). About a fifth relocated to the northwestern states where most commercial farms were located. This group earned an average of US$750 per month, about half of what the more educated migrants received.

If we extend this comparison to the U.S.-bound migrants in the MMP data in this period, the difference between the high- and low-education groups in earnings becomes less severe. The U.S. migrants with middle schooling or more earned about US$4,800 per month (in 2010 values) on average, while those with primary schooling or less were paid US$3,200. The jobs in the United States available to Mexican migrants, in other words, offered less of a premium for education. It is not incidental, then, that the majority of the U.S. migrants between 1965 and 1980 in our data came from among this less educated group in rural Mexico, who enjoyed the highest marginal returns on their move.

This pattern seems consistent with a rational choice model of migration behavior, that is, one that presumes individuals select the best alternative given their options. For the typical circular migrant—the rural farmer with no education—working in the United States appears to be the best choice, especially from the late 1960s to the early 1980s given the poverty in Mexico, the high wages in the United States, and the relatively porous border between the two countries.

Other patterns related to circular migrants, however, require further elaboration. Why, for example, does this group originate from central-western Mexico when the poorest regions are in the south of the country?

CIRCULAR MIGRANTS: ON THE BEATEN PATH?
THE REGIONAL PATTERNING OF U.S. MIGRANTS IN MEXICO

Between 1965 and 1980, 90% of circular migrants, and 87% of all first-time migrants to the United States in our data, originated from the central-western states in Mexico, which were poor but not the poorest in the country. This pattern is not just a particularity of the MMP data, which oversampled from the central-western states compared to the southern states in Mexico, but was observed in other nationally representative data sets as well.

Indeed, the geographic concentration of migrants in central-western Mexico is already evident in one of the earliest sources of large-scale data on Mexico-U.S. crossings. In 1925, more than half (57%) of the Mexicans who entered the United States via the three major entry points (San Antonio, El Paso, and Los Angeles) originated from just five states in central-western Mexico (Guanajuato, Jalisco, Michoacán, San Luis Potosí, and Zacatecas). This regional pattern changed little during the Bracero period from 1942 to 1964. Of the 4.6 million Bracero workers, about half were thought to originate from the same five central-western states in Mexico.

Scholars explain this pattern in two ways. First, they refer to the costs of migrating, which may be higher than what those in the poorest southern states can afford. Second, they point out the pattern of early railroad development in Mexico, which connected central-western states to the United States in the 1890s. Historians describe how recruiters used these railroads to reach Mexican workers and to bring them to the United States to build more railroads, to help in farming, and to work in factories.

Both explanations have face validity. The regional concentration of migrants in central-western Mexico might have its origins in its optimal level of poverty, in its earlier connection to the United States via railroads, or both. The initiating conditions notwithstanding, it is remarkable that the migrant flow from Mexico to the United States has retained its regional concentration for several decades.

Our data reveal that the central-western states still had a stronghold in the U.S.-bound migrant flow from 1965 to 1980. Figure 2.3 shows a map of Mexico where each state is color-coded to indicate the number of first-time U.S. migrants from that state between 1965 and 1980 as a share of 1,000 residents. The states in white are those not represented in the MMP data. There are eight states in black (Baja California, Colima, Durango, Jalisco, Michoacán, Nayarit, San Luis Potosí, and Zacatecas), and six of these are located in the central-western part of the country. Each state has at least 8.6 migrants per 1,000 residents, and together they account for 76% of all first-time U.S. migrants in our data between 1965 and 1980. The eight states in dark grey have between 3.3 and 8.5 migrants on a first U.S. trip per 1,000 residents and are located in the central-west (Aguascalientes, Guanajuato, Guerrero, México, and Querétaro) or the north (Chihuahua, Nuevo León, and Sinaloa). Finally, the eight states in light grey are home to less than 2.7 first-time migrants per 1,000 and are spread across the remainder of the country.

What explains the persistence of central-western Mexico as the major migrant-sending region to the United States over time? One explanation is that the same economic conditions present in the 1920s (and perhaps earlier) remained prevalent through the 1980s and continued to push individuals to migrate to the United States. Mexico's withdrawal from the agricultural sector in this period certainly ensured that the rural central-west would remain a locus of poverty.

Another explanation—and one that can be complementary to the first —is that the presence of earlier migrants from the region changed the decision-making environment for future migrants, making it more likely that they would also move to the United States. I now consider this latter explanation in greater depth.

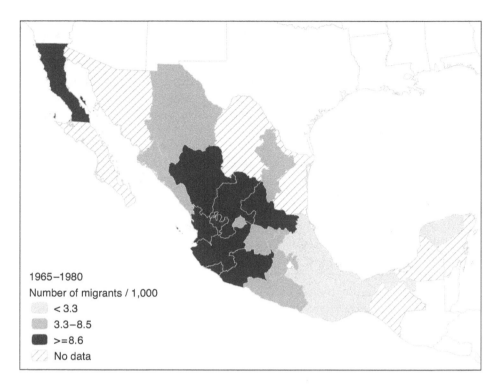

FIGURE 2.3. Map of Mexico with 24 states categorized into three groups
based on the number of U.S.-bound migrants out of that state between 1965
and 1980 per 1,000 residents in the MMP data
MAP BY Jeff Blossom, Center for Geographic Analysis, Harvard University

NETWORK EFFECTS IN MIGRATION

An extensive literature in sociology and anthropology has elaborated on
how prior migrants might inform or influence potential migrants in origin. In the 1960s, anthropologists wrote about "chain migration," a social
process by which each migrant pulls others from the origin to his or her
destination, forming new links in an ever-expanding chain. In the 1980s,
anthropologists talked of "migrant circuits," and sociologists of "migrant
networks," complex webs of social relations that connect migrants in destination to non-migrants in origin. These relations, scholars argued, make
future migration more likely, if not inevitable. Indeed, many empirical
studies that followed identified "network effects" in migration, which occur
when an individual's likelihood of migrating varies with the prior migrants
in his or her social network. Studies in the Mexican setting, for example,

found that individuals were likely to move to the United States if their family members had done so previously, or if they lived in communities with a high share of U.S. migrants.

Despite the proliferation of empirical work, however, scholars remain largely ambivalent about the mechanisms underlying the social influences in migration. What is it that prior migrants do that increases the chances that others will also migrate? For some scholars, prior migrants provide useful information or help that reduces the risks of migrating. For others, prior migrants create normative pressures that encourage new migrants to take on the journey. For others still, prior migrants contribute to the formation of institutions, like an ethnic community in destination, that increase the benefits one can expect from a move.

It is important to distinguish among generative mechanisms for network effects in migration because each mechanism might carry different implications for the continuity and growth of migration flows. Assume prior migrants provide resources such as help in crossing the border. These resources might be cut off if it becomes more difficult for prior migrants to return home, say, due to increased border enforcement. In that case, prior migrants might have less of an influence on potential migrants' decisions. Now assume prior migrants enable the formation of common resources, such as smuggling businesses that facilitate border crossing or recruiters that eliminate job searching. These resources allow for more migration regardless of how often individual migrants visit their home communities.

A TYPOLOGY OF GENERATIVE MECHANISMS FOR NETWORK EFFECTS

I introduce here an exhaustive typology developed jointly with Paul Di-Maggio. This typology distinguishes among three social mechanisms that might lead to network effects in migration. Each mechanism identifies a particular way in which prior migrants (or others observing migrants) inform or influence the migration decisions of those around them.

In the first mechanism, *social facilitation*, prior migrants offer useful information or help that reduces the costs associated with migration or increases the benefits that might be expected from it. An experienced migrant, for example, might give tips on crossing the border, and might help a new migrant find a job, which makes it less risky and more beneficial for that migrant to take the trip.

In the second mechanism, *normative influence*, prior migrants do not alter the intrinsic costs or benefits of the behavior but instead provide social rewards, or impose sanctions, to encourage or discourage it. Former migrants in the family, for example, might push another family member to migrate, offering to take care of her children while she is away. Or migrants in the community might shun their friend for not migrating, suggesting he is not brave enough.

In the third and final mechanism, *network externalities*, prior migrants generate a pool of common resources that increase the value or reduce the cost of migrating to potential migrants. These resources are institutionalized and need not be exchanged at an interpersonal level as in social facilitation. For example, the presence of a steady migrant stream from a community might attract smugglers and recruiters there, or it might create migrant enclaves or hometown associations in destination that make it easier for new migrants to complete the journey or to find a job.

These mechanisms are not mutually exclusive. A prior migrant can directly influence her friends by telling them about work options in the United States or by providing active encouragement, and she can indirectly affect their migration by working in a hometown association that helps new migrants.

It is possible, however, that different mechanisms become more or less salient in different periods or for different migrant groups in our data. Our qualitative data based on interviews with 139 migrants, migrant family members, and non-migrants in Mexico give us an opportunity to observe network effects in migration and also to identify the different mechanisms underlying them. Using these and other historical data, I trace how migrant networks have developed and operated during and after the Bracero period.

RAMÓN PÉREZ'S STORY

Ramón "Tianguis" Pérez, who migrated as a young man in the 1950s, and later wrote a book about his journey, describes how migration took off in his town in Oaxaca, a state in southwestern Mexico, after the Bracero program:

> The news of the Bracero program was brought to us by our itinerant merchants. . . . One of them came with the news that there were possibilities of work in the United States as a *bracero*, and the news passed from mouth to mouth until everyone had heard it.

Two merchants were the first to take up this opportunity, as Ramón recalled:

> From the day of their departure, the whole town followed the fate of those adventurers with great interest. . . . After a little while, the first letters to their families arrived. The closest kinsmen asked what news the letters contained,

and from them the news spread to the rest of the villagers. . . . The men's return home, six months later, was a big event because when they came into town they were seen carrying large boxes of foreign goods, mainly clothing. Their experience inspired others. . . . I, too, joined the emigrant stream.

The first migrants played a crucial role in Ramón's town by providing information about what it is like to work in the United States. They did not need to say much actually; the boxes they carried with them upon return communicated to everyone in town that it was worthwhile to take the trip across the border. And Ramón did so himself.

The network effects here worked mainly through social facilitation according to our typology, where prior migrants provided information that signaled to others the efficacy of migration. And many of Ramón's townsmen traveled to the United States as *braceros*. But, over time, network effects came to operate also through externalities, the resources that a strong migrant flow often creates or attracts.

Smugglers and recruiters began to frequent Ramón's town to find more workers to take to the United States. These actors became crucial to sustaining the flow when the Bracero program came to an end in 1964. As Ramón recalls, at that time, "the *coyotes* [smugglers] kept working on their own. They looked for employers in the U.S. and supplied them with workers illegally."

Ramón's story reveals two mechanisms at work—social facilitation and externalities, which turned prior migration into an engine feeding future migration flows in his town. These mechanisms were also important to circular migrants in our data in the post-Bracero period.

NETWORK EFFECTS AT A TIME OF CIRCULAR MIGRATION

Circular migrants—the group that predominated among first-time migrants in our data from 1965 to 1980—worked mostly in agriculture in the United States, taking the seasonal jobs once filled by the *braceros*. The seasonality of work, and relative openness of the border at the time, allowed these migrants to circulate, that is, go to the United States for about a year at a time and then return to Mexico.

This circularity—as in the Bracero period that Ramón writes about—must have enabled migrants to more directly share their experiences with others in their families and communities compared to migrants of a later period. Indeed, among our respondents, those migrating in this earlier period (before the U.S. border became better guarded starting in the mid-1980s) are likely to refer to face-to-face contact or direct help from prior migrants as being important to their decisions. This help reduces the uncertainty of the journey for new migrants. "You risk a lot to go make another peso because you are not sure if you will come back or if you will actually do okay over there," a migrant tells us. "That is the important thing," another adds, "[for] somebody to give you a hand."

Many migrants consider migrating only after securing help from a family member or a trusted friend. For example, one respondent tells us how her husband at first did not see migrating to the United States as an option "because nobody from his family was there" to support him. He only decided to go when the respondent's siblings offered to take the husband along.

Migrants typically travel in groups, which allows new migrants to learn the ropes from the more seasoned migrants. Traveling together also makes the journey safer for everyone, as the mother of a migrant elaborates: "It is like a way to protect themselves on the way. . . . They gather exactly because of that. . . . Because they know they will have to go through a lot, and that is a way to help one another."

Migrants from a community also often share living quarters in the United States, as one respondent explains: "They all gather . . . and rent an apartment. In a two-story apartment . . . live six, seven guys. . . . They all divide the expenses." This allows migrants to save money and send more of it back to their family in Mexico. It also allows new migrants to easily adjust to the United States. It is not uncommon for the new migrants to receive an initial loan from the other migrants until they can stand on their own feet. One migrant explains this system:

> Sometimes the friends living with me in the apartment, they would say "Hey, my brother is coming, lend me money for the *coyote* or the rent" . . . so I would pay their rent, meals, and re-adjust [their payments] when they started working. If there were five of us [living together], we each got to pay a certain amount and we helped each other that way.

Prior migrants personally help many new migrants in crossing the border, finding accommodation in the United States, and securing a job. Prior migrants can also inspire new migrants through visible signs of their success in the United States, like newly acquired land or a house, which can encourage others to migrate as well. Such signs reduce the uncertainty of migration and suggest its value as an economic strategy.

A migrant's wife, for example, tells us how her own family's success— conveyed through the purchase of a new house—inspired her husband's move:

> My mother lived with the same things [as us]. . . . Like, at the beginning, we only had a little room and a tiny kitchen. And as soon as my brother left [for the

United States], they built her a house . . . because they [migrants like my husband] do observe [others]. . . . They say, "You can see the results [of migrating]."

Another respondent concurs that observing other migrants encouraged him, and other first-timers, to travel to the United States: "Back then, everyone that left did well. Many acquaintances, neighbors, and friends did fine. They started their own businesses and bought land here."

The resources of direct help or information surely matter for all first-time migrants in our data. But such resources are particularly significant for circular migrants. Circular migrants have more opportunities to give (and receive) help or information personally because they make more frequent trips back home. Circular migrants are also more likely than the other groups to rely on word-of-mouth for information, as they concentrate in an earlier period when alternative sources of information (like news media, pamphlets from the government, the Internet, phone calls to migrants in the United States) are either not available or not accessible to those in rural Mexico.

The increased likelihood of circular migrants relying on other migrants is apparent in our survey data. The household heads among circular migrants (a group for which we have more detailed information) are significantly more likely to live with migrants from their origin community on their last trip (the only occasion this information is recorded) compared to the other migrant groups (66% vs. 61%, $p<0.05$). Earlier circular migrants—those migrating prior to 1975—are also more likely to live with their townsmen (67% vs. 61%, $p<0.05$) compared to their later counterparts moving in or after 1975.

The interpersonal exchange of information or help, or what I call social facilitation, is the main mechanism for network effects in circular migration. But it is not the only one. Externalities, institutionalized resources like smugglers or recruiters, are also relevant to sustaining circular migration.

About 80% of the household heads among circular migrants report relying on a smuggler to cross the border in our survey data. This share, although quite high, is actually significantly lower than the share (84%, $p<0.05$) among the other migrants in our data. Circular migrants use smugglers less not just because they can rely on prior migrants who tend to visit frequently, but also because they mostly migrate in a period when the border control is weak in the United States and smuggling operations are still rather small-scale in Mexico, typically taken up by former migrants themselves.

There is another mechanism for network effects, normative influence, that works through rewards or sanctions offered by social relations to encourage migration. This mechanism is different from the other two in that the alters—typically friends or family—have a stake in the person's decision to migrate. They are not just providing resources like information or help in a neutral way, but also are actively trying to convince the person to migrate. This mechanism works through social pressures that can be exerted directly by an alter (e.g., a family member voicing approval of the decision to migrate) or indirectly in a community (e.g., through a shared understanding that migration is a necessary stepping stone into adulthood).

Anthropologists observing Mexico in the 1980s write about a social norm taking hold in some communities, where migrating to the United States becomes a "rite of passage" that most young men take up without question. Those that stay in Mexico are sanctioned, often seen as non-enterprising or unsuitable for marriage.

Many migrants of the post-Bracero era among our respondents mention being actively "encouraged" by family and friends to go to the United States. Some migrants talk about a powerful image of migration in their communities at the time. "You just work to buy a broom over there," as one migrant describes it, "and sweep up the dollars."

This image diverges from the reality in the United States, even for those earlier migrants who faced relatively little difficulty in crossing or in finding a job on the fields. But the image mostly survives, because migrants can exaggerate life prospects in the United States, or "sweeten the truth," as the mother of a migrant puts it, and thus sustain the widespread belief in the value of migrating in sending communities.

Several migrants describe a rude awakening when they realized the discrepancy between what others had told them about the United States and what they actually experienced. A male respondent, who first migrated in 1974 at the age of 29, tells us:

> [Migrants] came and told stories that were not real. . . . "Over there I have . . . Over there I am." And they were all lies. . . . When I left, I went with friends who had [spent] years over there and noticed that they hardly had anything to eat. They had been there for years, and people here thought they were millionaires . . . but it was all a lie.

The glorified view of migration is hard to challenge, especially at the time of circular migration since prior migrants serve as the singular source of information on life in the United States. Migrants who do not succeed end up internalizing their failure. Many, as one respondent put it, do not return to their home "out of shame." These migrants inadvertently conform to a collective narrative about migration, although their personal experiences strictly diverge from that narrative. Their conformity, in the end, convinces many others to consider migration as a viable—and sometimes the only viable—path to success.

But, as we will see in subsequent chapters, the truth comes out sooner or later as new information sources become available about the possible perils of migrating. One former migrant talks about the "different perspectives" that migrants today have compared to those in the past. "Nowadays, people go with eyes wide open," he says.

For circular migrants, then, frequent visits home allow prior migrants to directly help migrants-to-be, to provide an example of success, and sometimes to feed (or simply not challenge) unrealistic hopes about the prospects in the United States. For this group, network effects mainly operate through social facilitation and normative influence with respect to our typology, and to a lesser extent through externalities.

As expected, network effects lead to migrant chains or networks that connect specific communities in Mexico to specific target destinations in the United States. Jorge, the migrant who was introduced in the beginning of this chapter, emphasizes these linkages. "People go where their family is, where their friends are, where their relatives are . . . where any acquaintance is." Many from his town go to Chicago, because "three of four people [first] went there, those people helped another five, and those five bring ten." Because of these chains, Jorge adds, "each town, each state [in Mexico] knows where their people are."

Migration as a path-dependent process

Prior migrants provide resources or influence that makes it easier for others in their families and communities to migrate. These so-called network effects make migration a path-dependent process, where past migration increasingly determines the size and direction of future movement. Prior migrants can create other changes in origin and destination that similarly make future migration more likely.

Prior migrants can buy land in the origin setting with their earnings, driving prices up, and forcing others to migrate in order to afford land for themselves. Prior migrants sometimes invest in agricultural technologies, reducing the demand for manual labor in origin, and leaving others no option but to migrate. Prior migrants and their earnings can induce a general sense of relative deprivation in the origin community, inspiring others to migrate as well.

Migrants can alter perceptions in destination too. The presence of a migrant group in a certain occupation might stigmatize that occupation for natives, creating a persistent demand for migrant labor there. This is why, economist Michael Piore argues, even temporary migrant worker agreements, like the Bracero program, can have permanent implications.

Sociologist Douglas Massey calls this self-feeding character "the cumulative causation of migration." Each migration act alters the context in both the sending and receiving societies in ways that make future migration more likely. Migration flows become self-perpetuating over time and even disconnected from the economic or political conditions that created them in the first place.

Is migration unstoppable once started?

Cumulative causation represents a new paradigm to understand migration. The theory alerts us to internal dynamics that perpetuate migration flows rather than external factors, such as wage differentials, that can initiate movement. The theory provides a corrective to the neoclassical economics model in this way. It also provides a plausible explanation for the stickiness of the regional origins of Mexican migrants for much of the twentieth century. But cumulative causation implies migration flows that grow ad infinitum. The theory cannot really account for change.

As the analysis here and in subsequent chapters will show, the internal dynamics of migration are neither unstoppable nor constant in their generative mechanisms over time. While the same central-western states in Mexico identified in historical work largely retain their status as the main suppliers of migrants in our data, for example, new regions also begin to emerge and gain in importance over time.

This tension is visible in figure 2.4, which shows the number of U.S. migrants from each of the 24 Mexican states in 1925 as a percentage of the population in that state in the 1930 Census (according to Foerster's historical data) against the same percentage in 1975 in the MMP data. Many states high in the 1925 share of migrants are also high in the 1975 share, but the relationship is far from perfect. Several states fall far from the estimated line in the figure given by a linear regression model that uses the 1925 share of migrants as a predictor of the 1975 share.

This simple analysis suggests migration as a possibly path-dependent process, but it is not a predetermined one. An established history of migration facilitates future movement out of a region but by no means makes it that region's destiny. As we will see in subsequent chapters, the changes in the economic conditions in Mexico, and their spatial loci, can create major shifts in the regional distribution of the migrant stream, as well as its composition over time.

Migration determined by economic differentials and social networks

There is an important theoretical takeaway here. The neoclassical economics and cumulative causation provide largely complementary views on migration: The former sets up the exogenous conditions that initiate

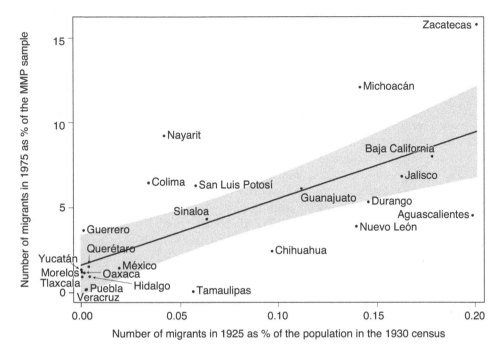

FIGURE 2.4. Prevalence of U.S. migrants in 24 Mexican states in 1925 versus 1975

movement and the latter, the endogenous dynamics that end up sustaining
the flow. One can see this complementarity perfectly in the case of circular migrants. The neoclassical model is crucial to understanding the fluctuations in the number of circular migrants. Their diminishing presence
over time only makes sense when we consider the falling real wages in the
United States, the rising incomes in Mexico, and the increasing enforcement on the border. But the cumulative causation model is also essential
here to understanding why circular migrants mostly originate from the
central-western states, and in particular, from families with prior migrants
or communities with already high levels of migration.

CIRCULAR MIGRANTS: PERFORMING
FAMILY AND GENDER ROLES?

The analysis so far explains why circular migrants appear in our data in a
particular period and in a particular region of Mexico. It answers the questions of when and where, in other words. One question remains, however.

Who are the circular migrants? The group includes a large majority of men (84%). This is perhaps not surprising. Men are the primary migrants because, in the post-Bracero years in which circular migrants prevail, most jobs are in agriculture in the United States. These jobs demand male workers. But, men are also the primary migrants in this period, I argue, because of their role as the primary breadwinners in the household.

In the 1960s, Mexico was still very much a patriarchal society with a traditional division of labor. Especially in rural areas, men were typically the heads of, and sole earners in, households. Women's responsibilities centered on household tasks and child care. The expected births per woman stood at an astounding 6.7 in 1970. Women obtained little schooling then, and only a small share reported being employed outside the home.

Our interviews suggest that the role of men as the head of and provider for the family often shapes their views on migration. Migrant men generally talk about their responsibilities to their wives and children. "Imagine yourself with young children, and having to pay for their schooling," a former migrant tells us. "They depended on me one hundred percent." Many household heads, especially those circulating back and forth between Mexico and the United States, state having specific goals in migrating, and not just for themselves, but also for their family. "You go with a certain purpose," a migrant man tells us. "If you don't have a house, your purpose is to build a house." Migrants like that "come back," he adds, "because they are better off being with their family [in Mexico]."

What is best for the family is not always obvious, however. For most, being a migrant means being away from the family. "Cut in half," explains one migrant about how he felt when he left his family for the United States. Another described it as "a great punishment." For household heads, the goal of providing for the family clashes with the desire of living with them. "One feels very empty," one migrant told us about his time in the United States. He described constantly asking himself why he "needs so many things" if it means being "alone" in the United States. But, as one respondent puts it, migrants have to "sacrifice some things to get others."

This trade-off must be salient for circular migrants in our data. A large share of the migrant men in this group were married (47%) and with children (44%), but an overwhelming majority among them (95%) still chose to migrate without their spouses. But most of them also migrated in a period when it was still possible to visit home frequently, even without documents for border crossing.

Knowing that one can come back within a few months makes it easier for migrants to forego being with their families and migrate to the United States. In fact, many of our respondents who migrated during this era attribute their decision to return to Mexico for good to the heightened border security that made it harder to go back and forth as frequently.

We saw in earlier analysis that circular migrants decline in prevalence over time, a trend that runs nearly perfectly counter to increasing budget spent on border control in the United States. As it becomes more difficult to cross the border without documents, circular migration becomes almost impossible. Household heads are now required to be separated from their family for much longer periods, which makes many consider returning to Mexico.

"You can lose your wife and your children," a former migrant tells us when explaining why he stopped going to the United States. "Some come back and the family is no longer there, they are gone," he says. "That is very sad for an immigrant." Fathers, even when they do not lose the family, often sacrifice the affection of their children. "When he comes," a former migrant's wife tells us, "the children do not love him. They do not want to talk to him. [Our son says,] 'He is not my father.'" A former migrant tells us about his sorrow when his teenaged son lashed out at him, saying, "I never asked you to go to the United States. I would rather have you stay here."

Wives play a key role in convincing husbands to return to Mexico by pleading with them to stay. As one migrant's wife tells us, "I tell [my husband,] 'It is better for you to stay with your children.'" Some women take jobs in Mexico to contribute to household earnings so that their husbands do not need to go. A return migrant's wife, for example, talks about selling tortillas in her village to help her husband. "We will not die of hunger," she says. "If you earn a little, you spend a little."

Women often have a say—but rarely the final word—in the migration decisions in the household, especially in the 1960s and 1970s when patriarchal family relations were the norm in rural Mexico. "Before it was another time," a migrant's daughter tells us when describing her father's abrupt departure to the United States in 1943 without consulting her mother. "Women used to do what men wanted," she adds. "But now we are living life in a different way." Indeed, as we will see in subsequent chapters, women take up an increasing share of the migrant flow in the years to come, not just following their husbands, but migrating independently for work as well.

However, women make up only a tiny fraction (16%) of circular migrants. Among the spouses of households in this group (for whom the survey records detailed information), the majority (54%) are migrating with or after their husbands. One reason for this state of affairs is that women have less power in the household at the time. Wives are under the supervision of their husbands, and daughters of their fathers, and are hardly free to decide for themselves. Another reason is that women face greater dangers in crossing the border without documents, including the risk of sexual abuse by migrant men or smugglers. Many respondents bring up this point. "I have heard that . . . a lot of girls got raped," a migrant's sister tells us to explain why she did not follow her brother. "I was terrified, and so I thought 'I am comfortable here.' "

Men in the post-Bracero period not only have work opportunities in the United States, but also the possibility of returning to Mexico frequently. This combination allows them to migrate for higher earnings, to aim for a specific target in Mexico (like a house), and to fulfill their roles as the main provider for and head of the families. They are able to do this without long periods of separation from their families, which could jeopardize their authority in the family, as well as their wife and children's affection. It is not incidental, then, that circular migrants contain the highest share of household heads among the four groups in our data (61%). The specific context of migration at the time allows household heads to align their economic goals with their roles in the family.

CONCLUSION

In 1965, a particular group dominated the migrant stream from Mexico to the United States, and it comprised nearly 70% of all first-time migrants. The group contained a large share of men—many of them household heads who were married with children—from rural central-western communities in Mexico. Migrants in the group typically had little education, worked in agriculture in both Mexico and the United States, and took multiple trips of short duration. I called this group the *circular migrants*. Circular migrants declined both in absolute numbers and in relative size over time, accounting for less than 10% of new migrants by 2010.

The trend in this group followed closely the economic trends in Mexico and the United States. Circular migrants declined in numbers as incomes in Mexico rose, real wages in the United States fell, and the budget dedicated to securing the border grew exponentially between 1965 and 2010. These changes increased the expected costs and decreased the expected benefits of migrating, altering the calculus around migration.

Circular migrants followed not just this economic logic, but also a well-paved path set by earlier migrants. They largely originated from the central-western states in Mexico, a high-migration region historically. They relied on information or help from other migrants to cross the border, used smugglers on occasion, and acted according to social expectations that set migration as a rite of passage. Circular migrants responded to economic opportunities, in other words, but those opportunities were mostly visible and accessible to them through earlier migrants.

Circular migrants were a product not just of the economic and social setting, but also of the cultural expectations that assigned particular roles to men and women. This group, more than any other group in our data, was comprised of men and of household heads. This was no coincidence. In the 1960s, when most circular migrants appeared in our data, men were often the sole breadwinners for, and the heads of, rural households. In the same period, it was not as difficult for migrants to go back and forth between Mexico and the United States. This meant that household heads could migrate to earn a living in the United States without being separated from the family for long periods. They could remain the provider, in other words, without risking losing their control over the family.

The economic, social, and cultural landscapes that made circular migration the dominant logic through the 1970s changed dramatically in subsequent decades. The Mexican economy was tested with a number of crises in the 1980s. Through the 1970s, the U.S. economy began to shift from manufacturing to services. Women increasingly moved into the labor market in both settings. Their roles in families started to change. All of these changes were reflected in the migrant stream between the two countries, as we will see in subsequent chapters.

Chapter 3

"WE LEAVE TO HELP OUR PARENTS ECONOMICALLY"

Crisis Migrants

FIGURE 3.1. Father of a current U.S. migrant in his kitchen telling his son's story
PHOTO BY Patricia Martín

ÁLVARO AND MATEO'S STORY

It is after a picturesque drive through the countryside, with blue agave fields springing up like a mirage on the barren plains, that we arrive in Buenavista, a charming little town in Jalisco. The first order of the day is

FIGURE 3.2. Álvaro's home
PHOTO BY Patricia Martín

to present the head of the communal land commission (*comisariado ejidal*) with an official letter from the university to explain our project, and get his blessing, so to speak. It is easy to locate his house, a white-stained brick ranch with bare iron rods jutting out, possibly for a floor addition to come. Álvaro arrives soon after, parking his shiny pickup truck right next to a horse that is tied to a post. Álvaro kindly invites us into his kitchen, where our long conversation shifts slowly from our project to his son Mateo's story.

About a year ago, we learn, Mateo was offered a job to work as a wood-cutter in the forests of Oregon. The recruiter was a seasoned migrant from Buenavista, who had been taking his townsmen to work in the United States for the past 20 years. But, this time, he had an especially tempting arrangement, one that involved a short-term work visa. Mateo was not to "suffer like the others" to cross the border, Álvaro thought.

The decision to migrate was still a difficult one. Mateo was newly married with a toddler son. He also did not have enough money to cover the visa expenses, which amounted to 20 thousand pesos (about US$1,500 in 2011). That was when, Álvaro tells us, the family stepped in: "We told him, 'We support you if you want to go.'" Indeed, Álvaro continued, "everyone agreed" that migrating was the best decision. The family encouraged Mateo to go, offering to pay half the visa expenses and to take care of Mateo's wife and son while he was in the United States. Mateo, in turn, did his part. He sorted out his documents in Monterrey and went to work in Oregon. It has now been four months since he left.

Álvaro has great expectations for his son. He wants Mateo to save his money, send it to his family, and eventually, start building a house for himself. He hopes Mateo will send enough remittances for them to expand the family home and to invest in a new business endeavor in Buenavista. Álvaro has plans to build a pond—where visitors can fish or swim for a fee—on a lot he has inherited from his grandparents. Álvaro has been offered a million pesos (more than US$75,000 in 2011) for the lot, but he does not want to sell it. Instead, he is waiting for Mateo's remittances to put his grand plan in motion.

The conditions in Buenavista do not allow many opportunities to gather capital for investment. Álvaro, for example, cannot borrow money to build his pond. He has already applied to the local government for funding but could not stir up any interest in his project. Nor can he depend on his farming income. Most land in Buenavista is not irrigated, leaving the harvest at the mercy of the weather. Corn "is ruined completely" when it does not rain. There is "no crop insurance," Álvaro adds, to manage such risks.

Given the scarcity of credit and insurance, and the inherent uncertainty in rain-fed farming, many small producers in Buenavista either sell their land or rent it to a large strawberry producer in town, working in this same company during harvesting season. Others, like Álvaro's family, turn to migrating to the United States.

Migration has been a particularly attractive strategy since Buenavista joined the Magical Villages (*Pueblos Mágicos*) initiative in 2002. The initiative turned the town into a major tourist attraction and introduced a sudden shock to prices. "Cheese that used to cost 30–40 pesos," Álvaro tells us, now costs "50 pesos." "Meat is 100 pesos per kilogram," the equivalent of what one could earn "for a day's work" in town. Land is also "very, very expensive," Álvaro continues. "A small lot is around 60–70,000 pesos." The high prices in town are not manageable with the meager incomes that most people make, about "one thousand pesos [per week], and that is it." The situation "is not magical," Álvaro quips. "It is tragic."

This is why Álvaro thinks migration is the only opportunity for his family. His son, Mateo, "has been lucky to be able to go [to the United States]," Álvaro says, "so he can save [money] and send it here [to Mexico] where it lasts." Álvaro's plans for the future are tied to his son's earnings. What the family will be able to achieve "all depends on how long [Mateo] stays" in the United States.

Mateo's migration, in many ways, represents a coordinated familial effort. Everyone has a part to play, and presumably, something to gain in return. Coordination here is necessary given that it is costly to migrate, and there is little opportunity for economic advancement in Buenavista. Mateo needs the family to finance his trip and to care for his wife and son, and the family needs Mateo to send remittances to invest in a new business.

The conditions that led Mateo and Álvaro to devise this strategy—the gradual decline in agriculture, the lack of credit and insurance, and the sudden spike in commodity prices—might seem specific to Buenavista, a town experiencing a boom in tourism. Yet, similar conditions defined the larger economic climate in Mexico for more than a decade from the mid-1970s to the late 1980s, when the country faced two major economic crises (1976 and 1982) and experienced spells of high inflation, high interest rates, and high unemployment. Real wages declined in this period, credit became very expensive, and jobs disappeared. The subsidies to agriculture continued to decline. These conditions forced many households to seek alternative survival strategies. Migrating to the United States was one such strategy.

CRISIS MIGRANTS

It is in this context that a specific group came to dominate the Mexico-U.S. stream from 1980 to 1989, replacing the circular migrants as the majority group among all first-time migrants in our data. This group consisted of mostly young men—typically the youngest sons—from relatively well-off rural households; it peaked in numbers during the crisis years in Mexico. To highlight this pattern, I name this group the *crisis migrants*.

Crisis migrants differed sharply from the circular migrants that dominated the earlier decade. While circular migrants typically came from poor households with no assets, crisis migrants originated from relatively well-off households that owned some land or a business, as well as a house. The groups also differed in their demographic attributes. Crisis migrants contained not only a higher share of teenaged men compared to circular migrants (71% versus 22%), but also a higher share of women (19% as opposed to 16%), many of them in their late thirties.

The profile of crisis migrants is consistent with the conditions in Mexico in the 1980s, which put pressures on all households (including, and perhaps especially, those with assets) and pushed household members who had never before been employed (men in their teens and women in their late thirties) to work and to migrate.

The actions of crisis migrants also hint at the depth of their despair in migrating. Crisis migrants are not only more likely to cross the border without documents compared to the other migrants in the same period, but they are also more willing to accept significantly lower-paying jobs in the United States (see figure 3.4 below).

Two patterns suggest crisis migrants' moves were part of a household strategy. First, many crisis migrants receive help from the family to cover smuggler fees. Nearly a fourth of crisis migrants do so in our data. Second, crisis migrants are likely to send remittances to the family in the origin community, or to bring back savings upon return (about 78% do). (This information is available for a small share of crisis migrants (458 out of 5,214), most of whom are heads of households. The share receiving help for smuggler fees is likely to be much higher in the remainder of the sample consisting of mostly younger sons in the household.)

Crisis migrants, and the particular conditions under which they proliferate in our data, suggest a distinctive logic for migration—one that resembles Álvaro and Mateo's reasoning above. The mobility of this group stems from the constraints in the Mexican economy, some persistent (like insufficient credit or insurance) and some periodic (like high inflation). Moving to the United States for this group often involves an elaborate arrangement, where the household members cover the costs of migrating, like fees for smugglers, and the migrant, in turn, sends remittances.

I now review the economic and political landscape in Mexico and the United States that gave rise to this family-centered logic in the 1970s and made it the dominant one among new migrants in the 1980s.

MEXICO, 1970–1980

Let's recap where Mexico stood in the 1970s. From 1940 to 1970, the economy had grown at an annual rate of about 6%; the inflation rate had remained at an average of 7% per year; and poverty had declined considerably. The fruits of this economic growth, however, had not been shared evenly. Agriculture was in decline, and rural areas—especially those in the central and southern parts of the country—were still very poor. President Echeverría (1970–1976) set out to correct the sectorial and regional imbalances in Mexico, but some argue that his policies also made the economy more vulnerable to external shocks, paving the way for the economic troubles to come.

Peso devaluation in 1976

During Echeverría's term, public spending increased at about 12% per year, nearly twice the economy's growth rate. The fiscal deficit reached 10% of the GDP in 1975, four times its share in 1971, and was covered partly by foreign debt, which climbed from US$7.5 billion to US$24 billion between 1971 and 1976. For the first time in almost two decades, the inflation rate in Mexico reached double-digit levels and the real exchange rate, pegged to the dollar, suffered a persistent appreciation. The private sector, in anticipation of a peso devaluation, began to take its assets and money out of the country. This capital flight was the last straw before a balance-of-payments crisis in 1975. The response came in August 1976, when the Echeverría government devalued the peso by more than 40%, abandoned the fixed exchange rate policy, and turned to the International Monetary Fund (IMF) for financial assistance.

THE DISCOVERY OF OIL

The tide seemed to turn quickly for Mexico, however. Shortly after becoming president, López Portillo (1976–1982) announced the discovery of vast oil reserves in southern Mexico. Between 1976 and 1981, confirmed oil reserves increased by more than tenfold (from 6.3 billion to 72 billion barrels). The oil revenues helped adjust the balance of payments, turning a deficit of 51.7 billion pesos in 1977 to a surplus of 17.5 billion pesos in 1980. The economy grew at an average rate of 8.4% from 1978 to 1981, emboldening the government to embark upon ambitious social programs to alleviate poverty and promote agriculture. The fiscal deficit was once again on the rise, reaching 14% of the GDP in 1981. Inflation remained in the double digits, and the peso was still overvalued, leading to another spell of capital flight in 1981. Even the massive oil revenues could not make up for the disequilibrium in the balance of payments.

PESO DEVALUATIONS IN 1982 AND 1985

The disaster hit again when oil prices, which had almost doubled in real terms from 1978 to 1981, began to decline in mid-1981. Nearly half of Mexico's foreign debt was due for payment or refinancing in the next year. With mounting internal and external pressures, the government devalued the peso by more than 70% in February 1982, and again in August of the same year. The government also announced a 90-day suspension on foreign debt payments, signaling the beginning of a debt crisis that would diffuse to the rest of the world. In September, López Portillo went on to nationalize the Mexican banking system, mere months before handing the presidency to Miguel de la Madrid (1982–1988).

A slowdown in the economy, and a spike in inflation rates, followed the 1982 crisis. The economic climate in the world—high interest rates, low oil prices, and scarcity of credit—made Mexico's recovery slow and painful.

Another peso devaluation in mid-1985 became inevitable to keep the balance of payments in check. The inflation rate reached more than 130% in 1987, and interest rates hit 96%. Real wages dropped at an annual rate of nearly 10% between 1983 and 1987.

POVERTY STILL CONCENTRATED IN RURAL CENTRAL-WEST AND SOUTH

The prolonged recession in the 1980s, considered the "lost decade" for both Mexico and many Latin American countries, brought about more poverty. From 1984 to 1989, the number of moderately poor Mexicans increased from 20 million to about 26 million; those in extreme poverty jumped from 10 million to nearly 14 million. The gap between the rich and poor also deepened in this period, with the top 10% of earners in the population increasing their share of the total income from 43% to 50%. The Gini coefficient, a measure of inequality, rose from 0.58 to 0.62 in five years.

Extreme poverty in the 1980s continued to be concentrated in rural areas, and in the central-western and southern parts of Mexico. In 1984, rates of rural poverty (29%) were six times higher than those of urban poverty (5%). In 1989, poverty rates had increased in both rural (35%) and urban (6%) areas, but the relative ratio of rural to urban poor had remained unchanged. Between 1984 and 1989, the incidence of poverty rose sharply in the central-west, south, and southeast—the historically poor regions in Mexico—while it remained more or less stable in the rest of the country.

The share of the extremely poor increased dramatically among farming households, reaching nearly one-half in 1987. Those working communal plots (*ejidos*) were hit especially hard, with subsidies to the sector being cut and rising interest rates making credit less accessible.

Middle-income households, in some respects, lost more than the poorest in the post-crisis period. From 1984 to 1989, households in the bottom third of the income distribution kept their share of the total income at around 4%. Households in the middle third, by contrast, saw their income share drop from nearly 20% to 17%, possibly due to the drastic decline in wage income on which these households depended.

SURVIVAL STRATEGIES DURING THE ECONOMIC CRISES

Many households turned to informal employment in the aftermath of the 1976 and 1982 crises. In urban areas, poor and middle-income households devised various strategies to support household budgets. Some households increased their labor market participation, for example, by involving adult women or young men; others simply increased household production, or reduced consumption. These strategies paid off. In Guadalajara, one study found, households lost only 11% of their total income between 1982 and 1985, while individual wages fell by more than a third.

In rural areas, subsistence and small-producer households intensified their off-farm activities in the post-crisis era, which not only contributed significantly to household earnings, but also provided insurance against risks to rain-fed agriculture. This strategy was especially prevalent in the central-western region for several reasons. First, many small farmers in the region produced for the market (unlike the subsistence farmers of the south and southeast) and thus needed more cash to sustain their activities. These farmers largely lacked access to credit, as most relied on the *ejido* plots, which, by law at the time, could not be used as collateral for obtaining loans. Second, many farmers in the region still employed traditional methods and, given insufficient irrigation, were highly dependent on the rainfall (which, as Álvaro noted, is still the case in Buenavista, a central-western town). Crop insurance, already inadequate, was becoming even scarcer over time.

Many rural families in the central-west, research shows, turned to wage labor or self-employment. Households were still quite large on average, given the high fertility rates of the past decades, and they could ration their labor force between domestic and international markets. The household head and older sons typically oversaw farming activities, while daughters moved to the cities in Mexico for factory and service jobs and younger sons migrated to the United States. The established history of U.S. migration in many families and communities in the central-west surely facilitated this movement.

WOMEN'S RISING PARTICIPATION IN THE LABOR MARKET

The economic recession of the 1980s pulled more women—especially more married women—into the labor market in Mexico. Women in rural areas moved in increasing numbers to the cities to take jobs in the service sector or in factories. Some worked in private households as domestic workers and others in the export assembly plants on the northern border, known as *maquiladoras*, which hired almost exclusively women at the time. Many women concentrated in the informal sector.

Women's entry into paid employment was possible in part due to lower fertility rates in Mexico, which averaged around 3.4 children per woman in 1990, down from nearly 7 children per woman in 1970. About a third of women aged 15 or older in Mexico worked in 1990, a share that would reach almost half in 2010. Women's increasing participation in the labor market began to alter the patriarchal relations in Mexican households. Men were no longer the sole providers in many households, but they still retained much of their power over their wives and children. This power, in fact, often extended to children's families, as most young couples lived with the husband's parents until they gained economic independence (just like the arrangement between Mateo and Álvaro that we saw in the beginning of the chapter).

THE UNITED STATES, 1970–1980
Changes in the manufacturing sector

At the end of World War II, the American economy was defined by the strength of its manufacturing operations. But global competition was also intensifying. This competition led many industries to relocate, to fragment their operations, and to de-skill their workforce in order to reduce production costs in the 1960s and 1970s.

The food-processing industry in the United States, for example, started moving to rural areas in the 1960s and restructured its production processes to reduce its reliance on skilled workers. By the mid-1970s, the garment industry no longer included firms with large workforces but instead comprised a series of subcontracting arrangements. The automobile and electronics industries changed in similar ways.

The changes in the manufacturing sector created growth in jobs characterized by manual work, low pay, and lack of benefits. These jobs, economist Michael Piore argues, were often not attractive to the natives and instead were filled by migrants, mostly undocumented Mexican workers in the 1970s and 1980s.

Growth in the service sector

The dispersion of manufacturing operations across the country (and the globe), according to sociologist Saskia Sassen, necessitated a concentration of management and finance services in a few "global" cities, such as Los Angeles and New York. The increase in the number of professionals in the cities led to an increase in demand for personal services. Migrant workers filled the new jobs in restaurants, hotels, domestic work, child care, and the like.

The service sector was growing not just in the "global" cities, but also in the U.S. economy at large. In the decades following World War II, the number of workers in goods production—agriculture, mining, manufacturing, and construction—continually lost ground to sharply rising numbers working in the service sector. The expansion in higher education in the United States in the postwar period facilitated the shift from manufacturing to services.

The number of state and community colleges increased significantly, as did the amount of federal grants and loans available to students. These changes enabled the country to train workers for the advanced service sector. The entry of female workers into the labor market also fed into the growth in the service sector, and vice versa.

Women's growing participation in the labor market

The labor shortages in the United States during World War II had pulled many American women into employment. This trend continued in the postwar period. Between 1950 and 1990, the number of women in the labor force tripled from 17.5 million to 53.5 million, while the number of men increased by only half (from 42 million to 64 million). The share of mothers with young children who worked outside the home increased from one in five in 1966 to nearly two in three in 1990.

Women's entry into paid employment was the result of expanding educational opportunities for all, the availability of jobs in the service sector that rely less on brute strength, new laws against gender discrimination in the United States, declining family sizes, and increasing rates of family dissolution. It was also a result of stagnating real wages in the United States after the 1970s, which forced many households to assume a two-earner model in order to maintain or improve their standards of living.

Women started to work, but their responsibilities in the home did not diminish, often requiring what sociologist Arlie Hochschild calls a "second shift." To balance their dual roles in the workplace and in the family, many women turned to hiring domestic workers to manage household tasks and child care. Migrant women were the most likely domestic workers; they not only provided a cheap source of labor that could be hired informally, but they also conformed to ideas of "traditional" motherhood.

Diversification of the migrant workforce

The changes in the economy in the 1970s and 1980s allowed the incorporation of a growing migrant workforce in the United States, and also made that workforce more diverse. Migrants in this period no longer concentrated in seasonal agricultural work but found year-round jobs in factories, hotels, restaurants, private households, and in the growing service sector at large. Women also comprised a growing number of migrants.

The increasing numbers of migrants in certain jobs, the economist Michael Piore argues, makes those jobs socially unacceptable to native workers, which creates a persistent demand for migrant workers. As a result, migrants' entry into new lines of work in this period might have paved the way for a continuing need for migrant labor in the decades to come.

INCREASING RESTRICTIONS TO LEGAL MIGRATION

As the economy came to rely more and more on migrant workers in the 1970s and 1980s, immigration policies in the United States did not become any less restrictive. In 1968, Mexican migrants, for the first time in history, were subject to a hemispheric ceiling of 120,000 visas annually. In 1976, new amendments to the Immigration and Nationality Act imposed another limit. Mexican citizens could now receive at most 20,000 visas per year, and they would still compete with the other countries in the Western Hemisphere against an overall cap of 120,000. In 1978, a worldwide ceiling of 290,000 replaced the separate hemispheric caps. In the 1980s, that ceiling dropped to 270,000.

These restrictions reduced the legal entries from Mexico to just 45,000 in 1977, the lowest level since the end of the Bracero program in 1964, and a mere tenth of the 450,000 annual visas granted to Mexicans at the height of that program.

The restrictions were accompanied by increasing enforcement on the U.S. side of the border. Between 1965 and 1986, the size of the Border Patrol more than doubled from 1,500 officers to 3,700 officers. The number of apprehensions on the border in the same period increased by about thirty-fold, from 55,000 to 1.7 million.

Despite these restrictions, however, most Mexican migrants that made it to the border eventually crossed. Researchers estimate that, in the 1970s and 1980s, the odds that an undocumented migrant would be apprehended averaged around one in three. Given that migrants were willing to try to cross multiple times, they would almost surely get in eventually. The difficulty of crossing in this period, however, skewed the stream toward those most willing to bear such hardship—young men who were yet to form families of their own. It also increased the chances that migrants would hire professional guides or smugglers on the border.

SUMMARY

Between 1976 and 1985, Mexico experienced multiple peso devaluations, which led to spells of inflation and unemployment, devastating poor and middle-income households alike. Households devised different coping strategies in this period, incorporating women into paid work (and thus allowing them to increase their power in the household) or sending migrants to cities in Mexico or to the United States.

The U.S. economy in this period changed in ways to support a more diverse migrant workforce than in the past. Manufacturing operations became more fragmented and subcontracting arrangements more common, multiplying jobs that offered low pay and no benefits. The service sector increased its share in the economy, opening new lines of work for migrants. Women joined the labor market in growing numbers, raising the need for domestic workers to manage household tasks and child care.

CRISIS MIGRANTS: MANAGING SUDDEN ADVERSITY?

In the 1980s, a group that I call the crisis migrants peaked in our data. This group consisted mostly of young men from relatively well-off families in rural communities. In the late 1960s, the group accounted for only one in ten first-time migrants in our sample. In the mid-1980s, the share of the group among new migrants had climbed to a half, making the group the majority among all migrants.

The rise of this group in the 1980s certainly coincides with the various changes in the Mexican and U.S. contexts in the same period. But it seems particularly related to the shocks to the Mexican economy, a conclusion supported by the analysis in appendix G. This analysis uses a regression model to relate the size of the crisis migrants to macro-level indicators that capture various economic, demographic, and policy changes in the Mexico-U.S. context. One relationship in particular stands out in the results from the model, one that is so robust that it is visible in the raw data plots shown in figure 3.3.

Figure 3.3 displays the number of crisis migrants over time (solid line with values on the left y-axis) simultaneously with three trends in Mexico (dashed line with values on the right y-axis across the three panels). The trend on the top panel is the Mexican inflation rate (included in the regression model in appendix G). The trends in the middle and bottom panels are the annual change in the value of Mexican peso against the U.S. dollar (i.e., the rate of devaluation), and the interest rate in Mexico, respectively (neither are included in the model in the appendix because of their high correlation with the inflation rate).

The brief history above described the oscillations in the Mexican economy through the 1970s and 1980s perpetrated by severe currency devaluations in 1976, 1982, and 1985. The devaluations were accompanied by high inflation rates that remained in the double-digits from 1973 through 1982, grazing triple-digit levels in 1983, 1987, and 1988. Interest rates, consistent with the inflation rate, remained high through the same period, making credit more expensive and less accessible to Mexicans.

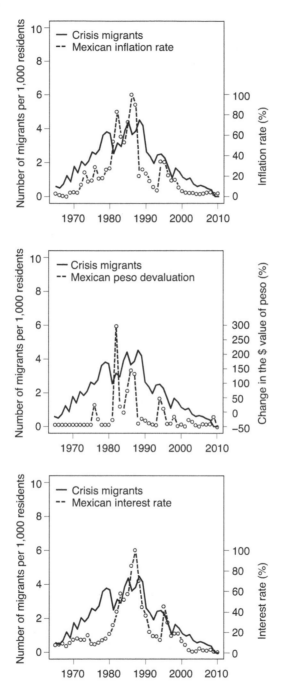

FIGURE 3.3. Trends in the number of crisis migrants, the Mexican inflation rate, the annual change in the dollar value of the Mexican peso, and the Mexican interest rate, 1965–2010

The bouts of devaluation, high inflation, and high interest rates in Mexico, the figures show, also correspond to periods of acceleration in the number of crisis migrants. Indeed, peaks in the rate of devaluation, or the corresponding increase in the rate of inflation (like after years 1976, 1982, 1986, 1987, and 1994), are often followed by peaks in the rate of crisis migration (like in years 1978, 1984, and 1998). The correlation between the rate of inflation and the rate of crisis migration is a striking 0.70, and the former accounts for about half the variation in the latter.

This pattern, one can argue, validates the name I have given to this group—the crisis migrants. The number of migrants in this group responds strongly and positively to the adverse economic conditions in Mexico in the aftermath of the 1976 and 1982 crises.

The regression model in the appendix suggests that the number of crisis migrants also responds strongly, but negatively, to the U.S. Border Patrol enforcement budget. That is, all else equal, a lower number of crisis migrants appears in our data in years that the United States spends more on controlling the border. This result explains why crisis migration did not increase quite as much after the economic crisis in 1994 in Mexico (an event I will cover in another chapter). There is a peak in the number of crisis migrants right after the crisis in 1994 (see figure 3.3), but the peak is not nearly as high as that after the crisis in 1976 or 1982. Heightened levels of enforcement on the U.S. border seem to curb mobility for crisis migrants, as it did previously for circular migrants.

CRISIS MIGRANTS: RESPONDING TO REGIONAL EVENTS?

The correspondence between crisis periods in Mexico and the peaks in the number of crisis migrants is certainly suggestive. But if crisis migration is really a response to sudden misfortune, one should observe it not just after national events, like peso devaluation, but also after more localized disasters. And the regional locus of those disasters should correspond to the regional locus of crisis migrants.

I explore this idea with two events with localized impact: the coffee crisis in the 1990s that affected the southeastern regions of Mexico, and the earthquake in 1985 that hit mostly the central and central-western areas. I expect that the number of crisis migrants will increase at a significantly higher rate in the impacted areas in the aftermath of these events than it will in other areas of the country.

Let us start with the coffee crisis of the early 1990s. In 1989, the International Coffee Agreement—in which members agreed to constrain coffee exports to boost prices—came to end, causing a sharp decline in prices. Growers in Mexico, who received an average of 80 cents per pound in 1990, could only get 58 cents in 1992. Four states in the southeast—Chiapas, Veracruz, Oaxaca, and Puebla—accounted for more than 90% of the coffee production in Mexico. The sudden fall in prices had a direct effect on the income of the poor, mostly indigenous, inhabitants of these states, who lacked the safety nets to weather such external shocks.

In Veracruz, Oaxaca, and Puebla—the coffee-growing states for which we have data—the number of crisis migrants headed to the United States doubled between 1990 and 1992, rising from 0.3 to 0.6 migrants per thousand. In the rest of the country, by contrast, the number of crisis migrants dropped by a fourth during the same period, from 2.6 to 2.0 migrants per thousand.

Now consider another event with strong regional impact—the devastating earthquake that hit the Pacific coastline of Mexico in 1985, killing at least 10,000 people, injuring 50,000, and rendering 250,000 homeless. The earthquake caused significant damage in Mexico City and neighboring areas. The MMP surveys do not cover Mexico City itself, but they do include individuals from the surrounding states of Jalisco, Colima, Guerrero, Michoacán, and México that suffered some damage, and perhaps a loss of job opportunities in the city, as a result of the earthquake.

The earthquake seems to have created a short-term peak in U.S. migration rates out of the affected regions. From 1984 to 1985, the number of crisis migrants jumped by one-half in the regions upset by the earthquake, while it increased by a mere tenth in the overall data. This rise quickly dissipated in 1986 when migration levels out of this region returned to their pre-earthquake levels and consistently declined afterward.

In both examples, we see a disproportionate increase in crisis migrants in areas of localized adversity compared to the rest of Mexico. This pattern coheres with the idea that this group might indeed be seeking relief from a crisis by migrating to the United States, where the earnings—not only higher, but also unaffected by the events in Mexico—provide a safeguard that is often lacking in the local economy.

CRISIS MIGRANTS: MIGRATING NO MATTER WHAT?

Crisis migrants in our data seem to respond to sudden adversities in Mexico and seek relief from U.S. migration. The desperation that pushes them to migrate also becomes evident in two patterns in our data. In the period following the 1982 currency devaluation—the most devastating years for the Mexican economy—crisis migrants are not only more likely to accept much lower wages in the United States compared to the other migrant groups in our data, but they are also more likely to be undocumented when crossing the border.

Figure 3.4 shows these trends. The plot on the left displays the average monthly wages in the United States separately for crisis migrants (solid line)

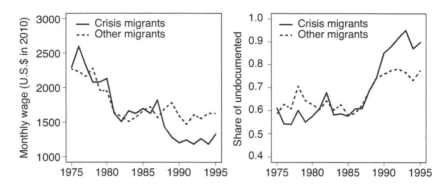

FIGURE 3.4. Trends in the monthly wage and share of undocumented in the United
States among crisis migrants and other migrants in the MMP data, 1975–1995

and those in the other three clusters combined (dashed line). In 1975, both
groups earn an average US$2,300 (in 2010 values) per month, which falls
slowly to about US$1,500 by 1980, following the secular decline in low-
skill wages in the United States (see figure 2.2, bottom plot). In the mid-
1980s, crisis migrants experience a sharp drop in their earnings, to about
US$1,100, while other migrants maintain the US$1,500 average through
the mid-1990s. The fact that this group accepts significantly lower (at the
95% confidence level) wages in the United States precisely in the post-
crisis period in Mexico—despite retaining the exact same age and education profile as in the pre-crisis era—points to the severity of the circumstances sending this group in search of U.S. jobs.

The plot on the right in figure 3.4, which shows the share of crisis migrants crossing the U.S. border without documents, permits a similar interpretation. This share (solid line) fluctuates around 0.60 from the mid-
1970s to the mid-1980s for crisis migrants, as it does for the other migrant
groups (dashed line). In the post-crisis era, the share of the undocumented
increases in both groups, but the rate of increase is significantly higher
among the crisis migrants (at the 95% confidence level). In the early 1990s,
nearly all crisis migrants entered the United States without documents,
again signaling the unique circumstances that made migration possibly the
last resort for this group.

CRISIS MIGRANTS: RETURN OR SETTLE?

Compared to the circular migrants in the preceding chapter, crisis migrants
are significantly younger on average (19 vs. 26 years old, p<0.05) and more
likely to be unmarried on their first trip (71% vs. 26%, p<0.05). The group,
as a result, has less incentive to return to Mexico. Crisis migrants spend a

median of 24 months in the United States on the first trip, while circular migrants stay for a median of 12 months.

Crisis migrants also find a more diverse set of work options in the United States compared to circular migrants. These options include not just seasonal work in agriculture, but also year-round jobs in factories, services, or construction. Crisis migrants, as a result, are less likely to work in agriculture compared to circular migrants (27% do compared to 33% among circular migrants, p<0.05). Crisis migrants contain a larger share of women compared to circular migrants (19% vs. 16%) because of the severity of the economic conditions pushing more women to work in Mexico, and also because of the receding patriarchal norms against women's employment or migration. Some of the migrant women in the United States work in the service sector (27%), some in manufacturing (17%), and most remain unemployed (41%) on the first trip, suggesting that they might have migrated as part of a couple.

For a portion of our data—that supplied by married household heads with information on spouses—we can discern if a married couple crossed the border in the same year. In this sample, we can see that a small share of crisis migrants (21%), but still significantly larger compared to circular migrants (5%), moved to the United States with their spouses.

All of these patterns—the predominance of unattached men in the group, the availability of year-round jobs in the United States, and the presence of couples migrating together—suggest a firmer basis for settling in the United States for crisis migrants compared to circular migrants. In our data, however, the majority of crisis migrants (55%) still return eventually, measured as staying in Mexico for at least three years following their final trip.

It is possible, however, that this large share is an artifact of the MMP data, which come mostly from communities in Mexico and thus oversample migrants that have either returned or that still retain ties to origin communities. To test this possibility, I compare two groups among the crisis migrants: those whose information was obtained in Mexico (about 92% of the sample) and those who were interviewed in the United States. And the return rates turn out to be almost identical in both samples (55% in the former and 56% in the latter).

CRISIS MIGRANTS: FROM AGGREGATE CONDITIONS TO INDIVIDUAL DECISIONS?

The analysis so far links the rise of crisis migrants in our data in the 1980s to the economic conditions in Mexico at the time. The sudden onset of high inflation and interest rates in this period, combined with high unemployment, hurt both middle-income families with modest investments and poor families barely getting by, pushing them to migrate to the United States.

Sociologist Pierrette Hondagneu-Sotelo interviewed one such migrant, María Mendoza, whose family migrated to the United States after the crisis in 1982. María described how the decision came about:

> With the peso devaluations [in 1976 and 1982], we had many losses. And we lost a very good business due to a bad investment my husband made when he added a shoe store to our furniture factory and store. That was the beginning of our failure. That was in 1980. We were left with many debts . . . we paid off most of our debts and we came here [the United States].

For María's family, the economic crisis was the last straw that brought the end of their business in Mexico. But for many families in Mexico, the risks to livelihoods are not limited to the periods of economic crisis. Álvaro and Mateo's story in the beginning of the chapter demonstrates this point.

In 2011, at the time of our interviews in Mexico, Álvaro was still talking about his inability to borrow money that would allow him to start a new business venture, and about the risks to his crops if it did not rain that year. These chronic issues in the community—the lack of credit and the lack of insurance to protect against crop failure—are pushing families to consider sending migrants to the United States even today.

Several respondents from other communities also mention the difficulty of supporting their economic activities on their own in Mexico. A migrant's wife, for example, tells us, "You own your piece of land, but having extra [money] is important." Migrating to the United States allows the family to raise the funds necessary to continue farming and also to expand their business. The family is growing coffee. With the migrant's income, the family has been able to buy a roaster for coffee beans, and now, is planning for "something bigger": to open a shop to sell their produce directly. The wife tells us that she would rather her husband stay in Mexico since "one is always calm here working in the ranch." But, "if there is no money to support your sowing," she adds, "you cannot work."

A former migrant expresses similar reasoning to explain why people migrate to the United States from his town. "If you want to start a business," he says, "there is no money . . . and if there is money, they lend it at a very high price. That is when one says, 'I better leave.'" In the past, this migrant adds, the Mexican government provided more help to farmers. He talks about how he built his house with loans from a government program. Now, he laments, "they give you no options" but to migrate.

It is not only costly to farm, a respondent tells us, but it is also risky given that the land in his town is not irrigated. "The crops have to be watered twice [a week] while they are growing. The weather here has changed a lot, too much. Sometimes it rains a lot, sometimes it doesn't at all. . . . Nobody here has a well where we can get water." Because farmers depend on steady rainfall, they can lose all their income in the case of a drought. One respondent tells us about a year their crops "did not turn out okay" and the family "started owing money because [the crop yield] was not enough to pay the bills." That is when, she adds, her brothers "had to emigrate" to the United States.

These stories suggest that families use migration as a way to obtain credit to support domestic economic activities in Mexico and as a means to manage the risks to those activities. This idea forms the backbone of a particular paradigm in migration research, the so-called New Economics of Labor Migration (NELM) theory.

MIGRATION AS A RESPONSE TO MARKET FAILURES

The NELM perspective views migrant flows as a response to uncertainty in developing economies like Mexico. Given the inadequacy of formal institutions (for example, well-established capital markets or insurance schemes), households in these settings need to protect themselves against possible reversals of economic fortune. One strategy households can employ is to send migrants to a different country, where the earnings—not subject to the whims of the origin economy—provide a hedge against the risks to domestic income.

The new economics perspective seems related to the risk diversification paradigm prominent in finance at the time, attributing a similar motive to migration behavior. Such a motive does not preclude income maximization, the main incentive for migration according to the neoclassical economics view. In other words, migrants might be helping their families diversify their sources of income while also increasing said income above levels that could be achieved in their home community alone. But the former goal requires a more elaborate arrangement than the latter.

Consider a family only seeking to maximize earnings. It is sufficient for that family to send a member to a destination where the expected returns are higher than those in origin. Now consider a family seeking to diversify risks to earnings in origin. In this case, the family needs to continue its economic activities in origin, and also send a migrant to a destination where the risks to earnings are uncorrelated with those in origin. The migrant's earnings provide a hedge against the risks to the family earnings, and vice versa. Note how this strategy requires coordination in the family, or a "contract," as the NELM scholars refer to it. This contract, scholars assume, is self-enforcing, as the family and the migrant need one another to protect against the risks in the origin and destination, respectively.

Many scholars have questioned this assumption of family unity. Our qualitative data, as we will see in a subsequent section, suggest strong power differentials in the family that can make this contract involuntary, one from which migrants cannot wait to free themselves eventually.

Setting that discussion aside for now, a number of patterns for crisis migrants seem consistent with the predictions of the NELM theory. First, crisis migrants proliferate in an acutely volatile period in Mexico, when households are likely to face added pressure to diversify income streams. The crisis conditions exacerbate the chronic issues for rural households—for example, the inadequate credit or insurance that rural households often bring up during our interviews and seem to seek relief by sending migrants to the United States.

Second, the observed division of labor, and the sharing of the costs and returns of migration, are largely in line with the family strategy presumed in the NELM theory. Crisis migrants contain a large majority of younger adults in their teens (71% between 15 and 19 years old), not the main breadwinners in the family, which suggests migration might be a potential complement to—rather than a substitute for—domestic economic activities. Crisis migrants who cross the border without documents (86% of the total) in some cases do so with financial help from the family. (Recall that one-fourth of the household heads in the group receive part of the smuggler fees from household members. Our qualitative data suggest that this share is likely to be much higher for younger sons for whom we have no information on smuggler fees in the survey data.) Crisis migrants also send remittances in similar amounts to the other groups, despite earning much lower wages starting in the 1990s (see figure 3.4), suggesting a heightened concern for household welfare.

Third, the large representation of middle-class families, and families in regions of sudden or chronic risks to livelihoods among crisis migrants can be taken as evidence for a risk diversification motive underlying migration. Recall that crisis migrants originate mostly from relatively well-off households with endowments (land or a business) that are worth protecting during times of economic turmoil. Crisis migrants spike in numbers in regions facing unfortunate events, like the states hit by the coffee crisis of the early 1990s or those affected by the earthquake in 1985. Crisis migrants are also overrepresented in regions of chronic economic vulnerability, such as among the cash-strapped and rainfall-dependent farmers in the rural central-west.

These patterns all suggest that crisis migrants might be the family-centered actors moving to the United States to manage particular risks to livelihoods in Mexico, an assessment in line with the NELM perspective. But crisis migrants are also very much social actors following a well-paved path carved by the migrants before them. The regions of economic deprivation supplying this group, perhaps not surprisingly, also happen to be the ones with a well-established migration history. I now turn to this particular pattern, and explore how the presence of prior migrants in families or communities shapes the mobility patterns of crisis migrants.

CRISIS MIGRANTS: HELPING HANDS?

In the preceding chapter, I defined a typology of mechanisms that can lead to network effects in migration, where prior migrants alter the odds of migrating for new migrants. Using qualitative evidence, I suggested that, for circular migrants, network effects worked mainly through *social facilitation*, where prior migrants—who typically made frequent trips to their origin communities—passed on information or provided direct help that facilitated crossing the border or finding a job in the United Sates for new migrants. Network effects for circular migrants also worked through *normative influence*, where peers exerted social pressures to migrate. Some prior migrants, for example, exaggerated the prospects in the United States or blatantly provided false information that convinced others to migrate. Finally, for circular migrants, inter-linked migration behavior also occurred through *network externalities*, where prior migrants helped create institutions like smuggling networks or ethnic businesses in destination that sustained more migration. Such institutions, however, were not yet commonplace for circular migrants, most of whom moved in the 1960s and 1970s.

Things were different for crisis migrants, many of whom left Mexico from the mid-1970s through the 1980s, when migrants tended to stay for longer stretches in the United States, and thus had less frequent contact with family and friends in origin communities. Social facilitation, for this group, likely worked through immediate family members—who could be trusted and to whom the good deeds could be reciprocated—rather than extended family or community relations. Compared to circular migrants, network externalities were more essential to crisis migrants, many of whom relied on formal guides or smugglers. And normative influence, still a crucial mechanism, was likely different in form than for circular migrants. It was not just migrants' friends who socially pressured this group to migrate, but also family members who needed migrant earnings given the dire circumstances in Mexico at the time.

As I discuss in greater detail below, the underlying mechanisms for network effects might have changed from the era of circular migrants in the 1970s to the period of crisis migrants in the 1980s, but the magnitude of such effects remained substantial in both periods. Crisis migrants, like the circular migrants before them, originated from the rural central-west, the region that had supplied the majority of migrants from Mexico to the United States from the early 1900s through the Bracero era.

SOCIAL FACILITATION: RECIPROCITY AND
TRUST EASIER TO ENSURE IN FAMILIES

Circular migrants—as the name suggests—went back and forth between Mexico and the United States, maintaining frequent contact with their family members and friends. The frequent contact gave these migrants not only the opportunity to help others migrate, but also the incentives to do so. Most circular migrants expected to return home, so it made sense for them to accumulate "chits" by helping other migrants, which they could claim in the future. The circularity allowed for expectations of reciprocity.

Crisis migrants, by contrast, proliferated in a period when migrants stayed in the United States for longer durations, on average, relative to the earlier years. The longer durations were the result of tougher border enforcement, as well as the new lines of work that offered year-round employment to migrants in the United States. Some of these migrants started to establish roots in the United States and to sever ties to Mexico.

Our qualitative data provide examples of how migrants "change" in the United States. "The money goes to their head," said one respondent who was forced out from a distant family member's house in the United States. "On the fourth, fifth day" of staying with someone in the United States, another former migrant commented, "They come to you and say . . . 'You should go find somewhere else [to live]'. . . . They throw people out to the street."

When help from friends or extended family, or what sociologist Mark Granovetter refers to as "weak ties," becomes less accessible or less enforceable, migrants-to-be turn to their immediate family members, or "strong ties." The importance of strong ties is evident for the crisis migrants in our data. A significantly larger share of crisis migrants (77%) have household members who have already migrated to the United States, compared to circular migrants (20%, significant at the 95% confidence level). This difference is in part owing to the fact that crisis migrants concentrate in a later time period, when more Mexicans have had a chance to obtain U.S. migration experience. But the difference also suggests a potential change in the social facilitation mechanism over time, where new migrants increasingly draw on the experiences of immediate family members rather than more distant relations in the extended family or community.

There are numerous examples of this transition from weak to strong ties as sources of help in our qualitative data, especially as the migrant stream becomes younger and more inclusive of women over time. A father of four migrant daughters, for example, tells us that he allowed his daughters to migrate only because he knew they would be safe in the United States with his brother, or their uncle. "They did not go for an adventure," he emphasized. "To try their luck by themselves? No. They had the support of [family members] there."

Family relations allow for trust and reciprocity. Migrants-to-be know they can trust the helping migrants, and the helping migrants know that their favor could eventually be reciprocated. This is why those relations are crucial to the mobility of crisis migrants—a more vulnerable group with less opportunity to interact with migrants outside the family compared to circular migrants.

Network externalities: increasingly indispensable

As social facilitation becomes less common (or more restricted to immediate family) over time, externalities—generalized resources created by a persistent flow—become more important to new migrants. A large share of crisis migrants (73% among the household heads), for example, rely on smugglers, an externality of past migrant flows, as well as of rising border enforcement that seeks to curb those flows.

Researchers note this shifting pattern in the Mexico-U.S. stream. Massey and colleagues, for example, show that the share of first-time migrants using a smuggler has increased from 40% in 1965 to more than 70% after 1975. This pattern suggests that, over time, the cumulative dynamics of Mexico-U.S. flows are more likely to be driven by institutionalized resources, like smuggling networks, than by interpersonal exchange of help between prior and potential migrants. The efforts to deter undocumented migration, perhaps ironically, make that migration all the more professionalized.

Normative influence: pressure from the family rather than the community

For circular migrants, normative influence worked mostly through the ideas perpetrated by prior migrants that glorified migration and made it a necessary rite of passage for young adults. Migrants-to-be were often "encouraged" to migrate by friends who "sweetened the truth" of what life in the United States was like, as one respondent put it.

For crisis migrants, normative influence worked not just through the norms that took hold in a community, but also through the active support offered by the family that had a vested interest in migration. Recall how Álvaro recounted his son Mateo's migration decision to us: "We told him, 'We support you if you want to go.'" And he added, "Everyone agreed. Nobody said 'no.'" The family not only convinced Mateo to go to the United States, but they also offered the money necessary to cover the visa expenses and agreed to take care of Mateo's wife and son. It was a common pattern in our qualitative data for families to intervene in the migration decision, especially for younger migrants. Fathers often used their authority and influence to persuade their sons to migrate.

CRISIS MIGRANTS: PERSUADED BY THE FAMILY?

Crisis migrants appear in periods and regions of economic volatility in Mexico. Crisis migrants also come from middle-income households, those most likely to suffer from the lack of credit or the abundance of risk in such settings. Crisis migrants often receive support from the family to migrate and send remittances back to the family. These patterns are all consistent with the NELM, the perspective that views migration as a coordinated strategy in the family to overcome credit or insurance constraints in developing economies.

In our qualitative data, there are many examples of this apparent coordination between the migrants and their families back home. A return migrant, who has five other siblings in the United States, referred to his parents to explain why they all migrated: "We leave . . . to help our parents economically." The parents paid the smuggler fees for the eldest sibling first, and that sibling then paid the smuggler fees for the next sibling, and so on. The siblings now all send money back to their parents and also support one another in the United States.

In another family, siblings came up with a similarly elaborate arrangement to support the family. Three of them migrated to the United States via two different routes to maximize their chances of crossing the border, while another one of them stayed behind to take care of their parents and the family's taco business. The sister in Mexico told us how this strategy helped the family: "[Before] we only had a very small room and a tiny bathroom. . . . Between all of us, we started to make [the house] bigger. . . . We are better off in that respect because they [migrants in the U.S.] send us [money] and we earn money here."

But things do not always work out so smoothly. Our qualitative data provide examples of disagreement in the family about migration. The examples of disagreement are not quite as numerous as the cases of apparent

agreement. It is important to highlight "apparent" here, as our data collection strategy is more likely to capture agreements than disagreements
in the family. Recall that our team did not observe negotiations in the
family in real time—as an ethnographer participating in local life over a
long period would—but only asked migrants and family members about
them. Our team also interviewed most respondents only once, perhaps not
enough to establish rapport for such intimate revelations.

Our data, however, still contain admissions of conflict in families. Such
conflicts suggest that the "contract" that is presumed to exist between the
migrant and the family in the NELM theory is not always amicable or
"self-enforcing," as suggested in earlier research. Power differentials in the
family sometimes leave young members no option but to comply with suggestions to migrate. Power, however, can shift to the migrant over time.
Migrants can form their own families or garner enough connections in the
destination community to ultimately extricate themselves from obligations
to the origin family.

FATHERS' AUTHORITY

Patriarchal relations in the family subvert not just the wife and the daughters, but also the sons, to the authority of the father. Younger sons—the
most typical status among crisis migrants in our data—provide the ideal
migrant for a family for several reasons. First, as mentioned previously, the
father and the elder sons are often in charge of land or business holdings
in origin, leaving younger sons as the only available source of flexible labor
in the family. Second, younger sons are more likely to succeed in crossing
the border given the harsh conditions awaiting undocumented migrants.
As a migrant's father tells us, "When you cross rivers, walk in the desert . . .
an older guy is not going to make it." Third, younger sons are typically
single, have "no responsibilities," as a migrant's mother put it, and their
allegiance lies with the parental family. They are likely to respect their
father's authority.

It is not easy to capture how fathers exert their will on their sons given
our data collection strategy. Most fathers among our respondents described migration as a mutual agreement between them and their sons.
Still, some implied their authority over the decision in subtle ways. Álvaro,
for example, suggested that, for migration to be a successful endeavor, fathers need to keep a watchful eye over their sons. "If the father doesn't tell
[the migrant] to do something [with his money], he won't do much. He is
just going to spend his money. We have to communicate." Immediately
after this statement, Álvaro reemphasized the role he played in Mateo's

migration, as well as the expectations he had of his son: "Just like [my son] asked 'Can I go?' and [I said,] 'Yes, you can go.' . . . We helped him. . . . He helps us too."

It is important for fathers to retain their authority in the family. For some, this concern guided the decision to send their sons as migrants rather than migrating themselves. A migrant's father voiced this sentiment when we asked him why his son migrated and not him. "I am the boss around here," he said. "If I go there [the United States], I will be bossed around."

Shifting allegiances

Family in Mexico might have the power to influence a member to migrate, but it can hardly expect to retain that power indefinitely. As a migrant's mother put it: "You have your children when they are young. When they grow up, they have their own way." For many migrants, marriage is a critical juncture, releasing them from their obligations to their parental family. Jorge, the migrant from the preceding chapter, described this transition as follows: "My dad taught us that. If you got married . . . your family was first. If you had extra, then you give some money to your parents."

Parents did not always appreciate their children's changing priorities. A migrant's father complained that his children, after getting married, "have forgotten about me." He later added bitterly, "One should help those who helped them get an education, right?" In such cases, severing of economic ties—the remittance flows from the migrant to the family—implied the severance of intimate family ties as well.

Implications

These examples, where household members disagree about migration, or agree at first but then have a change of heart, complicate the idealized conception of the household in the new economics perspective as a cohesive social unit. This point, however, should not be overstated. Any general theory, by its very design, relies on simplifications of the real process. My goal here is not to present these deviations as a challenge to the theory, but as examples of the real-life heterogeneity worth investigating in their own right.

It is also worth reiterating that the new economics theory—like all other theories of migration—is not so general as to be uniformly applicable. Many of its implications seem to hold, but under specific conditions and for a specific group of migrants we identified as the crisis migrants.

CONCLUSION

Between 1980 and 1990, a new migrant group replaced the circular migrants as the predominant group among the first-time Mexican migrants to the United States in our data. The group consisted mostly of young men—often the younger sons—from relatively wealthy rural households, and peaked in numbers following the economic crises in Mexico. I called this group the *crisis migrants*.

Crisis migrants accounted for just one in ten new migrants in the 1960s. The share of the group climbed to one-half in the mid-1980s, and dropped to one-fifth by the late 1990s. The trend in this group tracked almost perfectly to the inflation rates in Mexico, capturing the volatile economic environment in the country in the aftermath of the peso devaluations between 1976 and 1985. The group also responded to regional events like the coffee crisis in the early 1990s and the earthquake in 1985, increasing disproportionately fast in the affected regions compared to the rest of the country.

A more diverse set of opportunities were awaiting the crisis migrants in the United States, including jobs in a fragmenting manufacturing sector and a growing service industry. These jobs, unlike the seasonal agricultural work that many circular migrants did, offered year-round employment and, thus, a firmer basis for staying in the United States. Given also the stronger border enforcement at the time, crisis migrants remained in the United States for more prolonged periods when compared to circular migrants of the earlier era.

Crisis migrants, and the conditions that seem related to their rise, reveal a particular logic for migration. This logic is informed more by the constraints in Mexico (e.g., a chronic lack of credit and insurance that became particularly acute after the economic crises) than the opportunities in the United States. The logic often involves an elaborate arrangement, whereby the migrant and the family share both the costs (e.g., smuggling fees) and returns (e.g., remittances) of migration.

Crisis migrants, like the circular migrants before them, walked a well-traveled path set by past migrants, originating mostly from the central-western states that had historically high levels of migration. Crisis migrants relied heavily on help from immediate family members rather than distant relations, while also depending on professional smugglers to cross an increasingly well-guarded border. Heightened border security extended the time Mexican migrants spent in the United States, limiting their contact with their origin communities. Crisis migrants also faced significant pressures from family members, especially their fathers.

Thus, crisis migrants were an outcome not just of the economic conditions in Mexico at the time, or the social connections that made migrating easier out of the central-west, but also of the patriarchal relations that subjected younger sons to the authority of their fathers. However, those relations often lost their hold once migrants formed their own families or became firmly established in the United States, leading to the severance of their ties to their parental household.

The configuration of the economic, social, and cultural contexts that made crisis migrants the majority group in the 1980s did not stay put for long. The Mexican economy achieved more stability over time. The locus of poverty began to shift from rural to urban regions. U.S. immigration policy experienced a major change in 1986, opening the path to legalization for more than 2 million Mexicans. As we will see in the following chapters, these changes would dramatically alter the migrant stream between the two countries in the years to come.

Chapter 4

"YOUR PLACE IS WHERE YOUR FAMILY IS"

Family Migrants

FIGURE 4.1. A migrant's mother with her granddaughter in Mexico
PHOTO BY Patricia Martín

THE IMMIGRATION REFORM AND CONTROL ACT OF 1986

On September 26, 1986, the U.S. House of Representatives voted 202 to 180 not to take up a bipartisan immigration bill sponsored by Senator Alan Simpson, a Wyoming Republican, and Representative Peter Rodino, a New Jersey Democrat. This was the third time Senator Simpson was championing an immigration bill that would prohibit employers from hiring undocumented migrants and offer legal status to many undocumented migrants already in the country. The first two bills had sailed through the Senate in 1982 and 1983, only to perish amid strong lobbying from Hispanic groups, who supported the legalizations but opposed the employer sanctions, and growers' organizations, who feared a depletion in the supply of migrant workers on which they had come to depend to harvest their crops.

On September 26, it seemed that this immigration bill would face a similar fate. But the tide turned quickly. In less than two weeks, Representative Charles Schumer, a New York Democrat, worked out a compromise solution that seemed agreeable to both growers and workers' rights advocates. The new amendments to the bill provided a temporary worker program in agriculture while authorizing legal status to some migrants who worked in perishable crops. By October 17, both the House and Senate had approved the compromise bill, with its core provisions subjecting employers who hire undocumented workers to civil penalties and granting legal status to undocumented migrants who have lived in the country since before January 1, 1982.

On November 6, President Reagan signed the bill, the Immigration Reform and Control Act (IRCA), hailing it as "the most comprehensive reform of our immigration laws since 1952." "Future generations of Americans" the president added, "will be thankful for our efforts to humanely regain control of our borders and thereby preserve the value of one of the most sacred possessions of our people: American citizenship."

Not everyone was as optimistic as President Reagan, however. Even Representative Schumer, who had helped break the deadlock over the bill, called it "a gamble, a riverboat gamble. There is no guarantee that employer sanctions will work or that amnesty will work. We are headed into uncharted waters."

. . . AND THE AFTERMATH

A gamble it was. A few years into its implementation, many skeptics questioned whether IRCA succeeded, or would ever succeed, in its ultimate goal of curtailing the influx of undocumented migrants to the United States. After all, it was the great upsurge in the undocumented entries—estimated to be around 28 million between 1965 and 1986—that had set the stage for the legislation. About 70% of undocumented migrants in the country in 1986 were thought to be of Mexican origin.

At a congressional hearing in 1989, Alan Nelson, the commissioner of the Immigration and Naturalization Services (INS), claimed that a steady decline in the number of undocumented people apprehended at the border "continues to demonstrate that the law is working." The figures on apprehensions along the Mexico-U.S. border did show a dip after IRCA, from 1.6 million in 1986 to less than 0.9 million in 1989, but the effect diminished with time. By 1993, the number of undocumented migrants apprehended on the Mexican border had climbed back to 1.3 million.

Perhaps IRCA could not stop undocumented migrant flows in the long run, but it did change the lives of 2.3 million Mexicans by granting them a path to American citizenship. Nearly nine out of ten IRCA applicants eventually became permanent residents. A majority of them were men, who could now petition to bring their wives and children to the United States. The number of petitions filed by Mexican-born IRCA applicants increased consistently through the early 1990s, reaching nearly 700,000 applications in 1994.

In the early 1990s, studies began to note the ripple effects of IRCA's legalizations when women and children's likelihood of migration from Mexico to the United States increased dramatically. Many of these women, scholars argued, were migrating to join their husbands or family members who had obtained legal status through IRCA.

"YOUR PLACE IS WHERE YOUR FAMILY IS."

This is how Carmen explained why she first went to the United States, and why she eventually returned to Mexico. Her husband Julio was working in California when Carmen found out she was pregnant with their first child. She was a university student in Guadalajara then but did not hesitate to leave that behind to be with Julio.

It was not easy transitioning into life in the United States. For several days, Carmen remained "locked in" their apartment. "I did not speak the language, and I was even afraid of the children," she told us. Her husband encouraged her to do things on her own. "He would make me an appointment [with the doctor] to go by myself to check the baby," she recounted. "If I needed to go to the grocery store, he would push me to go alone." Julio's cousins, who were already settled in the United States, were helpful during this difficult period. Carmen started "to become independent, a little more" every day.

Carmen had a good education, but she never worked in the United States. She raised her two kids and supported Julio as he became a successful entrepreneur. But their relationship eventually soured and divorce became inevitable. At that point, Carmen decided to return to Mexico with her children and live with her parents.

When we asked Carmen if she would go back to the United States, she replied: "If the opportunity presents itself again, yes. . . . If I had a partner, and if we could support each other. I wouldn't go by myself."

For Carmen, migration remains a possibility, but only with a prospective partner. This preference accounts for her initial decision to move to the United States to be with her ex-husband, Julio, and also for her immediate return to Mexico upon divorce. Carmen's choices are not universal, perhaps not even the most typical among the women we interviewed in Mexico. But her story—at least the initial part—matches the experience of many Mexican women who migrated to the United States to join husbands and partners already there.

We met one of them, Teresa, in the first chapter, who left for the United States accompanying some relatives to be with Tomás, a U.S. migrant she serendipitously got to know while he was visiting her village in Mexico. "Men and women go through a very strong phase of nature," Teresa's father joked, recounting their story to us, "so there [in the United States] they got together and started a life project." It was 1989, and Tomás, as it turned out, had just obtained legal status through IRCA. The two got married and Teresa obtained U.S. residency shortly thereafter. Teresa became a homemaker and a mother to two children.

The story, sadly for Teresa's father, did not end there. "One left," he told us, "and after that one, the others followed." Teresa first helped her brother, and eventually her four sisters, to migrate to the United States. "How can you stop a person [from leaving]," the father pondered while explaining his current predicament. "Well, I'm retired, and I take care of my wife, who's ill. . . . I'm the one who's responsible for everything: I prepare the meals; I bathe her, put the clothes in the washing machine. . . . I don't have children here; they left for the United States."

LEGALIZATIONS REUNITING FAMILIES AND EXTENDING MIGRANT CHAINS

By granting legal status to millions of undocumented migrants, IRCA created incentives for new migrants—and more women and children than ever before—to join family members already in the United States. The incentives to migrate were especially strong for immediate family members (spouses and children) who could apply for legal status through the newly legalized migrants. The incentives were also substantial for members of the extended family, who, although not eligible to apply for legal status, could still count on the legalized migrants for help and support in the United States, just like Teresa's siblings did after she joined her husband-to-be, Tomás.

After IRCA, women increased their share among new migrants from Mexico to the United States. In the decade before IRCA, from 1975 to 1985, women comprised 27% of first-time migrants in the Mexican Migration Project (MMP) data. In the decade after IRCA, between 1986 and

1996, women made up 32% of first-timers in the migrant flow. Much of this increase came from an upsurge in the number of women reuniting with their spouses in the United States. Among migrant women married to household heads—a subgroup for which we have more detailed information—the share joining a husband already in the United States rose from 29% in the pre-IRCA era to 39% in the post-IRCA period.

Following IRCA, children migrated in greater numbers too. Between 1975 and 1985, 121 children (1.8% of those age 17 or younger) in the MMP data took a first trip to the United States. Between 1986 and 1996, this number quadrupled to 483 (5.8%). Among migrant children of household heads (93% of the sample of children), about 84% had a parent already in the United States in the post-IRCA decade, slightly higher than the 81% of children in the pre-IRCA period.

Also in the post-IRCA period, individuals with ties to legalized migrants saw a spike in their likelihood of migrating to the United States. A simple comparison in the MMP data shows the cascading impact of the legalizations on migration out of the recipient households in Mexico. Before the passage of IRCA, the MMP data show that there were more than 6,500 households with a migrant, defined as someone who has been to the United States at least once. Only one-fifth of these households had a migrant that ultimately qualified for legalization. After IRCA, the likelihood of sending a new migrant—someone who had never been to the United States—was twice as high in households with a legalization-eligible migrant as it was in those with a migrant who did not benefit from the legislation.

FAMILY MIGRANTS

The trends following IRCA—namely, the increasing presence of women, children, and individuals with ties to U.S. migrants in the Mexico-U.S. stream—are reflected in the rise of a particular group of first-time migrants in our data. This group—the third cluster from our analysis in the first chapter—includes mostly women who live in households with prior U.S. migrants and in communities with high rates of migration prevalence.

The composition of this group stands in stark contrast to the circular or crisis migrants in the preceding two chapters. It contains a clear majority of women (64%), whereas men invariably predominate the other two groups (at least 81%). The group also includes the highest share of migrants in the older age brackets. Almost three-fourths of the migrants in this group are twenty-five or older compared to less than one-half of circular migrants, and only one-tenth of crisis migrants. A large share of the migrants in this group (70%) are married during their first U.S. trip. This proportion is at a similar level in circular migrants (74%), yet significantly lower in crisis migrants (29%).

The most striking characteristic of the migrants in this group, however, is their degree of connectedness to former U.S. migrants. Prior to the first U.S. trip, more than 80% of the migrants in the group have at least one person in their family who has migrated to the United States, and 20% are related to someone with permanent resident status there. Moreover, about 80% of the migrants in the group come from a community with a high level of migration prevalence. All three shares are significantly higher than those in the other migrant groups in our data. To characterize this distinct pattern, I call this group the *family migrants*.

Family migrants display a unique configuration that reflects a deeply gendered dynamic shaping migration out of Mexico. It is no coincidence that the only female-dominated cluster in our analysis also stands out in its relative maturity, denser family ties to prior migrants, and high marriage rate. This configuration reveals the high barriers to women's migration in Mexico, which is seen as riskier than men's, and as a result, encouraged more if it is associational (that is, following the migration of a partner or a family member).

But not all migrant women in our data display this configuration. About half are spread across the three migrant clusters dominated by men. Women in the men-predominated clusters are quite different from those in the women-predominated cluster: significantly younger, more educated, less likely to be married, less likely to have family ties to former migrants, and more likely to work in the United States.

Our inductive categorization, in other words, uncovers a more complex patterning of migrants than could be detected with a simple male-female dichotomy used in prior work. Women in our data appear both as independent migrants moving mainly for work, as well as family migrants moving in association with partners or other family members. The former tend to be dispersed across the three men-predominated clusters in our classification—such as the circular or crisis migrants from the preceding chapters—and the latter are more concentrated among the female-predominated family migrants.

FAMILY MIGRANTS: ON THE RISE AFTER IRCA

Family migrants comprised less than 10% of new migrants in 1965, gradually rising to 20% by 1985. After IRCA, this group doubled both in absolute size and in relative share, accounting for nearly 40% of all first-time migrants from Mexico to the United States in the early 1990s.

The sudden spike in the family migrants occurred within a few years of IRCA's legalization program that granted legal status and rights to bring family members to millions of undocumented migrants. The statistical analysis in appendix G suggests a link between the rise of the family mi-

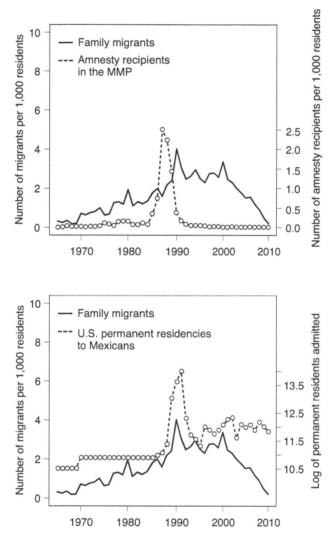

FIGURE 4.2. Trends in the number of family migrants, the number of amnesty recipients in the MMP data, and the number of U.S. permanent residencies given to Mexicans, 1965–2010

grants and IRCA's legalizations. This analysis shows that the number of family migrants—and family migrants only, not the other three migrant clusters—is significantly associated with the number of permanent residencies given to Mexicans in the United States, net of other determinants of migration flows, such as demographic factors or economic differentials.

The relationship between the family migrants and IRCA's legalizations is also clearly visible in the raw data plots presented in figure 4.2. The figure shows the trend in the number of family migrants (solid line with values on the left y-axis) along with two trends capturing the U.S. policy context (dashed lines with values on the right y-axis). The number of family migrants increased slowly but steadily between 1965 and 1985, from about 0.3 to 1.8 per 1,000 residents. The pace quickened considerably after IRCA. Between 1990 and 1999, our data contain about three family migrants in 1,000 residents per year, nearly double the number from the previous decade.

The jump in the size of family migrants followed a spike in the number of migrants legalized by IRCA in the MMP data, which reached five in 1,000 in 1987, as shown in the panel at the top. The jump also overlapped with a peak in the number of permanent residencies given to Mexicans (most of them legalized by IRCA) in the United States in 1990, as displayed in the panel at the bottom.

The growth in family migration was long-lived relative to the fleeting rise in the amnesties or permanent residencies granted to Mexicans. New migrants continued to join this cluster at high rates through the 1990s, dropping to their pre-IRCA levels only in the mid-2000s. Because of the sustained flow of family migrants—many of whom qualified for legal status through reunification—the number of permanent residencies given to Mexicans settled at a higher equilibrium in the post-IRCA period, never returning to its pre-legislation level.

FAMILY MIGRANTS: LEGALIZATION, SETTLEMENT, AND WORK OUTCOMES

The rise of the number of family migrants—a group containing a large majority of women with family ties to U.S. migrants—seems related to the distinct incentives IRCA supplied for legalization, family reunification, and settlement in the United States. Indeed, compared to the other migrant groups in our data, family migrants are less likely to enter the United States without documents (especially in the post-IRCA period), less likely to make repeated trips to Mexico, and more likely to obtain legal status in the United States. Family migrants are also significantly more likely to be unemployed on their first trip relative to the other migrants in our data.

The plots in figure 4.3 display these comparisons between family migrants and the other migrant groups. The panel on the top left plots the share of undocumented entrants to the United States among family migrants and other first-time migrants in our data over time. The share is significantly lower in family migrants (at the 95% confidence level) but only between 1992 and 1995, the period during which the petitions filed

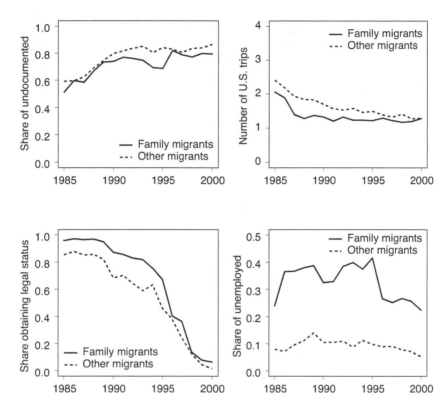

FIGURE 4.3. Trends in the share of undocumented, number of U.S. trips, share obtaining legal status, and share of unemployed in the United States among family migrants and other migrants in the MMP data, 1985–2000

by Mexican-born IRCA applicants to bring family members to the United States increased dramatically.

The panel on the top right shows the average number of trips taken by migrants entering in each year, which hovers around one for family migrants and remains significantly lower than that for migrants in the other clusters from 1987 to 1995. There is a notable secular decline in the average number of trips for both groups. Research links this decline to the tightening border control after IRCA, which, ironically, has not only failed to reduce undocumented entries in the long run, but has also provided a reason for those migrants to make fewer trips of longer duration, and perhaps even to settle permanently in the United States.

The bottom-left panel in the figure shows the share obtaining legal status among family migrants (solid line) and those in the other clusters (dashed line) over time. (Time here corresponds to the year of first migration, not to the year of legalization.) The legalization rate is significantly higher in the former group than the latter between 1985 and 1995, reaching nearly 100% in the first half of the period. The rate no longer differs between the two after 1995, and falls markedly for both as the year approaches the present, leaving less time for newly entering migrants to obtain legal status.

And finally, family migrants contain a relatively higher share of non-working migrants in the United States compared to the other groups. The bottom-right panel in figure 4.3 shows the share of unemployed people among the family migrants (solid line) and those in the other groups (dashed line). Between 1986 and 1994, nearly 40% of the migrants in the former group report not working compared to just 10% in the latter. The difference between the groups, although still statistically significant, shrinks after 1994, when the IRCA-induced legalizations are beginning to slow down.

FAMILY MIGRANTS: CONNECTED BUT NOT DEPENDENT

The share working is lower among family migrants compared to the other migrant groups, but it is still higher than the share not working. More than 60% of the family migrants in our data are actually employed on their first U.S. trip. This observation is important to emphasize. Most family migrants might be joining their spouses or parents in the United States under the unique circumstances of IRCA, but that does not mean those migrants are not economically active there.

And, while the share of associational migrant women in our data (that is, those following spouses already in the United States) increased with IRCA, it never reached the majority. Among migrant women married to household heads at the time of our survey—a subgroup for which we have more detailed information—the share of associational migrants rose from 29% in the pre-IRCA era to 39% in the post-IRCA period. The share of migrant women moving contemporaneously with their husbands declined from 25% to 21%. The share of those traveling independently (single or before their husbands) also declined slightly, from 46% to 41%, but still remained the largest among the three groups.

FAMILY MIGRANTS: MISSING IN THE MMP DATA?

The comparison of associational and independent migrants is based on a portion of the MMP surveys that was administered to the spouses of households in about half of the 143 communities. These data might not be representative of all migrant women in those communities. Moreover, about 90% of the MMP data on migrants comes from communities in Mexico, and only 10% from respondents in the United States. The data likely underrepresent migrants who have moved their entire family to the United States with no relatives left in origin communities in Mexico. Missing data can be especially problematic for family migrants—a group that has a higher number of family members already in the United States compared to, say, the circular or crisis migrants.

Despite potential missing data issues, however, the patterns we observe in the MMP data are largely consistent with the trends established in other data sets. Researchers have observed the rise in the number of women and children migrants after IRCA, for example, in the border apprehension statistics as well as in the surveys administered in the United States. Researchers have also repeatedly noted the growing rates of employment among Mexican women in the United States. In earlier work, scholars observed that Mexican wives in the United States were likely to work only if their husband's income was not sufficient to cover household needs, and if they could delegate housework or child care to other household members. In more recent studies, however, scholars identified a growing presence of Mexican migrant women who chose to work in the United States, regardless of husbands' employment status or income.

This trend is in line with our observations—that independent migrants outnumber associational migrants among Mexican migrant women, and that the majority of migrant women work even among the so-called family migrants (who are more likely to be associational migrants). The trends, according to sociologist Pierrette Hondagneu-Sotelo, reflect Mexican women's desire to obtain status in migrant households, as well as their intentions to settle in the United States to retain that status.

Family migrants—a group predominated by women with ties to prior migrants—reveal a distinctive logic for migration that is as much about reuniting families as it is about reaching economic goals. Family migrants are not just improving earnings like the circular migrants, or managing economic uncertainties in Mexico as the crisis migrants, but they are also resolving a dilemma that migration presents between economic desperation on the one hand and family separation on the other.

Family migrants are a result of the unique policy environment in the United States, but also of the changing role of women in Mexican families through the 1980s. The review below places family migrants in these specific contexts. The theoretical discussion that follows considers the social processes at work that connect the mobility of family migrants to that of earlier migrant groups. And, finally, qualitative data that follow reveal how the larger contexts and processes shaped individuals' thinking about U.S. migration.

MEXICO, 1980–1990
WOMEN ARE MORE POWERFUL IN HOUSEHOLDS

The preceding chapter provided a review of the economic crises in Mexico from the mid-1970s through the 1980s that forced many households to send migrants to the United States in order to manage the constraints and risks to their budgets. The same conditions, the review showed, pulled many women into the labor market.

Women's responsibilities in the home were declining in this period with the falling fertility rates, and their educational opportunities were increasing with the expansion of higher education in the country. Women's entry into paid employment—accelerated by the crises threatening household incomes—increased their power in households, where men had traditionally been the sole breadwinners. Patriarchy started to lose its stronghold in Mexican society. This is not to say that women always had full control over their fate, but at least their word carried more weight in the household.

WOMEN GAIN MORE CONTROL OVER MIGRATION DECISIONS

As discussed in the preceding chapter, women started to affect migration decisions in the family to a greater degree over time. Women, however, continued to face higher barriers to migrating compared to men. Research shows that women—unlike men—were positively selected on education to migrate. Women were also more dependent on social ties to prior migrants to migrate relative to men. And yet, as we will discuss below, those ties were not always accessible to women, nor did they always facilitate migration as they did for men.

Despite these impediments, women's mobility increased over time. Research identifies a generational shift in Mexican women's migration patterns in the MMP data. Whereas spouses of the household head often migrated to join their husbands already in the United States, daughters tended to move independently for work. Research also shows Mexican women's odds of both documented and undocumented migration to the United States increased after IRCA.

THE UNITED STATES, 1980–1990
STRUCTURAL CHANGES TO THE U.S. ECONOMY

The preceding chapters described three trends in the U.S. economy in the post–World War II period that increased the demand for migrant workers. First, manufacturing operations became increasingly fragmented, and subcontracting arrangements more common. This led to a growth in jobs that offered little pay and few benefits, which were attractive mostly to migrant workers. Second, although the service sector grew over time, it also became increasingly polarized with respect to pay and benefits. Professional and managerial positions on one end of the spectrum were filled by native workers (and perhaps high-skilled migrants); on the other side of the spectrum, jobs in personal services attracted mostly less-skilled migrants. Third, women entered into paid employment in greater numbers—increasing their share in the labor force from less than one-third in the 1950s to nearly one-half in the 1990s—and drove up the need for domestic workers that migrant women met.

RESTRICTIONS ON LEGAL IMMIGRATION

The increasing demand for immigrant labor in the United States was simultaneous with growing restrictions on legal immigration from Mexico. First, the amendments to the Immigration and Nationality Act in 1965 subjected Mexican citizens to a hemispheric cap of 120,000 visas per year. Additional amendments in 1976 imposed a per-country limit of 20,000 visas per year. Given these restrictions on legal entry, the share of Mexicans entering the United States without documents increased through the 1970s despite the stronger enforcement on the border.

The structural changes in the U.S. economy in the 1980s—the stagnating real wages of manufacturing workers, in particular—continued to feed a restrictionist sentiment against immigration. These changes, as we saw above, also fueled more demand for immigration. This was a paradoxical combination, according to sociologist Kitty Calavita, which differed starkly from the past, when the structural forces feeding a restrictionist sentiment, like high unemployment, reduced the demand for immigration. And this paradoxical combination gave rise to IRCA, a law full of contradictions.

PASSAGE OF THE IMMIGRATION REFORM AND CONTROL ACT

As we saw in the beginning of the chapter, passing IRCA required a number of compromises by the U.S. Congress. The sponsors of the bill had a particular vision of enacting employer sanctions to reduce undocumented immigration. The 1952 McCarran-Walter Act had already deemed it illegal to "harbor, transport or conceal illegal entrants," but an amendment known as the Texas Proviso exempted employers from harboring undocumented workers. It was not politically feasible to enact employer sanctions alone, however. Advocates of ethnic and religious groups also pressed for a legalization program for the undocumented migrants already in the country. IRCA, even when it combined employer sanctions and legalizations, seemed unlikely to pass until Congressman Schumer added provisions into the bill related to agricultural labor. These provisions ensured critical support from the southwestern and Californian delegations.

As passed in October 1986, IRCA consisted of three components. First, the employer requirements and sanctions made it illegal for an employer to knowingly hire undocumented workers. Second, the legalization provision enabled undocumented migrants who had been in the United States since before 1982 to apply for legal residence under the Legally Authorized Workers (LAWs) program. And third, the Special Agricultural Workers (SAWs) program allowed undocumented migrants who worked in agriculture up through 1986 to apply for legalization. A replenishment clause provided for additional farmworkers to be admitted if a shortage of farmworkers were to develop.

IRCA, in addition to its three pillars, included anti-discrimination safeguards to prevent employment discrimination against foreign-looking and foreign-sounding citizens and legal aliens, grants to aid states with the costs of legalization, a program to check the eligibility of non-citizens for federally financed welfare, and increased enforcement against undocumented migration with funds for the U.S. Immigration and Naturalization Service and the U.S. Department of Labor. IRCA was more than an immigration law, sociologist Frank Bean and his colleagues argue. It was a major piece of legislation that influenced employment, agricultural labor, civil rights, and welfare policies.

The effect of the legislation was a topic of contentious debate among scholars and the public alike. Kitty Calavita, for example, argued that the employer sanctions would remain "a symbolic measure with little impact on immigration flows." Other provisions, such as the replenishment clause for agricultural labor, she continued, would "predictably add to the stock of immigrant workers."

But the legislation had to include these contradictory components to be passable. In other words, it had to resolve the apparent conflict between the political pressures to restrict immigration and the economic pressures to supply employers with immigrant labor. Employer sanctions responded to the former—although remaining a mostly symbolic act, as we will see below—and the replenishment provisions for farm labor addressed the latter.

Legalizations after IRCA

Legalizations after IRCA involved two major steps. In the first step, eligible persons had a window (1 year for LAWs and 18 months for SAWs) to apply to receive *temporary resident status*, which gave them privileges to stay and work in the United States. Under the LAWs program, eligible persons included undocumented immigrants who had been residents in the United States since before January 1, 1982. Under the SAWs program, eligible persons included undocumented agricultural workers in perishable crops who had worked 90 person-days in either (i) each of the three years prior to the bill (1984–1986), or (ii) in the year ending May 1, 1986 alone. The former group needed to wait a shorter period (1 year rather than 2 years) to change from temporary to permanent resident status.

In the second step, temporary residents, after a waiting period (of 18 months for LAWs and 1 or 2 years for SAWs), had a one-year window to apply for *permanent resident status*. Failure to do so would revert immigrants back to undocumented status. To become permanent residents, immigrants needed to show English language and civics knowledge, and to meet certain health and criminal standards. Once they became permanent residents, immigrants could sponsor a spouse or children for permanent residency, and become eligible to apply for U.S. citizenship in five years.

A total of 1.77 million immigrants applied to the LAWs program, and 1.31 million applied to the SAWs program. The latter number exceeded expectations and instigated accusations of widespread fraud. Nearly all applicants (98% of the LAWs and 94% of the SAWs) were still approved. The majority of applicants were Mexican, about 70% of the LAWs and 82% of the SAWs.

Men made up the majority of the SAWs applicants (83%), perhaps unsurprisingly since the program targeted agricultural workers, a predominantly male labor force. But men also comprised the majority of the LAWs applicants (57%). The gender difference in IRCA legalizations cannot be attributed solely to the composition of the undocumented migrant population at the time. Estimates suggest a male-to-female ratio of 1.14 among the undocumented population in 1980, one that is lower than the sex ratio of 1.38 observed among the LAWs applicants. Sociologists Jacqueline Hagan and Susan Gonzalez Baker connect the lower representation of women among migrants legalized through IRCA to the kinds of occupations immigrant women typically take on, like domestic work, that make it hard to establish the six-year paper trail of employment and residence in the United States needed for legalization.

Employer sanctions after IRCA

IRCA made it illegal to knowingly employ undocumented workers. The provision applied to all employers, including those who subcontracted their work, and to all workers, including temporary workers. The law required employers to ask all employees for documentation proving their identity and eligibility to work in the United States. Penalties ranged from $250 for first offenders to $10,000 plus a possible prison sentence for repeat offenders.

Before the passage of IRCA, many doubted the potential efficacy of the employer sanctions. After all, the INS had the capacity to monitor only a small fraction of the nation's approximately 7 million employers each year. Proponents of the sanctions believed they would have a deterrent effect through voluntary compliance. After the enactment of the law, INS commissioner Alan Nelson declared that most employers were obeying the law simply because it is the law.

However, scholars observed in fieldwork how easy it was for immigrants to obtain fraudulent documents that they could then present to employers. And because the law put the burden of proof on the immigrants rather than the employers, it made it easy, in sociologist Jacqueline Hagan's words, for employers "to follow the letter of the law without carrying out the spirit of the law."

The Illegal Immigration Reform and Immigrant Responsibility Act (IIRIRA) in 1996 changed this state of affairs. It set up a system that enabled employers to verify by telephone, and later on an Internet-based platform called "E-verify," the immigration status of their workers, curtailing the use of fraudulent documents. But, until that time, employer sanctions had limited impact on undocumented migrant flows to the United States.

Undocumented migration after IRCA

Border Patrol apprehensions along the Mexico-U.S. border declined in the first few years after IRCA, from more than 1.7 million in 1986 (fiscal year) to about 950,000 in 1989. This decline occurred during a time when INS funding for enforcement activities rose from $361 million in fiscal year 1986 to $541 million in 1989, and the number of Border Patrol personnel jumped from 3,687 to 4,919.

Some observers took the decline in apprehensions as evidence of the deterrent effects of the increased border enforcement and employer sanctions. It turned out, however, that the decline was attributable more to IRCA's legalization programs—whereby many formerly undocumented migrants crossing the border periodically obtained documents—than to employer sanctions. And surely, by 1990, border apprehensions were on the rise again, growing 26% over the previous year. The number of undocumented Mexicans in the United States would increase consistently thereafter, from an estimated 1 million in 1990 to 4.5 million in 2000. (See figure 1.3.)

IRCA also attempted to deter undocumented flows with employer sanctions. But these sanctions could not be effectively enforced, as discussed above, well into the 1990s. Employers continued to hire undocumented workers, but paid them less than documented migrants who had increased in supply with IRCA's legalizations. Several studies found that the wages of undocumented and documented immigrant workers, although at similar levels prior to IRCA, diverged after the legislation, with the former group earning significantly less than the latter.

Family reunification after IRCA

The preceding statistics showed that men made up more than two-thirds (68%) of the applicants to IRCA's legalization programs. The applicants began receiving permanent resident status in large numbers in the 1990s and petitioned to extend that status to their spouses and children. The number of petitions by IRCA migrants increased consistently, from nearly 270,000 in 1992 to 740,000 in 1993, and to more than 850,000 in 1994.

Family reunification continued to be a major incentive for female migrants to come from Mexico to the United States in this period, but it certainly was not the only one. Studies found that Mexican women were not only more likely to migrate legally to the United States after IRCA, but they were also more likely to cross without documents compared to the pre-IRCA period. Different data sources all suggested an increasing share of women in the Mexico-U.S. stream in the early 1990s. Studies attributed this change in part to the differential impact of employer sanctions on men and women. While the sanctions decreased undocumented men's wages and hours worked, they had little impact on undocumented women, who worked mostly in the domestic sphere (e.g., cleaning houses, caring for children or the elderly), where those sanctions were more difficult to impose.

Connections to mexico after IRCA

IRCA granted many undocumented migrants legal status and, consequently, the option to bring immediate family members to the United States. These opportunities, one can argue, provided those migrants with a firm basis to settle in the United States, and gradually, to cut ties to Mexico. Legal status also gave migrants the right to travel freely between Mexico and the United States, which, research shows, was one of the strongest incentives to legalize. There is a debate about whether IRCA legalizations strengthened or weakened migrants' ties to Mexico, with no clear resolution. Some studies show that legalized migrants continue to travel frequently and invest in their communities of origin, others find that legalized migrants remit back home less and less over time.

SUMMARY

The economic conditions in the United States in the 1980s generated both greater demand for immigrant labor and growing pressure to restrict immigration. The response to these conflicting forces was the 1986 Immigration Reform and Control Act, a major piece of legislation that, on the one hand, legalized about 3 million undocumented migrants and instituted a special workers program to replenish any shortages in agricultural labor in the future, and on the other, imposed sanctions on employers hiring undocumented workers and increased border enforcement.

IRCA had a limited effect on deterring undocumented migration flows, which, after a brief decline in the late 1980s, continued to rise through the 1990s. The legislation, however, changed the lives of more than 2 million Mexican migrants, who could now work and travel freely, and bring their families to the United States.

IRCA increased the share of women in the Mexico-U.S. stream, and also the share of family migrants—a distinctly female group among the first-time migrants in our data that also stands out for its dense connectivity to former migrants through family or community ties.

Family migrants represent a particular logic for U.S. migration, one that not only seeks to solve economic problems, but also works to keep families together. Family migrants go the United States to eliminate the trade-offs in migration. Their mobility, more than that of any other group in our data, is predicated on the presence of former migrants in the United States. Now, let us turn to a theme from the preceding chapters, and consider these social connections between migrants and their family and community members in origin that tend to encourage more migration. How do such network effects operate in the post-IRCA period? And how do network effects in migration work for family migrants in particular, a group unlike any other in the prevalence of women?

FAMILY MIGRANTS: THE STRONGEST
CASE FOR NETWORK EFFECTS?

The preceding chapters contained ample evidence for positive network effects in migration, whereby prior migrants increase the likelihood that more people in their families and communities will migrate. Network effects work through three principal mechanisms, which are not mutually exclusive. Prior migrants provide useful information or help that reduces the uncertainty of migration, leading to what Paul DiMaggio and I have called *social facilitation*. Prior migrants (or others observing them) actively encourage migration, making it a social expectation, and thus exert *normative influence*. Prior migrants also generate *network externalities* like recruiters, smuggling networks, or ethnic enclaves in destination that help sustain more migration.

Each of these mechanisms works for each migrant group in our data, but to different degrees, depending on the context of migration as well as the characteristics of the migrant group. Social facilitation is the major mechanism for circular migrants, for example. In the 1970s—when most of the circular migrants appear in our data—Mexicans worked mainly in seasonal agriculture jobs in the United States and traveled back and forth between Mexico and the United States relatively easily, given the weak enforcement on the border. These migrants could pass on useful information to others in their families and communities, or take new migrants along with them. Normative influence was also at work for some circular migrants that were pressured into migrating by prior migrants, who presented a glorified view of migration, or by family members, who bought into that view. Finally, externalities like smugglers were not quite as common, or necessary, given the low level of border enforcement for most circular migrants.

For crisis migrants—teens peaking in the 1980s—social facilitation was important but worked more through trustworthy family ties than community relations, given the relative youth of the group and the relative difficulty of crossing the border at the time. For crisis migrants, recruiters and smugglers became crucial for the same reasons. Smugglers were externalities not just of the prior migration flows, but also of the stronger border enforcement those flows gave rise to on the U.S. side. Normative influence was present for this group as well, but mainly in the form of pressure from family members.

Network effects are arguably the strongest for family migrants among all groups in our data. Social ties for this group are not just inspiring or facilitating migration, as they do for the other groups, but those ties are often the very reason for migration. For many family migrants, the goal is not just to move, but to move to be with family members in the United States, especially after those members gain legal status with IRCA.

For family migrants, network effects continue to work through social facilitation, normative influence, and externalities. After IRCA, social facilitation perhaps becomes more common, especially through newly legalized migrants in the United States, who can travel freely to Mexico and bring others with them, if they choose to. After IRCA, externalities also gain in importance in inducing future flows. The reasons for this are twofold. First, levels of border enforcement increased after the legislation, which allowed professional smuggling businesses to thrive. Second, the large number of newly legalized migrants in the United States created more ethnic businesses or associations that could act as a resource for future migrants.

The trends in network effects—or in the relative importance of the mechanisms leading to them—apply to all migrant groups, not just the family migrants. But certain patterns in network effects are likely to be different for family migrants compared to the other three groups in our data. After all, family migrants are the only group predominated by women. A vast body of research in sociology shows how social networks are gendered, both in their composition and in their effects. Research in migration, too, finds that migrant networks can shape men's and women's migration differently.

Our discussion of network effects in the preceding chapters did not get into such gendered patterns because the migrant groups covered in those chapters were comprised overwhelmingly of men. But the rise of family migrants—and the share of women migrants in our data with them—give us an opportunity to discuss how network effects can operate differently for men and women. The discussion below is mostly theoretical; it draws on existing research for empirical evidence, as well as some examples from my qualitative interviews in Mexico.

NETWORK EFFECTS AND GENDER
SOCIAL FACILITATION

The three mechanisms underlying network effects in migration are all likely to be gendered, or in other words, to work differently for men and women. Let us start with social facilitation, which is based on the information or help prior migrants provide. The willingness or ability of prior migrants to help can vary by their gender, or by the gender of the prospective migrants seeking help.

In many settings, migrant women are found to be more willing to help other migrants compared to migrant men. In their study of rural Thailand, Sara Curran and colleagues found that ties to migrant women increased the likelihood of migrating to urban areas for both men and women. Ties to migrant men, however, increased the odds of migrating for men but not for women. This pattern, the authors argued, reflects the gendered cultural norms in Thailand, where women are expected to be more caring and more committed to the well-being of others in their families and communities. In Mexico, Sara Curran and Estela Rivero-Fuentes observed similar patterns: Prior internal migration trips by women increased the likelihood of migration for both men and women in households, but trips by men had no impact on the migration of men or women.

Our qualitative data reveal these gendered dynamics in an interesting way. Several migrant men, for example, mentioned having no ties to their families or communities in Mexico until they were married. In each case, the wife's strong commitment to her family inspired the migrant to get in touch with his own family and to help his relatives or friends in the community to migrate. Jorge, whom we met in the second chapter, was one of these migrants who were convinced by their wives to help others. "To everybody we knew, we helped," Jorge told us, "even to people we did not know." "My wife is like that," he added, "she does not like seeing people suffer."

Prior migrants' willingness to help can vary also by the gender of the recipient. Among Mexican migrants, sociologist Pierrette Hondagneu-Sotelo observed that women were often excluded from the predominantly male migrant networks in their origin communities and needed to rely on their own, mostly female connections. Sociologist Anju Mary Paul, in her study of Filipino migrant workers, also found help-giving to be a differentiated process, based not just on the gender of the prospective migrants, but also on perceptions of how interested, trustworthy, and reliable those migrants are.

The gender of prospective migrants can also determine what constitutes help, both for the migrant and for the person providing it. In the preceding chapters, we saw that "help" for prospective migrant men typically involves traveling with experienced migrants from the community or living temporarily in their shared space once in the United States. "Help" for prospective migrant women, by contrast, often means securing safe passage to the United States, as well as safe, continuous accommodation there. The higher bar set for acceptable help reflects the higher risks—real or perceived—of migrating for women in Mexico. During our interviews, both men and women constantly brought up the dangers of migration for women, which include getting "raped" or "beaten," "being left behind," and facing "a lot of cruelty." These dangers made migrant women reluctant to leave without securing reliable support on the way to, and once in, the United States. Many migrant women among our respondents used borrowed documents, such as passports of look-alike friends, to enter the United States; this strategy allowed them to avoid dangerous routes or smugglers (the typical perpetrators of violence against women). Family members also worked hard to find dependable helpers for migrant women, typically immediate relatives in the United States who could be trusted to take care of the migrant. For example, Teresa's father—whose migrant daughter I introduced at the beginning of this chapter—would not agree to his daughter's departure until he was assured that she had someone's passport to cross the border, and that she would stay with her uncle in the United States until she got her own place with her husband-to-be Tomás. His daughters, including Teresa, "did not go for adventure," the father emphasized during our conversation, "to try their luck by themselves? No." They "had the support of [family members] there."

Prior migrants' ability to help others—in addition to their willingness to do so—can also vary by their gender. Migrant occupations are segregated by gender in the United States. Migrant men typically work in collective settings, like factories, fields, or construction sites, which gives them opportunities to recommend other migrants for work. Migrant women, by contrast, are usually employed in small establishments or private homes, which limits their ability to recruit other migrants. Sociologist Jacqueline Hagan, in her ethnography of the Maya in Houston, Texas, found that women's private work settings not only constrained their ability to help others, but also hurt their own prospects in the United States. Unlike men, who established ties to natives in their workplaces, and later used these ties to secure affidavits to qualify for IRCA's legalization programs, women had few non-Maya ties in their networks, and faced difficulties in collecting the required documentation.

Migrant living spaces in the United States also differ by gender. Most migrant men among our respondents lived with other migrant men from their communities to minimize costs, and could offer prospective migrants accommodation, even if temporarily. Migrant men also had a rotating-credit system, where each would contribute to hosting a new migrant until that migrant could establish himself. Recall how a migrant described this system in the second chapter:

> Sometimes the friends living with me in the apartment . . . would say "Hey, my brother is coming, lend me money for the *coyote* or the rent" . . . so I would pay their rent, meals, and re-adjust [their payments] when they started working. If there were five of us [living together], we each got to pay a certain amount and we helped each other that way.

Migrant women, by contrast, typically lived with immediate family members, which not only delayed their initial move until a close relative agreed to host, but also constrained women's ability to offer accommodation to prospective migrants. The familial living arrangements, like the private work settings, also restricted the reach of women's social networks in the United States, delaying their adaptation to the new setting.

Finally, prior migrants' ability to help others can also vary by the gender of the recipients. Because migrant men and women work in different sectors of the economy, each might be limited in its capacity to help the other in finding a job, for example.

In sum, social facilitation mechanism—or information or help from prior migrants—works quite differently for prospective migrant men and women. Men generally need less help to move compared to women, and more of it is available because there are more migrant men, and because those migrant men typically work and live in collective spaces, making it easy to share resources related to migration.

Normative influence

Normative influence works through the social rewards or sanctions bestowed upon prospective migrants by peers, family, or community members. This mechanism is highly gendered in the Mexican setting. A desire to migrate meets with strong social approval for men, while generating certain objections for women.

Men are typically the heads of, and main breadwinners for, households, especially in the traditional rural areas of Mexico from where most U.S. migrants in our data originate. Even when women work outside the home, they are responsible for the bulk of the domestic tasks and are the main caregivers for children and the elderly. Migration aligns with men's role as providers, while it clashes with women's role as caregivers. Thus, it is usually encouraged for men and discouraged for women.

For example, many respondents in our qualitative data argued that women "should not migrate." One respondent offered a qualifier: A woman should leave "only if she is a single mother" and hence the sole provider for her household. Contrast these examples to those in the preceding chapters, where migrant men were actively persuaded by their friends and family to migrate.

The normative influence mechanism—or encouragement through social rewards or sanctions—works in favor of migration of men but against that of women in Mexico. Gendered social expectations, then, help generate gendered network effects in migration.

Women can challenge these expectations, however, as more of them assume the provider role alongside their husbands in Mexican households, and as more women join the migrant stream. Sociologists Pierrette Hondagneu-Sotelo and Peggy Levitt, in the Mexican and Dominican Republican settings, respectively, showed how migrant women act as agents of change in their origin communities, providing role models for prospective migrant women, and encouraging their mobility.

Women, in some cases, go along with the gendered expectations, and instead reframe the migration decision as an extension of those expectations. Sociologist Anju Mary Paul, in her study of Filipina migrants, observed how women overcame the objections to their migration by performing— rather than countering—gender norms. These women emphasized their roles as daughters and mothers, and their respective duties to support parents and children, to justify their move overseas.

Network externalities

Network externalities represent generalized resources that an established migration flow creates, like recruiting or smuggling networks or ethnic businesses in destination communities. These resources, in theory, should be equally accessible to migrant men and women. But, in reality, even externalities can work differently for men and women.

Smugglers, for example, can be more expensive for migrant women compared to migrant men. First, in the Mexican setting, women typically choose smuggling routes that are less risky and thus more costly. Migrant women in our qualitative data frequently reported using entry points along the border—arguably the least risky crossing strategy—instead of more dangerous routes, such as crossing through the river or the desert. Second, a family member often accompanies women, even when they hire a smuggler. Of the number of women crossing the border with a smuggler, 43% report having a family member with them in the MMP data, as opposed to just 22% of men.

Ethnic businesses, another externality of past migration flows, can also be more useful to men than women, given that migrant occupations are segregated by gender, and that most former migrants from Mexico have been men.

Network effects and gender after IRCA

The preceding discussion suggests that network effects in Mexico-U.S. migration are likely to work more positively for men than for women. Men are more prevalent in the initial migrant stream, which allows them to establish networks that then help further that advantage. Women are excluded from those networks or benefit less from them. Men also face positive pressures to migrate in their social settings, while women encounter objections to their migration. The gendered roles in the family and community structure this differential response. And finally, men benefit more from institutionalized resources, like smugglers or concentration of migrants in destination communities, that are more costly or less accessible to women.

All three mechanisms for network effects—social facilitation, normative influence, and network externalities—seem to accrue more advantages to men, exacerbating the initial differences between men and women in the probability of migrating.

IRCA's legalizations present a shock to this cumulative dynamic. The legalizations, as well as the family reunification following it, allow more women than ever to migrate. Migrant women can establish their own networks, challenge the normative expectations in their communities, and pull more women into the migrant stream. IRCA, however, only quickens a process already under way, whereby women are gaining more power in households and have more of a say in household decisions, including migration. We can trace some of these patterns with the qualitative data.

FAMILY MIGRANTS: WOMEN REDEFINING THEIR ROLES

The steady rise of family migrants in our data from the 1960s onward follows from certain trends in Mexican society that helped redefine women's roles. Educational levels increased in this period, fertility rates declined, and women entered the labor market at an accelerated rate, especially after the economic crises in 1976 and 1982. Women gained more power in households and affected important decisions such as migration.

Our qualitative data capture these trends, and their impact on how women think about migration, mostly in generational comparisons. In the second chapter, for example, a migrant's daughter talked about how her father departed for the United States in the 1940s without even consulting her mother. The mother had no choice but to accept the situation. "Women used to do what men wanted," the daughter pondered, "but now we are living life in a different way."

Many older women among our respondents lamented not having opportunities to go to school. The large family sizes at the time forced many of them to stay home to take care of siblings and to help their mothers. "While I was growing up I had ambitions to go to school," one respondent told us, but "I was never allowed to go because I had to take care of my younger sisters." This respondent would later insist that her daughter finish high school.

Smaller family sizes today, in addition to expanding educational opportunities, allow more young girls to complete their education. One of our respondents told us that she refused to have any more children so that she could finish her elementary school degree as an adult, for example.

Many of the married respondents talked about how they influenced their husbands' migration decisions. For instance, one young woman strongly opposed her husband's move and told him, "You won't go. We will eat beans and tortillas here together. If you do go, you are going to take us with you." In the end, the family migrated together. The contrast between this and the previous example—where the wife did not even get to voice her opinion on her husband's decision—is clear. In the second chapter, we also saw that some women started to work in Mexico so that their husbands would not have to migrate to the United States.

The discussions on migration were not always amicable in families. In some cases, husbands refused to take wives along with them. Such was the case for a young woman who turned to her sister, a migrant in the United States, for help. Only after hearing that his wife would migrate anyway with or without his help did the husband agree to take her to the United States. Another migrant woman made it across the border with her friend's help only to find that her husband had another family in the United States. "She suffered bitterly," her sister in Mexico told us, but she refused to "come back to Mexico defeated." The migrant found work in the United States and eventually sent for all her children to join her from Mexico.

Women not only increasingly affect migration decisions in the family, or migrate independently of the family, but they are also changed by migration over time. For example, after living in the United States for a while, a respondent's daughter refused to return to Mexico, where "women are beaten by their husbands." She enjoyed the more egalitarian gender relations in the United States, which she took as a model for her own marriage.

Such examples should not distract us from the fact that patriarchal relations still reign in most Mexican households. These relations become apparent in the comments respondents make about women as "facing greater risk," not just in migrating, but everywhere, such as "walking here [in the city] at night." The need to protect women is a common theme in our interviews. A father tells us, for example, that he never migrated because he has "always kept an eye on [his] children, especially because they are girls." One male migrant mentions that, sometimes, "a woman's parents won't let her go" to the United States. He describes the case of one woman, whose mother thinks she should not work because, "with three little girls, how could she? They are girls, so she has to be aware of what they do. It is more dangerous if she neglects them while working." These comments reveal that patriarchy is still alive and well in Mexico, although certainly not as pervasive as in the past.

CONCLUSION

In the brief three-year period between 1987 and 1990, a particular migrant group doubled in size, as well as in its relative share among first-time migrants from Mexico to the United States. This group encompassed more than one-third of all migrants at its peak in 1991 and contained a large majority of women and migrants with family ties to previous U.S. migrants. To underscore these ties, I called the migrants in this group the *family migrants*.

The sudden increase in the number of family migrants occurred right after the enactment of IRCA in 1986, an immigration law that opened the path to legalization for more than 2 million undocumented Mexicans in the United States. Legalized migrants acquired permanent resident status within a few years, as well as the right to extend the same status to their spouses and children.

Family reunification was a major factor that pulled family migrants from Mexico to the United States. The group included a large share of wives and daughters joining their husbands and fathers, who were already there. As a result, compared to the migrants in the other groups, family migrants were more likely to enter the United States with documents, and also more likely to eventually acquire permanent resident status. Family migrants followed husbands and fathers to the United States, but they did not remain dependent on them there. The share not working among family migrants was the highest among all migrants groups but still lower than the share working.

Family migrants suggest a specific logic for U.S. migration that combines the dual goals of economic survival and family integrity. By moving to the United States, family migrants were solving their economic problems in Mexico while also keeping their families together in the United States. This logic was certainly facilitated by IRCA's legalization provisions, but also by women's changing roles in Mexican families and communities, which gave them more input in family economic decisions, including migration. Compared to the earlier eras, women in this period increasingly chose to have fewer children, to work outside the home, and to push for family integrity, either by having the family remain in Mexico all together or by moving as a family to the United States.

In the years leading up to IRCA, women were already gaining prevalence in the U.S.-bound migrant stream. But their mobility was still more constrained than that of men. Women had less access to migrant networks, which were composed primarily of men, and thus, were more helpful to men, given that men and women remained mostly separated in their working and living spaces in the United States. Women were also encouraged to migrate less frequently—if not completely discouraged from it—given traditional gender roles that viewed them as caregivers. But IRCA, by granting legal status to millions of women—some directly and some through their husbands—greatly expanded women's networks in the United States and helped reduce the gender gap in such network effects in migration.

IRCA redefined the context of migration between Mexico and the United States, and also generated a long-term dynamic facilitating women's migration. But its effects on migration would soon be overshadowed by other economic processes and events, as we will see in the next chapter.

Chapter 5

"PUTTING DOWN ROOTS"

Urban Migrants

FIGURE 5.1. A migrant in his home in Mexico
PHOTO BY Patricia Martín

FATHER ANTONIO'S ACCOUNT

It is the first day of our fieldwork, and in some ways, the most difficult. San Marco, a busy urban neighborhood in Guadalajara, is not an easy place to navigate. The streets are crowded, and it is harder to blend in. The people we talk to seem suspicious of researchers asking questions, and understandably so, given that extortion schemes have become rampant in recent years. Providing any information about relatives in the United States brings with it the danger that you might receive a phone call someday telling you that your relatives are being held hostage for a ransom.

Leo, one of our interviewers and a local of this neighborhood, is our best asset here. He suggests that we focus on the "safe" streets and interview people in pairs, while one person walks up and down the street, keeping track of who is in which house and for how long. These precautions seem necessary given that crime is an issue in San Marco. There are gangs involved in drug trade and frequent turf fights. Father Antonio, the priest of the neighborhood church and one of our first respondents, describes the situation lightly as "worrisome." "Someone is killed every week," he says. "Every Saturday, someone dies, as if per contract."

It is mostly teenagers who are involved in the gangs, Father Antonio tells us, and many of them are the sons of rural migrants. San Marco has settlers from many villages and towns in the area, including from the surrounding states of Nayarit, Zacatecas, Aguascalientes, Hidalgo, and Michoacán. Migrants from different regions bring "different communal experiences, different traditions, and different habits," which sometimes "complicates co-existence," Father Antonio explains. Many rural migrants face difficulties in adjusting to city life. "Coming here [San Marco] meant selling their ranch, and they have never forgotten that," Father Antonio suggests. "They carry an uprootedness. . . . Many do not feel that they are a part of this neighborhood; they only live here." Some inevitably turn to U.S. migration, which has "serious repercussions" for the family and compounds this sense of disintegration and isolation.

Guadalajara is the second largest city in Mexico and a major destination for internal migrants. Between 1970 and 1990, the city population increased from just under 1.2 million to more than 1.6 million. About one-fifth of domestic migrants in the city originated from Michoacán in 1990, and slightly smaller shares came from the Federal District and Zacatecas. Guadalajara not only attracts internal migrants from other regions of Mexico, but it also sends international migrants to the United States.

The exodus from Guadalajara to the United States is not about a lack of employment, according to Father Antonio. "If one looks at the job databases, one finds seven or eight pages full of job offers." San Marco's residents have seen considerable improvements in their welfare over the past 30 years, Father Antonio argues, judging from the "cars parked outside" most houses. To be sure, the city's economy has grown remarkably in the past several decades. The growth, however, has been accompanied by a shift in the employment structure. The share of workers employed in manufacturing, for example, has dropped from 32% in 1970 to 25% in 2000. The share in the service sector, by contrast, has climbed from 35% to 43%.

It is the implications of these trends in the community that makes Father Antonio ask rhetorically: "Is there a lack of jobs? Or is there a lack of skills for those jobs?" The latter seems to be the major challenge in San Marco. There are jobs available, but most require skills that the neighborhood residents do not have. There are training programs as well, but too few to accommodate San Marco's growing population, which is driven by an influx of rural migrants.

SAN MARCO: A MICROCOSM FOR URBAN MIGRATION?

To explain contemporary migration from his city neighborhood to the United States, Father Antonio invokes two factors. First is the prior internal migration to the city, which, in his view, generates a pool of "uprooted" people with little connection to the area. The second factor is the skills required for jobs in the city, which limits the opportunities available to its residents. Father Antonio also mentions rising crime rates in the city, but he does not link this phenomenon to emigration explicitly. Father Antonio's observations are based on a single community, San Marco. But this community may represent a microcosm for understanding the rising levels of emigration from urban communities in Mexico to the United States.

URBAN MIGRANTS

While urban communities came to surpass rural regions as the main providers of new migrants to the United States, a particular migrant group gained prevalence in our data, rising to majority status among all first-time migrants in the early 1990s. This group—our fourth and final cluster—contained a large majority (68%) of migrants from urban communities, standing in stark contrast to the circular, crisis, and family migrants that included mainly residents of small villages or towns. To call attention to its distinctive origins in Mexico, I refer to this group as the *urban migrants*. Urban migrants in our data went from containing less than one-fifth of all new migrants in 1965 to accounting for more than one-half of them in 2000, and nearly 70% by 2010. (See figure E.1 in appendix E.)

This trend is not just an artifact of the MMP sampling strategy, which became more inclusive of urban communities over time. Many researchers have observed a rising share of U.S. migrants from urban regions in Mexico over time with nationally representative data, attributing this pattern in part to the urbanization in the country. Riosmena and Massey estimated that 30% of U.S. migrants in Mexico between 2001 and 2006 originated from metropolitan communities (>100,000 residents), and another 15% came from small urban areas (15,000–100,000 residents). The authors combined first-time and repeat migrants, however. The share from urban origins is likely to be higher among first-time migrants, and closer to that estimated in the MMP data.

CHARACTERIZING THE URBAN MIGRANTS

Urban migrants are distinct from the three migrant groups discussed in the preceding chapters in their regions of origin. Only 35% of migrants in this group come from the historical migrant-sending states in central-western Mexico, compared to at least 80% of circular, crisis, and family migrants. The urban-migrants group—like the circular and crisis migrants—contains a large majority of men (81%). It also contains more educated migrants, compared to both the other migrant groups and non-migrants. This pattern is consistent with findings from other data that show recent Mexican migrants to be positively selected on education, a shift from past flows containing Mexicans with less-than-average levels of schooling.

Nearly 75% of urban migrants have completed middle school or more, compared to just 12% of circular migrants, 33% of crisis migrants, and 19% of family migrants. The difference between urban migrants and the other three groups is robust to period effects; that is, these differences are not just a function of increasing education levels in Mexico over time. (See figure 1.5 in chapter 1, as well as the analysis in appendix F.)

URBAN MIGRANTS: WORK, WAGES, AND DESTINATIONS IN THE UNITED STATES

Urban migrants also differ from the other migrant groups in their outcomes in the United States. This group is more likely than the others to work in manufacturing, construction, or service industries; to command higher wages, on average; to end up in new migrant destinations; and to make fewer return trips to Mexico. Some of these differences become less significant over time as all migrant groups move to non-agricultural jobs, choose new migrant destinations, and become "caged in" the United States due to increasing border enforcement.

Figure 5.2 displays the trends over time for urban migrants and the other three groups combined. The top-left panel shows the share of migrants working in manufacturing or construction in the United States separately for urban migrants (solid line) and the other three clusters (dashed line). The top-right plot displays the average monthly wages for the two groups. The

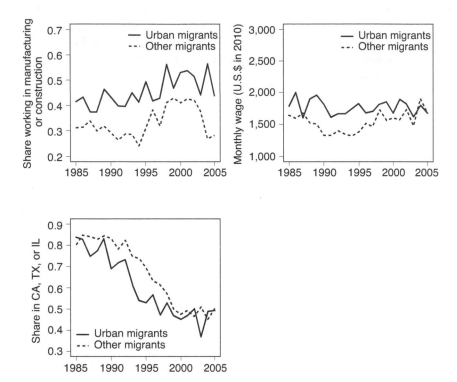

FIGURE 5.2. Trends in the share of migrants working in manufacturing or construction; monthly wage; share going to California, Texas, or Illinois among urban migrants and other migrants in the MMP data, 1985–2005

differences between urban migrants and the other groups are statistically significant (at the 95% level) in the overall data, as well as in most of the individual years.

The bottom-left panel in figure 5.2 shows that urban migrants are less likely than the other three migrant groups to end up in the traditional migrant destinations of California, Texas, and Illinois. While all migrant groups have gradually shifted to new destinations, urban migrants were the quickest to do so through the 1990s. Urban migrants were also the fastest in switching from rural to urban locales in the United States. Between 1995 and 2005, 25% of urban migrants ended up in a U.S. city of 100,000 people or more, compared to 20% in the prior decade. The rates for the other three groups remained at 21% in both decades.

These findings are consistent with patterns identified in recent work on origin-destination pairings in Mexico-U.S. migration. Research finds that earlier migrants from Mexico originated from rural regions and headed to rural areas in the United States. Recent migrants, by contrast, come from urban places in Mexico and choose to go to urban areas in the United States. These patterns, researchers argue, reflect the increasing concentration of work in cities in both countries.

Nearly one-fourth of urban migrants crossed the border with authentic documents. This share is close to that among family migrants, and significantly higher than the share (about one-tenth) among the circular and crisis migrants. It is easy to see why family migrants tend to be documented. The group, as we saw in the preceding chapter, contains mostly women with family members in the United States, who are likely to benefit from the family-reunification provisions of IRCA. The relatively high documentation rates among family migrants, in other words, are a direct reflection of changes in U.S. immigration policies in the 1980s. Interestingly, the high documentation rates among the urban migrants also likely result from the direct actions of the U.S. government in the post-NAFTA period, as we will see shortly in our review of the policy context.

What explains the mobility of urban migrants? What explains their differential outcomes in the United States? As I will argue below—and as Father Antonio's remarks hinted above—the rise of urban migrants resulted from the economic and spatial dislocations that followed Mexico's increasing integration into the world economy. The country's growing cities became at once attractive to internal migrants and a starting point for international migrants. The changing structure of work in the United States pulled urban migrants increasingly into manufacturing, construction, and service jobs and to new destinations. The increasing enforcement on the border did not seem to deter urban migrants, but it did force a settler logic on the group, especially to those without documents. I now turn to the context in Mexico and the United States that created this group and gave it wings to predominate the U.S.-bound migrant stream in our data from the 1990s through the 2000s.

MEXICO 1990–2010
The opening of the economy

The 1980s mark a major shift in Mexico's economic strategy from an import substitution industrialization model to an export-processing regime. After decades of protectionism and state interventions, the country embraced a neoliberal economic model based on trade liberalization, privatization, and deregulation. The initial impetus came from the 1982 balance-of-payments crisis. To avoid such incidents in the future, Mexico needed to become a more efficient economy capable of generating sufficient foreign exchange.

In 1983, Mexico removed import license requirements, and in 1986, joined the General Agreement on Tariffs and Trade (GATT), currently known as the World Trade Organization, opening its economy to trade and market competition. In 1989, the government eased restrictions on the rights of foreigners to own assets. It started to privatize state-owned enterprises and to remove entry restrictions in many industries. Trade quotas were replaced with tariffs, which were also lowered gradually. Trade barriers were lifted even further with the signing of the North American Free Trade Agreement (NAFTA), which created the largest regional market in the world between Mexico, Canada, and the United States. The agreement opened several sectors of the Mexican economy to foreign capital.

Trade liberalization and economic integration surely brought many benefits. One was to reduce Mexico's dependency on oil revenues (the volatility of which had contributed to the 1982 crisis). The share of oil revenues in the Mexican GDP declined from 14% to 7% between 1983 and 2000, while the share of exports rose from about 12% to 35%, and the share of imports increased from 6% to almost 38%. The share of foreign direct investment (FDI) also grew consistently in the same period, reaching almost 6% of the GDP in 1998.

Foreign investments into Mexico came mostly in the form of *maquiladoras*, factories that import components duty-free, assemble them into goods, and then export the goods. Most factories assembled one of three goods: apparel, electronics, or auto parts. *Maquiladoras* were first established in 1965 to provide work for the Bracero migrants that returned to Mexico when the labor-recruiting program ended in the United States. A majority of *maquiladora* jobs, however, went to women, not to former *braceros*.

THE GROWTH OF THE NORTH

Between 1965 and 2000, *maquiladoras* expanded exponentially, from 12 plants with 3,000 workers to 4,000 plants with 1.3 million workers. These plants were located primarily along the northern border of Mexico, the region that provided the lowest-cost access to the U.S. market (both to consumers and to parent firms, which kept offices in the U.S. border cities). In 1998, the northern region accounted for more than 85% of all *maquiladora* employment in Mexico. The region also grabbed a large share of total manufacturing employment, which increased from 21% in 1980 to 34% in 1998.

The regional patterning of *maquiladoras*, some argue, exacerbated the North-South divide in Mexico. Between 1996 and 2000, the states along the northern border enjoyed a combined annual growth rate of nearly 7%, the highest rate across all regions, and they increased their share in the country's GDP from 21% to 24%.

This was a major change for the country. Until the mid-1980s, three states—Mexico City (the Federal District), Jalisco, and Nuevo León—had accounted for more than three-quarters of industrial activity and enjoyed the highest levels of GDP per capita. These states also had attracted the lion's share of internal migrants.

In the open economy period, roughly starting with Mexico's entry into the GATT in 1986, the tables began to turn. Newly emerging industrial hubs on or near the border—such as the states of Chihuahua, Baja California Sur, Sinaloa, and San Luis Potosí—began to catch up to Mexico City in economic growth. These states solidified their economic reign with the signing of NAFTA.

The northern region began offering higher wages, on average, compared to the rest of the country, and thus, easily attracted domestic migrants. Between 1970 and 2000, the share of internal migrants to the border states increased by one-third, while the share headed to other large cities (Mexico City and Guadalajara) declined by more than one-half.

Migrants to the border region included mostly rural workers strained by the commercialization of land and reductions in agricultural support, as well as some urban dwellers leaving the saturated labor markets of Mexico City. Migrants included both women seeking work in the *maquiladoras* and men pursuing job opportunities in other manufacturing plants.

THE CONTINUING EMIGRATION TO THE UNITED STATES

The shift to the export-processing development model, coupled with Mexico's rapid integration into the world economy, led to rapid growth in the border states, and to an influx of internal migrants there from the economically deteriorating rural and urban areas. These changes, however, did not stop emigration from Mexico to the United States. Between 1996 and 2000, the number of Mexicans in the United States increased by nearly a third, from 6.4 to 8.4 million.

The marked increase in the number of Mexican migrants in the United States in the post-NAFTA period defied the expectation that an open and integrated economy would eventually curb labor flows to the United States. This was in fact a political selling point for NAFTA in both Mexico and the United States. "Without the free-trade agreement," Mexican President Salinas had warned, "you will witness millions of Mexicans crossing the border and looking for work." Janet Reno, the U.S. attorney general at the time, had similarly chimed in: "We will not reduce the flow of illegal immigrants until these immigrants find decent jobs, at decent wages, in Mexico. Our best chance to reduce illegal immigration is sustained, robust Mexican economic growth. NAFTA will create jobs in Mexico—jobs for Mexican workers who might otherwise cross illegally into America."

Indeed, optimism abounded when NAFTA was signed. Many researchers predicted that the benefits would accrue mostly to Mexico, the member with the smallest economy. Equalizing the price of traded goods, trade theory in economics implied, would bring about convergence in wages between Mexico and the United States. Employment in Mexico would rise, and migration to the United States would decline.

But, many others expected NAFTA to increase levels of migration, at least in the short run. A number of mechanisms were likely to bring about this effect. The agreement, for one, would lift barriers to agricultural imports. This, combined with the reductions in agricultural support well under way, would put pressure on rural workers to migrate to internal or international destinations.

The sweeping reforms, a second mechanism went, would bring structural changes to the economy. Firms would try to increase efficiency by reducing labor, leading to unemployment in the short run. Many inefficient industries would shut down, contributing to even higher rates of unemployment. New industries would have different skill requirements, and thus would be unable to absorb the displaced workforce. These changes would all lead to more migration within, and out of, Mexico.

NAFTA would increase income levels, a final mechanism implied, raising both Mexicans' aspirations and ability to migrate to the United States. This mechanism charted an inverted-U relationship between development and migration. Specifically, in the immediate aftermath of NAFTA—the early phases of Mexico's development—emigration would increase as more people could afford the costs of an international trip. But once opportunities in Mexico became more abundant, emigration would decline.

In the first decade after NAFTA, the income disparity between Mexico and the United States defied initial expectations; far from closing, it grew by more than 10%. Between 1994 and 2002, the Mexican economy lost 1.3 million jobs in agriculture. In the same period, the economy added half a million jobs in manufacturing, but the shift in industrial composition continued to displace workers. The real wages declined, on average, but were higher than before for the unskilled workers and for those in the border region.

How did these changes impact migration rates to the United States? Some scholars argued that NAFTA led to an increase in migration, at least in the short run. Others suggested that NAFTA was associated with a modest decline in U.S. migration, which rose due to other economic events. Of particular importance was the crisis in 1994, which briefly derailed Mexico's upward economic trajectory.

The 1994 economic crisis

The Mexican economy appeared quite solid in the early 1990s. President Salinas (1988–1994) was closely adhering to a program his predecessor Miguel de la Madrid established to stabilize the economy and to bring down inflation. This program, known as the Economic Solidarity Pact (the *Pacto*), combined wage and price controls with a tight fiscal and monetary policy and a stable peso fixed to the dollar. The program, as we saw above, was accompanied by increasing liberalization, deregulation, and privatization. Mexico's economy responded well to these changes.

During the Salinas presidency, the GDP grew at an average annual rate of nearly 3%, inflation fell from 60% to 7%, and real interest rates receded from nearly 30% to 7%. But the exchange rate pegged to the dollar led to an increasingly overvalued peso. The lower interest rates, combined with an expansion of consumer credit, fueled a rise in consumption, especially of imported goods. As a result, the growth in exports (almost 90% from 1987 to 1993) remained far below the rise in imports (nearly 250% in the same period), leading to a trade deficit of US$13.5 billion in 1993. Mexico financed this deficit with foreign investment. But much of the capital inflows came in the form of portfolio investment (in bonds and stocks rather than direct investment in plants and equipment), which increased as a share of total foreign investment to 87% in 1993, up from just 13% in 1989. The high mobility of portfolio investments meant that Mexico was now vulnerable to shifts in investor expectations and confidence.

Portfolio investments dropped sharply in 1994, partly as a response to rising interest rates in the United States. The political climate in Mexico, the Chiapas rebellion against NAFTA in January, the assassination of the Revolutionary Institutional Party (PRI) presidential candidate Luis Donaldo Colosio in March, and the pending elections in August, did not help allay investors' concerns; they demanded higher interest rates to compensate for the political uncertainties. The government, instead of raising interest rates, turned to converting its peso-denominated debt to dollar-based bonds, thus assuming the exchange rate risk previously borne by investors.

In December 1994, foreign reserves had dropped to a record low and were not nearly enough to cover the dollar-based bonds that were to mature in 1995. Investors began to expect that the government would run out of reserves and be forced to devalue the peso; they thus started to shift away from Mexican investments, trading pesos for dollars. On December 22, 1994, the peso was allowed to float freely, and within ten days, had depreciated by 55%.

The peso devaluation had deleterious effects on the Mexican economy. The GDP dropped by more than 6% in 1995, unemployment doubled, and real wages declined by nearly 13%. The number of workers in formal employment sank from 10 million to 9 million. One in two workers was now employed in the informal sector. Poverty rates, not surprisingly, also increased after the crisis, almost tripling in urban areas between 1994 and 1996 (from 7% to 20%) and increasing by one-half in rural regions (from 30% to 43%).

The recovery from the crisis was rather swift—thanks to a rescue package of nearly US$50 billion from the United States, Canada, and international financial institutions in February 1995. The country's GDP was soon on the rise again, growing at an average annual rate of 5.5% from 1996 to 2000. Formal employment was up to 12 million in 2001. But the recovery was nowhere near complete. The average real wage in 2000 was still below that in 1990, and both urban and rural poverty were well above their pre-crisis values.

RISING CRIME RATES

Drug-trafficking organizations have grown considerably in Mexico in the 2000s and have branched out into a host of illegal activities, including kidnapping, protection rackets, money laundering, and migrant smuggling. Drug trade–related homicides are often cited as the source of the sudden increase in homicides in the country, from less than 9,000 per year in 2007 to more than 27,000 in 2011. Data compiled by media organizations in Mexico suggest that 45–60% of homicides in 2012 bore the markings typical of organized crime groups, including the use of high-caliber automatic weapons, torture, dismemberment, and explicit messages.

Extortion schemes by drug traffickers have also escalated in Mexico in recent years, targeting not just the relatively wealthy, but also the poor. The increase in these activities has affected the lives of many Mexicans. Indeed, in recent opinion polls, respondents were more likely to select public security as their most pressing concern, rather than the economy.

The rising insecurity in Mexico might be a determinant of migration to the United States. Recent work, however, finds no link between homicide rates in Mexico and migration flows to the United States. This result might not apply to the urban migrants in our data, however—a group with particular attributes. Indeed, some of the border states where homicides have increased most markedly are also the states where a large share of U.S. migrants falls into the urban-migrants group. (Compare the map in figure 5.3 to that in figure 5.5.) It is important to note, however, that nearly all urban migrants in our data (98%) took their first trip before the escalation in crime in 2007. Thus, the growth in crime rates is an unlikely explanation for the rise in the urban migrants in our data.

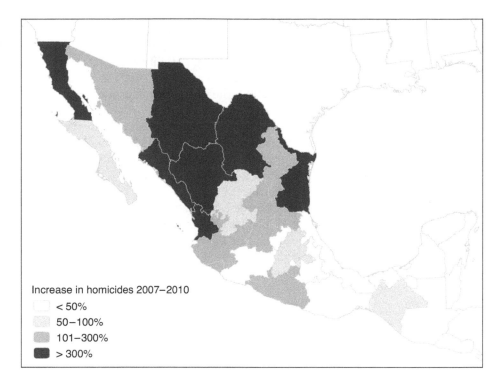

FIGURE 5.3. Map of Mexico with states categorized into four groups based on the increase in intentional homicide rates between 2007 and 2010
MAP BY Jeff Blossom, Center for Geographic Analysis, Harvard University

SUMMARY

In the 1990s, the Mexican economy increasingly opened to trade and foreign investments. The jobs lost in agriculture were partially offset by those gained in manufacturing. The northern region grew faster than the rest of the country in this period, thanks in part to the expansion of *maquiladoras*, or assembly plants for exports. The region offered higher wages, on average, and attracted domestic migrants from the economically deteriorating rural regions and the migrant-saturated urban areas such as Mexico City. In 1994, the Mexican economy experienced another peso devaluation, but it quickly recovered after a bailout engineered by the United States. Migration to the United States continued to increase during this period due to changes created by NAFTA, according to some scholars, and due to the economic crisis, according to others.

THE UNITED STATES, 1990–2010
THE GROWTH AND DOWNTURNS IN THE ECONOMY

During the "roaring 1990s," as economist Joseph Stiglitz refers to the decade, the U.S. economy grew at an impressive rate. From 1993 to 2000, 18 million new jobs were created. In 2000, the unemployment rate hovered below 4%, its lowest level in three decades.

These conditions created an additional pull for Mexican migrants, who increasingly moved to non-farm occupations. In the MMP data, 47% of the migrants working in the United States for the first time in the 1990s took jobs in manufacturing and 36% in services, up from 40% and 25%, respectively, in the previous two decades.

Job expansion in these years exceeded population growth even when the inflow of migrants is factored in. The fertility rates in the country had dropped considerably after the end of the baby boom era in 1964, dipping to 1.7 in the 1970s and slowly climbing back to 2.1 (population replacement level) in 1990. The lower fertility in the 1970s affected the number of workers available two decades later.

The demand for less-skilled workers remained high in the 1990s (although it started to shift in its origins from manufacturing to the service sector). Yet the number of native-born workers in that skill category continued to decline. Between 1990 and 2010, the number of younger (aged 25 to 44), less-skilled (high school degree or lower), native-born workers shrank by nearly 2%. This decline was owing to lower fertility rates of the 1970s, to the aging of baby boomers (the earliest of whom had reached the age of 45 in 1990), and also to the educational upgrading in the country. In 2010, those with more than a high school degree made up almost 60% of the population aged 25 or older, up from about 5% in 1950. The decline in the younger, less-skilled, native-born population in the United States, and the continuing demand for workers in physically demanding jobs, created a gap, one that only migrant workers could fill.

The economic growth of the 1990s came to a halt when technology stocks plummeted and this decline spilled over to the rest of the economy. In March 2001, the U.S. economy was officially in recession. The unemployment rate jumped to 6% and more than one million Americans fell below the poverty line. To stimulate employment, the Federal Reserve lowered interest rates, which, according to some economists, laid the groundwork for the 2007 financial crisis. The U.S. economy slipped back into recession. From 2007 to 2011, full-time employment dropped by 8.7 million. Considering that nearly 7 million new workers would have joined the labor force in this period, economists estimate the true job deficit to be in excess of 15 million.

INCREASING BORDER CONTROL AND EMPLOYER SANCTIONS

As we saw in the preceding chapter, the immigration legislation in 1986 (IRCA) introduced provisions to increase border enforcement and to impose sanctions on employers hiring undocumented workers. In the post-IRCA period, border enforcement increased continually. From 1990 to 2000, the budget available to the United States Border Patrol (USBP) more than tripled in real terms. In the same period, the number of agents overseeing the southwest border sectors increased from 3,226 in 1990 to 8,525 in 2000. Border enforcement budget rose an additional 157% in real terms from 2000 and 2011, and the number of agents on the southwest border more than doubled to 18,506. The USBP also began using more advanced technologies over time, including ground sensors and remote video surveillance.

In the 1990s, the USBP also launched several site-specific crackdowns to deter undocumented migrants: Operation Hold the Line in the El Paso sector in 1993; Operation Gatekeeper in San Diego in 1994; Operation Safeguard in Nogales, Arizona in 1997; and Operation Rio Grande in South Texas in 1997. Each operation reduced the number of apprehensions in its respective sector by pushing undocumented migrants to more dangerous routes, which led to a higher death toll on the border.

In the early 1990s, the number of apprehensions increased at the border, but undocumented migration still continued. Apprehended migrants were swiftly released, and simply tried again until they made it across the border. Repeat crossers could not be identified easily, as a migrant could give a different name at each apprehension.

This situation changed dramatically with the Illegal Immigration Reform and Immigrant Responsibility Act of 1996 (IIRIRA). The new legislation provided the basis for "consequence policies," or harsher punishments for undocumented border crossers. IIRIRA instituted expedited removal, interior repatriation, and 3- and 10-year admission bars for previously undocumented immigrants seeking to be admitted legally to the United States. Repeat crossers could also now be more easily identified with universal fingerprinting.

IIRIRA also established a system for employers to verify the legal status of their employees over the phone and, later, on the Internet using the "E-verify" platform. The system curtailed the use of fraudulent documents, shifting the responsibility of proving documentation status from the immigrants to the employers. The system also allowed for the more effective imposition of sanctions on employers hiring undocumented workers.

A final component of IIRIRA facilitated greater state and local involvement in immigration law enforcement. The attorney general now could sign written agreements with state and local jurisdictions to deputize officers to enforce federal immigration law. In 2013, 80 states and local law enforcement agencies had entered into such agreements.

Another 1996 law, the Anti-terrorism and Effective Death Penalty Act (AEDPA), permitted state and local enforcement officers to arrest individuals who have previously been convicted of a felony and deported. The Act also authorized the inclusion of information related to criminal immigration violations into the National Crime Information Center database (NCIC), which enabled local police to make immigration arrests during routine police-civilian encounters.

Together, these acts expanded the capacity of state and local law enforcement to enforce immigration law and contributed to the criminalization of immigration. The number of deportations increased by 64% in one year—from 69,680 in 1996 to over 114,000 in 1997—and has continued to rise since then.

The implications of these reforms became more apparent after September 11, 2001. The NCIC database started to include not just criminal but also civil immigration information, significantly extending the repertoire of sanctions available to the police. These and other initiatives enabled states and localities to emerge as actors in immigration policymaking, complicating life for undocumented immigrants living in the United States.

INCREASING VISAS AFTER NAFTA

As undocumented migrants faced greater dangers on the border and an increased risk of deportation in the United States, documented migration became a possibility for a larger number of Mexicans. Through the 1990s and 2000s, the U.S. Congress quietly passed legislation to increase the number of temporary work visas available to Mexican nationals. Between 1994 and 2010, entries by temporary Mexican workers went up from nearly 24,000 to more than 500,000. In the same period, entries by Mexican H-visa holders increased from about 14,000 in 1995 to nearly 225,000 in 2010. More Mexicans qualified for other kinds of temporary visas thanks to NAFTA. From 1994 to 2010, entries by treaty investors and traders (E visas) rose from fewer than 300 to over 98,000; entries by intra-company transferees (L visas) increased from about 4,000 to nearly 78,000; and entries by temporary NAFTA professionals (TN visas) grew from less than 30 to more than 77,000.

The congressional legislation and NAFTA, then, contributed to a spike in the level of guest worker migration. Transnational corporations acted as intermediaries in providing visas to workers, creating what Lucassen and Smit call organizational migrants." Indeed, research finds that, in cities such as Tijuana, the U.S.-owned *maquiladora* plants offered sponsorship to obtain papers for their workers, and thus, contributed to higher rates of documented migration.

CHANGING DESTINATIONS FOR MIGRANTS

In recent years, Mexican migrants have moved away from traditional destinations, such as those in the Southwest and the Chicago Metropolitan area, to so-called new destinations. For example, nearly 60% of Mexican migrants went to California until the 1990s. By the latter half of that same decade, however, the share of new migrants to California declined to one-third. Most of the "missing" migrants ended up in states like North Carolina, Georgia, Florida, Iowa, Nebraska, Colorado, Nevada, and Pennsylvania. Researchers attributed this geographic shift to several factors, such as the mobility of newly legalized migrants after IRCA, the relocation of many industries in the United States (most notably, food processing), and deteriorating living conditions in traditional migrant destinations.

The conditions in Mexico and the United States together set the stage for the urban migrants in our data. Greater visa availability after NAFTA allowed a lucky few to enter the United States with documents, while more stringent border enforcement forced the undocumented majority to enter the country with the assistance of professional smugglers. The decline in younger, less-skilled workers in the native-born population opened new opportunities for urban migrants in manufacturing and service sectors where such workers were greatly needed. Urban migrants moved increasingly to non-farm jobs and to new destinations in the United States, diverging from the circular and crisis migrants prevailing in earlier periods. While the conditions in the United States just reviewed largely shaped how migrants would enter the country, what jobs they would take and where, those in Mexico were crucial for determining who the migrants would be. Beginning in the 1990s, when Mexico joined the GATT and became a signatory to NAFTA, it opened itself to foreign investments and trade. The north of the country became a hub for internal migrants, as well as a source of international migrants to the United States, the urban-migrants group in particular. How were foreign investments linked to internal and international migration flows? The answer requires first establishing the theoretical links between globalization and international migration.

LINKING GLOBALIZATION AND
INTERNATIONAL MIGRATION

Sociologist Saskia Sassen views rising internal and international migrant flows as an inevitable result of the globalization of production. This idea has its roots in the world systems theory, which links the mobility of people to the mobility of capital. The process begins with the movement of capital from advanced industrial economies, like the United States, to smaller countries, like Mexico, that are not yet fully integrated into the world economy. Increasing trade, foreign investment, and market competition disrupt existing economic and social arrangements and displace workers from traditional livelihoods. In turn, workers are pushed to search for new ways of earning income, either within their own country or in other international destinations.

Saskia Sassen has studied how this pattern unfolds in many regions of the world. First, foreign investments concentrate employment in export-processing zones. Second, commercial agriculture begins to replace subsistence production in rural regions. Some small farmers turn to wage labor, while others resort to domestic migration. Export-processing zones become the focal destinations for rural migrants. But these zones typically employ women, who are seen as a cheap and docile workforce, easily adaptable to repetitive assembly-line work and easily replaceable once that work takes its physical or mental toll after a few years. The women who are displaced, and the men who are mostly unemployed, turn to international migration.

This process, perhaps counter-intuitively, suggests that foreign investments, while leading to employment growth in a country, can still bring about more emigration, especially if such investments alter existing labor market structures.

Foreign investments can also trigger more emigration through the largely invisible cultural and ideological linkages they create, according to Sassen. Workers in export-processing plants in a developing country become familiar with the work practices and lifestyles in industrialized nations. This familiarity reduces the barriers to emigration. The population at large also becomes more "westernized" over time, and consequently, more prone to moving.

Sassen describes several economic changes within industrialized nations that create a chronic need for immigrant labor. The deployment of manufacturing to the developing world brings about an expansion of the service sector in industrialized countries, and by extension, the concentration of management operations in "global cities" such as New York or Los Angeles. These changes create a bifurcated labor market structure in which there is a small share of high-paying jobs and a large share of low-paying ones; very few jobs are found in between.

Economist Michael Piore was the first to suggest this "segmented labor market" structure in advanced economies, although he did not link it explicitly to the globalization of production like Sassen did. Piore argued that advanced economies contain a capital-intensive sector, inhabited by native workers receiving high wages and stable employment, and a labor-intensive sector, reserved mainly for immigrant workers willing to accept low pay and precarious work conditions. This structure is a direct result of the duality of capital and labor as factors of production. The former is fixed and costly to the employer if misallocated. The latter can be varied with layoffs and is costly only to workers. Employers, then, invest their capital to cover the most certain component of their demand—creating stable and rewarding employment along the way—and manage the uncertain components by deploying cheap and flexible labor, supplied in most cases by immigrants.

Both Piore and Sassen describe migration as a result of a global system of capitalist development and expansion. Here, migration is not just about differences between countries in employment or economic institutions, as suggested in the neoclassical or new economics theories; it is also about the linkages between developing and advanced economies. Rural migrants in Guadalajara, or the Mexican migrants in the United States, from this perspective, are all responding to changes brought on by globalization, namely the increasing economic coordination and integration of nations through investments and trade.

FOREIGN INVESTMENTS IN MEXICO AND THE RISE OF URBAN MIGRANTS

These ideas potentially explain some of the mobility patterns in the Mexican case. Trade and foreign investments in Mexico began to increase after the country entered the GATT in 1986, and they really took off after the signing of NAFTA in 1994. The rise of these flows to Mexico runs parallel to the rise of a particular migrant group in our data—the urban migrants.

Figure 5.4 shows the trend in the number of urban migrants (solid line with values on the left y-axis) along with two trends (dashed line with values on the right y-axis across the two panels) that capture the total foreign direct investment in Mexico and the level of trade with the United States.

In the 1970s, one out of 1,000 residents in the MMP data was joining the urban migrant stream annually. This number increased to four per thousand in 1990 and to six per thousand in 2000. The number dropped sharply to one per thousand between 2000 and 2010, reflecting the general decline in the number of Mexican migrants to the United States as a result of heightened border enforcement and more severe sanctions on employers who hired undocumented workers. (The *share* of urban migrants

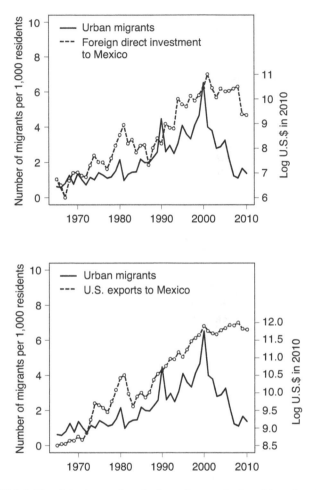

FIGURE 5.4. Trends in the number of urban migrants, the logarithm of total foreign direct investment to Mexico, and the logarithm of U.S. exports to Mexico, 1965–2010

among new migrants, however, continued to increase through the 2000s—see figure E.1 in appendix E. Indeed, this group solidified its majority status between 2000 and 2010, increasing its share among all first-time migrants from 50% to nearly 70%.)

The trend in the number (and share) of urban migrants is highly correlated with the growth in the volume of foreign direct investment to Mexico (in logarithm of U.S. dollars in 2010), as shown in the panel at the top. The trend in the size of the urban migrant group also runs parallel to the steep increases in the volume of exports (in logarithm of U.S. dollars in 2010) from the United States to Mexico, as shown in the bottom panel.

The latter association is one of the strongest results from the aggregate statistical model in appendix G, which relates the number of urban migrants to several macro-level trends. Other possible associations—for example, between rates of urban migration and fluctuations in Mexican or U.S. employment levels—are not statistically significant.

These results differ from some of the findings in the literature. As we saw in the review above, some scholars associate NAFTA with a modest decline in Mexico-U.S. migration rates. My results suggest an increase in migration rates after NAFTA but only for the urban migrants.

The results here, as in prior research, are all correlational; that is, they establish a co-movement in trends rather than a causal effect of one trend on the other. To establish a causal effect, one needs a source of exogenous variation in foreign investments (or any other macro-level indicator) that is not directly related to migration levels to the United States. Lacking such a source, researchers typically turn to meso-level analyses to obtain corroborating evidence, as I do here.

Meso-level analysis: regional patterning

One strategy is to look at different states and regions in Mexico—which differ in their exposure to foreign investments—and observe the variation in the rates of emigration. For example, economist Gordon Hanson ranks Mexican states with respect to their exposure to globalization, which he measures with the share of the state GDP that comes from foreign direct investments, imports, or *maquiladoras*. The top three states are, unsurprisingly, all in the border region: Baja California, Chihuahua, and Nuevo León. But Hanson detects no association between exposure to globalization in a state and rates of emigration from that state to the United States.

My analysis suggests otherwise, and the reason for this difference is simple: Hanson pools all migrants together while I divide migrants into four groups and study each one separately. I also focus on first-time migrants only. I find that a state's exposure to globalization is highly correlated with the emigration of the urban-migrant group in the MMP data.

The map in figure 5.5 shows this pattern. The colors on the map distinguish three categories of the 24 Mexican states surveyed in the MMP data. In the eight black states, urban migrants are the most prevalent group, making up at least 65% of all first-time migrants between 1965 and 2010. In the dark grey states, urban migrants still constitute the majority in six out of eight cases but account for 28– 57% of all new migrants. In the light grey states, urban migrants are a minority and contain less than one-fifth of all first-time migrants.

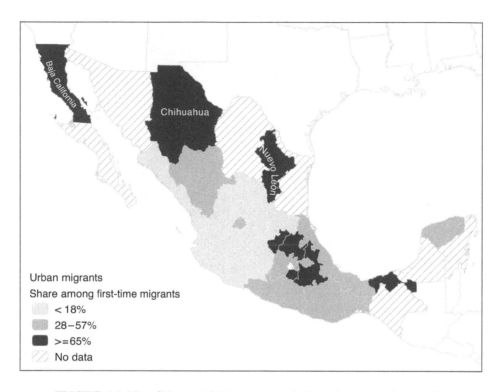

FIGURE 5.5. Map of Mexico with 24 states categorized into three groups based on the
share of urban migrants among all first-time migrants from that state between 1965 and 2010
MAP BY Jeff Blossom, Center for Geographic Analysis, Harvard University

Quite revealingly, then, in the states with high exposure to globalization in Hanson's assessment, I observe high shares of urban migrants.
For example, in the state most exposed to globalization in Mexico—Baja
California—urban migrants make up nearly 90% of all first-time migrants.
Similarly, in Chihuahua and Nuevo León—the second and third most glo-
balized states according to Hanson—there is a high share of urban migrants, 70% and 80%, respectively. In all three states, the number of urban
migrants per 1,000 of the population increases significantly with NAFTA,
at least doubling in size within just a couple of years. The fact that FDI
and trade are more localized in their effects—that is, occur in the regions
that are most influenced by these flows—gives more credence to Sassen's
theory than an average effect would. Exposure to foreign investments—or,
in Hanson's terms, "globalization"—might not change the overall rate of
migration out of a state, but it does increase the rate of first-time migration
of the relatively educated urban-migrant group in our data.

Meso-level analysis: intervening mechanism of internal migration

The border states attract not only foreign investments but also domestic migrants. In Sassen's theory, domestic and international moves are intricately connected. Foreign investments in developing countries often concentrate employment into export-processing zones, which become major points of attraction for internal migrants. Given the selective hiring and high turnover rate in these zones, however, many internal migrants eventually turn to international migration.

The review above showed that foreign investments in Mexico supported the expansion of *maquiladoras* along the border. The rate of internal migration to the region increased as a result. *Maquiladoras* hired mostly women and kept their turnover rates high—around 100% per year—hiring two workers to keep one slot filled. The plants also reduced their average pay over time.

These patterns all seem consistent with the idea that the same conditions (i.e., new but precarious work in the *maquiladoras*) might be mobilizing both internal migrants, and then turning them into international movers. In our data, about three-fourths of the urban migrants in the border states were born in a different state. About one-third of these internal-then-international migrants were women.

Alternative links between internal and international migration

It is not yet certain that both internal and international moves were a response to external events (such as the flow of foreign investments to Mexico). Indeed, Sassen argues that working in export-processing zones might change the aspirations of internal migrants, or familiarize them with international work settings, and thus prepare them for a move overseas.

Geographers Ron Skeldon and Russell King elaborate on this and other possible pathways through which internal moves could be precursors to international flows, or vice versa. One pathway, possibly the most common one, involves rural migrants moving to a city in their own country in an effort to accumulate financial resources and social contacts, which then allows them to cross to another country.

Scholars observe this "stepwise" migration strategy in many developing countries. In Mexico, for example, researchers argue that jobs in the *maquiladoras* or export-oriented agriculture in the border region serve as a "school for El Norte." Rural migrants gain specific skills in these jobs, collect necessary resources, and eventually move to the United States, where they receive better wages for doing similar kinds of work. Many cities in northern Mexico, as a result, serve as a "trampoline" for international moves.

Skeldon and King describe a second pathway, which they call "knock-on effects," linking internal and international moves. These effects describe how one kind of migration by one group could lead to another kind of migration by another group. For example, the entry of immigrants to a particular area could dry up the opportunities for natives there, pushing them to migrate to other destinations in their country. International migration knocks on an internal flow in this case. Similarly, the influx of domestic migrants to an urban area could restrict the jobs or wages available to city residents, forcing them to move to another country. In this example, internal migration knocks on an international stream.

The latter mechanism is evident in northern Mexico. As noted above, the region experienced swift economic growth in the 1980s and 1990s, becoming a magnet for internal migrants. The resulting population growth created a steep and increasingly unmet demand for housing, infrastructure, and services. The living conditions in the region deteriorated quickly. In 1990, more than one-third of the population in the border cities reported living in very poor housing compared to less than one-fifth in Mexico City, and about one-tenth in Guadalajara. Social expenditures, which had benefited urban populations in the 1970s and 1980s, shifted to rural areas, and thus could not counter increasing urban poverty. These conditions, researchers argue, all contributed to rising emigration from urban areas to the United States, especially among those people living in the border region.

These patterns suggest complex connections between foreign capital flows, urbanization, and emigration. In Sassen's argument, foreign capital (and related globalizing trends) are largely responsible for both urbanization and emigration trends. In Skeldon and King's analysis, by contrast, urbanization can also be the reason underlying emigration. It is hard to disentangle these alternative mechanisms, which are not mutually exclusive. In fact, both mechanisms seem consistent with the rise of the urban migrants from the border states, which received both the highest share of foreign investments and the highest share of domestic migrants beginning in the 1990s.

MESO-LEVEL ANALYSIS: INTERVENING MECHANISM OF RURAL DECLINE

Not all states with a high share of urban migrants are along the border, however. Indeed, of the eight black states in the map in figure 5.5, one is in the central region (Querétaro), three are in the central-south (Hidalgo, Puebla, and Morelos), and one is in the southeast (Tabasco). These regions—which include many of the dark grey states as well—supply nearly half of all the urban migrants in our data.

The number of urban migrants out of the communities in the central, central-south, and southeast—like those in the border states—spikes in the

1990s, increasing from 0.33 to 0.73 per 1,000, 0.23 to 1.6 per 1,000, and 0.34 to 0.94 per 1,000, respectively, between 1990 and 2000. But the urban migrants in these communities are slightly different from those in the border region. Most importantly, a sizable proportion comes from non-urban locales.

The "urban" label represents the majority of cases (68%) in the group, but not the remaining 32% that originate from communities of smaller size (<10,000 residents). Interestingly, more than three-fourths of the "non-urban" minority in the urban-migrant group concentrate in the central, central-south, and southeast regions.

The urban-migrant group, then, encapsulates two streams: the truly urban stream from the border, and the more mixed stream from the central, central-south, and southeastern regions of Mexico. What explains the latter stream? Sassen might argue that the commercialization of agriculture in Mexico, coupled with the opening of the economy to exports in crops, turned subsistence farmers into international migrants.

Research provides evidence for the first part of this argument. Some scholars have found that Mexico's importation of subsidized crops from the United States (such as corn), as well as the open commodity markets for crops (such as coffee), depressed agricultural prices in Mexico after NAFTA. Others view this decline as part of a long-term trend rather than a direct consequence of the trade agreement. Whether attributable to NAFTA or not, the decline in agriculture is a source of rural unemployment and poverty, especially in the central and southern regions of the country.

Researchers refer to these trends to make sense of increasing rates of U.S.-bound migration from these regions beginning in the 1990s. Riosmena and Massey report that the central and southern regions (encompassing the central, central-south, and southeast parts of Mexico in my categorization) accounted for 46% of U.S. migrants in 2006, up from just over 20% in 1992.

These regional trends are consistent with the increasing presence of central- or southern-origin migrants in our data. The fact that these migrants cluster in the urban-migrant group—which increases in size with the level of U.S. exports and foreign investments in Mexico—seems in line with the Sassen hypothesis, although is not a conclusive test of it.

MESO-LEVEL ANALYSIS: INTERVENING MECHANISM OF JOB LOSSES

Another strategy for establishing the plausibility of the Sassen hypothesis is to consider the mechanisms through which foreign investments yield more out-migration, and to observe whether those mechanisms are at work in the Mexican setting. For example, Sassen argues that foreign investments lead employment to concentrate in certain industries, displace workers in others, and turn them into international migrants.

Let us focus on the first part of this argument—the link between foreign investments and employment. The review above showed that foreign investments supported the expansion of *maquiladoras*, export-processing plants, located mostly in northern Mexico. This region enjoyed a growth in jobs and wages as a result, especially after NAFTA. But the region also experienced the highest employment volatility in the country. The variance in employment (due either to shifts within an industry or between industries) increased by almost 20% in the north after NAFTA, while it remained 7% or less in the rest of Mexico. The border region also became more sensitive to fluctuations in the U.S. economy after NAFTA. For example, the region experienced zero growth rates in 2001 and 2002 when the U.S. economy slowed and many U.S.-owned *maquiladoras* shut down. In fact, by 2004, about one-third of the *maquiladora* jobs created in the early 1990s had disappeared.

I now turn to the second part of the Sassen argument—that displaced workers become international migrants. Sociologist Rubén Hernández-León observes some of these patterns in Monterrey, the capital of the border state of Nuevo León and the third-largest city in Mexico. The shift from heavy to light manufacturing in the city, coupled with declining wages, job security, and benefits, he argues, has turned the residents onto emigration, which provides "a coping strategy to fully substitute for employment lost at home."

Our data provide similar evidence from 143 urban communities in 24 states. About 44% of household heads among first-time migrants (the sample with complete life history information) have experienced a job loss lasting six months or more in one of the five years preceding their first move, compared to only 6% of household heads that have never migrated. About 40% of household heads among the urban migrants have been unemployed at least once within the previous five years of their first trip, a slightly lower share than the other migrant groups (45%) but still significantly higher than the non-migrants.

These analyses suggest a link between the rise of the urban migrants and Mexico's integration into the global economy. The accession into the GATT and signing of NAFTA, coupled with parallel reforms in the country, ensured ever-growing capital and trade flows. As a result, existing economic arrangements in rural and urban areas were disrupted, ensuring movement from the former to the latter, and eventually, to the United States.

The resulting migrant group—the urban migrants—varied from the groups presented in the preceding chapters in its non-traditional regions of origin, its higher levels of education, and its occupational concentration in manufacturing in Mexico. This group also varied from the other migrant groups in the network dynamics that fueled its mobility. I now turn to these dynamics.

URBAN MIGRANTS: OFF THE BEATEN PATH?

Network effects in migration work through three principal mechanisms. In each mechanism, prior migrants alter the context in origin or destination, typically in ways that make future migration more likely. In *social facilitation*, prior migrants offer useful information or help that reduces the risks and increases the benefits of migrating for potential migrants. In *normative influence*, prior migrants shape collective views on migration, often by glorifying and encouraging it. In *network externalities*, prior migrants directly or indirectly contribute to collective and institutionalized resources—such as smugglers, recruiters, or ethnic communities in destination—that enable more migration.

As we saw in the preceding chapters, these three mechanisms work for each migrant group, but to different degrees and in different combinations. Social facilitation, for example, is a major mechanism for all groups, but it requires stronger relations (such as immediate family ties) for crisis and family migrants—the two groups with relatively vulnerable populations (teenagers and women, respectively)—compared to circular migrants. Normative influence is stronger for the male-predominated clusters of circular and crisis migrants than it is for the majority-female family migrants. Network externalities are important to all groups, and increasingly so over time. Smugglers, for example, become indispensable to undocumented migrants as immigration enforcement tightens along the Mexico-U.S. border. In brief, not only do network effects in migration vary across the migrant groups, but how they matter also changes over time.

The social facilitation and normative influence mechanisms are unlikely to work as well for urban migrants as they did for the other three migrant groups. First, urban migrants originate from regions with historically low levels of migration. Circular, crisis, and family migrants, by contrast, all concentrate in regions of high migration prevalence. There is simply a lower number of prior migrants, and hence fewer resources, available to urban migrants relative to the other groups. As a result, social facilitation for this group is likely to be limited.

Second, urban migrants live mostly in large, urban communities while other migrant groups concentrate in small, rural ones. The relatively selective and sparse social ties in the former setting (as opposed to the pervasive and dense ties typical in the latter) make it hard to establish and enforce shared views on migration. The normative influence mechanism, then, is also likely to be weaker for urban migrants when compared to the other groups.

It is difficult to identify these mechanisms with survey data, let alone test their prevalence for each group over time. While our qualitative data cannot accomplish the latter task either, they do allow us to observe the different mechanisms at work.

Past research provides some evidence consistent with the implications of the ideas above. Elizabeth Fussell and Douglas Massey, for example, used the MMP data to show that prior migrants in a community have a smaller positive effect on individuals' odds of migrating in urban settings when compared to rural areas. Bryan Roberts and colleagues relied on qualitative data to further bolster this claim, showing how a lack of social support in urban regions in Mexico pushes rural-to-urban migrants to rely on their social ties in their old rural communities to migrate to the United States.

Urban migrants are distinct not just in being urban, but also in the time period in which they proliferate. Three-fourths of urban migrants take their first trip in the post-IRCA period, which is when border enforcement started to become more stringent and to push undocumented crossers to more dangerous paths. Most migrants without documents in this period had to rely on professional guides or smugglers, as we saw earlier.

Network effects in migration in the post-IRCA period worked mostly through mediating institutions, such as smuggling businesses, which resulted from both a sustained migration flow from Mexico over time and policy responses on the U.S. side to curb that flow. These institutions, or network externalities, provided crucial assistance to aspiring migrants, especially to the urban migrants in our data. These individuals not only lacked social ties to past migrants available to those in most rural communities, but they also moved at a time when it was harder to cross the border alone.

Hiring a smuggler in the post-IRCA period, however, was no easy task. First, smuggling fees rose consistently over time. According to the MMP data, the average fee quadrupled between 1986 and 2000, from about $500 (adjusted to 2014 values) to $2,000. The fee reached almost $2,500 in 2010. In order to afford a *coyote* (smuggler), many families we interviewed had to borrow money from loan sharks or take out a second mortgage on their home. Some families paid smugglers in installments, but that arrangement could be risky. "The main thing is to pay the *coyote*," a migrant's wife told us, "or your family might be 'charged' in a different way here."

Second, smuggling operations became increasingly tied to organized crime. For example, some drug-trafficking organizations diversified their portfolio of illicit activities in the 2000s and began offering *coyote* services. Not only did urban migrants have to confront an increasingly well-guarded border, but they also had to survive the potentially dangerous smugglers they hired to cross into the United States.

Many of our respondents expressed fears of being robbed by smugglers, being left behind, and even getting killed. Some told us stories that justified those fears. Smugglers often carried guns, one respondent reported, "in case [a migrant] tries to run." Smugglers abandoned one migrant in the desert after stripping him of his money and his shoes. The migrant survived only because he happened upon a pair of shoes on a dead body (probably that of another migrant) in the desert and continued his walk to the border.

Reaching the border does not guarantee a migrant's safety, however. One former migrant told us how his group was kidnapped right at the crossing by "people thieves," who "steal" migrants from smugglers, cross them over the border, and demand payment for their services. Another migrant was "sold" by his smuggler to another one at the border.

In response to the dangers *coyotes* pose, migrants have devised strategies to ensure safety. Many respondents were adamant about delaying payment until after they have been successfully crossed into the United States. They also described how they would not carry the money to pay the smugglers' fees with them. Instead, our informants reported having a friend or a relative bring it to the smugglers on the U.S. side. Those who "pay upfront," one migrant commented, "are the ones who die." Migrants also often relied on their social ties to find a trustworthy and competent smuggler.

The perils of border crossing, and of dealing with smugglers, shaped how our respondents thought about migration in the post-IRCA period. It was not just the difficulty of getting into the United States, but also of finding work there, that made many respondents reluctant to leave Mexico.

URBAN MIGRANTS: "THE ONES THAT DARE"

We asked the more recent migrants among our respondents—those closest to urban migrants in the circumstances they faced—to compare their experience to that of earlier migrants to the United States, and vice versa. The comparisons consistently brought up two issues: the border, and work conditions in the United States.

"It was easier before," a former migrant told us, referring to the border crossing. Another migrant likened going to the United States these days to "going to war." "There should be signs at each kilometer leading up to the border," this migrant continued, "warning [new migrants] not to do it."

"It is no longer the same," a migrant's wife commented on the work conditions in the United States. Her husband could get work "wherever he wanted" before the economic crisis in 2007. All he needed to do was to wait on a corner where employers came to pick up day laborers each morning. Now, not only is the work scarcer, but it is "no longer convenient to be standing" on the street waiting for work "because *la migra* (immigration enforcement) can come and take them." "And yes," the wife added, "it was more difficult [to cross and to find a job] every time."

It was hearing of such hardship—increasingly advertised by the media in Mexico—that discouraged many of the non-migrants in our data from migrating. "We all want to improve, logically, but at what cost?" asked a respondent. "What if I cannot cross, if I die on my way there, if I cannot get to my family?" "It is the fear of crossing," said another respondent to explain why she never considered going to the United States. "The collective thought is that it is more dangerous to cross now."

The difficulty of crossing disheartened even the more seasoned of migrants. One female migrant, after a menacing encounter with a smuggler, decided: "Without papers, I won't go back. I won't dare again." Another former migrant, and a father of two sons, worried not about the difficulty of going to the United States, but about that of coming back to visit his family. With the border conditions now, he told us, "going means that I would leave [my family] for at least 3 or 4 years." "It feels wrong," he added. "I'd rather stay here."

Other respondents mentioned the deteriorating U.S. economy as a reason for not migrating. "Going there is not appealing to me," the sister of two migrants told us. "Migrants in the United States have been through a lot. I don't envy them at all, or what they have. . . . They have gotten that through tears, suffering, and humiliation." Her siblings in the United States lost their home after the 2007 recession and now live in a trailer. "I saw those difficult situations," she explained. "Life is not as it used to be in the United States. . . . It is harder to get by now." A return migrant echoed this sentiment: "There is no life for the ones over there. . . . I would rather work on a street corner selling tomatoes here."

Young people are "the ones that dare" to migrate nowadays, as one father of a migrant told us, "even if there are no jobs there." Migrating to the United States gives young migrants independence, and an opportunity for new experiences. Rubén Hernández-León interviewed young urbanites in Monterrey, Mexico, many of whom claimed to migrate for adventure. Some of our respondents displayed this logic as well, connecting their desire to migrate to "the temptation of knowing what it is like to be there," "curiosity," "more of an experiment," and finally, to seeking "adventure."

These cases, although not numerous, display the varying motivations underlying migration, some of which diverge markedly from the predominant calculus.

CONCLUSION

Between 1965 and 2010, one group continually increased its share among the first-time migrants—from less than 10% to nearly 70%—in the Mexico-U.S. stream in our data. This group included a large share of men, mostly from urban communities in the border, central-south, and southeastern regions of Mexico rather than the traditional migrant-sending rural communities in the central-west. To characterize this distinctive pattern, I called this group the *urban migrants*. Urban migrants were significantly more educated compared to the circular, crisis, and family migrants in the preceding chapters, and also relative to non-migrants at their time. The group worked mostly in manufacturing and construction in the United States, earned significantly higher wages than the other migrant groups, and made fewer return trips to Mexico.

The rise of urban migrants in our data occurred contemporaneously with Mexico's integration into the world economy. By joining GATT in 1986 and signing onto NAFTA in 1994, Mexico experienced an influx of foreign capital and U.S. exports; the trend in urban migrants ran parallel to these trends. Several mechanisms likely intervened in this relationship. First, the rural decline in the open economy period forced many rural peasants to migrate to the cities. Second, the export-assembly plants expanded in the northern part of Mexico, which attracted the displaced peasants, but also provided precarious employment. Many city workers, including former internal migrants, thus turned to international migration.

Urban migrants increased their share in the migrant stream in the 2000s but, like the other migrant groups in our data, declined in absolute size. Heightened border enforcement and more severe employer sanctions in the United States, coupled with the economic downturns in 2001 and 2007, contributed to this decline. Tighter immigration control at the border also accounted for the urban migrants' lower rates of return to Mexico when compared to the groups that were prevalent in the earlier eras.

Since urban migrants originated mostly from non-traditional sending areas in Mexico, they were less likely than the other migrant groups to have access to help or information from prior migrants. Urban migrants were also less likely to be exposed to strong normative pressures to migrate, which were more typical of the densely knit rural communities in the historical sending areas. Undocumented urban migrants, however, were more likely than any other group to rely on professional guides and smugglers precisely because they lacked personal ties to prior migrants and had to cross a more dangerous border.

The perils of clandestine migration beginning in the late 1990s made it a mostly male enterprise. Women's share among the urban migrants declined consistently over time, from 26% in the 1970s to 19% in the 1990s, and to 14% in the 2000s, when the death toll on the border started to rise.

Once again, it was the economic, social, and political contexts in Mexico and in the United States that shaped not only who migrated, but also how and for how long. As the increasingly destitute cities in Mexico pushed urban migrants out, the border control regime forced them to rely on smugglers and to stay in the United States for longer periods of time, if not indefinitely. This strategy differed dramatically from the return-oriented logic guiding the circular migrants, the immediate but temporary conditions pushing crisis migrants, and the family-centered reasoning that brought the family migrants to the United States.

I now tie these patterns together in the concluding chapter.

Chapter 6

WHERE DO WE GO FROM HERE?

Conditional Theories and Diverse Policies

FIGURE 6.1. Three migrants walking toward the border in Tijuana
PHOTO BY Patricia Martín

DIEGO

One Friday morning in November 2006, Diego received a phone call from his mother. Her friend, Carlos, had a job opportunity in Fort Worth, Texas and would be taking a group of migrants there in a few days. Diego needed to act quickly. He talked to his wife, Cristina. Reluctant at first, Cristina gave in when Diego brought up their three children. Not only did Diego's salary barely cover their subsistence, but the family home was in desperate need of repair and required an additional bedroom for the kids.

Diego quit his job that day and took out a loan to pay Carlos, who—as a family friend—would charge him only US$900, a bargain compared to the regular *coyote* (smuggler) fees of US$1,500 or more. On Sunday, Diego was on a bus to Piedras Negras, a border town on the Rio Grande River and across from Eagle Pass, Texas, his backpack filled with canned foods, cookies, and bottled water.

On Monday morning, Diego, Carlos, and six other migrants started walking toward the Rio Grande. In three hours, they were on an inflatable raft, crossing the river, for an additional 500 pesos (about US$45 in 2006) per head. The cost worried Diego. He had only 2,000 pesos with him and he had already spent one-fourth of them.

Once on land, Carlos instructed the group to walk, never telling them how long the journey would be. "We are almost there," he replied whenever someone dared to ask. They walked for five days, resting only intermittently. By Friday, they were running out of food and water. Splitting the last box of cookies among eight people, they continued to walk, their feet covered in blisters.

That night, the group found themselves in the middle of a large field. "We have crossed," Carlos announced, pointing to the bright lights of a town visible in the distance. But Diego noticed another set of lights—those from a Border Patrol watchtower—shining on them. The group quickly hid behind the bushes. Once the lights moved on, Carlos instructed them to run toward a house where they would take shelter. The landlady there charged Diego 600 pesos for the night, putting him up with all the other migrants in a tiny bedroom and offering no food. At the very least, Diego thought, he had made it to Texas.

The next morning, a driver came in a van to take the group to Fort Worth. They had barely spent five minutes on the road when the Border Patrol started chasing them. Pulling over to the emergency lane on the highway, the driver told everyone to run, a feat for a group that had been walking for five days straight. Diego ran as fast as he could, but he twisted his ankle while jumping a fence. Though in pain, Diego continued to flee. When he finally stopped, there was nobody left around him. Lost in the fields and starving, Diego started heading back to the highway. He was lucky to run into the driver of the van. At least now he could find his way back to the shelter house.

It began raining hard, and soon, Diego and the driver were soaked to the bone. They entered an empty hunting cabin to rest. "I was very cold," Diego recounted. "I had been wet all day." They "tore away the carpet" to cover themselves, and rested on the floor. Once it stopped raining, they returned to the shelter house, paying another 600 pesos to the landlady. Diego now had no money, and he had not eaten in two days. He called Carlos. He learned that all the other migrants had been caught and sent back to Mexico. But Carlos had made it to Fort Worth. He offered to send a car for Diego and to find him a job, but for a price. "There is no compassion there, only business," Diego said to us bitterly. At the end of his rope, Diego agreed to pay Carlos US$1,000, which, for now, he would owe to him. The next day, Diego was at work on a construction site with his twisted ankle and blistered feet. He thought himself lucky to have a job.

Diego saved US$5,000 in one year and returned to Mexico for good. He did not want to be separated from his children any longer. "The children will grow up," he explained, "and what will they say about me?" His savings were enough to fix the family home and to buy a taxi. "It paid off," he told us. "It did not fulfill all my wishes, but it did help." But the things he saw on the trip also scarred him for life. "It was rough," he said, "but [at least] I am here talking about it."

Diego told us that he would never go back to the United States. "The main thing is the danger," he said, "because it is harder to go [now]." "If I were like most people, I'd say, 'I want to have my van, I want to have my big house'. But I say, 'What for?' I am doing just fine here. One is better off with the family."

MIGUEL

The youngest of eight siblings, Miguel did not expect that the responsibility of supporting his parents would fall on his shoulders. But it did. By the time Miguel finished middle school in 1989, six of his siblings had left for the United States; some already had families there. "Sometimes they sent money," Miguel told us, and "sometimes they did not." "Because they are married," he offered when asked to explain this variability. But Miguel needed certainty. His mother had diabetes. "It is expensive and it is every day," Miguel told us. "You cannot say, 'Now, I will take [the medication] and now I won't.'"

Miguel dropped out of school and started working in construction with his father. But the money was still not enough. "I wanted to help my father and my mother," Miguel told us; that is why he decided to migrate. He was only 17 years old. His first thought was to apply for a tourist visa, but it was difficult to gather the required documents and, even if he could, getting the visa was far from guaranteed. Instead, Miguel turned to his siblings to ask for a loan to pay the *coyotes*. Two brothers gave him the money. Miguel waited until the last minute to tell his parents about his plans. "They never agreed," he told us. "They both suffered when I left."

On November 27, 1991, Miguel arrived in Mexicali, a city bordering Mexico and California, with a name that blended the two places (just like Calexico, its neighboring city on the other side). But he could not cross that day. The border control seemed heavier than usual, and the *coyotes* sent everyone to a nearby house. "There were more than 70 of us in a small room," Miguel recalled. "There were a lot of young people like me, but also couples, little children, and even babies." Everybody waited for his or her turn to cross; Miguel's came four days later.

The *coyote* asked Miguel and the twin sisters that would accompany him a simple question: "Do you want to try to climb the wall?" "I only want to be in the United States," Miguel replied. But when he actually saw "the wall"—the steel barriers separating Mexico from the United States— Miguel was scared. "I wanted to go back. You feel alone and sad. You want to cry, to give in to despair." Miguel saw that all the migrants around him were in the same situation, and fought his fear. He and the twins climbed over the wall, none of them realizing they had become covered in cuts and blood. "In that moment, you don't even feel it," Miguel said. "You feel the adrenaline; you don't want the Border Patrol to catch you."

The *coyotes* put Miguel in the trunk of a jeep, under a wooden board covered with blankets. Miguel remained there for 18 hours until he reached his final destination. "It felt like a year," he said. "When I got out, I felt like I couldn't breathe because of the fear." But then Miguel saw his brothers waiting for him. He had made it.

Miguel stayed with his brothers only for a short while. He moved to San Jose and started working in construction. He worked continuously for 16 years. His only break was when he fell while working on a building, injuring his neck and shoulders, and dislocating his spine. He never told his mother about this accident. "I did not want her to worry about it," he explained. "Since she was sick, it was better to say that everything was fine."

Miguel was so concerned about his parents that he sent a large share of his earnings to them, about US$400 each month. "It was a relief for me [to send the money]," he told us. "It helped them a lot. My mother's medicine is very expensive." Miguel also sent money so that his parents could fix their house, put new tiles on the floor, and buy a new roof.

Miguel never thought he would return to Mexico. He was earning well in the United States and helping his parents back home. But then the crisis in 2007 struck. "We could not send money because they did not pay us on time. We could feel the crisis," he told us. When his employers skipped his paycheck for the fourth time in a row, Miguel decided that was it. "The economy was very bad. I had to dip into my savings to eat. Everything was tumbling down, so I decided to come back." He has been living in Mexico ever since.

PATRICIA

Patricia left her neighborhood in Guadalajara early one morning in February 2003 to catch a plane to Tijuana, a bustling city on the border that was just across from San Diego. This would be Patricia's third attempt to cross the border to meet up with her husband, Alejandro, who was in the United States. Her first attempt to cross through Nogales ended in a detention center in Arizona. Her second attempt to cross through a port of entry with a fake birth certificate led to her deportation.

But today Patricia was hopeful. Following the instructions given to her, she arrived at a dingy hotel room in Tijuana to meet the *coyotes*, as well as nine other migrants that would accompany her on the journey. The *coyotes* seemed "very organized"; they ordered the migrants into a van and, after a short drive, pulled into a garage. One by one, migrants passed through a small window into the adjacent house, invisible to any onlooker, to rest for the night—the only reprieve they would get before the treacherous trip ahead.

Early the next morning, their long walk through the desert began. It was easy during the day but, at night, temperatures fell close to freezing. Patricia hid under a blanket, walking as close to the others as possible to stay warm. Sleep was out of the question. They needed to make it to the border without being detected; and the closer they got, the more careful they had to be. At some point, the *coyotes* became very cautious, starting to put blankets on the ground so that migrants would not leave any footprints on the sand.

It was three in the morning when Patricia first saw the fence marking the border. The *coyotes* guided all the migrants to a tunnel underneath, and one by one they crossed to the other side. But then "things became more difficult." The truck that was supposed to pick them up was nowhere to be seen. When Patricia looked up, she saw a helicopter circling with a light beaming on the ground. She heard the Border Patrol dogs barking in the distance. She hid behind the bushes with all the other migrants, becoming stiff from the cold and dizzy with hunger. When the truck arrived five hours later, they could hardly move, let alone run to it. But run they did.

The truck took all the migrants to a house to spend the night. The next morning, anxious to see her husband, Patricia was ready for the final leg of her journey from San Diego to Los Angeles. She was not quite expecting to see the *coyote* dressed in a suit, carrying a laptop, and standing next to a convertible Porsche. But that was the cover they needed to go through the Border Patrol checkpoints between San Diego to Los Angeles. Patricia got into the trunk with two other migrants, and after a three-hour drive, she was finally with her husband. Alejandro paid the *coyote* nearly US$3,000 and took Patricia to her new home.

Before embarking on the trip, Patricia knew how dangerous it was to cross through the desert. "You can become dehydrated, you can get hypothermia, or they can rape you," she told us. But she still took on the journey to be reunited with her husband.

Patricia and Alejandro lived and worked together in the United States for 8 years. They made a good life for themselves. But they both missed their families in Mexico. "My husband made barbecue every Saturday," Patricia recalled, "but he was alone in the garage next to the grill." "One feels empty," she added. "As time goes by, you start feeling remorseful. Your parents are getting older, family members are dying, and you are in the United States."

In 2011, Patricia and Alejandro took all their savings and returned to Mexico with their two daughters. "It was family that brought me back here [Mexico]," Patricia told us, just as it was family that made her go to the United States in the first place.

THREE BORDER CROSSERS, THREE OUTCOMES

In both research and policy, we treat Mexican migrants to the United States as a homogenous group. We assume they all move to the United States to do better or to have more opportunities. We presume they will cease to migrate if it gets harder to cross the border or to find work in the United States. But the three stories above show us how varied migrant experiences can be: in their rationale, in their response to various policies, and in their potential ending.

Diego, Miguel, and Patricia all crossed a perilous border to make it to the United States. But each had a different reason. Diego wanted to save enough money to meet his wife and children's basic needs. Miguel aspired to help his mother with her medical expenses. And Patricia wished to reunite with her husband, a U.S. migrant.

Diego, Miguel, and Patricia all returned to Mexico eventually. Diego reached his goal within a year and wanted to be with his family in Mexico. After working in the United States for 16 years, Miguel could see his job opportunities drying up after the economic crisis in 2007 and thought he could put his savings to good use in Mexico. Patricia had lived in the United States for eight years when she finally decided that she was tired of being away from her extended family.

Different reasons mobilized each of these migrants. For Diego and Miguel, the reason was money; for Patricia, it was family. The difficulty of crossing the border did not deter Diego, Miguel, or Patricia on their first trip. It did make Diego, who had young children, reluctant to try crossing again, however. A policy that deterred one, in other words, was not at all effective for the other two.

This is the main premise of this book: We need to recognize that there might be different logics for migration, seek to identify the conditions under which each logic becomes salient, and devise diverse policies to achieve specific outcomes.

"THE MORE WALLS THEY BUILD, THE MORE WALLS WE WILL JUMP."

This is what Felipe Calderón told the press as the presidential candidate of the National Action Party in May 2006 in response to U.S. efforts to build more physical barriers along its border with Mexico. (He would go on to become the president of Mexico from 2006 to 2012.) Shortly thereafter, in October 2006, U.S. President George W. Bush signed the Secure Fence Act, which authorized and partially funded the possible construction of 700 miles of fencing and other hurdles along the border. "This bill will help protect the American people," President Bush declared. "This bill will make our borders more secure." By 2009, the Department of Homeland Security (DHS) had erected 613 miles of fencing and other barriers on the border.

Starting in 2006, the DHS also invested about US$1 billion to create a "virtual fence"—a suite of cameras and radars to enhance surveillance along the border. After numerous delays and glitches, the DHS canceled the virtual fence project in 2011, stating that the project is ineffective and too costly.

Between 1965 and 2010, the United States dedicated almost US$40 billion (adjusted to 2010 values) to the Border Patrol budget. The funds supported not just the fence and the various technologies to prevent clandestine crossings, but also more than 20,000 officers patrolling the border in 2010 (up from about 4,000 in the early 1990s). Despite these efforts, the number of undocumented migrants from Mexico increased from an estimated stock of 2.2 million in 1986 to 6.9 million in 2008, declining slightly thereafter to 6.5 million in 2010.

Was President Calderón right? Did building walls have no deterrent effect on undocumented migration from Mexico to the United States? Or would the undocumented flow have been much larger had there been little or no enforcement on the border? It is hard to say. But one thing is quite clear: Heightened security on the border has pushed undocumented migrants to less guarded and more dangerous routes along the border. It has also moved migrant smuggling activities—once taken up by former migrants themselves—into the domain of organized crime. The Mexico-U.S. border, as a result, has become a riskier place for migrants and immigration officers alike.

ONE THEORY, ONE POLICY?

The efforts to prevent undocumented migration still largely center on border enforcement. The focus on the border, some critics argue, reflects an inherent "hypocrisy" in immigration policymaking. Politicians in wealthy nations like the United States are often caught between the economic realities that make immigration inevitable, and the public pressures that deem it undesirable. Politicians, as a result, often turn to highly visible but mostly "symbolic" instruments, like border enforcement, that appear to control immigration without really stopping it.

Symbolic or not, border enforcement as a policy instrument, some scholars argue, reflects a particular perspective on the root causes of migration. This perspective comes from neoclassical economics and asserts that individuals migrate if the expected benefits of migrating (e.g., higher earnings in destination) exceed the expected costs. Individuals will not migrate if the costs are too high, for example, when crossing the border is dangerous or finding work in destination is difficult.

This simplistic perspective, sociologist and political economist Stephen Castles argues, feeds "the idea that migration can be turned on and off like a tap by appropriate policy settings." But the numbers above already tell us that migration can hardly be turned "on and off." The undocumented migrants from Mexico tripled from 1986 to 2010, even though the amount spent on border control in the United States increased more than tenfold during this same period. One could assume that the benefits of migrating in this period were still higher than the costs, even with heightened border enforcement. Or one could think of alternative motives for migration, including those that are not captured in the individual-maximizing-utility model.

MULTIPLE THEORIES, MULTIPLE POLICIES?

Much of migration research in the past three decades has moved in the latter direction—that is, away from the neoclassical model and toward alternative theories of migration. But these other theories have not been able to suggest straightforward policy prescriptions like the neoclassical model, and thus, have had limited impact on policy.

The first important advance in theory came when researchers began to see migration as a decision taken up by families, not individuals. In many settings, including Mexico, anthropologists and sociologists had noted how family members came together to determine not just whether they would send a migrant, but also whom they would send. Economists used these insights to develop the "new economics of labor migration" in the 1980s.

This model asserted that families could send a migrant not just to increase their earnings, but also to minimize the risks to those earnings. A farming family could protect against weather conditions that would ruin their produce, for example, if a son were to move to a place unaffected by the misfortunes at home. Researchers found that this model worked particularly well in developing countries where formal mechanisms to manage such risks were not fully functioning.

Another major advance in theory occurred when scholars started to describe migration as a social process. Prior migrants, the argument went, offer useful resources, like information or help, or sheer inspiration to aspiring migrants, which make migration an easier decision for them. According to this "cumulative causation" model, past migration becomes the best predictor of future movement over time, overriding the economic factors that might have initiated a flow in the first place. Researchers observed this dynamic in many different settings, including in Mexico-U.S. flows.

Researchers also pointed to structural factors, for example, the capitalist expansion from "core" countries like the United States to "periphery" countries like Mexico, which disrupt local economies in the latter, and create cultural and ideological linkages to the former, facilitating migration in-between. Others identified a "segmented labor market" structure in advanced economies like the United States that diverted natives to the capital-intensive sector and required immigrants to occupy the labor-intensive jobs.

Inspired by the proliferation of theories, empirical researchers began to test each theory in different settings. But employing different theories in different settings led to a fragmented set of findings. In addition, each theory left out a component that was critical to another theory. "Economic factors are important, but hardly ever sufficient to understand any specific experience," Stephen Castles wrote. "No analysis of migration to Britain," he continued, "could be complete without an understanding of the history of British colonialism." Researchers then began to combine different theories to explain migration in particular settings. But some scholars cautioned against bringing together theories that operate at different levels of analysis. "Contrary to much conventional wisdom to integrate microstructural and macrostructural theories," sociologist Alejandro Portes argued, "in the case of immigration, the two levels are not fungible."

In the early 1990s, a multidisciplinary team led by sociologist Douglas Massey undertook a major attempt to clarify, compare, and link theories of international migration. Their conclusion encouraged scholars to be circumspect in how strongly they advocated for one theory over another: "All theories play some role in accounting for international migration in the contemporary world, although different models predominate at different phases of the migration process, and different explanations carry different weights in different regions depending on the local circumstances of history, politics and geography."

The field, then, converged on the idea that different theories can work in different settings, in different combinations, and for different groups of individuals. The challenge, Massey and Taylor argued, is "test[ing] various theoretical explanations comparatively . . . to determine which ones prevail under what circumstances and why." In other words, the challenge is not theoretical but empirical. It is about identifying what theories work in which settings, in what combinations, and for which groups of individuals. The "major obstacle," Castles wrote, is "the complexity and diversity of migration experiences . . . if there are so many factors at work [in migration], the possible combinations become infinite."

The combinations, however, need not be infinite. Take the three migrants discussed at the beginning of this chapter. The conflation of different events and circumstances led Diego, Miguel, and Patricia to different paths. Are these isolated stories, or are they representative cases for different groups in our data? In other words, are there other individuals similar to Diego, Miguel, or Patricia? More generally, are there different groups of migrants that are responding to similar sets of circumstances? It is these questions that guided the first step of my analysis.

IDENTIFYING GROUPS AMONG MIGRANTS

There are different ways of identifying "groups" of migrants. One can categorize migrants along a single characteristic such as gender, education, or origin community type. But a characteristic can acquire different meanings when combined with other characteristics. For example, having low education might not mean much for one's livelihood in a farming community, but it might influence one's life chances in a city. Low education, then, might be more predictive of migration behavior in the latter context than in the former.

To capture the diversity in migration experiences, rather than any single attribute, I studied configurations of multiple characteristics at the same time. I assumed that individuals who share similar configurations face similar opportunity structures, both in Mexico and the United States. Consider an uneducated farmer in a small rural community. The conditions awaiting this person in Mexico or the United States will be similar to others like him but quite different from those available to, say, a college-educated female engineer in the city.

I chose attributes like age, sex, education, household wealth, and community type—those that are known to shape migration behavior in the Mexico—U.S. context. I then used cluster analysis to discover the groups of migrants with similar configurations of these characteristics. Cluster analysis is an inductive method; it relies on data to determine the most typical configurations, and then assigns each case to different groups based on those configurations.

DATA AND ANALYSIS STRATEGY

I used data from the Mexican Migration Project (MMP) surveys, a binational data collection effort between Mexico and the United States. Between 1982 and 2013, the MMP team visited 143 communities in major migrant-sending areas in Mexico. In each community, the team surveyed all members of about 200 randomly selected households, collecting detailed migration histories and basic demographic and socioeconomic information. The team also followed up with migrants from these communities in the United States through snowball sampling.

The MMP data provide a representative sample of Mexican migrants to the United States. The data possess several advantages over alternative data sets: In particular, they contain information that spans a long time period on different kinds of migrants (those moving for work, family, or otherwise), including on those with and without documents. Because the data originate mostly from Mexico, however, they might underrepresent migrants with no relatives back home. I have compared the patterns in the MMP data with those based on other data sets throughout the book and have not encountered any major discrepancies between them.

The MMP sample includes 145,276 respondents, about 13% of whom have migrated to the United States at least once. I used the retrospective migration histories to reconstruct the characteristics of migrants during their first U.S. trip. I considered only the first trip to avoid the endogeneity issue, that is, to make sure that migrants' characteristics (e.g., wealth or education) are not a result of prior U.S. trips. My sample, in the end, consisted of 19,243 individuals observed during their first U.S. trip sometime between 1965 and 2010.

I first focused on migrants alone and identified different groups among them with cluster analysis. I then compared the characteristics that set each migrant group apart from the other groups as well as from non-migrants. I confirmed that the different migrant groups in the data were not just an artifact of a changing Mexican population, but reflected different selection mechanisms into U.S. migration. Finally, I investigated the particular conditions under which each group proliferated in the Mexico-U.S. stream. Using a statistical model, I related the size of each migrant group to major economic, policy, and demographic trends in Mexico and the United States. I found the numbers in each migrant group to be associated with a different set of factors in the larger context.

This analysis confirmed my initial intuition that migrant groups—defined by different configurations of characteristics—encounter different opportunity structures. It also gave me a way to externally validate the migrant groups, that is, to test their meaning outside the data that generated them.

I also used qualitative data to understand how individuals think about migration and how migrants actually migrate. In 2011 and 2012, with a local team in Jalisco, Mexico, we conducted in-depth interviews with 139 migrants and non-migrants in four communities previously surveyed by the Mexican Migration Project. These interviews allowed me to connect the larger patterns from the statistical analysis to particular logics individuals use to evaluate migration. The interviews also allowed me to study social interactions in migration behavior, interrogating how individuals can be inspired or influenced in their decisions by other migrants (or non-migrants) around them. Finally, the interviews gave me a full picture of migrants' journeys, from their initial decision (reported from multiple perspectives, not just that of the migrant) to their first time crossing the border, and from finding work in the United States to finally returning home (or not). These stories, like the three that opened the chapter, helped me understand migration as a holistic process and scrutinize certain patterns with quantitative data later on.

The compilation of methods in this book is inspired by migration, but it is general in its applicability. Many other behaviors show similar diversity in their origins and in the explanations provided for those origins. It is possible that each explanation may work in different settings or periods, or for different subsets of individuals. Classification tools, like cluster analysis, might prove useful in partitioning the data into substantively meaningful groups, and regression analysis might aid in scrutinizing whether different groups are subject to different causal regimes. Qualitative data can then highlight the mechanisms, the individual-level logics, underlying each regime.

FOUR GROUPS OF MIGRANTS

Cluster analysis revealed four groups among first-time Mexican migrants to the United States between 1965 and 2010. The first group included almost all men with no education, the majority of whom came from poor households in poor communities in central-western Mexico. These migrants were likely to send regular remittances and to make frequent trips back home, more so than the other groups. I characterized this distinctive pattern by naming this group the *circular migrants*.

In 1965, circular migrants were the majority group, accounting for two-thirds of all first-time migrants. The group declined in size thereafter, making up one-third of new migrants in 1980 and just one-tenth of them in 2010.

From 1980 to 1989, a second group attained the majority status among first-time migrants in our data. Migrants in this group were mostly men, typically the sons in the household, and almost all of them were teenagers. This group was thus much younger, on average, when compared to migrants in the other groups. Migrants in this group were also relatively wealthy; many came from households that owned some property, as well as a plot of land or a small business.

In 1965, the second group made up less than one-tenth of new migrants. Through the 1970s, the group increased in size, reaching its highest level in the mid-1980s. Because the group peaked in this period of severe economic hardship in Mexico (a relationship I confirmed with subsequent analysis), I called them the *crisis migrants*. In 1985, crisis migrants accounted for nearly half of all new migrants but lost their relative share gradually thereafter. In 2010, the group contained less than one-tenth of new migrants.

The third group in our data included the largest share of women, and the largest share of migrants with family ties to former or current U.S. migrants. The group, labeled the *family migrants*, grew slowly but steadily at first. From 1965 to 1985, family migrants went from containing just 5% of new migrants to about 15% of them. In the five years that followed, the group would double in absolute size and in relative share, accounting for more than one-third of new migrants by 1990 and retaining that level from that point on.

The final group consisted mostly of men from urban communities, which contrasts with the other groups whose migrants originated mostly from small villages or towns. The group also included the most educated migrants overall. I called the group the *urban migrants* to highlight their distinctive origins in Mexico.

Urban migrants consistently increased in size over time. In 1965, the group accounted for less than one-fifth of first-time migrants to the United States; in 2000, it contained more than one-half of them, and by 2010, almost 70%.

DIFFERENCES NOT A RESULT OF TEMPORAL TRENDS

Each migrant group was present in each time period. But each group also displayed a clear temporal signature. Circular migrants dominated the 1970s, while crisis migrants became prevalent in the 1980s. Likewise, family migrants experienced a sudden spike in the early 1990s, and urban migrants reached majority status through the 2000s.

The defining characteristics of each group, however, were not just a reflection of these temporal signatures, as my analysis showed. Urban migrants, for example, are not more educated than the others because they concentrate in a later period in our data, when education levels are generally higher in Mexico. Urban migrants are more educated compared to the other migrants, and also compared to non-migrants, in *each year* (possibly because of the more expansive educational opportunities in cities compared to rural areas). The differences between the migrant groups, in other words, are real, and not just an artifact of temporal trends in Mexico.

FOUR CONTEXTS AND FOUR LOGICS FOR MIGRATION

Each migrant group displayed a distinct configuration of characteristics, responded to a distinct set of conditions in Mexico and the United States, and, I argued, followed a distinct logic in migration.

CIRCULAR MIGRANTS

Let us start with circular migrants—mostly men from poor households in rural communities. This group was the majority among new migrants in the 1960s but declined consistently over time, finally becoming a small minority in the 2000s. This group closely followed trends in wages in Mexico and the United States, as well as levels of border enforcement. Circular migrants shrank in numbers as incomes in Mexico rose, wages for less-skilled workers in the United States fell, and the budget for border security grew. This response was in line with the predictions of the neoclassical economics model: changes in the wage gap or in border control likely altered the calculus around migration, increasing its expected costs and decreasing its potential benefits.

CRISIS MIGRANTS

Crisis migrants—typically young sons from relatively well-off households—increased their share among new migrants through the 1970s, peaking in the mid-1980s, and declining in numbers thereafter. The rise and fall in the number of crisis migrants followed almost perfectly the trends in Mexican inflation rates and in the exchange value of the peso, suggesting that the group's mobility was tied to the volatile economic climate in Mexico between 1976 and 1985.

Crisis migrants were responding more to constraints in the Mexican economy than to opportunities in the United States. Indeed, the group accepted much lower wages, on average, in the United States compared to the other migrant groups, especially during years of economic crisis in Mexico.

Some of the constraints in the Mexican economy—such as a lack of insurance—were omnipresent. Likewise, small producers working non-irrigated land were constantly at the mercy of the weather. Other constraints, like high inflation, were episodic. Small business owners or farmers suddenly became limited in their ability to obtain credit to maintain their daily operations during an economic crisis.

Under such circumstances, sending a migrant to the United States served a dual purpose: It increased family earnings while also diversifying the risks to those earnings. If there were a sudden drought threatening the crops, for example, the family could rely on the migrant's earnings. Similarly, if the migrant lost his job in the United States, he could count on the support from his family.

Crisis migrants seemed to be part of such a family strategy to hedge against risks to earnings, consistent with the new economics perspective on migration. For one, the group, although present throughout in our data, especially proliferated during economic downturns in Mexico. The group also spiked in numbers in regions experiencing localized misfortunes, such as in the south-eastern states during the coffee crisis in the early 1990s and in central and central-western Mexico after the earthquake in 1985. The mobility of crisis migrants also seemed more of a coordinated, rather than an individual, effort. The family usually funded the migrant's trip, and the migrant, in turn, sent remittances to the family.

FAMILY MIGRANTS

Family migrants—mostly women with ties to prior U.S. migrants—grew gradually in numbers until 1990, which is when the number of first-time migrants in the group suddenly doubled. It would subsequently remain at that level. The spike in family migrants occurred right after the passage of the Immigration Reform and Control Act (IRCA) in 1986, a law that provided a path to legalization to more than 2 million undocumented Mexicans already in the United States. Within a few years, legalized migrants could obtain permanent resident status and the right to sponsor their spouses and children in the United States.

Family reunification was the main motive bringing family migrants to the United States. The group included a large share of wives and daughters joining husbands and fathers. Compared to the other groups, family migrants also included a larger share of migrants that entered with documents, as well as a larger share of individuals who would eventually become permanent residents. Although many family migrants followed husbands and fathers already in the United States, they did not necessarily remain dependent on them. A majority of family migrants found employment in the United States right away. Nevertheless, the women in this group were still more likely to be unemployed compared to those scattered across the other, male-predominated, groups. About half of the women among the family migrants group did not work, compared to about 40% of women among circular or crisis migrants. The latter, in other words, were more likely to be independent movers compared to the former, mostly associational migrants.

Family migrants represent a particular logic for U.S. migration that combines the goal of economic improvement with that of family integrity. This group moved to the United States not only to address their economic problems in Mexico, but also to keep their families together. This logic, although more viable and more common after IRCA, was already on the rise before the legislation, as border enforcement made it harder for migrants to visit their families in Mexico.

URBAN MIGRANTS

Urban migrants—consisting of mostly men from urban communities with relatively high levels of education—increased their share among new migrants consistently over time, from a small minority in 1965 to a large majority in 2010. The rise in urban migrants was concurrent with Mexico's integration into the global economy, represented first by its accession into the Generalized Agreement in Tariffs and Trade (GATT, the precursor to World Trade Organization) in 1986 and then its signing of the North American Free Trade Agreement (NAFTA) with the United States and Canada in 1994. Indeed, the trend in urban migrants closely followed the increasing trends in foreign investments and U.S. exports entering Mexico.

Three potential mechanisms link the opening of the economy in Mexico to the uprooting of people to the United States. One mechanism is the rural decline attributed, first, to the commercialization of agriculture (which wiped out small farmers), and second, to the entry of imported U.S. crops into the market after NAFTA (which drove out domestic producers). This decline pushed rural peasants to migrate to cities in Mexico or directly to the United States. Another mechanism is the expansion of export-assembly plants in northern Mexico, which attracted rural peasants, but offered mostly precarious employment. The displaced workers, many originally from rural areas, turned to U.S. migration. A final mechanism is the change in industrial composition in Mexico, and the resulting shift in skill requirements, which, again, pushed those who were out of work across the border and into the United States.

Urban migrants responded to these spatial and economic dislocations in a globalizing economy. Ever-growing Mexican cities attracted rural peasants at first, but they would then become loci of poverty and displacement in their own right. Ultimately, they became a "trampoline" for international migration. Urban migrants assumed a settler logic in the United States, given both the strict enforcement on the border that made it hard to go back and forth, as well as the longer-term jobs available in manufacturing and services that offered a more solid basis for putting down roots compared to the seasonal work in agriculture offered to earlier migrant groups.

HISTORICAL CONTINGENCY

The history of migration between Mexico and the United States mattered as much as the economic or policy context in structuring where migrants came from, where they were headed, how they migrated, and even with what purpose. It is no coincidence that the circular, crisis, and family migrants in our data all originated from central-western Mexico, for example. The region was certainly poor but not the poorest in the country. Yet it had high levels of migration historically, thanks to an early contact with the United States through railroads. Recruiters used these railroads in the early 1900s to reach Mexican workers, bringing them to the United States to build more railroads and to work in the fields and factories. The Bracero program—the temporary labor agreement between Mexico and the United States from 1942 to 1964—similarly drew its workers mostly from the central-west. As a result, the region remained rich in migrant networks -family and community ties that connect aspiring migrants to former or current U.S. migrants. These ties acted as conduits of information or influence that facilitated future movement.

NETWORK EFFECTS IN MIGRATION

Scholars of migration have long written about such "network effects," where prior migrants alter the odds of migrating for new migrants (as we have seen in the cumulative causation model mentioned above). But few studies have characterized the different mechanisms through which such network effects are generated. How is it that prior migrants (or non-migrants) shape the migration decisions of others around them?

Survey data and statistical methods are often inadequate to identify network effects in migration, let alone to study their underlying mechanisms. This is due to known difficulties with measuring social networks and with separating their effects from the processes that created the social connections in the first place. In this book, I relied on data from in-depth interviews to understand how network effects work, and how they change over time.

I relied on a typology for network effects developed jointly with sociologist Paul DiMaggio. This typology distinguishes among three mechanisms
through which prior migrants can inform or influence the migration decisions
of those around them. In the first mechanism, *social facilitation*, prior migrants
provide useful information or help that typically reduces the costs or increases
the benefits of migration. In the second mechanism, *normative influence*, prior
migrants (or others observing them) offer social rewards or sanctions that actively encourage or discourage migration. In the third mechanism, *network
externalities*, prior migrants lead to creation of common and institutionalized
resources like smugglers or recruiters that facilitate migration.

These mechanisms are not mutually exclusive, and in fact, often work
in combination in our data. But the mechanisms vary in their salience for
different groups and over time.

CIRCULAR MIGRANTS

For circular migrants, social facilitation is the major mechanism for network effects in migration. This group concentrated in regions of high migration prevalence, and thus, had easy access to information or help from
former migrants. The group also "circulated," that is, made frequent trips
back home, given the seasonality of their work and also the weakness of the
border enforcement in the 1960s and 1970s. The group, in other words,
had ample opportunities to help others migrate across multiple trips.

Normative influence was also a crucial mechanism for circular migrants,
or any other migrant of the earlier cohorts. Prior migrants were often the
only source of information on migration in the 1960s and 1970s. Ethnographies from that time, as well as our interviews with those who migrated in
that period, suggest that prior migrants often exaggerated the prospects in
the United States, feeding a glorified view of migration. Circular migrants
were particularly exposed to such views that made migration the social
norm, an expected rite of passage for young men, enforced by family and
community members alike.

Externalities, like smugglers, were not yet common during the era of
circular migrants, although recruiters still played an important role in pulling new migrants to work sites in the United States.

CRISIS MIGRANTS

For crisis migrants—teens peaking in the 1980s—social facilitation was important but available through trustworthy family members rather than weaker
community relations, given the relative youth and vulnerability of the group.
Crisis migrants, like circular migrants, were exposed to normative pressures to

migrate, especially from family members, according to our interviews. Compared to circular migrants, the group was more likely to report using smugglers in the survey data, an externality not just of prior migrant streams, but also of the border-enforcement reaction to those streams on the U.S. side.

FAMILY MIGRANTS

Network effects were arguably the strongest for family migrants. The reason for this is simple: Social ties were not just inspiring or facilitating migration, as they did for the other groups, but they were also typically the very reason for migration. This group moved mainly to be with family members already in the United States.

Family migrants, as the only female-predominated group, experienced network effects differently, our interviews suggest. Migrant women, in general, faced more restrictions to their mobility compared to men, and also benefited less from network effects relative to men. Since men comprised migrant networks historically, social facilitation worked better for men than women. A male worker in the fields in the United States, for example, could more easily recommend other male workers for his job than he could female workers. Normative influence was also typically strong (and almost always positive) for men, while it was weak and sometimes negative for women. A man's willingness to migrate was often met with social approval and encouragement, but a woman's desire to move raised questions and concerns. Externalities were also more powerful for men than women. Smugglers charged women more than men, a result of women typically choosing less risky, and thus more expensive, crossing routes.

The differences between men and women, both in migration and in the network effects on migration, diminished over time, although they did not quite disappear. IRCA, the legislation responsible for the spike in the number of family migrants, was an important turning point. The rising number of migrant women after the legislation helped expand the networks available to women; it also tempered the gendered norms around migration that had previously constrained women's mobility.

IRCA also changed the network effects on migration, not just for family migrants or women generally, but also for all migrants in the years to come. After IRCA, social facilitation became easier for newly legalized migrants, who could bring others in their extended families or communities, but harder for those without documents who could no longer travel back and forth because of the increasingly stringent border enforcement. After IRCA, externalities became more important for new migrants for the same reason. Research found that increasing border control in this period did not reduce undocumented migration, but it did make clandestine border crossers more dependent on professional smugglers. These trends in network effects, or in their underlying mechanisms, especially mattered for the urban migrants, most of whom crossed the border in the post-IRCA period.

URBAN MIGRANTS

For urban migrants, network effects mainly worked through externalities. The group was more likely than any of the others to rely on professional guides or smugglers because it concentrated in a period of strong border enforcement in the United States. The group also relied on these resources because social facilitation and normative influence mechanisms did not work as well for them as they did for the other groups. Urban migrants originated from regions with historically low levels of migration. With a smaller number of prior migrants, social facilitation is likely to be more limited for this group relative to the other three groups. Urban migrants also came from large, urban areas with selective and sparse social ties, where it is hard to establish and enforce collective views on migration. The normative influence mechanism, then, is also weak for urban migrants compared to the other three groups.

Network effects, in short, mattered for all migrants but to different degrees and in different combinations. Social facilitation, for example, required stronger relations (like immediate family ties) for crisis and family migrants—the two groups with members considered more vulnerable (teens and women, respectively)—compared to the circular or urban migrants. Normative influence was stronger for men than for women. Finally, network externalities, like smugglers, were important to all groups, and more so over time with increasing enforcement on the U.S. border.

CULTURAL EXPECTATIONS AND FAMILY ROLES

Economic conditions and the policy context, as well as the mechanisms for network effects in migration, differentiate the four migrant groups in the Mexico-U.S. stream. Gender and family roles also separate the four groups from one another and also from the non-migrants. First, three migrant groups are predominated by men, and only one group by women. Men, overall, are more likely than women to migrate from Mexico. Second, the four migrant groups include different members of the household. The first group contains mostly the heads, the second group the sons, the third group the wives and daughters, and the last group a combination of all of these. For each group, the logics guiding migration are intimately linked to the family roles the migrants occupy, and the cultural expectations that come with those roles. These expectations, of course, are not static, but they shift over time as the Mexican society changes and as more people migrate to the United States, altering the meaning of migration.

Circular migrants, for example, followed the cultural prescriptions of their time, which required men to be the heads of and sole breadwinners for their families. By migrating to the United States and making regular visits back home, this group not only could provide a better livelihood for their families, but also could remain in close contact with them.

Crisis migrants responded to severe economic conditions in Mexico, and migrated as part of a family strategy. The mobility of this group—most of them younger sons—was in part a reflection of family relations in Mexico that typically submit unmarried children to the authority of their fathers.

Patriarchal relations, and the expected role of women as caregivers in the family, constrained women's mobility in Mexico. But over time, women started to gain more status as fertility rates declined, education levels increased, and labor market opportunities became more abundant. Their higher status afforded women increased input in family economic decisions, like migration. This status also gave them greater decision-making power to become independent migrants. As a result, women's presence in the Mexico-U.S. stream began to increase over time, not just among family migrants, but also in the other groups in our data.

But women's mobility was still more constrained than that of men. Women had less access to migrant networks—which were made up by, and thus more helpful to, men—given that men and women remained mostly separate in their working and living spaces in the United States. Women were also less frequently encouraged to migrate—if not completely discouraged from doing so—due to their caregiver role in families. Finally, women were more cautious in undertaking migration beginning in the 1990s because of the perils that clandestine migration posed.

THE MEXICO-U.S. STREAM, 1965–2010

The analysis in this book identified four migrant groups in the Mexico—U.S. stream from 1965 to 2010. Each group responded to particular economic constraints and opportunities in Mexico and the United States, or to particular incentives created by policy. Circular migrants reacted to the wage differentials between the two countries but their prevalence decreased over time as the border control restrained circularity for those without documents. Crisis migrants moved in sync with the fluctuations in the Mexican economy that put domestic earnings at risk, even for those from relatively well-off households. Family migrants took advantage of family-reunification incentives after IRCA, a law that granted legal status to millions of undocumented migrants. And urban migrants were a product of the economic and spatial changes following Mexico's integration into the global economy.

Each group also followed a different line of reasoning given the larger structural conditions at work. For circular migrants, mostly observed in the 1970s in our data, migration was almost predicated on return. The goal was to go to the United States, to save some money, and to come back to Mexico to invest it. For crisis migrants, reaching their highest level in the mid-1980s, migration was also temporary, at least initially; it provided relief from an immediate catastrophe at home. For family migrants, migration meant becoming a family again, but now, in the United States; settlement was a possibility now, and perhaps the goal in migration. For urban migrants, migration might have been temporary, but it was the border enforcement that gave it its permanence. Given the difficulty of going back and forth, many in this group chose to stay in the United States, especially those without documents.

The logic of each group resonated with a particular theory of migration, but under certain specified conditions. For example, the possibility of making frequent trips across a relatively unguarded border, and the availability of help from fellow migrants, allowed circular migrants to react to the fluctuations in the wage levels in the United States, as expected by the neoclassical economics perspective. Thanks to social ties to migrants, and also a burgeoning migration industry, crisis migrants managed to respond to sudden economic hardships at times of crisis in Mexico, and provide temporary relief to their families back home, in line with the new economics of labor migration idea. With IRCA granting legal status to millions of undocumented Mexicans, family migrants could join their spouses, parents, or siblings already in the United States, as predicated by the cumulative causation dynamic. Each theory worked, in other words, but under specific economic, historical, and social circumstances, and for particular groups of individuals.

WHAT IS NEXT?

The explanation for migration in this book is highly contextual. Four migrant groups each proliferate under specific circumstances, and each reveals a distinct logic in migrating. This conditionality makes it difficult to arrive at generalized conclusions and predictions. If all migration is conditional on the context, then how will we know who the next group will be? If all migration theories can be conditionally true, then which one should we use to devise immigration policy? The analysis here does not yield a particular prescription, but instead, suggests general principles that can guide future research and policy.

The first point to take away, and it is not a novel one, is the conditionality of migration theories. Each theory highlights a particular aspect of migration. The neoclassical theory emphasizes wage and employment differentials between regions, while the new economics perspective underlines the exposure to risk in developing countries. Each theory is also limited by its scope conditions. It is not always true, in other words, but only "sometimes true," that is, under particular circumstances.

Wage differentials between countries, for example, can push people to migrate but only if people *can* migrate, that is, if they can cross an international border. The Mexico-U.S. case here is distinct because the two countries share a border, and with it comes the possibility of clandestine crossing. And, in our data, the one group that closely tracks with its size the fluctuations in the U.S. wages can do so because it concentrates in an earlier period, when clandestine crossing is relatively easy.

The exposure to economic risk, similarly, can only be an incentive for international migration if people are able to move internationally. For crisis migrants, the group peaking at times of economic crisis in Mexico, not only is clandestine crossing possible, but former migrants in the family and community, as well as a growing migration industry that includes smugglers between the two countries, also facilitate it.

The question one needs to ask, then, is: What are the necessary conditions for people to react to a particular economic condition? This question helps us set the scope conditions for any argument and open the horizon to a more encompassing explanation. This approach is quite different from "testing" theories against one another, or choosing one theory over the others in any way. It requires accepting the possibility that each theory might work under some conditions, and for some people. The approach seems in line with that of seeking "mid-range theories" (rather than a "grand theory" of migration) advocated by sociologist Alejandro Portes.

A second, related, point is the relevance of the social and cultural context. Given any set of circumstances, who would react to it given the social and cultural setting? Many people in Mexico might be exposed to conditions of poverty, for example, but only some respond to it by migrating to the United States. Gender and family roles often dictate who the migrants will be. But these roles can change over time and even vary across communities. It might be more acceptable, for example, for women to migrate in a community in Mexico where many women have migrated before than, say, in a community where men are the only migrants.

The actions of prior migrants, in general, set the stage for the decisions of future migrants. This process resembles "Coleman's boat," sociologist Jim Coleman's schematic description of how macro-level structure and micro-level decisions are linked. Structure shapes individual actions, but those actions in turn alter the social structure. This feedback mechanism describes the social process of migration in many migrant-sending settings. Prior migrants can provide help that makes it easier for new migrants to take on the journey. They may also contribute to a new set of expectations from young adults in communities, turning migration into a norm. All else equal, then, one can reasonably expect more migration out of communities or regions where migration is already prevalent. The individuals in such communities are likely to be the first respondents to any constraints in origin or opportunities in destination that create incentives to migrate.

A similar feedback mechanism likely operates in migrant-receiving settings where the size and composition of migrant streams can shape public responses to immigration and in turn inspire permissive or restrictive immigration policies. The analysis in this book considered such linkages only in the case of the Immigration Reform and Control Act in 1986, when the negative public reaction to the undocumented Mexican flows countered with advocacy from the growers' organizations and Hispanic groups led to a legislation with contradictory components, like tougher border control on the one hand and mass legalizations on the other. More work is needed to understand how the public reacts to the arrival of different migrant groups (for example, the recent dispersion of Mexican migrants to "new destinations"), and how that reaction shapes the political responses and policies pertaining to immigrants.

The third, and related, takeaway is about the importance of understanding both sending and receiving contexts. What are the opportunity structures in both settings? For example, if a sudden economic crisis were to leave many engineers in Mexico out of work, they will only migrate to the United States if there are opportunities desirable to them there. In other words, it takes two countries to have a migration flow, and unless one understands the conditions in each, it is hard to make sense of that flow. There are exceptions, of course, like a war creating a refugee stream that will go anywhere rather than stay in origin. But in most cases, a "transnational" lens is crucial to understanding migration, as advocated by many scholars in the field over the past two decades.

A fourth point regards the complexity of designing immigration policy. How can a nation develop an effective migration policy when the factors producing migration are largely transnational or global, that is, beyond the control of any single nation? How can a nation settle on a migration policy when there are different interest groups within the nation with divergent views, such as employers favoring migration and workers opposing it?

These difficulties, scholars argue, often lead to migration policies that are symbolic, or to those that have contradictory objectives, hidden agendas, or unintended consequences.

My findings suggest yet another source complicating migration policy: different migrant groups follow different logics, and react to different kinds of incentives or policy. Circular migrants, for example, remain high in numbers as long as the wages in the United States are high and the enforcement on the border is weak. The group, in other words, responds to both economic and policy incentives in the United States. Crisis migrants do not, at least not to the same degree as the circular migrants. To be sure, this group also migrates to take advantage of the higher earnings in the United States. But crisis migrants peak in the stream not when the prospects in the United States are the brightest, but rather when those in Mexico are the poorest. Family migrants increase in size immediately after IRCA, the legislation that created incentives for family reunification in the United States.

What does this plurality imply? It implies that migration policies will probably not have a universal effect on the migrant population. The rising enforcement on the border might deter the circular migrant who would rather stay with his family in Mexico than risk his life crossing the border (like Diego in the beginning) but perhaps not the crisis migrant who is escaping dire economic conditions at home. Similarly, the difficulty of finding work in the United States, due to an economic downturn or greater workplace enforcement, might discourage anyone migrating for work, but not those moving to join family members already there (like Patricia).

Any policy, then, should at least attempt to have a clear and well-circumscribed objective: What is it that the policy is trying to achieve? Who would respond to it, and in what way? It is perhaps naïve to raise this point given the realities of migration policymaking, including the conflicting interests guiding it or the political process diverting it. But it is equally naïve to ignore the point and assume that one policy will work equally well for everyone. If migrants are a diverse pool, then one needs diverse migration policies to manage that pool.

A related question worth raising is: What constitutes migration policy? Certainly, any legislation that concerns migrants or governmental office controlling these individuals' movement qualifies as migration policy. But international economic agreements can also create or relieve migration pressures between two countries, as NAFTA did between the United States and Mexico. Foreign aid that promotes development in a poor country and conflict resolution efforts that improve security in a violent region may also impact migration flows. In other words, migration policy encompasses social policy, international relations, and foreign aid policies, among other dimensions.

For the United States, migration policy should not just entail border enforcement. It should also involve broad policies that advance domestic economic interests and recognize basic commitments to human rights, to the bonds of family, and to the responsibilities that come with being a part of a community of nations in a densely interlocking region.

THE END OF MIGRATION FROM MEXICO?

This book emphasized change more than stability. The analysis focused on different migrant groups, or how different circumstances made salient different configurations of attributes for migration. But the migrant groups also shared many circumstances to which they gave similar responses. Each migrant group, for example, declined in numbers relative to the population after the year 2000. This downward trend owed to long-term demographic trends in Mexico, as well as to economic downturns and immigration policies in the United States.

First, over the past 50 years, family sizes have shrunk considerably in Mexico. The birth rate has dropped from an average of 6.7 births per woman in the 1960s to 2.3 in 2010. The slower population growth has allowed the domestic economy to better absorb the new cohorts into the labor market, thus reducing the pool of potential migrants to the United States. Second, the U.S. economy has experienced two major crises in the past decade, in 2001 and 2007, bringing high levels of unemployment and limiting the opportunities available to potential migrants. Third, U.S. immigration control has also tightened in this decade, both on the border and inland, and with an elevated number of deportations, it has become harder for Mexican migrants to get to and remain in the United States. Taken together, these conditions have brought the net migration flow from Mexico to the United States to a standstill in 2012, and to below zero in 2014.

Does the standstill or recent net loss in migrants mark the beginning of the end for the Mexico-U.S. flow? One could answer this question in the affirmative based on some of the conclusions drawn from mass migration from Europe to the United States between 1850 and 1914. That flow, economists Hatton and Williamson argue, reached a natural end when fertility rates dropped in Europe and wages converged to those in the United States. But the conditions in the Mexico-U.S. flow are not exactly comparable. First, while fertility rates are declining in Mexico, the average wages are significantly lower compared to the United States. Economist Michael Clemens and colleagues estimate that an average Mexican worker can more than double his earnings by simply moving to the United States, even after controlling for cost-of-living differences between the two countries. The wage gap, in other words, persists. Second, unlike the European countries, Mexico shares a border with the United States, and though it is much harder to cross without documents these days, it is still possible to do so with help from smugglers. Third, the aging and retirement of baby boomers (and the resulting decline in the size of the workforce), and educational upgrading (and the consequent drop in the population of less-skilled workers) continues to create demand for immigrant workers to fill arduous jobs, for example, in construction, cleaning, and the like.

Mexican migration to the United States could increase again in the future, especially if conditions in Mexico deteriorate suddenly, as they did in the 1980s. But, given the country's slower population growth now, a return to the mass-migration levels of the 1970s and 1980s seems unlikely.

It is not easy to anticipate what the future will bring. If there is one lesson to take away from this book, it is that different circumstances might continue to give rise to different migrant groups. One need not look further than this decade to understand this point. The migrant flow from Mexico slowed down in the 2000s, but a new—and quite unexpected—migrant stream emerged from Central America. This stream contained thousands of unaccompanied children from El Salvador, Guatemala, and Honduras. The number of minors apprehended at the border reached nearly 60,000 in fiscal year 2014 and surpassed more than 26,000 in the first part of fiscal year 2015 (from October 2014 to June 2015). Researchers argued that different reasons mobilize children from different countries. Child migrants from El Salvador and Honduras are migrating to escape the rising drug trade related violence in their countries, while those from Guatemala seem to be moving more for economic reasons.

Nobody could see the child migrants coming. And perhaps 50 years ago, nobody could see Mexican migration reaching the levels it did today. Nothing might prepare us for the future apart from "tacit abandonment of global solutions," as Nobel laureate Mexican essayist Octavio Paz wrote. There will never be a global explanation for migration, or a global solution for it (if one takes it as a problem, that is). Different explanations will work at different times and for different people. Different policies will be effective in different ways. Each migrant flow must be understood on its own terms, in its particular setting, without imposing any one theory on it a priori. When it comes to policy, what we need is "good sense," as Paz wrote, and to move "more and more towards limited remedies to solve concrete problems.

Appendix A

CLUSTER ANALYSIS: WHY IS
IT ON THE FRINGES OF SOCIAL SCIENCE?

Cluster analysis is not a part of the mainstream toolkit in the social sciences. This is surprising, especially in sociology, where there is a long tradition of identifying configurations that characterize "ideal" types. Today, this tradition survives mostly in qualitative studies. In quantitative work, "the statistical turn" in the last century has led to an almost exclusive focus on regression analysis.

There are a few possible reasons for this state of affairs. First, cluster analysis is mainly a descriptive tool. There is an aversion in many social sciences to pure description, which is seen as inferior to analytic thinking and as unscientific. Economists particularly refrain from description, a tendency economist Amartya Sen reveals and counters in his article, "Description as Choice." Most social scientists are more comfortable with methods, like regression analysis, that allow one to test hypotheses than those like cluster analysis that only describe the data.

A second, and related, reason is the prominence of *typological thinking* in the social sciences. There is always a tension between focusing on a typical case, on the one hand, and identifying the variation across cases, on the other. Historians of science refer to these two alternatives as *typological* and *population thinking*, respectively.

The roots of the former in social science can be traced back to the 1840s, to Adolphe Quételet, a Belgian mathematician, who applied statistics to study the "average man." The characteristics of the average man, he argued, are often stable and predictable, and thus, likely to reveal universal truths. "The determination of the average man," Quételet wrote, "may be of the most important service to the science of man and the social system."

These ideas have had an enduring influence on social science and remain popular today. Many typological thinkers still study the typical individual whose characteristics or behavior presumably generalize to the entire population.

Population thinkers, by contrast, focus on the variations from the typical individual. Such variations, they argue, reveal as much about the population as does the average case. Charles Darwin made these ideas central to biology with his work on population diversity and its role in evolution. But, it was his cousin, Francis Galton, who introduced population thinking to social science. Writing in the 1880s, Galton became engrossed with "how the quality is distributed" in a population. This led to his discovery of "correlation," and to the eventual development of regression analysis, the most widely used statistical tool in social science. These new tools, however, did not eradicate the ingrained typological thinking in social science. Many practitioners who used these tools continued to interpret the variations from the average case as "errors" in the measurement of a fixed quantity rather than an inherent quality of the population.

This is perhaps why, more than a century later, Otis Dudley Duncan, one of the most influential sociologists and demographers of our time, called population variability one of the "cardinal problems that social science has not yet come to grips with." James Heckman, in his lecture for the Nobel Prize in economics in 2000, referred to his life's work as "accounting for heterogeneity and diversity" in economic life against "the long-standing edifice of the average person."

These influential thinkers, among many others, made population variability a central problem in social science. Several methodological advances emerged as a result. Researchers began to use these tools to study how an outcome varies for different groups of individuals, in different contexts, or across different time periods. But these advances still remained in the realm of regression analysis and did not motivate the use of tools like cluster analysis to describe population heterogeneity.

A third reason for the unpopularity of cluster analysis is suspicions around its purchase for theoretical advancement. Cluster analysis produces typologies, and "typologies," sociologist Alejandro Portes emphasizes, while useful for heuristic purposes, "are not theories".

None of these reasons is sufficient to discard cluster analysis, or related methods, from the toolkit of social scientists, however. First, cluster analysis is a descriptive tool, but description, as Amartya Sen argues, is a vital scientific activity. It is also one that is difficult because it requires one to choose specific details to focus on while discarding others. Cluster analysis makes that task easier as it reduces the complexity of data into a few categories. Second, cluster analysis allows us to view differences across categories, in line with population thinking, and to develop typologies based on the data. Third, these data-driven typologies, although not theories by themselves, can be important heuristic tools for conceptualization, allowing us to see patterns that we otherwise would not be able to see.

Appendix B

THEORIES OF INTERNATIONAL MIGRATION

There are many ways to think about international migration. We can see the movement of people as a response to differences in opportunities between countries in wages, employment, or political freedoms. We can connect the movement to historical ties forged over time through conflicts, cooperation, or trade. We can also treat migration as an action of enterprising individuals or families who hope to do better in a new destination. There is no contradiction in these views. Differences in opportunities across nations, after all, will only lead to migration if individuals or families react to them. I review alternative explanations of migration below, moving from the macro- to the micro-level, descending from an aerial view of ties across nations to a close-up of individual motivations.

WHY DOES MIGRATION HAPPEN?
A GLOBAL SYSTEM

There is a global organization of power, according to the world systems theory. A set of nations makes up the "core" and other nations remain in the "periphery." Core nations expand outward in search of raw materials, cheap labor, or new consumers. This expansion alters traditional economic and social arrangements in the periphery, and creates a mobile population already familiar with the institutions of the core. The result is a reverse movement of people from the periphery to the core.

In the past, colonial regimes formed the core and expanded by gaining control of new territories considered to be in the periphery. Today, governments of industrialized nations and multinational corporations make up the core and bring developing nations into the periphery through foreign investments and trade.

Industrialized nations specialize in capital-intensive sectors that require a highly skilled workforce, outsourcing most labor-intensive production to developing nations in the periphery. For example, the United States, a core country in this model, focuses on the design, sales, and marketing of its many brand-name products that are often sourced, manufactured, or assembled in nations considered to be in the periphery, like Mexico, Thailand, or China.

This global division of labor determines both the flows of capital and flows of people. Sociologist Saskia Sassen argues that the movement of capital from industrialized to developing nations sets off a counter-movement of people from developing to industrialized nations. This process unfolds as follows.

Increasing investment in a developing country brings about fierce market competition that transforms the agrarian base. Farmers, under pressure to increase production and profits, have no choice but to consolidate land and mechanize production. Subsistence farmers turn to cash crops or sell their land. Many small landowners become wage laborers, and with increasing mechanization in agriculture, are forced to seek opportunities elsewhere. Some migrate to cities for work; some become international migrants.

It is not only the agrarian base that experiences a transformation. Foreign investments concentrate employment in export-processing zones in the periphery, like the *maquiladoras* along the U.S. border in Mexico. These zones become focal destinations for rural migrants, especially for women, who are the preferred workers since they accept lower wages and seem more adaptable to the repetitive assembly-line work. The recruitment of women into work threatens the gender hierarchy in patriarchal societies. Lacking commensurate opportunities at home, and not to be outdone by women, many young men turn to international migration. So do many women displaced from assembly-line work once that work takes its physical and mental toll on them.

Foreign investments thus lead to emigration, all the while creating more jobs in a developing country, especially if those investments disrupt existing work structures and gender relations. Foreign investments also trigger emigration through the cultural and ideological links they forge between countries. Workers in an export-processing plant in a periphery country, for example, become aware of the work practices and lifestyles in the core nations. The population at large also becomes more "westernized" over time. This familiarity, according to Sassen, reduces the barriers to emigration.

There are concurrent changes in industrialized nations that create a chronic need for migrant labor, providing the demand side of this global equation. First, the deployment of manufacturing to developing countries allows an expansion of the service sector in industrialized countries. The demand for less-skilled manufacturing work declines, while that for high-skilled service jobs increases. At the same time, high-skilled work becomes geographically concentrated. Management, consulting, and finance operations are increasingly consolidated in "global cities" (to use Sassen's term) like New York, London, and Tokyo that coordinate the complex network of economic relations across countries. The intensity of work life in these cities creates more demand for less-skilled service workers (cleaners, caretakers of children and the elderly, restaurant workers, and the like). And immigrants from developing countries in the periphery often meet this demand, for reasons we will see in a subsequent section.

The world systems theory alerts us to the importance of the connections between countries in explaining migration. There is a global system that links countries, assigning each a particular role. Industrialized countries form the core and developing countries the periphery. Money flows from the core to the periphery first; this flow alters existing social and economic arrangements in the periphery and pushes people to search for opportunities in the core. Money flows create a network structure through which labor flows occur but only in the reverse direction.

DIFFERENCES IN WORK OPTIONS

Not all theorists of migration take world systems scholars' grand-scale approach to explain the movement of people. For many economists, migration is a simple result of differences between countries (or regions within a country) in wages or availability of jobs. A move across a border is no different from a move from a small village to the city: both stem from a regional imbalance in work opportunities.

This viewpoint finds its sharpest formulation in neoclassical economics. Individuals move from a setting where wages are low and workers are plentiful, like Mexico, to a place where wages are high and workers are scarce, like the United States. This movement, the theory goes, eventually closes wage and employment gaps between regions. With many workers gained, wages drop in the United States. And with many workers lost, wages rise in Mexico. Wages eventually converge in the two countries, at which point it no longer makes sense for people to move in-between.

This formulation provides a simple and elegant description of migration. But its predictions on regional convergence better fit internal moves than international flows. This is because, unlike domestic migrants (or perhaps international migrants of an earlier era), workers cannot always move freely across a border due to visa requirements. Clandestine movement is difficult but possible in some settings (for example, between Mexico and the United States); it is unthinkable in others. The restriction on movement is an obstacle to regional convergence.

However, this qualification does not contest that bilateral differences in work options are a necessary condition for most labor migration. Indeed, numerous studies have shown how international migration flows match business cycles in receiving countries, spiking at times of economic prosperity and plunging in periods of economic hardship.

DIFFERENCES IN RISK PROFILES

In another formulation, also out of economics, scholars view migration as a response to risk in developing economies of the world. This risk may result from any number of factors. One is volatility in weather conditions in an agrarian society. If land is not fully irrigated and traditional cultivation methods are still prevalent, farmers are left entirely dependent on rainfall. An unexpected drought in such a setting could threaten an entire season's production, exposing small landholders to the risk of no earnings and subsistence farmers to the risk of going hungry.

Risk in a developing economy could also result from volatility in prices or in credit. A sudden economic crisis could leave many households unable to purchase basic commodities, unable to obtain new credit to sustain their land or business, or simply without work.

In advanced economies, such risks are managed through insurance, financial markets, or government protections. A farmer facing weather uncertainty, for example, could buy insurance or financial products like weather derivatives to protect his or her income or assets against a drought. A factory worker facing job loss could count on unemployment insurance, at least for a while. These protections are often lacking in developing countries, however.

Migration becomes a vital survival strategy for families in such settings, where livelihoods depend on circumstances for which one can hardly prepare. Sending a family member to a new place, where risks are less extreme, or just different in kind from the origin community, allows families to hedge their bets against hardship. If rainfall is not sufficient in Mexico, a rural family can rely on earnings from a migrant in Mexico City or in the United States. And if working conditions become precarious in the internal or international destination, the migrant can rely on the support from the family.

This view, called the new economics of labor migration (NELM), connects migration to differences in risk profiles across regions. The theory— like its neoclassical economics counterpart—does not distinguish between internal and international movements. In fact, some of the earliest work establishing this perspective relied on data from internal migration exclusively. This work argued that migration helps a family diversify risks as long as the migrant works in a different sector from the rest of the family —a sector where risks to earnings are uncorrelated with risks to earnings in the family's main line of work. A migrant does not need to move too far to achieve this outcome if, say, there is a factory where he or she can take up work near the family's farm. But, given that different sectors in a country are subject to at least some common risk, a migrant is better off hedging against that risk by moving to an international destination.

DIFFERENCES IN POPULATION STRUCTURE

Differences in work options or risk profiles matter for migration between countries, but so do the differences in population structure, demographers argue. Each country experiences a demographic transition as it becomes more developed. Birth and death rates are roughly equal at first. With improved food supply and health conditions, birth rates increase and death rates decline, leading to rapid population growth. Birth rates drop eventually as a country becomes more urbanized, its population more educated, and its workforce more gender-balanced, while death rates are stable or still falling.

Most developing countries are in the middle of this spectrum: Their populations are growing and the share of working-age adults is rising. Most developed countries, by contrast, fall at the end of the spectrum: Their population is shrinking and the share of working-age adults declining. This demographic differential creates a push out of developing countries, where working-age adults are plentiful and jobs are scarce, and a pull toward developing countries, where working-age adults are scarce and jobs are plenty. A demographic differential possibly manifests itself in a wage or employment differential between developing and developed nations, and thus, generates movement in exactly the same direction as would be expected by the neoclassical economic theory.

DIFFERENCES IN SECURITY

Regions of the world vary in the political freedoms or protections they offer to people. Migrants escaping political oppression, religious persecution, or ethnic conflicts are categorized as "asylum seekers" or "refugees." Migration theory considers these groups as different from labor or family migrants.

The boundaries between asylum seekers and labor migrants, however, are often blurred. Migrants escaping increasing violence in a country, say, due to a turf fight between drug cartels, might not be eligible for asylum-seeker status in their new destination. These migrants might enter a country under a work visa or without documents. Or migrants intending to work in a new country might still obtain asylum-seeker status if they happen to come from war-torn regions. Researchers call this phenomenon "categorical substitution," whereby restrictions on one migrant group lead to increasing numbers in the other groups. All else equal, a country receives more asylum seekers if its asylum policies are generous, more documented labor migrants if its visa policies open, and more undocumented migrants if both asylum and visa policies are restrictive.

The progression of theories, as I have presented them, started from the global gaze of world systems scholars, where people and money flow in opposite directions across a network of all nations, to a dyadic focus, where people move between specific country pairs to exploit differences in economic opportunity, demographic structure, or political safety and security. I now descend to the level of nations.

THE WILL OF THE STATE

The nation-state is an important actor in migration, although it is hardly recognized as such in migration theories. The state can regulate through its immigration and emigration policies the number and types of migrants it willingly receives and sends. States vary in their capacity to implement restrictive immigration policies, however. According to sociologist Douglas Massey, centralized states without strong constitutional protections and without an independent judiciary, like the oil-exporting states in the Persian Gulf, are possibly the only ones that can impose ironclad restrictions on immigration, given also the relatively low demand for entry into those countries. On the other end of the spectrum are liberal democracies, like Canada, Australia, and the United States, which lack a centralized state but have a strong tradition of individual liberty and an established culture of immigration. These countries have less power in enforcing restrictions on immigration, and restrictions are less likely to have an effect given the high numbers of people seeking to immigrate.

There is also an emergent global human rights regime that protects the rights of immigrants. Developed nations are more likely to abide by the rules of this regime, which further limits their ability to impose strict controls on immigration. But this global trend does not prevent immigration from being a top item on the public agenda in most developed countries. Politicians find themselves in a bind: On the one hand are the pressures from the electorate to limit immigration. On the other are the economic and demographic realities making immigration necessary, as well as the moral and judicial scrutiny preventing its restriction. A resolution to this tension is to use symbolic policy instruments, like border enforcement or limiting immigrants' access to social services, which only appear to control immigration.

Immigration policy is still not completely immune to public sentiment. Research finds that immigration policies closely follow business cycles in receiving countries, becoming more expansive at times of economic boom and more restrictive in periods of hardship. Increasing inequality, unemployment, and volume of immigration all facilitate more restrictions on immigration, until, that is, immigrants reach sufficient numbers to influence the electoral process.

Immigration policy focuses on controlling entry, while emigration policy is centered on screening exit and return. One can extend Massey's argument on the former to the latter: Centralized states without constitutional and judicial protections will be more successful in limiting citizens from leaving. A prime example is the communist regimes of the Soviet Union and China, which restricted the outmigration of their citizens well into the 1980s. At the other extreme are nation-states promoting the emigration of citizens through government-sponsored programs or bilateral labor agreements, such as the Philippines. In these settings, emigration often provides an escape valve that relieves the pressures of population growth and unemployment, and partially releases the government from the burden of providing relief. In between these two extremes are the laissez-faire attitudes of some countries, like Mexico, where emigration policy is not always deliberate, but rather an unintended consequence of other nation-building projects.

DIVIDED LABOR MARKET IN DESTINATION

International migration can result from an intrinsic demand for immigrant labor in developed countries. One thing that can drive this demand, as argued by Sassen earlier, is the global division of labor. Manufacturing operations move to developing countries, while management and banking services become consolidated in "global cities" in developed nations. These cities attract a high-skilled workforce along with less-skilled workers that provide basic services like food preparation, cleaning, or care work. Immigrants typically occupy the latter jobs. But one could ask why natives do not.

Economist Michael Piore offers a plausible explanation. Each job implies a certain social status. Natives are not motivated to work for less-skilled jobs since these jobs are at the bottom of the hierarchy and give little opportunity for upward mobility. Immigrants, on the other hand, view such jobs as a means to earning money rather than a means to obtain social status.

Theoretically, employers can raise wages to make less-skilled work more attractive to natives. But a raise given to the bottom group disturbs the accepted hierarchy, creating ripple effects from the bottom up. If, say, fruit-pickers get a raise, then field supervisors should also get a commensurate raise, and so on. To avoid a cascading increase in wages, or what economists call "structural inflation," employers turn to immigrants to fill the jobs considered to be at the bottom of the hierarchy.

Once certain jobs have been occupied by immigrants, however, they attain a negative stigma as "immigrant jobs" and become even more unacceptable to natives. This social labeling, according to Piore, contributes to a persistent demand for immigrant labor in developed countries.

The clear line between immigrant and native jobs is also reinforced by a segmented labor market structure, according to Piore. In most advanced economies, there is a capital-intensive "primary" sector offering high wages and stable employment, and a labor-intensive "secondary" sector with low pay and precarious work conditions. This structure is a direct result of the duality of capital and labor as factors of production. The former is fixed and costly to the employer if misallocated. The latter can be varied with layoffs and is costly only to workers. Employers, then, invest their capital to cover the most certain component of their demand, creating stable and rewarding employment along the way, and manage the uncertain components by deploying cheap and flexible labor. Natives fill the jobs in the primary sector, while immigrants meet the needs of the secondary sector.

A CUMULATIVE DYNAMIC IN ORIGIN

Economist Michael Piore describes a path-dependent process in receiving economies, whereby immigrants gradually become an indispensable component of the labor force. Sociologist Douglas Massey describes a similar path-dependent process in developing countries, where initial migration becomes a reason for more migration later on. This process, called the "cumulative causation of migration," works through several mechanisms.

Migrants send remittances, for example, which often increase income inequality and induce a sense of relative deprivation among non-migrants in the sending community. Remittances, if invested in labor-saving tools, also change agrarian organization and reduce local opportunities for employment in rural settings. Such changes create more incentives for migration.

Migrants also provide information or influence that makes other people in their family or community more likely to migrate. Terms like "migrant networks" or "chain migration" all convey the pull of social ties, where one migrant acts as a seed bringing several other migrants to the same destination. But how does this process actually work?

Researchers do not always agree on the social mechanisms underlying network effects in migration, which occur if prior migrants in a person's network alter the likelihood that the person will migrate. Some argue that prior migrants provide useful information or help that reduces the barriers to migration, encouraging new migrants to take on the journey. Others suggest that prior migrants alter social expectations in a family or community, and contribute to a "culture of migration," whereby moving to a particular destination becomes a norm, or rite of passage, for young adults.

Empirical studies in many settings have found migration to be more likely in families or communities with already-high levels of migration. Studies have also shown that individual or community characteristics, as well as the larger economic climate in origin or destination, matter less for migration in regions of high migration prevalence.

Urbanization in origin

The cumulative causation idea connects emigration out of a country to changes induced by past emigration. One can extend this idea to connect emigration out of a country to changes created by past internal migration in that country.

Ron Skeldon, with fellow geographer Russell King, identifies pathways through which internal moves could be precursors to international flows. One pathway, possibly the most common one, involves rural migrants moving to a city in their own country in an effort to accumulate financial resources and social contacts, which then allows them to cross to another country. Scholars observe this "stepwise" migration strategy in many developing countries. In Mexico, for example, researchers find that jobs in the *maquiladoras* or export-oriented agriculture in the border region serve as a "school for El Norte." Rural migrants gain specific skills in these jobs, collect necessary resources, and eventually move to the United States, where they receive better wages doing similar kinds of work. Many cities in northern Mexico, as a result, serve as a "trampoline" for international moves.

Skeldon and King describe a second pathway, which they call "knock-on effects," linking internal and international moves. These effects describe how one kind of migration by one group could lead to another kind of migration by another group. The influx of domestic migrants to an urban area could restrict the jobs or wages available to city residents, forcing them to move to another country. Internal migration, in this case, knocks on an international stream. These ideas suggest that international migration flows could follow from patterns of urbanization in a country.

The above theories tell us that international migration flows can be shaped by the actions taken by either sending or receiving states, by the structure of markets in a receiving country, or by prior internal or international moves that have altered the economic and social structures in a sending country.

These aggregate explanations tell us why migration happens, but not necessarily who does the migrating. I now turn to the micro-level explanations for migration, and describe individual or family-level motivations that inspire specific kinds of people to cross borders.

WHO DOES THE MIGRATING?

Most social scientists try to explain who migrates in one of three ways: by reference to individual desires to maximize income, to family strategies to diversify risks to income, or to social ties to migrants already in destination. These three ideas make up the micro-level counterparts of the macro-level explanations for migration above, corresponding respectively to the neoclassical economics, new economics of labor migration, and cumulative causation perspectives.

THOSE WITH MOST TO GAIN

Neoclassical economists view migration as a choice by rational actors seeking to maximize utility. The migration decision resembles an optimization problem. Individuals evaluate their skills—more specifically, what those skills are worth in their own country as compared to another. Individuals also consider the potential costs of migrating; these costs include anything from the psychological costs of separation from family to financial costs of completing the trip. Migrants are those individuals for whom the benefits exceed the costs, or, those who are able to maximize their expected income by migrating. Migrants are, in other words, those with most to gain by migrating.

THOSE WITH MOST TO LOSE

Sociologists and anthropologists have collected considerable evidence questioning the individualistic model of migration presented in the neoclassical economics theory. Many case studies reveal how family is actually the key unit where migration decisions are discussed, contested, and finalized. These ideas find traction in the new economics model of migration. Family, as a decision-making unit, is categorically different from the individual, as it has multiple members. Similar to an investor buying different types of assets, a family can allocate its members in different sectors of the economy to diversify potential risks to its earnings. This strategy is critical to family survival in developing countries, such as Mexico, where the risks are abundant, but the formal market mechanisms to manage them are still insufficient. Under such conditions, the model posits, it is families that face the greatest risk, those with most to lose in origin that send migrants.

THOSE WITH THE MOST CONNECTIONS

Both economic models disregard the social ties that connect migrants to those left behind. These ties, as the cumulative causation model posits, facilitate future movement by providing useful resources or by acting as purveyors of norms. In this alternative model, migrants are not necessarily those with most to lose in origin, or most to gain in destination, but those with the most ties to prior migrants.

WHERE DOES THIS BOOK FIT?

Theories of migration present a "fragmented" set of ideas, "sometimes segregated by disciplinary boundaries," argued Massey and colleagues in their landmark review of the literature almost two decades ago. In a later statement, Massey and Taylor identified the major challenge for migration research to be "test[ing] various theoretical explanations comparatively . . . to determine which ones prevail under what circumstances and why." This is what this book sets out to do. Specifically, the analysis herein shows that specific opportunities mobilize specific groups of people in Mexico, not everybody. And specific opportunities become more or less salient at different times. To the extent that theories emphasize such opportunities, they become more or less applicable at different times and for different groups of individuals.

NOTES ON QUALITATIVE METHODOLOGY

When I started this project, I had little experience conducting in-depth interviews. Earlier, for my PhD dissertation, I had designed focus group interviews to learn about the experiences of internal migrants in Thailand. I imagined that the issues I encountered in Thailand—recruiting and training local student interviewers; arranging the logistics of focus groups; finding respondents, and gaining their trust; all in an international setting—had prepared me well for fieldwork in Mexico.

But, I ran into many unfamiliar questions while in the field in Mexico. How do you recruit respondents, like undocumented migrants, who have legitimate reasons to suspect a researcher from the United States asking about their migration histories? How do you ask respondents about their family members abroad, when such information is routinely used to extort money in fake kidnapping schemes? How do you ensure the safety of your research team when searching for respondents in a crime-ridden area? These questions required fashioning ad hoc solutions. I often turned to colleagues, or the methodological appendixes in some of my favorite academic books (for example, *Black Identities* by Mary Waters) for practical advice that I could not find in more abstract texts on qualitative research methods.

I first needed to select the study site. I had analyzed the survey data from the Mexican Migration Project, and identified four types of migrants from Mexico to the United States. (I called these types circular, crisis, family, and urban migrants, respectively.) For qualitative fieldwork, I decided to select communities from the MMP. Each community would contain a clear majority of one of the four migrant types. By comparing the responses across communities, I would be able to see if migrant types varied in their stated motivations underlying migration.

To tap the full range of migrant experiences, I considered additional criteria for community selection. I wanted the selected communities to belong to different geographic regions, and also, to different historical regions of Mexico-U.S. migration identified by Jorge Durand and his colleagues. It was not too long before I realized how difficult—and how pointless—it was to try to optimize all these criteria at the same time. The quantitative sociologist in me wanted to have "representative" data, but I would never have enough cases to make meaningful comparisons across geographic or historical dimensions, let alone claim representativeness on a single dimension.

I decided to focus on the first criterion alone, and even that presented its own difficulties. The MMP had surveyed 143 communities. For each migrant type, I decided to select the community where that migrant type had the highest concentration. I ended up with four communities located in four different states. The farthest two were more than 450 miles apart. I was prepared to undertake the cost and other logistical difficulties of traveling across Mexico, but several colleagues pointed to a far more serious concern: safety. The crime rates were on the rise in Mexico, with drug cartels fighting for control in many regions.

While considering alternative options, in May 2011, I found out that I was pregnant with twins. This happy news presented new constraints—and a really strict deadline—for fieldwork. I was teaching in the fall, which meant I had to finish the fieldwork in the summer of 2011. I immediately applied for funding and also received approval from Harvard's Institutional Review Board. Given the short timeframe, I needed to recruit a large team of interviewers to complete the fieldwork. I contacted Doug Massey and Jorge Durand, the two directors of the MMP team, to see if they could help me recruit Mexican students. They generously offered to "lend" me the MMP team, six research assistants from the University of Guadalajara with extensive field experience.

Doug and Jorge also suggested that I constrain my fieldwork to the state of Jalisco, specifically the region surrounding Guadalajara, where they could handpick communities to ensure safety. Guadalajara, once protected from the illegal drug trade as the home to cartel leaders' families, had lost this status in 2010 with the rise of the Zetas, a breakaway criminal organization formed by ex-military members.

This suggestion sent me back to the drawing board. I came up with a list of twelve candidate communities in Jalisco, three communities for each migrant type. Jorge then reduced the list to four communities, one for each migrant type. I was quite uncertain about this process at this point: I was concerned about my own, and my team's, safety, of course, but I was also hesitant to give up the scientific purity of the site selection. My dilemma reached a swift resolution when Jorge told me that one of the communities in the original list was then the most dangerous place in Jalisco. I decided that safety had to be the first priority here.

This choice had implications for what I could learn from the data. Not all the selected communities contained a clear majority of a given migrant type. Only 40% of the migrants in the first community, for example, were circular migrants, according to my analysis of the MMP data. This rate was one of the highest rates across all communities in Jalisco, but it was not high enough to make the group the majority in that community. (Urban migrants were the majority.) This meant that I could no longer use community membership as a rough proxy for the observed migrant type. Neither could I compare communities, which would have automatically attributed the variation in responses to that in migrant types. But, I could use the variation in the community context, and evaluate its impact on individuals' motivations to migrate. I decided to aim for 30 interviews in each community, 120 in total, to have meaningful comparisons across communities.

After reorienting the project, I focused on organizing and training the research team. The task, initially, was quite easy. The MMP team already had an established leader, Karina, who took care of the logistics, distributed tasks, and checked the collected data for consistency. Before I set out for Mexico, I had several meetings with Karina via Skype and mapped out a detailed plan. We decided on how much to pay the research assistants (midway between what an RA would receive in Mexico versus in the United States), how to pay them (in cash), how to travel (rent a van for several weeks), and where to stay (in a hotel or a rented cabin).

Working with a local research team was my plan from the beginning. I spoke some French and Italian but was only a beginner in Spanish and could not do the interviews myself. This situation was not ideal. I worried that I would have little control over the flow of each interview. I would also miss some of the subtleties in the responses because I was not fluent in Spanish. I tried to overcome these issues in two ways. First, I traveled with a research assistant, and a dear friend, Patricia, who is a native Spanish speaker. Every evening, Patricia would listen to all the interviews conducted that day, and translate them for me. This way I could follow what was going on in the field, and offer suggestions for the next day's work. Second, after the interviews were transcribed and translated, I worked with two bilingual research assistants at Harvard, who checked the accuracy of the translations and included clarifying descriptions in parentheses, which helped me better grasp the subtle meanings that could otherwise be lost in translation.

In other ways, however, it was advantageous to work with a team of interviewers. First, the team members were all from Guadalajara; they easily gained entrée into the communities and established rapport with migrant families. Second, the team contained five interviewers and one supervisor, and thus was able to complete a large number of interviews, 123 in total, in just a month.

Our first team meeting took place in July 2011 at the University of Guadalajara. By that time, I had come to know the team supervisor, Karina, really well. But, I was meeting the rest of the team—Anabel, Bárbara, Gabriela, Leo, and Yonathan—for the first time. I knew they all spoke some

English but was surprised to see that they were reluctant to address me directly. Karina and Patricia both acted as translators, explaining my instructions to students, and translating their questions back to me. This state of affairs lasted for a few days until I started practicing my broken Spanish. I kept asking them about Spanish words, or colloquial ways of saying things, and this amused everyone. One specific sentence I learned, which later became a good joke, was to end every other sentence with "porque estoy embarazada con gemelos" (because I am pregnant with twins). I made a fool of myself at most times, but this seemed to relax the students, and it gave them courage to talk to me in English. They also became more at ease in voicing their questions or concerns about the interviews to me.

One issue that lingered throughout the fieldwork was how to train the research team in qualitative research methods. The team collectively had years of experience in surveying migrant communities. They knew how to approach potential respondents, how to explain the project, and how to gain their cooperation. But, they were also too immersed in the MMP survey methodology. This meant that they were used to asking many questions quickly, and encouraging short responses. I wanted them to shed these old habits. Before going off to the field, we had a daylong workshop on qualitative methods, specifically, on in-depth interviewing techniques. We went over my interview schedule (included at the end of this appendix), and discussed each question, and its purpose, at length. I explained to them that the questions were mere guidelines; our goal was not to ask each and every one of them, but to sustain a natural conversation around certain themes and to let the respondents tell their stories. The students were excited about this idea. They told me that they had encountered many respondents who wanted to talk more when administering the MMP but had to cut them short to follow the survey script exactly. It would be a nice change to hear them out.

This initial enthusiasm, however, did not automatically translate into the long and detailed interviews I was hoping for. In fact, the first few interviews completed did not last more than a half hour. We soon identified some structural obstacles that prevented respondents from talking to us longer. For example, we were visiting most homes in the morning, when women were cooking or taking care of their children. They did not have enough time to talk to us then. We were also asking that the respondents be alone, which, in many cases, was not possible due to cohabiting relatives or visiting neighbors. We fixed our protocol after a few days in the field. We made appointments with respondents, and agreed to come at the time that suited them best. We also allowed for others to be present during the interview. Despite these adjustments, many of the interviews were still short in duration (about 20 minutes). But one of the students, Gabriela, turned out to be a natural in fieldwork; her interviews were consistently long, and full of vivid details. Many of the stories I have used throughout the book come from her interviews.

Of the four communities we visited, three were small rural towns and one was a neighborhood in the city of Guadalajara. In rural towns, we first found the village headman (*comisario ejidal*) and presented them with an official letter from the University of Guadalajara that explained the purpose of our project. We also showed our identity cards, which showed the logo of the university and the MMP project. These documents seemed to help the headmen (and later the respondents) to make sense of our project.

Finding and recruiting migrants was not always easy. Our first community was the urban neighborhood, and there, we relied on the personal connections of Leo, a team member who happened to live there. Because the neighborhood was not very safe, we parked our car in front of the home of Leo's aunt, who kept an eye on it throughout the day. She also kindly allowed us to rest in her house. Leo directed us to the "safer" streets. Six students then split into pairs to ensure safety, and started knocking on doors to look for migrants or family members of migrants who could report on them.

We followed the same strategy in rural communities, where people seemed to be less busy and more eager to talk to our team. We noticed early on in the fieldwork that it was hard to find male respondents, who often worked during the day. To get around this issue, we made appointments with the wives to talk to the men in the evening, or turned up around lunchtime, when men were likely to return home to eat. We also spotted and interviewed migrant men in public spaces, like restaurants or parks. The team members were actually quite good at guessing if a person was a U.S. migrant from his or her clothing (Puma shoes were a big giveaway, for example). We were careful on such occasions to find a private space to interview the respondent so he or she could talk to us without being overheard or interrupted. A number of people we approached refused to talk to us, either because they did not have the time, or because they were reluctant to provide any information about family members, which—they thought—could be used in an extortion scheme later on. (Many people recounted stories where someone they knew had received a phone call from a stranger claiming to hold a family member hostage and asking for a ransom.)

In two communities, we talked to the priests, a brilliant idea suggested to me by Jackie Hagan. These interviews turned out to be very helpful; the two priests not only knew all the migrants in their communities, but both of them had actually lived and worked in other communities as well, so were able to draw interesting comparisons among migrants across places and over time.

There was only one major unfortunate event during our fieldwork, which happened on the last day (the only day I was not on the site to supervise the students). Gabriela, one of the students on the team, was interviewing a former migrant (and a self-confessed drug addict) on a street corner when a pickup truck pulled up after circling around them a few times. The driver forced Gabriela into the car, and asked her to explain what she was doing. (Our best guess is that he was a drug dealer concerned about us interviewing one of his clients.) Confused by her explanation, the man asked Gabriela to interview him, to which Gabriela obliged. When the man caught Gabriela eyeing a patrolling police car, he apparently said, "Don't worry—it won't stop. They owe me." Gabriela managed to remain calm, continue with the interview, and conceal the fear stirring inside her, she told me. In the end, the man let her go. But the incident affected me deeply. If this had happened on any other day than our last, I would probably have stopped the fieldwork to protect everyone, or at least moved on to a different community.

Another event, though much less remarkable, involved having my debit card information stolen. I had brought some cash with me to Mexico and wired some additional funds to Karina for fieldwork expenses. But I still had to use an ATM machine a few times in Mexico. I was careful to go to actual bank branches per Karina's recommendation. But, somehow, my debit card still must have gotten copied somewhere, as I found nearly $8,000 missing from my personal account upon my return to Boston. (Thankfully, my bank reimbursed me.)

The fieldwork went on for a while after I returned. I asked Gabriela, our best interviewer, to continue the interviews as her time allowed. (She had started working for a government agency then but still agreed to do the interviews on the weekends.) Per our IRB protocol, we had not collected any names or addresses to preserve the anonymity of our respondents. (The protocol did allow us to take photos of consenting respondents, however.) But Gabriela, having done the interviews herself, was able to visit two of our original respondents later on in order to ask more questions. She had established great rapport with them, and they were happy to continue the conversation, she told me. Per my request, Gabriela also completed 16 new interviews on her own during the summer of 2012. These interviews covered families that had no U.S. migrants, a subpopulation that was missing from our initial fieldwork.

I would not consider myself a qualitative researcher, but I was still very much compelled to go to Mexico. I had to see migrants and their lives for myself, at the very least. Going there and listening to migrants' stories, as they told them, gave me confidence to write about them and their lives in this book. But for a long time, I could not quite figure out how I would use the interviews and stories I had collected. The combination presented in this book came after many trials and errors.

I first decided to transcribe and code all the interviews with qualitative data analysis software (Atlas.ti). Two wonderful students at Harvard, Yvette Ramirez and Asad Asad, took on the arduous task of identifying common themes with me, and systematically coding the data for those themes. We analyzed the codes over and over, tried to establish connections between different themes, and so on. This practice was helpful in identifying common patterns, for example, how do most migrants cross the border? Or how do most people think about male migration versus female migration? Parsing the data this way appealed to the quantitative scholar in me. I could reduce almost everything to numbers.

But then I realized that I could use the data in a completely different way. To me, the most interesting aspect of the interviews was hearing people's stories in their entirety and in their own words. What does a person's life look like before migration? How does that person come to migrate? What happens to their family, and to the migrant's life, afterward? I started to read, re-read, and summarize these life histories. In so doing, I became intimately familiar with each of the respondents. I put myself in their shoes, so to speak. I decided to use their stories to allow other people to do the same, to understand what migrants are sacrificing by coming to the United States, what they are gaining, and how they are feeling about all of this. I wanted the readers to learn exactly what I had learned by doing the interviews. This reasoning led to the patchwork you see in the book: detailed individual stories in combination with general patterns from multiple stories obtained through a painstaking coding of the data.

There are a few lessons from this fieldwork that I will take with me into my next project. First, local information and support is crucial when working in a potentially dangerous setting. Second, the initial plan for a research project is not an immutable imprint for how the research should proceed. Initially, I had planned to select communities a certain way, but when that turned out to be infeasible, I did not hesitate to change the plan. I also had intended to use the data in a specific manner, but in the end, took a diversion. Third, it is fine to be ambivalent about the data and analysis even well into the project. We are accustomed to reading a certain kind of narrative in both qualitative and quantitative work that suggests a linear and direct relationship between research question, design, and execution. But in reality, we, as researchers, often snake through several options, hit dead ends, and restart several times. This happened many times in writing this book. And each time, I was relieved to read work that truthfully described the research process (like that of Stanley Lieberson, Mario Small, and Mary Waters). I hope I have provided a similarly honest account.

INTERVIEW GUIDE
A. FAMILY BACKGROUND

I am going to start with some questions about you and your family.

1. Please tell me a little about yourself. Where were you born? How long have you lived in this town?
2. Are you currently married?
   [IF YES] How old were you when you first married? What does your husband/wife do for work? Is he or she a U.S. migrant?
3. Do you have children?
   [IF YES] Please tell me about your children—how old are they, where do they live, what do they do for a living, and how much education do they have?
4. How old are you now? How old were you when you first migrated to the United States? What year was that? Did you have a family then? Who did you live with?

B. MIGRATION HISTORY

Now, I am going to ask some questions about your migration history.

5. Why did you decide to migrate to the United States? Why at that particular time? What was your goal on your first trip? Did you achieve that goal? When? Did your goals change as you continued to migrate?
6. Did your family members help you in making the decision to migrate? Did anyone support your decision? Did anyone object to it? What was their reaction?
7. On your first trip to the United States, did you go alone or with your family? Who did you go with?
8. What was your education—the highest level of school that you completed when you first migrated? Was that an important factor in your decision to migrate? Why? Would you migrate if you were more or less educated?
9. Did you work in your hometown before you went to the United States? Please tell me a little about your job then. About how much did you earn? Was that enough to cover your family's expenses? Was your pay here a factor in deciding to migrate? Would you still migrate if you had a better-paying job in Mexico?
10. What were the other members of your family doing at the time of your first trip? Did your family own a house? Did your family have any land or a business at the time?

[IF YES] Were you able to make enough money from your land or business? Did you need extra money at the time for the land or business? Who took care of the land or business when you were away?

[IF NO] Would you migrate if your family owned some land or a business?

11. Did your family have any debt around the time of your first trip? How much? Was that a factor in your decision to migrate? Would you migrate if you did not owe any money?

12. Was there an important event around the time of your first trip? For example, did someone in your family lose his or her job, have an accident, or fall ill?

[IF YES] Was this event important in your decision to migrate?

13. Did you consider going to another city in Mexico or to another country— maybe Canada, Spain, or somewhere else?

[IF YES] Why did you choose to go to the United States?

14. Were you the first one to migrate to the United States in your family?

[IF NO] Who had migrated before you in your family? Were they U.S. citizens at the time?

[IF THERE ARE OTHER MIGRANTS FROM THE HOUSEHOLD] Would you migrate if your family members were not already in the United States?

15. Had any of your friends or anyone from your hometown migrated to the United States before you? Did you know about their experiences? What was it like for their families here in Mexico? How did that affect your decision to migrate? Would you still migrate if you did not know about their experiences?

16. What was it like in your hometown before you went to the United States? Were there enough jobs? How did most people earn their living? Were there many U.S. migrants? Why do you think that was the case?

17. What was it like in Mexico then? How was the economy compared to today? Do you think the conditions in Mexico encouraged people to migrate?

C. First Trip to the United States

I will now ask you some questions about your first trip in the United States.

18. On your first trip, was it difficult to cross the border? Did anyone help you? Did you have to pay a *coyote* (smuggler) or anyone else? Did your family help with that payment? Did an employer or a friend give or promise you papers?

19. Where did you go in the United States? How did you select that location? Did you consider another city or place in the United States— [DEPENDING ON RESPONDENT'S ANSWER] maybe Texas, Florida, Los Angeles, New York, or Chicago?

20. How long did you stay in the United States on your first trip? Why? Where did you live? Did you live alone or with family, friends, or others from your hometown?

21. What was your first job in the United States? How did you get the job? How did you first hear about this job? Was it through a friend, a relative, a want ad, an employment agency, or what? What did they do to help you get it?

22. About how much did you earn at this job? Was it enough to cover your bills?

D. Remittance Behavior

23. On your first trip, did you send any money back home? Why? Did your family expect you to send?

[ASK REMITTERS ONLY]

24. How much did you send on your first trip? To whom? Why that person? How about the trips after the first?

25. Did you know you were going to send money home when you first migrated? When did you start sending? How did you decide?

26. Were there any families that were receiving remittances in your hometown before your first trip? Do you know how much?
      [IF YES] How do you know? How many families were receiving remittances? Was that an important factor in your decision to migrate? Would you still migrate if you did not know of those families?

27. Were your Mexican friends in the United States sending money to their families? How about your relatives in the United States—were they sending money? Do you know how much?
      [IF YES] How do you know? Did that encourage you? Would you still send money if your friends were not sending?
      [IF NO] Why were you sending?

28. How did your family members use the money you sent? Were you able to buy any land or a business in your hometown? Were you saving up to buy anything?

29. Was there a time when you had to stop sending money? What happened?
      [IF NO] What do you think would happen if you stopped sending money? How would your family react?

30. Was there a time when you had to send more money than usual—maybe because your family in Mexico was having a difficult time? What happened?

31. Were you ever without a job in the United States?
      [IF YES] How did you get by? Who helped you?

[IF NO] What do you think would happen if you suddenly lost your job in the United States? Who would help you? How?

32. Who took care of the household when you were away in the United States?

    [IF APPLICABLE] Who took care of your children or your parents?

33. What was it like to be living far away from your family? Did you talk or write to them while you were in the United States? How often?

E. Overall Experience in the United States

I will ask a few questions about your overall experience in the United States.

34. How many times have you been back to the United States since your first trip? How did you get back and forth on these trips?

35. Have you taken any friends or family members with you on any of those trips? Who were they? When did you take them? What did they do for a living in the United States?

36. Are you planning to go back to the United States?

    [IF YES] How long do you intend to stay there? Do you have any family members in the United States? Are you planning to take any family members with you?

37. Have you become a citizen of the United States?

    [IF YES] How did that happen?

    [IF NO] Do you think you will some day?

    Trying to find out legal status, based on information voluntarily offered:
        U.S. citizen
        Legal permanent resident
        Non-immigrant visa holder (e.g., H2)
        Legalized SAW (seasonal agricultural worker—1986 IRCA)
        Unauthorized immigrant

38. How well would you say you speak English—very well, well, okay, not well, or not at all? Would you like to speak English, or speak English better? Have you tried to learn more English?

F. Comparative Questions about Migration

Now I am going to ask you to compare your migration experience with the experience of other (younger or older) migrants.

39. [FOR OLDER MIGRANTS] Do you think the migrants at your time (when you first started to migrate) are different from the migrants today?

How? For example, are they more or less educated? Are they richer or poorer? Do they work in different kinds of occupations? Do they come from different kinds of communities? Do they have different goals? Why?

40. [FOR YOUNGER MIGRANTS] Do you think the migrants today are different from the migrants of ten or twenty years ago? How? For example, are they more or less educated? Are they richer or poorer? Do they work in different kinds of occupations? Do they come from different kinds of communities? Why?

Appendix D

CLUSTER ANALYSIS

———————————

There are several steps involved in cluster analysis. The first step, as described in the text, is choosing the attributes for partitioning the data. The second step is scaling the attributes. I chose to dichotomize the nonbinary attributes, converting values above the median to 1 and those below it to 0. This strategy standardizes the range of attributes and has shown superior performance in prior studies compared to other scaling methods that standardize the variance of attributes. Similar to past work, I found that the attributes standardized to the same scale (but not the same variance) led to the most well-separated and substantively meaningful clustering solution in the MMP data.

It might be worthwhile to make a side point here. In classical statistical estimation, converting continuous variables to binary attributes would lead to severe information loss. In cluster analysis, this approach is not only acceptable, but it is frequently used to de-noise high variance variables. More generally, because the goal in statistical estimation is to estimate or confirm a given quantity (e.g., a parameter), tuning data or methods to produce a result would lead to bias. By contrast, the goal in cluster analysis is to create categories that reveal new information; tuning data or methods until we learn something useful is therefore perfectly reasonable.

The third step in cluster analysis involves choosing an algorithm. I used the Matlab implementation of the K-means algorithm, a generic method that makes no assumptions about the data structure. Alternative methods typically assume a hierarchical clustering structure or rely on a probabilistic model of the data. The former (hierarchical) approach is useful if such a structure is substantively expected (e.g., evolutionary trees in biology), which is not the case in this study. The latter (model-based) approach is advantageous if the data conform to a probabilistic model and has proven useful in low-dimensional data sets. Yet, in my experience, the available software implementations of the model-based approach have poor performance with large and high-dimensional data sets like the MMP. Also, the K-means algorithm is equivalent to the model-based approach for certain probabilistic models of the data.

K-means algorithm iterates between computing K cluster centroids by minimizing the within-cluster variance and updating cluster memberships. Like all clustering algorithms, K-means relies on a measure of similarity, or dissimilarity, to assess how "close" cases are to one another in the attribute space. The fourth step in cluster analysis involves choosing this measure, which is typically far more consequential for discovering the clustering structure in data than specifying the algorithm itself. Although there are no generic guidelines, researchers typically base their decisions on the nature of the data and the substance of the question.

I used the city block distance to assess how close migrants are in various demographic, economic, and social attributes. This measure aptly deals with binary data and reflects our substantive preference to treat two individuals who share a trait (e.g., low education) as equally similar to one another as two individuals who both lack the trait. For every pair of individuals i and j, the city block distance, d_{ij}, is the sum of the absolute differences in the values x_{il} and x_{jl} of each attribute $l = 1, \ldots, p$,

$$d_{ij} = \left(\sum_{l=1}^{p} \left| x_{il} - x_{jl} \right| \right) (1)$$

The fifth, and final, step in clustering is determining the number of clusters in the data. The K-means method requires the researcher to supply that number, or K, to the algorithm. By construction, this algorithm locates K clusters even when no such structure exists in the data. To avoid obtaining artificial partitions, researchers use cluster validation measures to choose the optimal number of clusters. This process is similar to model selection in regression analysis, where researchers use the likelihood ratio, or another criterion, to select the best and most parsimonious model for the data.

I used eight different cluster validation measures to estimate the number of clusters in the MMP data (see figures D.1 and D.2). In six of these measures, the four-cluster solution emerges as the optimal choice, and in the remaining two, a reasonable option given a preference for parsimony.

The four panels in figure D.1 present four cluster-validation measures plotted against the number of clusters ranging from two to six. All measures are implemented in the *clValid* and *fpc* packages in R software. The *Goodman-Kruskal Gamma* compares each within-cluster distance to each between-cluster distance. A pair of distances are concordant (discordant) if the within distance is smaller than (greater than) the between distance.

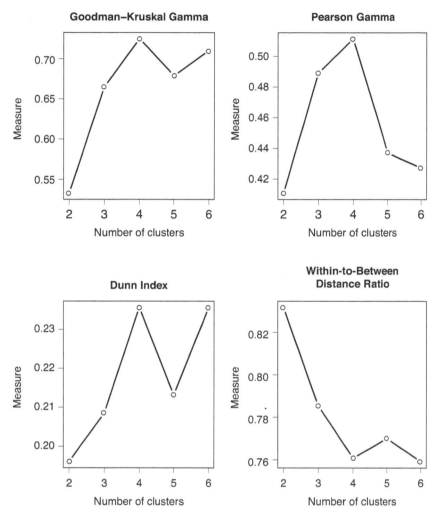

FIGURE D.1. Cluster validation measures

The index equals the proportion of net concordant pairs (i.e., the total concordant minus discordant) in all pairs. The *Pearson Gamma* evaluates the normalized congruence between two clustering partitions as a function of positive and negative agreements in pairwise cluster assignments. The *Dunn Index* is the ratio of the smallest distance between individuals in different clusters to the largest distance between individuals in the same cluster. *Within-to-between distance ratio* simply takes the ratio of the average intra-cluster distance to the average distance between clusters.

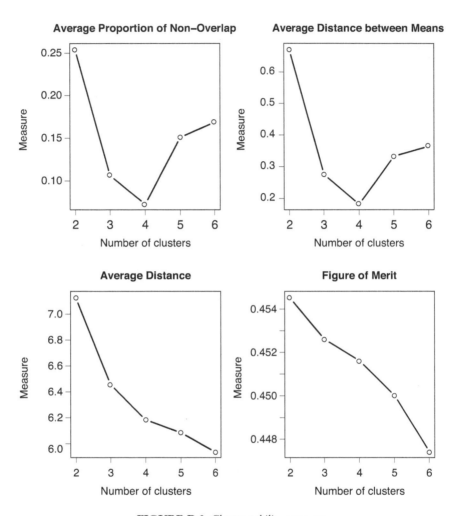

FIGURE D.2. Cluster stability measures

For the *Goodman-Kruskal Gamma* and the *Pearson Gamma* in the upper panels, and the *Dunn Index* in the lower left-hand panel, higher values indicate higher cluster quality. For the *within-to-between distance ratio* in the lower right-hand panel, lower values indicate higher cluster quality. All four measures obtain their optimal value for the four-cluster solution. For the two measures in the lower panels, the six-cluster solution yields the exact same value as the four-cluster solution.

Four additional measures, plotted against the number of clusters in figure D.2, capture the "stability" of clusters to changes in the attribute space.

Each measure compares the clustering based on the full data and clustering based on the data with one attribute removed. The *average proportion of non-overlap* computes the average proportion of observations not placed in the same cluster under both cases. The *average distance between means* measures the average distance between cluster centers for observations placed in the same cluster under both cases. The *average distance* computes the average distance between individuals who end up in the same cluster in both cases. The *figure of merit* measures the average variance in the removed attribute among individuals in the same cluster, when clustering is done with the remaining attributes.

For all four measures, lower values indicate a more stable clustering solution. For the *average proportion of non-overlap* and the *average distance between means* measures in the upper panel, the four-cluster solution yields the best score. For the *average distance* in the lower left, the six-cluster solution gives the best score, but the four-cluster solution is a close contender corresponding to an "elbow" where the index value decreases steeply beforehand but only gradually thereafter. For the *figure of merit* measure in the lower right, the six-cluster solution seems optimal.

Based on these results, and a preference for parsimony, I chose the four-cluster solution, which is optimum for six measures and reasonable for the remaining two. This broad agreement across various measures is actually rare in clustering applications and increases my confidence in the internal validity of the results.

Appendix E

TRENDS IN THE SHARE OF MIGRANTS
ACROSS THE FOUR CLUSTERS

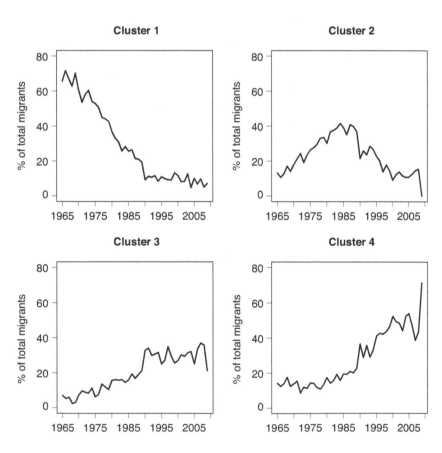

FIGURE E.1. Trends in the number of migrants (as a share of total migrants) across the four clusters

Appendix F

MICRO-LEVEL DETERMINANTS
OF MEXICO-U.S. MIGRATION

I used a statistical model to compare the determinants of migration be-havior in the overall sample, as well as in select samples that include non-migrants and each migrant cluster separately. I coded migration behavior on a binary scale (0 or 1) that indicates if a person makes his or her first U.S. trip in a given year. I then used a logistic regression model to relate this outcome to all individual, household, and community indicators used in discovering the four clusters in the first chapter, adding state and year indicators to account for possible regional or temporal variation in migra-tion behavior. I included in the overall sample all individuals in the MMP data (145,276 persons) observed annually from age 15 onward. I observed migrants (19,243 persons) through the year of their first U.S. trip and non-migrants (126,033) through the year of the survey.

This analysis was important to see if the attributes I used in identifying the four migrant clusters in the first chapter truly matter for migration be-havior. Imagine a hypothetical scenario: Each of 19,243 first-time migrants in our data has a twin, identical in all personal attributes but different in migration behavior. The four clusters among migrants, in other words, would be replicated exactly among non-migrants. These clusters would say nothing about migration behavior. In that case, the estimates in table F.1 would suggest no association between the selected attributes and the prob-ability of taking a first trip.

The reality, however, is far from this hypothetical case. Most of the indicators are associated significantly (at the 95% confidence level) with the probability of migrating. Table F.1 presents the coefficient estimates for the full sample (column 1) and samples including each migrant cluster separately (columns 2–5). Figure F.1 displays the same estimates for select indicators in a dot plot for ease of comparison. The y-axes show the names

TABLE F.1. ESTIMATES FROM LOGISTIC REGRESSION MODELS OF FIRST U.S. MIGRATION ON SAMPLES INCLUDING THE FOUR MIGRANT CLUSTERS IN THE MMP DATA (1965–2010)

Variable	MODEL 0	MODEL 1	MODEL 2	MODEL 3	MODEL 4
Sample includes non-migrants and . . .	All migrants	Cluster 1 migrants	Cluster 2 migrants	Cluster 3 migrants	Cluster 4 migrants
Age	−0.068** (0.001)	−0.051** (0.001)	−0.191** (0.003)	−0.018** (0.001)	−0.074** (0.002)
Male	1.007** (0.015)	1.587** (0.037)	1.554** (0.034)	−0.494** (0.033)	1.474** (0.036)
Years of education	−0.010** (0.002)	−0.109** (0.004)	−0.009* (0.004)	−0.011* (0.005)	0.078** (0.003)
Number of rooms owned	−0.030** (0.002)	−0.262** (0.009)	0.031** (0.004)	0.007 (0.004)	−0.024** (0.005)
Value of land owned (in log)	−0.003 (0.002)	−0.031** (0.004)	0.016** (0.003)	0.007* (0.004)	0.000 (0.004)
Number of businesses owned	−0.087** (0.017)	−0.276** (0.051)	0.001 (0.031)	−0.011 (0.035)	−0.172** (0.035)
Migrated in Mexico?	0.404** (0.023)	0.679** (0.035)	−0.387** (0.090)	−0.159 (0.089)	0.422** (0.050)
Number of U.S. migrants in household	0.274** (0.004)	0.272** (0.007)	0.228** (0.006)	0.265** (0.005)	0.345** (0.007)

	(1)	(2)	(3)	(4)	(5)
Proportion of U.S. migrants in community	0.685**	-0.927**	2.266**	1.841**	-1.895**
	(0.057)	(0.136)	(0.090)	(0.104)	(0.247)
Proportion of labor force in agriculture in community	1.136**	2.289**	2.623**	0.331	-0.115
	(0.074)	(0.134)	(0.163)	(0.202)	(0.186)
Proportion of labor force earning less than minimum wage in community	-0.019	0.609**	1.476**	-1.956**	-1.369**
	(0.075)	(0.135)	(0.159)	(0.200)	(0.183)
Metropolitan area (0/1)	0.008	-0.148**	-0.298**	-0.273**	0.735**
	(0.017)	(0.036)	(0.039)	(0.046)	(0.039)
Historic migration region (0/1)	0.837**	1.335**	2.150**	1.341**	-1.451**
	(0.061)	(0.123)	(0.165)	(0.222)	(0.148)
Border region (0/1)	0.229**	0.560**	1.498**	0.028	-0.774**
	(0.075)	(0.137)	(0.184)	(0.287)	(0.165)
Central region (0/1)	0.579**	0.289	-0.347	-0.113	0.484**
	(0.067)	(0.172)	(0.342)	(0.258)	(0.092)
State and year dummies included?	yes	yes	yes	yes	yes
Pseudo-R^2	0.104	0.161	0.260	0.118	0.148
N (person-years)	2,069,778	2,008,342	1,953,740	2,054,451	2,055,527

*$p<0.05$, **$p<0.01$ (two-tailed tests). Results are logit coefficients. Standard errors, in parentheses, are corrected for clustering at the individual level. Region definitions are based on Durand and Massey's (2003) classification; the reference regions are the Central-South and Southeastern.

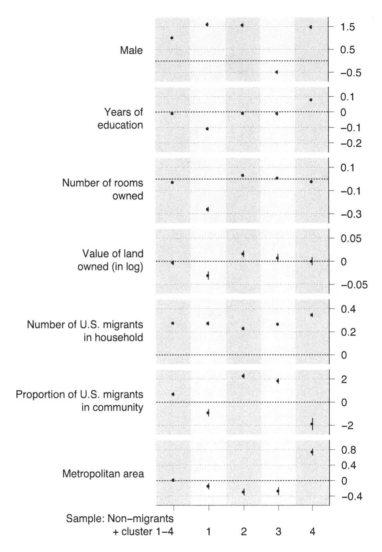

FIGURE F.1. The coefficient estimates from a logistic regression model of first U.S. migration on the MMP samples including non-migrants and migrants in each of the four clusters of indicators (left) and the range of estimates (right). A dashed line marks zero for each indicator. The dots represent the point estimates and the vertical lines, the 95% confidence intervals.

In the full sample (first column), individuals are significantly more likely to become a migrant if they are male; uneducated; poor in properties or business; and if they live in households or communities with prior U.S.

migrants. The relationships are similar, but stronger, in the sample including non-migrants and cluster 1 migrants only (second column). All of the estimates (except for age) here are significantly larger (at the 95% confidence level) in absolute size compared to those in the full sample. (Comparisons are based on seemingly unrelated regression with a linear probability model of migration in alternative samples.)

The same indicators, however, have different effects in the remaining three samples. These changes are apparent in figure F.1, where the dots indicating the coefficient estimates jump around across the five samples for each indicator. Individuals are more likely to become a cluster 2 migrant (third column), for example, if they own properties, the opposite pattern of cluster 1 migrants. Individuals are more likely to join the cluster 3 stream (fourth column) if they are female, and the cluster 4 stream (fifth column) if they are educated and live in a metropolitan area.

These patterns here are consistent with the earlier descriptions of migrant groups in chapter 1. The patterns, however, are also novel in establishing one crucial point: the attributes that distinguish each migrant group from other migrants (for example, property ownership for cluster 2 or urban origin for cluster 4) also distinguish that group from the non-migrants. This result confirms that the attributes I used for identifying different migrant groups indeed have significant associations to migration behavior. The fact that these associations vary across groups means that there might be diverse mechanisms shaping the migration behavior of each group.

Conventional analyses that pool all migrants together are bound to overlook this diversity. Take, for example, the opposing effects of land ownership on cluster 1 (negative) and cluster 2 (positive) shown in the second and third columns of table F.1, respectively. These effects offset one another in the full sample (first column), yielding an insignificant coefficient. Similarly, the differential effects of gender or education for each group disappear in the full sample, where the coefficients simply reflect average effects based on the relative group sizes.

Appendix G

MACRO-LEVEL DETERMINANTS
OF MEXICO-U.S. MIGRATION

Many studies in economics connect migration flows to regional differences in wages and employment rates. The intuition comes from neoclassical economics: Migrants are expected to flow from low-wage countries, like Mexico, where labor is plentiful but capital is relatively limited, to high-wage destinations, like the United States, where labor is scarce but capital is abundant. Empirical findings support many of these predictions. Scholars show, for example, migration rates between Mexico and the United States respond to relative wage and employment figures in the two countries.

An alternative view links migration flows to a dearth of credit and insurance markets in developing countries. This so-called new economics theory suggests households send migrants not only to access credit (a prediction consistent with the neoclassical theory), but also to insure against the risks to their earnings in origin. Empirical work provides supporting evidence: Migration rates to the United States are higher during times of economic volatility or credit shortage in Mexico.

The segmented labor market theory suggests migration flows are driven by persistent labor demand in destination, where certain jobs—once occupied by migrants—obtain a negative stigma and become unappealing to native workers. Research shows Mexican migration rates increase during periods of employment growth in the United States, a prediction consistent with this hypothesis (as well as the neoclassical theory).

The world systems theory proposes the grandest vision of migration flows as a result of capitalist penetration from core (the United States, here) to periphery countries. The theory implies that increasing economic integration between Mexico and the United States facilitates migration flows between the two countries by, for example, disturbing the local production in the former, and creating a mobile population that is already familiar with the institutions of the latter. Studies find support for these claims: Migration propensities increase as the foreign direct investment in Mexico grows and as the volume of trade between Mexico and the United States expands.

Researchers supplement these theory-driven observations with others based on demographic trends. Studies show that migration flows respond to changes in fertility rates or labor supply in Mexico. Migration to the United States slows down as family sizes contract in Mexico or when the share of young population declines.

Studies highlight the fluctuations in crime rates in Mexico as a potential determinant of migration flows to the United States. Studies also point to immigration policy in the United States, which can encourage more migration by allowing for family reunification, as after the Immigration Reform and Control Act in 1986, or discourage it via increasing border enforcement. The fact that immigration policy elicits these responses is sometimes taken as evidence for neoclassical theory, which, in its micro-level formulation, specifies migration as an individual choice based on cost-benefit analysis. Stricter immigration policy, according to this model, reduces migration by increasing its costs to individuals.

This gives a fairly long list of potentially important factors in Mexico—U.S. migration. My analysis included indicators for most: (a) average wages for low-skill production workers in the United States, (b) GDP per capita in Mexico, and (c) unemployment rates in Mexico and the United States, to test the key predictions of neoclassical theory; (d) inflation rate in Mexico to capture the responses to risk implied by new economics theory; (e) employment growth in the United States in specific industries where migrants are disproportionately employed (e.g., construction) for the segmented labor market hypothesis; (f) the value of U.S. exports to Mexico to consider the world systems idea; (g) birth rates lagged by 20 years to account for the shifts in labor supply; (h) the U.S. Border Patrol Enforcement budget, and (i) the number of U.S. permanent residencies given to Mexicans to control for the policy context. For parsimony, I excluded some other plausible measures that are highly correlated with those included or measures that are not available for the entire time period.

I started with a simple aggregate model that relates the annual number of first-time migrants (per 1,000 residents) in the MMP data to various macro-level indicators in the prior year. The data cover the period from 1965 to 2010. I scaled all indicators to a mean of 0 and standard deviation of 1 so as to compare their relative effects on the migration rate.

Figure G.1 shows a dot plot with error bars to present the coefficients from ordinary least squares regression models. The outcome in the first column (M0, for model 0) is the annual number of migrants to the United States per 1,000 residents in the MMP data; the outcomes in the remaining four columns (M1–M4) are the annual number of migrants in each of the

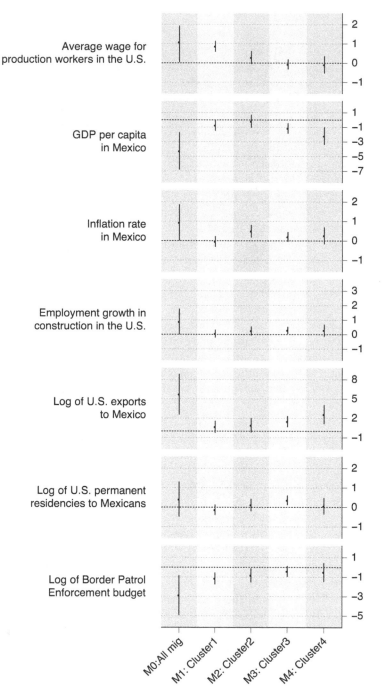

FIGURE G.1. Selected coefficient estimates from ordinary least squares regression models of annual number of first-time migrants per 1,000 residents (all and in each of the four clusters) from Mexico to the United States in the MMP data, 1965–2010

four clusters. The y-axis on the left lists the names of variables and that on the right shows the range of the coefficient estimates. The dots indicate the point estimates and the vertical lines the 95% confidence intervals. A coefficient estimate is statistically significant (that is, different from zero) if its vertical line does not cross the dashed line marking zero. The figure shows only the coefficients that were statistically significant in at least one model. The estimates for the other variables, such as unemployment rates in Mexico and the United States, the employment growth in farmwork in the United States, or the lagged birth rates in Mexico, are shown in the full regression results in table G.1.

What determines the rise and fall of migration from Mexico to the United States? The estimates in the first column of table G.1 suggest some general answers. These estimates do not establish causal effects in a statistical sense, but they do suggest strong correlations. More Mexicans migrate for the first time when the wages in the United States are higher and when the Mexican GDP per capita is lower, all else equal. The latter is more important (that is, has a larger coefficient) than the former. The economic conditions in Mexico, then, matter more for mobilizing new migrants than those in the United States. More Mexicans cross the border for the first time when the United States exports in larger volumes to Mexico, but fewer do so when it spends more on border enforcement.

Some of these patterns persist in the second column, which investigates the trends in circular migrants (cluster 1), a group that tends to be less educated and poorer than the rest of the migrants in the data. This group increases in size when the U.S. wages are higher, when the Mexican GDP per capita is lower, and when U.S. border control is weaker, all else equal. The U.S. wages seem relatively more important here (with a larger coefficient) than the Mexican GDP per capita, the opposite of the pattern for the overall migration rates in the first column.

The third column looks at the trends in crisis migrants (cluster 2), a group with mostly younger migrants from relatively wealthy households in rural Mexico. There are more migrants in this group when U.S. border control is weaker—like in the previous two models—and when the Mexican inflation rate is higher. Recall from the third chapter that this group was especially prevalent in the Mexico-U.S. migrant stream after the economic crises in 1976, 1982, and 1986 in Mexico, which led to steep increases in inflation rates.

The fourth column models the migration rates of family migrants (cluster 3), a group distinct in containing a large share of women who have ties to prior U.S. migrants. More migrants appear in this group when the Mexican GDP per capita is lower and when U.S. exports to Mexico are higher. Interestingly, migration rates of the group increase with the U.S. employment growth in construction, and also with the number of U.S. permanent

TABLE G.1. ESTIMATES FROM ORDINARY LEAST SQUARES REGRESSION MODELS OF ANNUAL NUMBER OF FIRST-TIME MIGRANTS FROM MEXICO TO THE UNITED STATES IN THE MMP DATA (1965–2010)

Variable	Outcome:	MODEL 0 Total number of migrants	MODEL 1 Number of cluster 1 migrants	MODEL 2 Number of cluster 2 migrants	MODEL 3 Number of cluster 3 migrants	MODEL 4 Number of cluster 4 migrants
Average wage for production workers in the United States		0.98* (0.48)	0.86** (0.13)	0.28 (0.16)	−0.07 (0.12)	−0.09 (0.22)
GDP per capita in Mexico		−4.27** (1.28)	−0.73* (0.36)	−0.18 (0.43)	−1.16** (0.33)	−2.20** (0.58)
Unemployment rate in Mexico		−0.68 (0.71)	0.17 (0.20)	−0.02 (0.24)	−0.33 (0.18)	−0.51 (0.32)
Unemployment rate in the United States		0.17 (0.60)	−0.17 (0.17)	0.17 (0.20)	0.08 (0.15)	0.09 (0.27)
Inflation rate in Mexico		0.93 (0.46)	−0.04 (0.13)	0.49** (0.16)	0.20 (0.12)	0.27 (0.21)
Employment growth in agriculture in the United States		0.19 (0.36)	−0.01 (0.10)	0.10 (0.12)	0.13 (0.09)	−0.03 (0.17)

Employment growth in construction in the United States	0.88 (0.43)	0.06 (0.12)	0.25 (0.15)	0.29* (0.11)	0.28 (0.20)
Birth rate in Mexico lagged by 20 years	0.32 (0.82)	−0.01 (0.23)	0.53 (0.28)	0.14 (0.21)	−0.35 (0.38)
Log of U.S. exports to Mexico	5.70** (1.58)	0.68 (0.44)	0.91 (0.53)	1.51** (0.40)	2.60** (0.72)
Log of permanent residencies given to Mexican-born in the United States	0.41 (0.45)	−0.13 (0.13)	0.12 (0.15)	0.36** (0.12)	0.06 (0.21)
Log of U.S. Border Patrol Enforcement budget	−2.89** (1.02)	−1.15** (0.29)	−0.83* (0.35)	−0.41 (0.26)	−0.51 (0.47)
Intercept	8.07** (0.26)	2.31** (0.07)	1.98** (0.09)	1.59** (0.07)	2.19** (0.12)
R^2	0.70	0.95	0.84	0.84	0.74
N	45	45	45	45	45

*$p<0.05$, **$p<0.01$ (two-tailed tests). Standard errors are in parentheses. All variables are lagged by a year to avoid simultaneity with the outcome. Number of migrants is given per 1,000 residents to adjust for changing sample size over time.

residencies available to Mexicans. The former pattern suggests a move initiated by labor demand in the United States (which would attract mainly the male migrants, about 35% of the group), and the latter one facilitated by possibilities for family reunification, like for the migrants legalized after the passage of the Immigration Reform and Control Act in 1986.

The fifth, and last, column shows the estimates for the trends in urban migrants (cluster 4), a group containing relatively educated migrants from urban areas in Mexico. The size of this group declines with the Mexican GDP per capita, and increases with the value of U.S. exports to Mexico.

A comparison of the model results here shows that the same macro-level factors have varying associations to the migration rates of different groups. Such variations remain hidden in the model of aggregate migration rates (M0), where the four clusters are pooled into a single group. The estimates in that model also have wider confidence intervals, meaning that they are less precisely estimated, than those in the cluster-specific models. The share of the variance explained in the aggregate model is also lower (0.70) compared to those in the models fit separately to migration rates of the four clusters (ranging from 0.74 to 0.95).

These comparisons suggest that the four clusters capture an important source of variability in the Mexico-U.S. stream. Taking into account this variability allows us to better understand the different factors that might be related to the rise and fall of each group over time. For example, while circular, family, and urban migrants increase in size when the Mexican GDP per capita is lower, this is not the case for crisis migrants, who instead become more prevalent when the Mexican inflation rate is higher, while the other migrant groups do not.

Prior research uses such relationships to evaluate theories of migration. Were I to take this approach, I would find varying support for different theories across the four migrant clusters. The trends in circular, family, and urban migrants, for example, and their negative association to the Mexican GDP, offer support for the neoclassical model, which connects migration rates to wage differentials between origin and destination. The trend in crisis migrants—specifically, its link to Mexican inflation—provides evidence for the new economics theory, which asserts migration to be a result of economic volatility in origin. The positive correlation of the trend in family and urban migrants to the value of U.S. exports to Mexico is consistent with the world systems theory, which relates capital inflows to migration outflows.

NOTES

INTRODUCTION

Page 1 The lyrics are from a *corrido*, a Mexican ballad, attributed to Cecilio Chavez in Taylor (1935).

Page 1 The story of the **Virgin** is from Durand and Massey (1995).

Page 1 The **paintings** are shown in Durand and Massey (1995).

Page 2 Cornelius (2001) reports 499 **migrant deaths** on the Mexico-U.S. border in 2000. This number is conservative, as it includes only the deaths reported to the Mexican Consulates along the Southwest border.

Page 2 The estimate of the **Mexican-born population** in the United States is based on the Current Population Survey in March 2011, adjusted for possible migrant undercount (Passel, Cohn, and Gonzalez-Barrera 2012).

Page 2 The figures on the **share of men among Mexican migrants** are based on my computations from the Mexican Migration Project (MMP) data on successive cohorts of U.S. migrants leaving 143 Mexican communities between 1970 and 2000. The sample contains migrants on the year of their *first* trip to the United States, and is weighted by the inverse of the sampling fraction employed in the study sites. The trends are slightly different from those in Durand, Massey, and Zenteno (2001, p. 121), who use the same data, but introduce migrants to the sample on the year of their *most recent trip*. The authors also use a smaller sample from 35 communities (those for which data were available at the time of their study) and do not report using sample weights.

Page 2 The figures on **the share of migrants from traditional migrant-sending regions** are based on my computations from the MMP, and are consistent with those based on Mexico's Encuesta Nacional de la Dinámica Demográfica (ENADID) data in Durand, Massey, and Zenteno (2001, table 1).

Page 2 **Increasing migration from Mexico City and the border cities** is reported in Fussell (2004a).

Page 2 **New migrant destinations**: Massey and Capoferro (2008, table 2.1); Riosmena and Massey (2012).

Page 2 **Shift from a sojourner to a settler strategy**: The pattern is based on Durand, Massey, and Zenteno's (2001, table 3) analysis of Mexico's ENADID data. Cornelius (1992) provided earlier evidence with his analysis of migrant workers in three Southern Californian counties. Marcelli and Cornelius (2001, table 2) similarly identified a trend toward settlement in their analysis of survey data from immigrant-dependent businesses in San Diego, where the percentage of Mexican migrants who viewed the United States as their main country of residence increased from 70% in 1970 to 87% in 1990. Most recently, Taylor et al. (2011, figure 2) analyzed the Current Population Survey, and found a higher tendency for unauthorized migrants to settle in the United States. In 2000, about 44% of unauthorized migrants (Mexicans or others) had stayed in the country for 10 years or more. In 2010, that share had increased to 63%.

Page 3 **Attention to human capital in economics**: In 1960, Theodore Schultz, the president of the American Economic Association, dedicated his presidential address to a discussion of human capital. He argued that the growth in investment in individual skills and knowledge "may well be the most distinctive feature of the [Western] economic system" (Schultz 1961). Gary Becker, the Nobel laureate in Economics in 1992, pioneered much of the theoretical and empirical work on returns to human capital investments, most notably, returns to schooling (Becker 1962, 1964). Jacob Mincer published a classic study that related earnings to the level of on-the-job training (Mincer 1974). These findings led economists to claim human capital as a major source for economic productivity and growth, as well as an explanation for growing earnings inequality in the United States (Becker 1993).

Page 3 **Migration as an income-maximization strategy**: Harris and Todaro (1970); Sjaastad (1962); Todaro (1980, 1969); Todaro and Maruszko (1987).

Page 3 **Family as the key unit for migration decisions**: Dinerman (1978); Harbison (1981); Pessar (1982); Roberts (1982); Wiest (1973); Wood (1981).

Page 3 **Risk diversification models in finance**: In the 1950s, Harry Markowitz (1952; 1959) developed the theory of portfolio selection in economics. The theory analyzed how households and firms can allocate financial assets optimally under uncertainty, or can maximize returns while diversifying risks. A decade later, William Sharpe (1964) used this theory as a basis to model price formation for financial assets, in his so-called Capital Asset Pricing Model. Both economists went on to win the Nobel Prize in Economics in 1990.

Page 3 **Migration as a risk diversification strategy**: Lauby and Stark (1988); Stark (1991a); Stark and Bloom (1985); Stark and Levhari (1982); Taylor (1986).

Page 3 **Chain migration**: Hugo (1981); MacDonald and MacDonald (1964); Ritchey (1976).

Page 4 **Social ties as resources**: Gurak and Caces (1992); Massey et al. (1987); Massey and García-España (1987); **as purveyors of norms**: Alarcón (1992); Massey (1986); Piore (1979); Reichert (1981).

Page 4 **Cumulative causation of development**: Myrdal (1957a, 1957b); **of migration**: Massey (1990a, 1990b).

Page 4 Migration resulting from a **dual labor market structure**: Piore (1979); from a **"world system"**: Sassen (1988, 1991); Wallerstein (1974).

Page 5 **Futile to search for universal explanations**: Portes (1997).

Page 5 **Cause-effect chains complex**: Abbott (2001); Ragin (1987); **data partial**: The data in the social sciences are often observational, not experimental, and cannot measure all the factors relevant to the behavior at hand.

Page 6 **U.S. average wages** are for production workers from the Bureau of Labor Statistics (Series: CES0500000008).

Page 6 **Growth in the U.S. economy**: Jones (2002).

Page 6 **Increases in construction**: Jorgenson and Stiroh (2000:164, table 2).

Page 7 **The MMP data provide an accurate profile of migrants**: Massey and Zenteno (2000).

Page 8 **Mechanisms that give rise to the diversity in migration**: For a more general treatment of the mechanisms-focused approach, see Hedström and Swedberg (1998); Morgan and Winship (2007).

CHAPTER I

Page 10 All individual and location names are pseudonyms.

Page 11 **Technical high school program**: The University of Guadalajara offers advanced high school training through its SEMS (Sistema de Educación Media Superior) program. More information is available at: http://www.sems.udg.mx.

Page 12 The presence of **multiple generations** of Mexican migrants in the United States complicates the assimilation process, Jiménez (2010, p.24) argues in *Replenished Ethnicity*, as the first generation migrants continue to come in and force the older generations to view their ethnic identity within "a prevailing narrative of Mexicans as foreigner." Gutiérrez (1995) makes a similar argument in *Walls and Mirrors*, where he traces the Mexican ethnic identity from the late nineteenth century onward. Telles and Ortiz (2008), in *Generations of Exclusion*, identify continuities across generations, for example, low levels of socioeconomic mobility among succeeding cohorts of Mexican migrants.

Page 12 **Multicultural identity**: In *Ethnic Options*, for example, Mary Waters (1990) shows how ethnic identification varies in its content and importance across generations.

Page 12 **Children of migrants' socioeconomic disadvantage**: Kasinitz, Mollenkopf, Waters, and Holdoway (2008); Suárez-Orozco and Suárez-Orozco (2009).

Page 12 **Mexican GDP per capita** figures are from the World Bank database (Series: NY.GDP.PCAP.KD). All values are reported in constant U.S. dollars in 2005.

Page 13 **Generalizations organized around social categories**: Research suggests that the human mind works more through classifications and inductive generalization than deductive logic; see Dawes (1998). **Certain attributes being singled**

out in creating categories and reaching judgments: Macrae and Bodenhausen (2000:113); Stangor et al. (1992). In *Categorically Unequal*, Douglas Massey (2007) connects these cognitive mechanisms—selective categorization and evaluation—to the process of social stratification.

Page 13 **Attributes of an average Mexican migrant**: Massey and Espinosa (1997).

Page 13 **How the attributes have changed over time**: The figures are based on Borjas' (1996) analysis of 1970 and 1990 U.S. Census data. They represent recent Mexican migrants who have been in the United States for five years or less.

Page 14 The phrase **"the situational and relational character"** of social categories is from Donato et al. (2006, p.18).

Page 14 The quote on **intersectionality** is from McCall (2005, p.1771). The literature on intersectionality problematizes not just the relationships between different social categories, but also the definitions of those categories, and thus often takes a very specific methodological stance. For an insightful discussion, see McCall (2005).

Page 14 The quote on how studying configurations is **"difficult without recourse to qualitative methods"** is from Donato et al. (2006, p.19).

Page 14 How **gender relations** shape access to migrant networks: Hondagneu-Sotelo (1994). How gender relations vary **by social class** or **across rural or urban settings**: Grasmuck and Pessar (1991).

Page 14 How **gender relations change** via migration: Hondagneu-Sotelo (1994) and Levitt (1998).

Page 14 Studying the **interactions between personal and contextual attributes** with survey data: Students of *intersectionality* have generally been critical of this approach for taking social categories, like gender, fixed across settings and time. McCall (2005), however, has argued for using these categories strategically to systematically document differences across multiple social categories.

Page 14 **Personal attributes matter less**: Massey, Goldring, and Durand (1994).

Page 15 **Difficult to make sense of the patterns**: Human beings can keep between 4 and 7 items (somewhat higher if those items are ordered hierarchically) in their short-term working memory (Cowan 2001; Miller 1956).

Page 15 **Cluster analysis** has led to the discovery of functional regions ("networks") of the brain (Fox et al. 2005) and of gene configurations connected to specific types of cancer (Tibshirani et al. 2002). The former has been critical to studying the onset of depression (Greicius et al. 2007) and Alzheimer's (Sorg et al. 2007), and the latter to testing gene therapy for cancer treatment (Sørlie et al. 2003).

Page 15 **Abbott and Ragin's work**: Abbott (2001); Abbott and Hrycak (1990); Ragin (2000, 2008).

Page 15 **Cluster analysis as a tool for conceptualization**: Grimmer and King (2009).

Page 16 **Same outcome through different causal pathways**: This idea is similar to what Ragin (1987) calls "multiple conjunctural causation"; there may be multiple causal bundles that lead to the same social or historical outcome, and those bundles may include various conditions that come together.

Page 17 **Neoclassical economics theory**: Harris and Todaro (1970).

Page 17 **New economics theory**: Stark and Bloom (1985).

Page 17 **Cumulative causation theory**: Massey (1990a).

Page 17 **Theories not mutually exclusive**: Massey et al. (1998); Massey et al. (1993); Massey et al. (1994).

Page 17 **Massey and Espinosa study**: Massey and Espinosa (1997).

Page 18 **Social science modeled after physics**: Lieberson and Lynn (2002).

Page 18 **Massey and Taylor critique**: Massey and Taylor (2004, p. 383).

Page 19 Difficulty of answering the **"why" question**: Richard Feynman, the Nobel Laureate physicist, provides a fun example to describe how difficult the "why" question is in his field. Basically, at each level of explanation, we can continue to ask why, which leads to infinite regress. See the "Aunt Minnie" example (Sykes 1995).

Page 20 **Social explanation should identify mechanisms**: Hedström and Bearman (2009b); Hedström (2005).

Page 21 **A brief history**: For a detailed account of the political economy of Mexico prior to 1965, see Moreno-Brid and Ros (2009). For a history of migration between Mexico and the United States prior to 1965, see Henderson (2011); Massey, Durand, and Malone (2003).

Page 21 **Settlers for the Spanish crown migrating to the United States**: Camarillo (1984).

Page 22 **The 1848 treaty ceding to the United States the northern Mexican provinces**: Massey (2007). A song by Los Tigres del Norte, an acclaimed Mexican band, refers to this historical point to put current migration in perspective. "I did not cross the border," the lyrics go (translated from Spanish), "the border crossed me."

Page 22 **Became migrants without migrating**: Alba, Jimenéz, and Marrow (2014) argue the long and complicated history of Mexico-U.S. migration makes it difficult to classify Mexicans in generational terms. Those incorporated into the United States with the 1848 treaty, for example, were never really migrants.

Page 22 **Mexican recruitment in the 1890s**: Cardoso (1980).

Page 22 **About 60,000 Mexicans**: The number is from Reisler (1976). The author notes that official records are collected after 1908, and estimates that between one-quarter and one-third of Mexicans remained in the United States in those years.

Page 22 **Four periods in Mexico-U.S. migration**: Camarillo (1984).

Page 22 **Mass deportations**: The estimates of deportations range from 400,000 to 1 million (Divine 1957; Johnson 2005).

Page 22 **Loss and shortage of farmworkers**: Craig (2015); Rosenblum (2003).

Page 22 **4.6 million Mexicans**: Cornelius (1978).

Page 23 **Apprehension numbers**: Massey, Durand, and Malone (2003).

Page 23 **Sources for figure 1.3**: 1850–1990 values of the total Mexican-born population are based on the decennial U.S. censuses as reported in Gibson and Lennon (1999, table 4) and Passel (2005, p. 37, for years 1940 and 1950). 2000–2011 values of the Mexican-born population (total and undocumented) are based on the annual Current Population Survey (CPS) as computed by Passel et al. (2012, tables A1 and A3) adjusting for potential undercount of migrants.

Page 23 **Operation Wetback**: Calavita (2010).

Page 23 **Undocumented into Bracero workers**: Calavita (2010).

Page 24 Detailed information on the **MMP** is available at: http://mmp.opr.princeton.edu/.

Page 24 **MMP consistent with the ENADID**: Durand, Massey, and Zenteno (2001); Massey and Zenteno (2000).

Page 26 **Inductive generalization rather than deductive logic**: Dawes (1998).

Page 26 **Grimmer and King quote**: Grimmer and King (2009, p. 2).

Page 26 **Proportion of individuals who have ever migrated in a community**: This measure, called "migration prevalence" in the MMP data, is computed using the date of birth of each individual and the date of the first U.S. trip. As described in detail in Massey, Goldring, and Durand (1994), migration prevalence is defined as the ratio of the number of persons aged 15 and older who had ever been to the United States over the total number of persons aged 15 and older in a given year. The numerator is computed retrospectively from the date of the first U.S. trip, and the denominator is computed from the date of birth. Fussell and Massey (2004) describe strategies used to address potential biases in the measure emanating from permanent out-migration or in-migration, which are reflected in the PREV measure included in the COMMUN file of the MMP.

Page 26 **Regional indicators**: Durand and Massey (2003) (DM hereafter) provide a regional classification scheme, which divides Mexico into four distinct regions of origin. I use this scheme with a slight modification. I separate the central group in the DM classification into two groups: the central and the central-south. The **central-west** (called "historical" in DM) includes the west-central states of Aguascalientes, Colima, Durango, Guanajuato, Jalisco, Michoacán, Nayarit, San Luis Potosí, and Zacatecas. Durand and Massey (2003, tables 3.3 and 3.4) show that this region provided at least half of all U.S. migrants from the 1920s onward. The **border** region, the second most important sending region until the mid-1990s according to DM (tables 3.6 and 3.7), includes the states of Baja California, Baja California Sur, Chihuahua, Coahuila, Nuevo León, Sonora, Sinaloa, and Tamaulipas. The **central** region includes the states of Distrito Federal and Querétaro, while the **central-south** region contains Guerrero, Hidalgo, México, Morelos, Oaxaca, Puebla, and Tlaxcala. These states went from providing less than 10% of all U.S. migrants until the 1980s to accounting for nearly 30% by 2000 (DM, tables 3.9 and 3.10). Finally, the **southeast** region includes Campeche, Chiapas, Quintana Roo, Tabasco, Veracruz, and Yucatán. This region also increased its share of the U.S. migrant population from about 2% in the 1990s to 7% in 2000 (DM, table 3.13).

CHAPTER 2

Page 40 **Overcrowded**: Estimates by CONEVAL (Consejo Nacional de Evaluación de la Política de Desarrollo Social) based on data collected by INEGI (Instituto Nacional de Estadística y Geografía) in the Census of Population and Housing 2005 and the National Household Income and Expenditure Survey 2005.

Page 40 The **ejido** land tenure system was a result of the Mexican Revolution led by Emiliano Zapata's call for land for the peasants. Before the revolution, less than 5% of the population owned more than 90% of the land. Article 27 of the 1917 Mexican Constitution allowed peasants to petition to distribute private land to *ejidos* (communal land) and to grant members the rights to work the land. By 1970, about half of Mexico's cultivated land were in *ejidos* (Martin 1997).

Page 43 **Growth rates for Mexican economy** are based on the change in the gross domestic product in real terms reported in Moreno-Brid and Ros (2009, table A.1). Growth rates in manufacturing are from INEGI (1999, table 13.1). Growth rates in agriculture are in Morton (2013, table 3.1).

Page 43 **Effective protection rates** are reported in Moreno-Brid and Ros (2009, table 5.3).

Page 43 Figures for **public investment and credit** given to agriculture are from Moreno-Brid and Ros (2009, table 5.5).

Page 43 **Mexican labor force in agriculture**: Morton (2013).

Page 43 **Average wage in manufacturing sufficient for the basic needs basket**: Latapí and Roberts (1991).

Page 43 **Social security coverage**: Roberts and Latapí (1997, p. 49).

Page 43 **Agriculture sector** numbers are from Lustig (1982) and Heath (1988, p. 138).

Page 43 **Income distribution** figures are from Moreno-Brid and Ros (2009, table 5.7).

Page 44 **Public investments in agriculture** figures are from Moreno-Brid and Ros (2009, table 6.1).

Page 44 **Number of poor**: Moreno-Brid and Ros (2009, table A.7, p. 265).

Page 44 **Fertility rate**: World Bank Database.

Page 44 **Labor supply and emigration rates**: Hanson and McIntosh (2009, 2010).

Page 45 **Bracero program**: Numbers on Bracero migrants and border apprehensions are from Massey, Durand, and Malone (2003).

Page 45 **Bracero contracts first favorable to workers**: Smith and Edmonston (1997, p.26); then **grower-friendly**: Calavita (2010).

Page 48 **Recession** periods are based on unemployment levels (Ginzberg 1994, p. 37). For relationship between business cycle and less-skilled wages, see Abraham and Haltiwanger (1995).

Page 50 **Internal migration figures** are computed from a panel data set created from the PERS data in the MMP survey. Internal migrants are defined as individuals for whom the year of the first or last domestic migration trip (the only trips recorded in the data) fell between 1965 and 1980. All percentages are based on the average percentage across all years in this period. A rural community is defined as one where at least half of the labor force is in agriculture; a poor community is one where at least half of the labor force earns less than the minimum wage.

Page 50 **Returns to internal migration greatest for the educated**: Stark and Taylor (1991, p. 1176) observe a similar pattern in their analysis of internal and international migration strategies in 61 randomly selected households in rural Michoacán. Individuals with high levels of education choose to migrate to urban destinations in Mexico (rather than to the United States) where they can obtain high returns to their skills.

Page 50 **Wage, occupation, and destination figures** are recorded for the *last trip* for both domestic and U.S. migrants in the MMP data. The analysis in the text is based on the last trips that have occurred between 1965 and 1980. The wage figures are obtained by aggregating hourly, daily, weekly, and bi-weekly wages to monthly values.

Page 51 **The U.S. migrants . . . earned**: Migrant earnings in the MMP data can be recorded at the hourly, weekly, bi-weekly, or monthly rate. The monthly figures in the text are computed by assuming that all workers are employed full-time.

Page 51 **Regional origins of Mexicans entering the United States**: For 1925 values, see Foerster (1925). For values during the Bracero period (1962), see Durand and Massey (2003, table 3.3, p. 74).

Page 52 **Railroads and migration**: Camarillo (2004); Woodruff and Zenteno (2007).

Page 52 I report information on **first-time migrants** because the MMP data record the timing of the first U.S. trip for *all individuals*. The data capture subsequent trips for household heads and their spouses, but this group may not be a representative sample of the migrant population at large.

Page 52 **States in dark grey**: Seven out of the eight states (Baja California being the only exception) are considered historic migration states in Durand and Massey's (2003, p. 74, tables 3 and 4) comprehensive analysis of various data sets (including the nationally representative Mexican survey, ENADID).

Page 53 **Chain migration**: MacDonald and MacDonald (1964); **migrant circuits**: Rouse (1991); **migrant networks**: Boyd (1989).

Page 53 **Identified network effects**: Empirical analysis often cannot distinguish social effects (i.e., individuals responding to the behavior or characteristics of the group) from "correlated" effects (i.e., individuals responding to the same environment). See Manski (1993) for a detailed discussion. See Munshi (2003) for a rare exception overcoming this problem from the migration literature.

Page 53 **Studies in the Mexican setting**: Cohen (2004); Curran and Rivero-Fuentes (2003); Davis, Stecklov, and Winters (2002); Jones (1995); Massey and Espinosa (1997); Massey and García-España (1987); Massey, Goldring, and Durand (1994); Massey and Zenteno (1999); Munshi (2003); Palloni et al. (2001). For a review, see Massey et al. (1994).

Page 54 **Mechanisms underlying social influences—information or help exchange**: Carrington, Detragiache, and Vishwanath (1996); Garip (2008); Kandel and Kao (2001); Mines (1981); Moretti (1999); Tilly (2007); Curran and Rivero-Fuentes (2003); Palloni et al. (2001); **normative pressures**: Cohen (2004); Hernández-León (1999); Kandel and Massey (2002); Mines (1981); Piore (1979); Reichert (1981); Wiest (1973).

Page 54 **Typology of social mechanisms**: DiMaggio and Garip (2012). De Haas (2010a) provides an alternative typology that differentiates between endogenous and contextual feedback mechanisms leading to network migration. The former works through the resources or ideas (e.g., information, help, or a different "culture") prior migrants bring, and the latter through the contextual changes (e.g., more inequality in origin, or more ethnic enclaves in destination) prior migrants instigate. The former is a mix of the social facilitation and normative influence mechanisms described in our typology, and the latter is a counterpart to network externalities.

Page 55 **Research on institutions representing network externalities in migration—smugglers and recruiters in origin**: Cornelius (2001); Singer and Massey (1998); **migrant enclaves in destination**: Castles, De Haas, and Miller (2014); Epstein (2008); Korinek, Entwisl, and Jampaklay (2005); Light and Bonacich (1991); Piore (1979); Portes and Sensenbrenner (1993); Zhou (2010); **hometown associations in destination**: Fitzgerald (2008, pp. 103–24); Goldring (2004); Levitt (2001b); Smith (2006).

Page 55 The quotes **"The news of . . ."** are from Ramón "Tianguis" Pérez's diary (1991, pp. 12–13). Parts are also published in Camarillo (2004, pp. 23–24).

Page 57 **Social facilitation through visible signs of migrants' success**: See, for example, Stark, Taylor, and Yitzhaki (1988); Stark and Taylor (1991).

Page 59 **Rite of passage**: Kandel and Massey (2002); Massey et al. (1987); Reichert and Massey (1979); Reichert (1981).

Page 59 **Conform to a collective narrative**: Scholars suggest that collective narratives can influence both individual and collective behavior (Ewick and Silbey 2003; Somers 1992; Tilly 2002). Frye (2013) uses this idea in a compelling empirical investigation of sexual relationships and school dropout rates in Malawi. Kirk and Papachristos (2011) employ a similar logic to understand persistence of crime in certain neighborhoods.

Page 60 **Prior migrants buy land**: Mines (1981); Reichert (1981); Wiest (1984); **invest in agriculture**: Massey et al. (1987); **induce sense of relative deprivation**: Stark, Taylor, and Yitzhaki (1988); Stark (1991); Stark and Taylor (1989); Taylor (1992).

Page 60 **Migrants stigmatize occupations for natives**: Piore (1979).

Page 60 **Cumulative causation**: Massey (1990a); Massey et al. (1993); Massey and Zenteno (1999).

Page 61 **Cumulative causation implies flows grow ad infinitum**: De Haas (2010a); Epstein (2008).

Page 62 **Figure 2.4**: Neither Foerster's (1925) data nor the MMP surveys provide an accurate estimate of the number of migrants out of each state. The former records only the legal border crossings and through three entry points. The latter captures only a few communities (typically those with the highest number of migrants) in each state. Yet, these two sources are the only ones available in the periods of interest. For later periods, studies show migration rates in the MMP data to be generally consistent with those observed in nationally representative data from Mexico. See Massey and Zenteno (2000), for example, for a comparison of the MMP data to the ENADID surveys.

Page 63 **Expected births**: World Bank Database.

Page 63 **Share . . . married and with children; majority . . . chose to migrate without a spouse**: Information on the marital status of migrants during their first trip is only available for household heads in the MMP data (LIFE file). We report the percentages for household heads among circular migrants between 1965 and 1980 (1,784 out of 2,860). For married household heads, the location of the spouse is recorded in select communities (community id: 33 to 143) in the MMP data (SPOUSE file). The share of circular migrating without a spouse on the first trip is computed for all married household heads in communities 33 to 143 (834 out of 1,784).

Page 64 **Women have a say but not the final word**: Research finds that women's bargaining power in Mexico varies significantly by age and position in the household (Ortiz 1996; Riley and Gardner 1993).

CHAPTER 3

Page 69 **Sell or rent land**: In 1992, President Carlos Salinas de Gortari amended Article 27 of the Mexican constitution and made it legal to sell, buy, rent, or lease *ejidos* (communal land), activities prohibited under the old agrarian law (Nuijten 2003).

Page 69 **Magical Villages Program** (Programa Pueblos Mágicos) is an initiative spearheaded by the Ministry of Tourism (Secretaría de Turismo) in Mexico to recognize towns or villages for their natural beauty or cultural or historical significance. Launched in 2001, the program has granted "magical village" status to 83 towns and villages spread across all 31 states in Mexico by 2014. There are five magical villages in the state of Jalisco. (More information is available at: http://www.sectur.gob.mx/wb2/sectur/sect_Pueblos_Magicos)

Page 71 **Information available for a small share**: This is recorded in the MIG and MIGOTHER files of the MMP. The former is collected from household heads that are migrants, and the latter from another household member in households where the head is not a migrant.

Page 71 **1940–1970** figures are from Moreno-Brid and Ros (2009). Average growth in Mexican GDP is given in table A.1. Inflation rate (based on changes in the wholesale price index in Mexico City) is computed from values in tables A.9–A.11.

Page 71 **Poverty rate**, based on a nutrition-based poverty line, declined from 61.8% in 1950 to 24.3% in 1968 (Moreno-Brid and Ros 2009, table A.7).

Page 71 **Economy more vulnerable**: Lustig (2000, p. 14).

Page 71 **Public spending** as a share of the GDP increased from 20.5% in 1971 to 32% in 1976 (Moreno-Brid and Ros 2009, table A.13 and chapter 6). **Fiscal deficit**: Zedillo (1986, table 4).

Page 71 **Foreign debt**: Moreno-Brid and Ros (2009, figure 6.1).

Page 72 **Inflation rate** reached 12% in 1973 and remained at double-digit levels for more than a decade. **Real exchange rate** (set to 100 in 1970) receded to 78.6 in 1975. Both figures are in Moreno-Brid and Ros (2009, table A.12).

Page 72 **Balance-of-payments crisis**: External factors, like the worldwide recession following the oil prices increases in 1973, also contributed to Mexico's plight. In fact, Zedillo (1986) estimates that those factors might have accounted for two-thirds of the disequilibrium in balance of payments in 1975.

Page 72 **Devalued the peso**: The value of the peso dropped from 8 cents to the dollar to about 5 cents (Lustig 2000, p. 19).

Page 72 **Oil reserves**: Rizzo (1984, p. 99).

Page 72 **Deficit to surplus**: Figures are based on Rizzo's (1984, table 5.2) computations from Banco de Mexico data, *Informe Annual*, 1978–1980.

Page 72 **1978–1981 GDP growth**: Moreno-Brid and Ros (2009, table A.12).

Page 72 **Social programs**: SAM (Sistema Alimentario Mexicano) was launched in 1980 to stimulate food agriculture and make Mexico self-sufficient in food production, and also to improve nutritional standards of the poor population. COPLAMAR (Coordinación General del Plan Nacional de Zonas Deprimidas y Grupos Marginados) was launched in 1977 to enhance social conditions in marginalized communities.

Page 72 **Fiscal deficit in 1981**: Lustig (2000, table 1.5). **Inflation rate** sustained an annual average of 22.5% from 1976 to 1981. Real exchange rate dropped to 77.6 in 1981 after being set to 107.6 with the peso devaluation in 1976. Both figures are from Moreno-Brid and Ros (2009, table A.12). **Capital flight** in 1981 amounted to US$11.6 billion in contrast to earlier years, where it remained less than US$3 billion from 1976 to 1980 (Lustig 2000, table 1–5).

Page 72 **Peso devaluations**: Between January and March 1982, the exchange rate (peso-to-dollar) dropped from 26.35 to 45.46 (Lustig 2000, p. 24).

Page 72 **Slowdown in the economy**: In 1983, Mexico's GDP contracted by more than 5% while inflation rose to 102% (Moreno-Brid and Ros 2009, table A.12).

Page 72 **Economic climate in the world**: The price of oil declined from US$31.3 per barrel in 1980 to US$11.9 in 1986. In 1990, the price of oil remained nearly 40% below its level in 1980 (Lustig 2000, table 2–2).

Page 73 **Devaluation in 1985**: The Mexican peso lost 20% of its value against the dollar (Moreno-Brid and Ros 2009, chapter 7). **Inflation and interest rates in 1987**: Lustig (2000, table 2–4). Interest rates are given on one-month treasury bonds (CETES).

Page 73 **Real wages dropped . . . between 1983 and 1987**: The minimum wage declined at an average rate of 9.8% yearly, while the average wage in manufacturing decreased by 8.1% (Lustig 2000, table 2–4).

Page 73 **"Lost decade"**: Centeno (2010).

Page 73 **Poverty and inequality** figures are from Lustig (2000, tables 8–1 and 8–2). Moderately poor individuals live on two US dollars or less; extremely poor live on a dollar or less.

Page 73 **Extreme poverty rates** by region and employment sector are from Lustig (2000, table 8–3). Extreme poverty rate is defined as the share of population living on less than about one US dollar a day. Between 1984 and 1989, extreme poverty rates increased in the central-west (from 16.6% to 22.4%), south (from 16.7% to 25.1%), and southeast (from 15.6% to 34%); rates remained similar in the northwest (6.4% in both years), northeast (6.6% and 6.8%, respectively), north (18.5% and 18.8%), and southwest (14.4% and 14.2%); they declined in the central region (from 19.7% to 14.9%). The share of the extremely poor among households where the head works in agriculture climbed from 37.9% in 1984 to 48.7% in 1989.

Page 73 **Ejido sector hit hard**: de Janvry, Gordillo, and Sadoulet (1997). For example, SAM (Sistema Alimentario Mexicano), though launched in 1980 to make Mexico self-sufficient in food production, was abandoned after the 1982 crisis. Credit available to agriculture fell in absolute terms between 1982 and 1984. Moreover, the public sector institutions provided less of that credit, with their share declining from 70% of the total in the 1970s to less than half in 1984–1986. Finally, credit eligibility requirements were tightened (Martin 1997, pp. 146–47).

Page 73 **Middle-income lost more than the poorest**: Figures are from table 8–3 and p. 93 in Lustig (2000).

Page 73 **Informal employment**: Between 1982 and 1985, the share of wage earners in the urban labor force dropped from 83% to 76%, while the share of self-employed (a signifier for informal employment) increased from 12% to 15% (Lustig 2000, p. 78).

Page 73–74 **Urban household strategies**: de la Rocha (1988). **Earnings in Guadalajara**: de la Rocha (2007, p. 52).

Page 74 **Off-farm activities**: de Janvry and Sadoulet (2001, table 1) present results from a nationally representative survey of the *ejido* (communal land) sector conducted in 1997. They find that off-farm activities (wage labor, self-employment, or migration) bring more than half of the household income in *ejido* households in Mexico, ranging from more than a third on the largest farms to more than three-fourths on the smallest.

Page 74 **Farmers produced for the market**: Degg (1989).

Page 74 **Ejido . . . as a collateral**: In 1991, the Mexican Congress reformed Article 27 of the Constitution, which, until then, had prevented *ejidatarios* (farmers working communal land) from selling, renting, or borrowing against the *ejido* land.

Page 74 **Crop insurance . . . scarcer**: From the 1980s to the1990s, for example, the share of planted area covered by public insurance went down from 44% to less than 7%, according to Bean and Stevens (2003, p. 46). During the Salinas presidency (1988–1994), the government's public crop insurance program, ANAGSA (Aseguradora Nacional Agrícola y Ganadera, S.A.), was abolished.

Page 74 **Rationing labor force**: de Janvry and Sadoulet (2001); Grindle (1988); Taylor (1984). See also Cornelius (1978); Roberts (1982); Wiest (1973).

Page 74 *Maquiladoras* **hired women**: Fernandez-Kelly (1983) reported that the share of women workers in *maquiladoras* ranged from 75% to 90%.

Page 74 **Women concentrated in the informal sector**: Arizpe (1977).

Page 74 **Mexican fertility rates**: World Bank Database.

Page 74 **Share of working women**: World Bank Development Indicators, labor force participation rate (data.worldbank.org).

Page 75 **Couples lived with parents**: De la Peña (1984).

Page 75 **Changes to the food-processing industry**: Leach and Bean (2008); **garment industry**: Bonacich (1993); Fernandez-Kelly and Garcia (1990); **automobiles and electronics**: Hossfeld (1990); Morales (1983).

Page 75 **Jobs with manual work**: Piore (1979); Portes and Bach (1985); **filled by migrants**: Piore (1979) argues that most advanced economies have a "segmented" labor market structure, that is, a separation between well-paying and secure jobs in the "primary" sector and low-paying and unstable employment in the "secondary" sector. Native workers in a country often compete for jobs in the primary sector, leaving the secondary sector to immigrant workers.

Page 75 **Rising service sector**: Ginzberg (1994).

Page 76 **Women in labor force**: Dutka (1994, p. 16), based on U.S. Bureau of Labor Statistics, Employment Estimates. **Share of mothers working and reasons for the increase**: Reich (2010); **links to migration**: Sinke (2006).

Page 77 **Visas to Mexicans and Border Patrol statistics**: All numbers are from Massey, Durand, and Malone (2003).

Page 77 **Odds of apprehension**: Espenshade (1990); Massey and Singer (1995).

Page 77 **Skewed the stream**: Massey et al. (1987).

Page 78 **Trends in Mexico**: Inflation rate is from Moreno-Brid and Ros (2009, tables A11 and A12) for the period 1965–1983, from Lustig (2000, Tables 2–4 and 6–1) for the period 1984–1997, and from the NATLYEAR series in the MMP data between 1998–2010. Inflation rate is the annual rate of change in the Mexican Consumer Price Index. The rate of devaluation is the annual change in the U.S. dollar value of the Mexican peso. Interest rate is the average cost of funds in Mexico. (All series in NATLYEAR are based on International Monetary Fund Financial Statistics Yearbooks.)

Page 80 **Peaks in the rate of devaluation . . . and rate of crisis migration**: The Mexican peso is devalued by more than half in 1976, 1982, 1984, 1986, and 1987. The largest annual increases in the number of crisis migrants occur in 1978 (by 30%), 1984 (32%) and 1998 (54%). **Rate of inflation accounts for . . . half the variation in the rate of crisis migration**: A simple regression of the lagged inflation rate on the number of cluster 2 migrants yields an adjusted R^2 of 0.52. Adding various macro-level indicators to the model brings the R^2 to 0.84. See appendix G for details.

Page 80 **Events with localized impact**: Another possible event to consider is the 1980s oil crisis. But it is harder to delineate the regional effect of this event for two reasons. First, more than 90% of the oil production is concentrated in two states (Sánchez Reaza and Rodríguez Pose 2002, table 2)—Campeche (74%) and Tabasco (20%)—and the MMP data omit the former and contain few observations from the latter. Second, the sudden drop in oil prices in 1982 and 1986 influenced the entire Mexican economy, precipitating nationwide crises, which, as I described above, can be related to the national rise in the number of crisis migrants.

Page 80–81 **Coffee prices**: International Coffee Organization website accessed on July 15, 2014. (http://www.ico.org/historical/1990–99/PDF/PricestoGrowers90–99 .pdf) **Coffee-producing states** are ranked according to their share in the production: Chiapas (33.2%), Veracruz (24.2%), Oaxaca (13.7%), and Puebla (19.2%). Information comes from Campo Mexicano website accessed on August 10, 2014 (http://w4.siap.gob.mx/sispro/portales/agricolas/cafe/Descripcion.pdf). **Effect on the income of the poor**: Coffee prices declined by more than 70% between 1984 and 1992, causing an estimated drop of 15% in the earnings of subsistence and small producers in Mexico according to the World Bank (Sánchez Reaza and Rodríguez Pose 2002, table 2). The most affected were those in indigenous communities, who constituted 65% of coffee producers in Mexico. The anti-poverty programs at the time, like PRONASOL (Programa Nacional de Solidaridad), did not provide safety nets to absorb external shocks. After the coffee crisis, there were no efforts to compensate workers for wage losses (1996).

Page 81 **1985 earthquake and its aftermath**: Lustig (2000, pp. 206, 218).

Page 81 Information on the **U.S. monthly wages** is missing for 3,643 individuals out of 5,214 in cluster 2, and for 9,083 out of 14,029 in the other three clusters combined in the MMP data.

Page 84 **María Mendoza's story**: Hondagneu-Sotelo (1994, p. 76).

Page 85 **NELM—Migration as a result of uncertainty**: Stark and Bloom (1985); Stark, Taylor, and Yitzhaki (1986); **as a risk diversification strategy**: Katz and Stark (1986); Stark (1984); Stark and Levhari (1982).

Page 86 **Question assumptions of family unity**: Boyd and Grieco (2003); de la Rocha (1994); Grasmuck and Pessar (1991); Hondagneu-Sotelo (1992); Hondagneu-Sotelo (1994); Pedraza (1991); Sen (1983); Sen (1990).

Chapter 4

Page 95 **Road to the immigration bill**: Robert Pear (1986, October 21). "The Immigration Bill: Step by Step." *New York Times*. Retrieved from http://www.ny times.com.

Page 96 **The amendments**: The temporary worker program involved expedited procedures for growers to hire migrant workers under the H2-A visa classification. A replenishment program promised to admit more workers after 1990 if newly legalized migrants abandon farmwork. And finally, a special legalization program granted temporary resident status to migrant workers in perishable crops who worked at least 90 days for three years (from 1984 to 1986, or 1986 onward), allowing a change to permanent status after one year (Bean, Vernez, and Keely 1989; Calavita 1989).

Page 96 **Core provisions of the bill**: IRCA, in addition to the Schumer amendments summarized in the note above, included (i) employer sanctions that involved civil penalties ranging from $250 to $10,000 for each undocumented worker hired, (ii) safeguards against employer discrimination against foreign-looking or foreign-accented citizens and legal residents, (iii) a legalization program to grant temporary resident status to undocumented migrants residing in the country since before 1982, and (iv) increased budget for border enforcement. For more details, see Bean, Vernez, and Keely (1989, chapter 3).

Page 96 **President Reagan's speech**: Retrieved from the website http://www.reagan.utexas.edu/archives/speeches/1986/110686b.htm.

Page 96 **Schumer quote**: Robert Pear (November 7, 1986). "President Signs Landmark Bill on Immigration." *New York Times*. Retrieved from http://www.nytimes.com.

Page 96 **Reasons for the upsurge in undocumented entries from Mexico**: In 1964, the United States terminated the Bracero program that had recruited almost 5 million Mexicans for short-term work in agriculture over 22 years (Durand and Massey 2003, table 3.3). This change, however, did not end growers' demand for cheap migrant labor, nor did it affect the entrenched division in the U.S. labor market, where agricultural work was socially associated with migrants, and thus undesirable to citizens (Piore 1979). Mexican migrants continued to cross the border for farmwork after the Bracero program, but additional obstacles made it impossible for most to obtain legal documents. In 1965, Mexican citizens became subject to a cap of 20,000 visas per year (excluding immediate family of U.S. citizens), and after 1978, even those were to be allotted in competition with migrants from other countries against a fixed worldwide cap of 290,000 (Jasso and Rosenzweig 2006). This context of increasing restrictions on legal migration with continuing demand for migrants in the United States and declining economic prospects in Mexico (especially from the mid-1970s onward, as we saw in chapters 2 and 3) led to an upsurge in undocumented migration after 1965 (Bean and Stevens 2003; Massey, Durand, and Malone 2003).

Page 96 The estimate for the **undocumented entries between 1965 and 1986** is from Massey and Singer (1995, table 3). The authors divide the annual number of apprehensions (provided by U.S. Border Patrol) with the probability of apprehension (estimated to be about 0.35 in the MMP data). The estimate for the undocumented stock in 1986 is from Woodrow, Passel, and Warren (1987). The total number of undocumented migrants is 3.2 million, and those born in Mexico, about 2.2 million. The authors use the "residual method," which takes the difference between the foreign-born population enumerated in the Current Population Survey in 1986 and the legally resident immigrant population. See Van Hook and Bean (1998) for an excellent discussion of alternative methods and estimates.

Page 96 **Set the state for the legislation**: The stagnating growth in real wages and increasing unemployment in the United States during the mid-1970s also created pressures for an immigration reform (Bean and Stevens 2003, figures 2.6 and 2.7; Bean, Telles, and Lowell 1987). Indeed, research shows that restrictionist calls against immigration often coincide with economic downturns in the United States (Espenshade and Hempstead 1996).

Page 96 **Alan Nelson quote**: Roberto Suro (June 18, 1989). "1986 Amnesty Law Is Seen as Failing to Slow Alien Tide." *New York Times*. Retrieved from http://www. nytimes.com.

Page 97 **Figures on apprehensions** are reported for each fiscal year by the U. S. Border Patrol on their website (accessed July 27, 2014): http://www.cbp.gov/ sites/default/files/documents/U.S.%20Border%20Patrol%20Fiscal%20Year%20 Apprehension%20Statistics%201960–2013.pdf.

Page 97 **IRCA and border apprehensions**: Raw apprehension data alone cannot provide an accurate assessment of IRCA's impact, as other factors—like economic conditions in Mexico and the United States—also affect migration flows, and by implication, the apprehensions along the border. Bean et al. (1990) and White, Bean, and Espenshade (1990) present careful analyses of the apprehensions to evaluate IRCA's effect net of alternative determinants of migration flows. Both studies conclude the legislation has reduced undocumented crossings from Mexico upon its enactment; the reduction is estimated to be 8 million in 35 months in the former, and about 2 million in 23 months in the latter. This effect, however, seems to have largely dissipated by 1990 (Bean, Edmonston, and Passel 1990). Using other data sources from Mexican communities, studies found that undocumented migration rates to the United States either did not change (Cornelius 1989; Donato, Durand, and Massey 1992b), or increased (Massey, Donato, and Liang 1990), after IRCA. Observing the crossings along the border, studies also reported little change in the count of undocumented migrants between 1986 and 1988 (Bustamante 1990). While studies disagreed on the immediate effect of IRCA on the undocumented flow, the consensus was that the effect, if one existed, had disappeared by the end of the 1980s (Bean, Edmonston, and Passel 1990).

Page 97 Of the **2.3 million Mexican** applicants to IRCA's legalization programs, 1.1 million were part of the special agricultural workers program (Bean, Vernez, and Keely 1989, pp. 68–69).

Page 97 **Path to citizenship**: IRCA's amnesty program received 3 million applicants from Mexico and other countries (Rytina 2002, exhibit 1). 2.7 million applicants eventually received legal permanent resident status, and 1.1 million of those were naturalized as of 2009. Naturalization rates were somewhat lower among Mexican-born applicants (46% among pre-1982 migrants and 28% among special agricultural workers) compared to those from other countries (68% and 60%, respectively) (Baker 2010, table 1).

Page 97 **Petitions to bring spouses and children** by IRCA migrants increased from 268,818 in 1992 to 853,382 in 1994 (Woodrow-Lafield 1994, table 1).

Page 97 **IRCA and migration by women and children**: After IRCA, Bean et al. (1990) noticed an increase in the number of women and children apprehended at the border. Similarly, Richter, Taylor, and Yúnez-Naude (2007) found that migration shares among rural Mexicans declined twice as more among men than they did for women. Donato and Sisk (2015) found that children's (aged 17 or younger) odds of migration increased by 42% in the post-IRCA decade compared to the 1970–1986 period.

Page 99 The three groups I identify among **migrant women married to household heads** map onto three migration strategies identified by Hondagneu-Sotelo (1994): (i) family stage migration, where wives follow husbands to destination, (ii) independent migration, where men or women migrate as single individuals, and (iii) family unit migration, where husbands and wives migrate together. In my categorization, independent migration includes also wives who migrate before their husbands. The numbers are computed from the PERS file of the MMP data, which records the year of first migration for household heads and their spouses (usyr1) as well as the marital status of each (usmar1) in that year. This information is available only for the respondents in communities 72 to 143, giving us a small sample of women ($N = 284$, ~ 6% of all women migrants in the time period) to draw conclusions from. One can construct an alternative sample by identifying the couples in households using the indicator for each respondent's relationship to the household head in the PERS data (relhead). Some couples are straightforward to locate with this indicator (e.g., head and head's spouse, head's mother and head's father, and so on) while others require restricting the sample to certain cases (e.g., matching head's brother to head's sister-in-law in households where only one of each exists). These couples are identified with the information provided at the time of the survey. To compare the relative ordering of the husband's and wife's migration in a couple, then, one further needs to assume that the couple existed before either the husband or the wife migrated to the United States. This is a strong assumption, and that is why the text reports only the statistics computed from a smaller sample where no such assumption is needed. But, it is still worth noting that this larger data set, covering 1,223 of the 4,225 (29%) migrant women in the time period, yields qualitatively similar trends to those in the text. Between the pre- to post-IRCA decades (1975–1985 and 1986–1995), among the migrant women in our sample, the share joining a partner in the United States increased from 63% to 69%, while the share moving independently (single or before their husbands) declined from 23% to 16%.

Page 99 **Cascading impact of the legalizations**: The numbers are based on the PERS file in the MMP data. Of the 1,339 households with an amnesty recipient, 680 (50%) sent another migrant between 1986 and 1996. Of the 5,174 households with a migrant prior to 1985 but ineligible for the amnesty, 1,351 (26%) sent a new migrant in the same period. (Pearson chi-square test is significant at the 99% level.)

Page 99 **Migrants . . . married during the first U.S. trip**: This information is available for the household heads in all 143 communities in the MMP data and for the heads' spouses in communities 72 to 143. We have 1,602 observations in the third cluster (out of 3,916), and 7,173 in the other clusters (out of 15,327).

Page 100 **Women as independent or family migrants**: Earlier research sought to provide evidence against the prominent idea that most Mexican women are family migrants driven to cross the border to be with partners or family members already there. Reichert and Massey (1979), for example, studied one community in Mexico and found that 90% of women migrated to the United States for work. Hondagneu-Sotelo (1994) offered a useful typology to distinguish independent and family migration and to study the conditions leading to each. The author also identified an alternative motive that led Mexican women to migrate: reducing patriarchal control and gaining autonomy in the family by moving to a more gender egalitarian setting. Grasmuck and Pessar (1991) noted this motive earlier in women's migration from the Dominican Republic to the United States. The increasing independence of women migrants or the feminization of migration became a major theme in recent research (e.g., Donato et al. 2011; Donato and Gabaccia 2015; Hugo 2000).

Page 102 **The jump in family migrants coinciding with a peak in the number of U.S. permanent residencies**: This correlation is confirmed also in the regression model in appendix G, which relates the size of each cluster to various macro-level factors suggested in migration research. The number of U.S. permanent residencies (in logarithm form) is significantly associated with the size of family migrants, but not with the sizes of the other three groups in our data.

Page 102–103 **Petitions . . . increased dramatically**: Woodrow-Lafield (1994, table 1).

Page 103 **Border control and settlement**: Massey, Durand, and Malone (2003); Massey, Durand, and Pren (2016).

Page 105 **Rise in the number of women in border apprehension data**: Bean et al. (1990); **in surveys in the United States**: Marcelli and Cornelius (2001).

Page 105 **Women work if husband's income not sufficient**: Long (1980); Segura (1991); **if could delegate housework**: Stier and Tienda (1992); Tienda and Angel (1982); Tienda and Glass (1985); Wong and Levine (1992); **regardless of husband's employment**: Donato (1991); Donato (1993).

Page 106 **Women's entry into employment**: de la Rocha (1994); Tiano (1984).

Page 106 **Women affect migration decisions**: Ortiz (1996); Riley and Gardner (1993); **positively selected on education to migrate**: Kanaiaupuni (2000); **more dependent on social ties**: Espinosa and Massey (1997); **ties not accessible to women**: Hondagneu-Sotelo (1994).

Page 106 **Generational shift in women's migration**: Cerrutti and Massey (2001).

Page 106 **Women's odds of migration increase after IRCA**: Bean et al. (1990); Donato, Durand and Massey (1992b); Massey, Donato, and Liang (1990).

Page 107 **Jobs with little pay or benefits**: A study by economists Barry Bluestone and Bennett Harrison for the congressional Joint Economic Committee found, for example, that nearly 60% of the workers added to the labor force from 1979 to 1984 earned less than $7,000 per year (cited in "Minimum Wage Hike's Real Payoff" by David Gordon for the *Los Angeles Times*, May 12, 1987).

Page 107 **Share of women in labor force**: Dutka (1994). **Drove up the need for domestic workers that migrant women met**: Based on data from the 1990

U.S. Census, Hagan (1998) reports that native-born employment in private household domestic work declined by 27% between 1980 and 1990, while foreign-born employment increased by 73%.

Page 107 **Share without documents increased**: Massey, Durand, and Malone (2003).

Page 107 **Stagnating wages**: Between 1973 and 1985, individual wage and salary income fell 10% in real terms in the United States. In the same period, the proportion of households earning less than $20,000 a year increased by 8% (cited in "America's Dwindling Middle Class" by A. Gary Shilling for the *Los Angeles Times*, May 26, 1987).

Page 107 **Paradoxical combination**: Calavita (1989).

Page 107 **IRCA**: For details of the legislation and how it was passed: Bean, Vernez, and Keely (1989); Calavita (1989)

Page 108 **IRCA more than an immigration law**: Bean, Vernez, and Keely (1989).

Page 108 **Employer sanctions "symbolic"**: Calavita (1989, p. 41).

Page 108 **Details of IRCA legalization process**: Bean, Vernez, and Keely (1989); Hagan (1994).

Page 109 **Applicants to the LAWs and SAWs programs**: All numbers are compiled from Bean, Vernez, and Keely (1989, pp. 36, 69).

Page 109 **Male-to-female ratio among the undocumented**: Passel and Woodrow (1984); **among LAW applicants**: Hagan (1994),

Page 109 **Lower representation of women among legalized**: Baker (1990); Baker (1997); Hagan and Baker (1993); Hagan (1998).

Page 110 Debate on the **efficacy of employer sanctions**: Calavita (1994).

Page 110 **"Follow the letter of the law"**: Hagan (1994, p. 167).

Page 110 **Apprehension numbers**: Bean et al. (1990); **INS budget and Border Patrol personnel numbers**: Bean, Vernez, and Keely (1989).

Page 110 **Decline attributable to legalizations**: Crane et al. (1990); Donato, Durand, and Massey (1992a); **border apprehensions on the rise**: Massey, Durand, and Malone (2003, p. 91); **increase in the number of undocumented**: The 1990 number is from Warren (2000); the 2000 number is from Passel, Cohn, and Gonzalez-Barrera (2012).

Page 110 **Sanctions not effectively enforced**: Fix and Hill (1990).

Page 111 **Wages of documented and undocumented diverged**: Donato, Durand, and Massey (1992a); Donato and Massey (1993); Sorensen and Bean (1994).

Page 111 **Number of petitions**: Woodrow-Lafield (1994, table 1).

Page 111 **Women more likely to migrate legally**: Cornelius (1989); **also to cross without documents**: Bean et al. (1990); Donato (1993).

Page 111 **Increasing share of women in the early 1990s**: Marcelli and Cornelius (2001, table 1) report two data sources: (i) 1996 UCSD San Diego County Immigrant-Dependent Business Establishment Survey and (ii) 1994 USC-COLEF Los Angeles County Household Survey. The authors compare the share of women in both data sets in 1985–1989 versus 1990–1992. The share of women rises from

30% to 44% in the UCSD data, and from 47% to 56% in the USC-COLEF data.

Page 111 **Decline in undocumented men's wages and hours worked**: Donato, Durand, and Massey (1992a); Donato, Durand and Massey (1992b); **little impact on undocumented women**: Bean et al. (1990); **women's legal entry**: Donato (1993).

Page 111 **Right to travel freely as an incentive**: Hagan and Baker (1993).

Page 111 **Debate about IRCA legalizations and migrants' ties to Mexico**: Baker (1997) found that about two-thirds of respondents to a survey of newly legalized migrants with IRCA send remittances to their origin countries. Amuedo-Dorantes and Mazzolari (2010) showed remittances to be declining over time in data from the Legalized Population Survey (LPS), a nationally representative sample of the population that legalized through IRCA's general amnesty program.

Page 114 **Networks, gendered composition**: Marsden (1987); McPherson and Smith-Lovin (1987); McPherson, Smith-Lovin, and Cook (2001); **gendered effects**: Burt (1997); Burt (1998); Lin (2000); Renzulli, Aldrich, and Moody (2000), for a review, see England and Folbre (2005); **in migration behavior**: Cerrutti and Massey (2001); Curran and Saguy (2001); Curran et al. (2005); Curran and Rivero-Fuentes (2003); Davis and Winters (2003); Donato and Kanaiaupuni (1999); Kanaiaupuni (2000). For reviews, see Boyd (1989); Donato et al. (2006); Mahler and Pessar (2005); Pessar and Mahler (2003).

Page 114 **Women more willing to help**: Curran et al. (2005); Curran and Rivero-Fuentes (2003).

Page 115 **Willingness to help varies by gender of the recipient**: Hondagneu-Sotelo (1994); Paul (2013).

Page 116 **Ethnography of the Maya in the United States**: Hagan (1998).

Page 117 **Migrant women as agents of change**: Hondagneu-Sotelo (1994); Levitt (2001).

Page 117 **Women reframe the migration decision**: Paul (2013).

Page 118 **Exacerbating initial differences**: This idea is an application of a larger argument that Paul DiMaggio and I have developed on how network effects can generate and increase intergroup inequality. See DiMaggio and Garip (2011); DiMaggio and Garip (2012).

CHAPTER 5

Page 123 **Guadalajara population**: IX Censo General de Población 1970, INEGI XI and XII Censos General de Población 1990 and 2000.

Page 124 **Rising share of U.S. migrants from urban regions**: Durand and Massey (2003); Durand, Massey, and Zenteno (2001); Flores et al. (2012); Fussell (2004a); Lozano-Ascencio (2001); Lozano-Ascencio (2000); Lozano-Ascencio, Roberts, and Bean (1999); Marcelli and Cornelius (2001); Roberts and Hamilton (2007); Unger (2005).

Page 125 **More educated . . . consistent with other data**: Chiquiar and Hanson (2005), for example, use the Mexican Census to show that recent streams of U.S. migrants are more educated on average than the Mexican population. Studying all migrant groups in the United States, not just Mexicans, Jasso, Rosenzweig and Smith (1998) also observe an increasing influx of educated migrants starting in the 1990s. **Shift from past flows**: Borjas (1987); Borjas (1991); Borjas (1996); Borjas (1999).

Page 125 **"Caged in"**: Massey, Durand, and Pren (2015) find that undocumented migrants are increasingly constrained in their mobility (and thus caged in) in recent years with the increasing border enforcement.

Page 126 **Switch from rural to urban locales**: Waldinger (1989) observes the increasing concentration of Mexican migrants in metropolitan labor markets in the United States.

Page 126 **Origin-destination pairings**: Flores et al. (2012); Riosmena and Massey (2012).

Page 127 **Enforcement did not deter**: Aguilar et al. (2010); Dávila, Pagán, and Soydemir (2002); Gathmann (2008); Massey and Riosmena (2010); Redburn, Reuter, and Majmundar (2012, p. 34).

Page 128 **Privatizations**: The number of state-owned enterprises went from 1,155 in 1982 to 433 in 1988. The privatizations continued in the 1990s, when the state sold major industries like telecommunications, airlines, and banking (Aspe 1990).

Page 128 **Quotas to tariffs**: Bravo Aguilera (1989).

Page 128 **Largest regional market**: NAFTA, when signed in 1994, integrated a population of 372 million, with a combined GNP of US$7 trillion (Wise 1998, p. 4). NAFTA expanded on the bilateral Canada-U.S. Free Trade Agreement (CUFTA) signed five years earlier.

Page 128 **Share of oil revenues, exports, and imports in GDP**: Moreno-Brid and Ros (2009, tables A12–A17); **share of FDI**: Sánchez Reaza and Rodríguez Pose (2002, table 1).

Page 128 **Foreign investments into *maquiladoras***: About half of the FDI in 1998, for example, went into *maquiladoras* according to official statistics (CNIE 1998).

Page 128 ***Maquiladoras* . . . export the goods**: To ensure compliance, *maquiladoras* were required to buy a bond equal to the value of imported goods that would be returned to them once they had exported all the final goods. This is why *maquiladoras* are sometimes referred to as in-bond assembly plants. NAFTA eliminated the in-bond arrangement by giving all Mexican firms, including the *maquiladoras*, duty-free access to the U.S. market (Hanson 2007).

Page 128 **Apparel, electronics, or auto parts**: These three industries accounted for 80% of total *maquiladora* exports to the United States (Hanson 2003, p. 7, footnote 2).

Page 128 **Majority of jobs to women**: Women were cheaper to hire, viewed as more passive and disciplined, and more suited in general to assembly work, which required patience and dexterity. Almost 80% of workers in *maquiladora* plants were women in 1975. The share of women gradually dropped to 60% in 2000 (Anderson and Gerber 2009, p. 132, figure 6.4).

Page 128 *Maquiladoras* expanded: Martin (2003, p. 13).

Page 128 **Northern region** encompasses the six states on the border: Baja California, Chihuahua, Cohauila, Nuevo León, Sonora, and Tamaulipas. *Maquiladora* employment shares are from Sánchez Reaza and Rodríguez Pose (2002, Table 3). Overall manufacturing employment shares are from Hanson (1998, p. 428, table 2); Hanson (2003, p. 9).

Page 128 **North-South divide**: The regional disparities, which had been narrowing in the ISI (Import Substitution Industrialization) years, started to grow again, a pattern some economists attribute to processes of trade liberalization and economic integration (Sánchez Reaza and Rodríguez Pose 2002).

Page 129 **Border states—GDP growth rates**: Hanson (1996); Randall (2006, table 8.2).

Page 129 **Mexico City, Jalisco, and Nuevo León—share of industrial activity, GDP per capita**: López Malo (1960); **share of internal migrants**: Villarreal and Hamilton (2012, p. 1277).

Page 129 **The region offered higher wages**: Flores et al. (2012, figure 9.3, p. 169); Mendoza (2002, table 13).

Page 129 **Share of internal migrants**: Villarreal and Hamilton (2012, p. 1277).

Page 129 **Commercialization of land**: Article 27 of the Mexican constitution limited commercial farmers to a maximum of 100 hectares of irrigated land to grow grains and corn, 300 hectares of irrigated land for orchards, or enough land to maintain 500 head of cattle. In 1992, an amendment to the article removed the restriction and allowed selling of the communal land plots (*ejidos*) to domestic or foreign corporations (Martin 1993).

Page 129 **Reductions in agricultural support**: Through the 1990s, Mexico phased out price subsidies for 11 field crops, slowly dismantling the state-run National Company of Popular Subsistence (CONASUPO), and cutting agricultural credit (Yúñez-Naude 2003). Instead of price guarantees, new agricultural policies, like PROCAMPO, offered income transfers.

Page 129 **Number of Mexicans in the United States**: Bean et al. (2001).

Page 129 **Salinas quote** is from *Sacramento Bee*, April 7, 1991, mentioned in Cornelius and Martin (1993, p. 485).

Page 129–130 **Reno quote**: "Attorney general Reno sees NAFTA benefits in creating jobs, stopping drugs and illegal immigration from Mexico." (Press release). The White House, Washington, DC, October 12, 1993, available at www.ibiblio .org/pub/archives.

Page 130 **Optimism about NAFTA**: Many economists viewed NAFTA as part of foreign policy to foster Mexico's economic development and its political stability (Krugman 1993). A newspaper ad given by a bank in the United States read "300 economists, 136 newspaper editors and 6 presidents support NAFTA" (Fairbrother 2014, p. 1344, figure 2).

Page 130 **Employment to rise, migration to decline**: Hufbauer and Schott (1992, pp. 47–64), for example, estimated a 2% increase in Mexican employment, and a 9% increase in wages, within a year of the agreement's passage. Markusen and Zahniser (1997) claimed that the higher employment and wages would reduce migration from Mexico to the United States.

Page 130 **NAFTA expected to pressure rural workers to migrate**: Hinojosa-Ojeda and Robinson (1992), for example, projected the number of displaced workers to be around 1.4 million, and expected an increase of more than half a million in the number of undocumented migrants to the United States in the five years following NAFTA. Cornelius and Martin (1993), however, challenged these projections, arguing that many rural workers had already moved out of agriculture, and while those newly displaced could move to the border cities, only a small share of them would continue on to the United States.

Page 130 **NAFTA expected to increase unemployment**: Pastor and Wise (1998), for example, find that much of Mexico's growth from 1989 to 1994 is attributable to increases in productivity rather than job creation.

Page 130 **The inverted-U relationship between development and migration** has been observed in in Italy, Ireland, and Taiwan (De Haas 2005, 2010b). In line with these observations, in the Mexican case, Martin (1993) projected an initial "migration hump" after NAFTA, where emigration from Mexico to the United States would increase at a rate of 10–30% annually over 5–15 years. This hump, he argued, would be offset by the decline in emigration thereafter due to both economic and demographic changes in Mexico.

Page 130 **Income disparity grew**: Stiglitz (2007, p. 64).

Page 130 **Jobs in agriculture and manufacturing (1994–2002)**: Audley et al. (2003, p. 6).

Page 130 **Shift in industrial composition**: The change in the composition of manufacturing exports from 1988 to 2003 was equivalent to about a third of their total volume. The labor reallocation process was also slower than anticipated (Feliciano 2001; Hanson and Harrison 1999).

Page 130 **Real wages declined**: Hanson (2003) showed a decline in real wages for workers between 1990 to 2000, from US$1.3 per hour (in 1990 values) to $1.1 for men and from $1.2 per hour to $1.1 for women. Chiquiar (2008) observed an increase in real wages but only for unskilled workers in the same period. The increase was steepest in the border region, that is, in the states that were most integrated to the U.S. economy. Fairris (2003, p. 483) attributed the decline in real wages partly to the weakening of unions with bouts of privatization and deregulation in the 1980s. The share of workers in the formal sector covered by the unions, for example, dropped from 31% in 1996 to 21% in 1984.

Page 130 **NAFTA led to increase in emigration**: Martin (2003). **Modest decline in emigration**: Richter, Taylor, and Yúnez-Naude (2007) analyze a representative sample of rural households in Mexico and find that NAFTA slowed down the upward trend in emigration. NAFTA, the authors conclude, relieved emigration pressures, but its effect remained lower than other macroeconomic factors.

Page 131 **Salinas presidency economic indicators**: GDP growth rate: Lustig (2000, table 6.1, p.145); inflation (December to December change in consumer prices) and real interest rate (on one-month CETES): Lustig (2000, table 2.4, p. 40, table 6.1, p. 145).

Page 131 **Exports and imports; portfolio investment share**: Pastor (1998, pp. 124–25, figure 3.1).

Page 131 **Chiapas rebellion and assassination**: On January 1, 1994—the day NAFTA came into effect—a group called the Zapatista National Liberation Army revolted in Chiapas, occupying some towns and entering into intense combat with the national army. The government soon declared a ceasefire and began negotiations with the insurgents. The political turmoil did not end there, however. In March 1994, the PRI (Partido Revolucionario Institucional—Revolutionary Institutional Party) presidential candidate Luis Donaldo Colosio was assassinated in Tijuana. The crime was thought to be the work of an individual and not an organized conspiracy, but in any case led to chaos within the PRI. Pedro Aspe, Minister of the Treasury, and Salinas's favorite to replace Colosio as the presidential candidate, could not be nominated since he could not meet the constitutional requirement of the period of separation from public office. Ernesto Zedillo, a former Minister of Education, won the candidacy in the end and also the presidential elections (Rodríguez Kuri 2011).

Page 131 **Peso depreciated**: Audley et al. (2003, p. 19).

Page 131 **Peso devaluation—alternatives**: Some argue that the crisis could have been averted through a slow and controlled devaluation earlier in 1992, when the exchange rate began to lose parity, and speculate that President Salinas delayed the devaluation to ensure the passage of NAFTA and his party's win in the 1994 elections (Pastor 1998).

Page 131–132 **Changes in GDP, unemployment, and real wages**: Lustig (2000, tables 7.2 and 7.3). **The number of workers in formal employment** includes those enrolled in the pension program (Martin 2003). The share of workers in **the informal sector** is from Audley et al. (2003, p. 24).

Page 132 **Poverty rate** reported in Hanson (2007, table 10.1) equals the share of population with per capita income below threshold necessary to achieve minimum caloric intake.

Page 132 **Rescue package**: The United States offered US$20 billion in loans and loan guarantees; the IMF added nearly $18 billion, and Canada contributed another billion (Lustig 2000, p. 182, table 7.1).

Page 132 **GDP growth 1996–2000**: Moreno-Brid and Ros (2009, table A.16). **Formal employment in 2001**: Martin (2003). **Average real wage and poverty rates**: Hanson (2003); Hanson (2007, table 10.1).

Page 132 **Branched out into a host of illegal activities**: Guerrero Gutiérrez (2011); Ríos (2013).

Page 132 **Homicides and share by organized crime**: Molzahn, Ríos, and Shirk (2012).

Page 132 **Targeting the poor**: 24–40% of households participating in the Oportunidades program for poverty alleviation reported that they had been extorted by traffickers (Díaz-Cayeros et al. 2011). **Public security concerns**: Dell (2015).

Page 132 **No link of homicide to migration**: Alvarado and Massey (2010). Ríos (2014) shows some counter-evidence linking increasing violence in Mexico to a rising migration to the U.S. border cities between 2006 and 2010.

Page 134 **"Roaring 1990s"**: Stiglitz (2004).

Page 134 **Job expansion exceeded population growth**: Bean, Brown, and Bachmeier (2015, chapter 8).

Page 134 **Fertility rates**: World Bank Database. Numbers are total fertility rates, that is, average number of children a woman would be expected to have if her childbearing followed the fertility pattern in any given year.

Page 134 **Demand for less-skilled high**: Bean, Brown, and Bachmeier (2015, chapter 8); **shifting in its origins**: Freeman (2007).

Page 134 **Younger, less-skilled, native-born workers shrank**: Bean, Bachmeier, and Brown (2014); **the decline owed to . . .** : Bean, Brown, and Bachmeier (2015, chapter 8).

Page 134 **Unemployment rate and numbers below poverty line**: Stiglitz (2004); Stiglitz (2010); **low interest rates laid the groundwork**: Reich (2010); Stiglitz (2010); **full-time employment dropped**: Bureau of Labor Statistics, Employment Situation, available at http://www.bls.gov/news.release/empsit.toc.htm, accessed June 20, 2014). **True job deficit**: Stiglitz (2012, p. 10).

Page 135 **Border patrol budget, agent numbers, and new technologies**: Carriquiry and Majmundar (2012).

Page 135 **Death toll on the border**: Cornelius (2001); Eschbach et al. (1999).

Page 135 **Apprehensions increased**: Orrenius (2001); **apprehended tried again**: Kossoudji (1992); **give a different name**: Koslowski (2002).

Page 136 **States entering agreements**: Watson (2013).

Page 136 **NCIC database**: Gladstein et al. (2005); Sullivan (2009).

Page 136 **The number of deportations**: Moinester (2015) based on U.S. Immigration and Customs Enforcement Data.

Page 136 **NCIC includes civil immigration information**: Gladstein et al. (2005); Wishnie (2004).

Page 136 **U.S. Congress passed legislation**: Massey, Durand, and Pren (2015).

Page 136 **Entries by visa type**: Data compiled by Massey, Durand, and Pren (2015) from U.S. Office of Immigration Statistics website: http://www.dhs.gov/immigration -statistics.

Page 137 **Organizational migrants**: Lucassen and Smit (2015).

Page 137 *Maquiladoras* **offer sponsorship**: Fussell (2004b).

Page 137 **Move to new destinations**: Donato et al. (2007); Durand, Massey, and Capoferro (2005); Malone et al. (2003).

Page 137 **Share to California**: Durand, Massey, and Capoferro (2005); Massey and Capoferro (2008).

Page 137 **Reasons for the geographic shift, mobility of newly legalized migrants**: Durand, Massey, and Capoferro (2005); Durand, Massey, and Parrado (1999); Neuman and Tienda (1994); **relocation of industries**: Griffith (2005); Hernández-León and Zúñiga (2000); Kandel and Parrado (2005); **deteriorating living conditions**: Fennelly (2005); Hernández-León and Zúñiga (2000).

Page 138 **Globalization of production and migration**: Sassen (1988); Sassen (1998); **world systems theory**: Wallerstein (1974).

Page 138 **Physical and mental toll**: The average tenure in export-processing plants seems to be around 5 years (Sassen 1988).

Page 138 **Growth and emigration**: De Haas (2010b) discusses various mechanisms that generate a nonlinear relationship between economic development and emigration.

Page 138 **Global cities and migration**: Sassen (1991).

Page 139 **Segmented labor market**: Piore (1979). See Massey et al. (1993); Massey et al. (1994) for a review of theoretical and empirical work in this area.

Page 141 **Ranks Mexican states**: Hanson (2007).

Page 143 *Maquiladoras* **hired . . . mostly women; turnover rates high**: Martin (2003, p. 13); **reduced pay over time**: The average pay in dollar terms in 2002 was lower than that in 1994 (Martin 2003).

Page 143 **Pathways linking internal and international migration**: King and Skeldon (2010).

Page 143 **Stepwise migration strategy**: King (1976, pp. 70–72) observes this pattern in Turkey, and Skeldon (2006, pp. 22–24) notes it in Thailand. Paul (2011) shows a similar resource-collection strategy guiding multiple international moves by Filipino migrants.

Page 143 **Stepwise migration in Mexico**: Cornelius and Martin (1993); Cornelius (1992); del Rey Poveda (2007); Lindstrom and Lauster (2001); Lozano-Ascencio, Roberts, and Bean (1999); Zabin et al. (1993); **"school for El Norte"**: Zabin and Hughes (1995, p. 413); **"trampoline"**: Durand and Massey (2003).

Page 144 **Knock-on effects**: International migration from a particular region could knock-on internal migration to that region (King and Skeldon 2010). This knock-on effect works through jobs international migrants leave behind or through the new jobs they help stimulate through their remittances, which makes their areas of origin attractive for internal migrants (Skeldon 2006, p. 150). One example of this pattern is seen in Jalisco, a central-western state in Mexico, which started to receive internal migrants from Chiapas, a southern state, who replaced those leaving Jalisco for the United States (Fitzgerald 2008, p. 150).

Page 144 **Population growth**: The population in Tijuana, for example, grew at an annual rate of 5.4% in the 1980s, while that in Mexico City expanded by only 1% (Roberts and Latapí 1997, p. 55).

Page 144 **Population in very poor housing**: Roberts and Latapí (1997). Very poor housing is defined as housing without piped water and with non-solid construction materials.

Page 144 **Increasing urban poverty**: Lustig (2000); Roberts and Latapí (1997).

Page 144 **The conditions . . . contributed to rising emigration**: Cornelius (1991, p. 162); Roberts and Latapí (1997).

Page 145 **Depressed agricultural prices**: Audley et al. (2003); Nevins (2007); Zepeda, Wise, and Gallagher (2009); **long-term trend, not a consequence of NAFTA**: Yúnez-Naude and Barceinas (2002); Yúnez-Naude and Barceinas (2003); **source of rural unemployment and poverty**: Hanson (2003); Polaski (2004); Zepeda, Wise, and Gallagher (2009).

Page 145 **Researchers refer to these trends**: Durand and Massey (2003); Durand, Massey, and Zenteno (2001); Riosmena and Massey (2012).

Page 145 **Central and southern regions account for 46% of U.S. migrants**: Riosmena and Massey (2012, Table 2) use data from the 2006 Mexican National Survey of Population Dynamics (ENADID), a nationally representative survey where a migrant is defined as someone who has been to the United States during the 5 years prior to the survey; **up from 20%**: Durand, Massey, and Zenteno (2001, table 2) use data from the same survey conducted in 1992.

Page 146 **Growth in jobs**: *Maquiladora* employment increased 110% over NAFTA's first six years, compared to 78% over the preceding six years. See Gruben (2001).

Page 146 **Variance in employment**: Flores et al.'s (2012) computations from comparisons of pre- and post-NAFTA periods (1987–1993 to 1994–2002).

Page 146 **Sensitive to fluctuations in the U.S. economy**: This partly results from the reliance of the northern state economies on *maquiladoras*, a large share of which are U.S.-owned. Three states right on the border (Baja California, Chihuahua, and Tamaulipas), for example, derived almost one-fifth (18%) of their state GDP from *maquiladoras* in the 1993–1999 period. Two other states on the border (Coahuila and Sonora) extracted more than 8% of their GDP from this industry. The remaining states received less than 5% of their GDP from *maquiladoras* (Hanson 2007, p. 424).

Page 146 **Zero growth rate**: Randall (2006, pp. 125–27). About 800 *maquiladoras* closed between 2001 and 2003, most in the northern region.

Page 146 *Maquiladora* **jobs disappeared**: Polaski (2004).

Page 146 **Patterns in Monterrey**: Hernández-León (2008). The quote is from p. 29.

Page 148 **Evidence consistent with the implications**: Fussell and Massey (2004); Roberts, Frank, and Lozano-Ascencio (1999).

Page 148 **Smuggling fees**: The MMP, "Border Crossing Costs" 1975–2012, mmp.opr.princeton.edu/results/001costs-en.aspx

Page 149 **Diversified illicit activities**: Guerrero Gutiérrez (2011); Ríos (2013).

Page 150 **Migrate for adventure**: Hernández-León (1999).

CHAPTER 6

Page 159 **Calderón quote** is from "Some in Mexico See Border Wall as Opportunity," by Ginger Thompson for the *New York Times*, May 25, 2006.

Page 159 **Secure Fence Act**: White House news release. Available at http://georgewbush-whitehouse.archives.gov/news/releases/2006/10/20061026–1.html; accessed on June 29, 2015.

Page 159 **613 miles of fence**: "U.S.-Mexico fence building continues despite Obama's promise to review effects," by April Reese for the *New York Times*, April 16, 2009. **Virtual fence ineffective and costly**: Janet Napolitano, the secretary of Homeland Security, quoted as saying the project "does not meet current standards for viability and cost effectiveness," in "Homeland Security Cancels 'Virtual Fence' After $1 Billion Is Spent," by Julia Preston for the *New York Times*, January 14, 2011.

Page 159 **Border Patrol budget**: Author's computations based on the numbers in the NATLYEAR file of the MMP data. The budget in each year is converted to constant US$ in 2010 and then summed up. **Number of officers**: From U.S. Customs and Border Protection website, http://www.cbp.gov/sites/default/files/documents/BP%20Staffing%20FY1992-FY2014_0.pdf, accessed on July 16, 2015.

Page 159 **Number of undocumented migrants** in 1986 is from Woodrow, Passel, and Warren (1987). Numbers in 2008 and 2010 are from Passel, Cohn, and Gonzalez-Barrera (2012).

Page 160 **Symbolic instruments**: Andreas (1998); Andreas (2012); Calavita (1989); Calavita (1994); Cornelius, Martin, and Hollifield (1994); Massey (1999).

Page 160 **Policy . . . reflects a particular perspective**: Castles (2004); Massey, Durand, and Malone (2003); Massey, Durand, and Pren (2016).

Page 160 **Castles quote**: Castles (2004, p. 858).

Page 160 **Budget increased tenfold**: The 1986 budget for the Border Patrol was around US$300 million (in constant 2010 values); the 2010 budget was more than US$3.5 billion. Source for the data is the NATLYEAR file in the MMP data.

Page 160–161 **Neoclassical model**: Harris and Todaro (1970); **new economics of labor migration**: Stark and Bloom (1985); **cumulative causation**: Massey (1990a); **core periphery**: Sassen (1988); Wallerstein (1974); **segmented labor market**: Piore (1979).

Page 161–162 **Castles quotes**: Castles (2010, p. 1573).

Page 161 **Portes quote**: Portes (1997, p. 810).

Page 161 **Massey et al. quote**: Massey et al. (1998, p. 281).

Page 162 **Massey and Taylor quote**: Massey and Taylor (2004, p. 383).

Page 170 **Ethnographies from that time**: Reichert (1981); Reichert and Massey (1979).

Page 171 **More dependent on smugglers**: Massey, Durand, and Malone (2003).

Page 175 **"Sometimes true" theories**: This is the notion used by sociologist James Coleman (1964). Many complex social phenomena cannot be captured in a single theory, Coleman argues. But one can vary the conditions under which such phenomena exist, and produce several models, which are all true "sometimes," that is, under the specified conditions. See Swedberg (2014) for a useful discussion of this concept.

Page 175 **"mid-range theories"**: Alejandro Portes (1997) used this concept— initially suggested by Robert Merton—to argue against a "grand theory" of migration. Such a theory, he suggested, would be too general to be useful. Instead, researchers should aim for "mid-range theories" that can explain specific empirical findings in specific contexts.

Page 176 **Coleman's boat**: Coleman (1986, 1994). This visual representation has become popular with the recent attention to mechanism-based explanations in sociology. To understand change in the macro-level structure, the argument goes, one needs to first specify the micro-level mechanisms that produce that change. See also Hedström and Bearman (2009a); Hedström and Swedberg (1998); Hedström and Ylikoski (2010).

Page 176 **Transnational lens**: Cornelius, Martin, and Hollifield (1994); Levitt (2001a); Levitt (2001b); Levitt and Schiller (2004); Portes, Guarnizo and Landolt (1999); Schiller, Basch and Blanc (1995); Vertovec (2004).

Page 177 **Policies that are symbolic**: Andreas (2012); Calavita (1989); **with contradictory objectives and unintended consequences**: Calavita (1989); Castles (2004).

Page 177 **Migration policy encompasses** . . . : See Castles (2004); Zolberg (1989).

Page 178 **Reducing the pool of potential migrants**: Hanson and McIntosh (2010) estimate that the declining size of cohorts entering the Mexican labor market accounts for about 40% of the temporal variation in migration to the United States. Hanson and McIntosh (2009) report projections that show the decline in cohort growth will continue into the future in Mexico.

Page 178 **Net migration to a standstill**: Passel, Cohn, and Gonzalez-Barrera (2012); Krogstad and Passel (2014); **below zero**: Gonzalez-Barrera (2015).

Page 178 **Double earnings by moving to the United States**: Clemens, Montenegro, and Pritchett (2008).

Page 179 **Crossing still possible**: Andreas (2012) writes that new border enforcement tactics are often countered with more sophisticated crossing strategies by smugglers, like using more remote entry points, paying off corrupt officials, or relying on fraudulent documents.

Page 179 **Continued demand for immigrant workers**: Bean, Brown, and Bachmeier (2015).

Page 179 **Unaccompanied children**: The numbers are from the U.S. Customs and Border Protection website, http://www.cbp.gov/newsroom/stats/southwest-border -unaccompanied-children, accessed on July 13, 2015; **reasons for the rise in numbers**: Gonzalez-Barrera and Krogstad (2015).

Page 179 **Octavio Paz quote**: "In Search of the Present," Nobel Lecture, December 8, 1990. http://www.nobelprize.org/nobel_prizes/literature/laureates/1990/paz -lecture.html.

APPENDIXES

Page 181 **Tradition of identifying ideal types in sociology**: Weber ([1922] 1978) and Lazarsfeld (1937).

Page 181 **"The statistical turn"**: Camic and Xie (1994).

Page 181 **Aversion to description**: Abbott (2001, pp. 121–22); Swedberg (2014, p. 41).

Page 181 **Typological and population thinking** categories are defined by Mayr (1982).

Page 181 **The roots of typological thinking** in the physical sciences go much further back to Plato, the philosopher of ancient Greece, who lived around 400 BC (Mayr 1982; Xie 2007).

Page 181 **"The determination of the average man"** quote is from Quételet (1842).

Page 182 **Population thinking** started with Darwin (1859) in biology and Galton (1889) in social science. See Hilts (1973); Xie (2007). Galton was also a pioneer in eugenics, coining the term itself, and defining it as "science which deals with all influences to improve the inborn qualities of a race" (Galton 1904). In the first half of the twentieth century, eugenics gathered a strong following, not just in academia, but also in the social and political spheres. Its main premise—nature over nurture (also terms coined by Galton)—was misused to attribute social distinctions to biological merit, and to justify policies to segregate, sterilize, and even kill certain groups in Nazi Germany.

Page 182 How **new tools** (like regression) are used in typological versus population thinking: The difference here is quite subtle; it is not in the application of the tools, but in their interpretation. See Xie (2007) for an insightful discussion.

Page 182 **Duncan quote** is from a personal communication between Otis Dudley Duncan and Yu Xie dated 30 July 1996 and mentioned in Xie (2007).

Page 182 **Heckman quote** is from the Nobel Memorial Lecture in Economic Sciences, December 8, 2000, re-published in Heckman (2001).

Page 182 **Methodological advances** to study population variability: Specific models were developed to address specific kinds of variability. Duncan's (1982) Rasch models consider the variability in survey responses across items and individuals. Raudenbush and Bryk's (1986) multi-level models focus on the variability in outcomes across individuals in different contexts or periods. Following the precursor models by Lazarsfeld and Henry (1968) and Goodman (1974), D'Unger et al.'s (1998) latent-class models and Muthén and Muthén's (2000) growth curve models estimate the variability in outcomes across unknown latent groups or trajectories, respectively.

Page 182 **Typologies not theories**: Portes (1997, p. 806).

Page 182 **Description as vital**: Sen (1980).

Page 183 **Typologies based on data**: For earlier references, see Bailey (1973); Lazarsfeld (1962).

Page 183 **Typologies for conceptualization**: Grimmer and King (2011); Portes (1997); Swedberg (2014).

Page 184 **World systems theory**: Castells (1989); Portes and Walton (1981); Wallerstein (1974).

Page 185–186 **Flows of capital linked to flows of people**: Sassen (1988); **global cities**: Sassen (1991).

Page 186 **Neoclassical economics, differences in wages result in migration**: Harris and Todaro (1970); Todaro (1976).

Page 187 **Regional convergence**: Hatton and Williamson (1998) observe wage convergence between Europe and the United States over a period of eight decades when movement was relatively free.

Page 187 **Migration flows match business cycles**: For earlier work, see Easterlin (1968); Kuznets (1958); Thomas (1941). For more references, see Hatton and Williamson (1998); Massey et al. (1994).

Page 187 **New economics of labor migration**: Stark (1984); Stark (1991); Stark and Bloom (1985); Stark and Levhari (1982); Taylor (1986).

Page 188 **Demographic differential**: Hatton and Williamson (1998); Hatton and Williamson (2005); Zelinsky (1971).

Page 189 **Categorical substitution**: Czaika and De Haas (2013); De Haas (2011).

Page 189 **Nation-state an actor**: Massey (1999); Zolberg (1989).

Page 189 **Global human rights regime**: Cornelius, Martin, and Hollifield (1994).

Page 190 **Symbolic policy instruments**: Andreas (1998); Calavita (1989); Calavita (1994); Espenshade and Calhoun (1993).

Page 190 **Policies follow business cycle**: Meyers (2000); Timmer and Williams (1998).

Page 190 **Influence electoral process**: Lowell, Bean and De La Garza (1986).

Page 190 **Emigration policies, Philippines**: Battistella (1995); Hugo (1997); **Mexico**: Fitzgerald (2008).

Page 191 **Segmented labor market structure**: Piore (1979).

Page 191–192 **Cumulative causation**: Massey (1990a); **through relative deprivation**: Stark and Yitzhaki (1988); Stark and Taylor (1989); **agrarian change**: Reichert (1981); **social networks**: Massey et al. (1987), see Boyd (1989) for a review; **culture of migration**: Kandel and Massey (2002); Reichert (1981); **empirical evidence**: Massey and García-España (1987); Massey and Zenteno (1999), see Boyd (1989); Massey et al. (1994) for reviews.

Page 192 **Internal migration and emigration**: King and Skeldon (2010); Skeldon (2006).

Page 193 **Migrants as rational actors maximizing utility**: Harris and Todaro (1970); Sjaastad (1962); Todaro (1980); Todaro (1969); Todaro and Maruszko (1987).

Page 193–194 **Family as the key unit for migration decisions**: Dinerman (1978); Harbison (1981); Pessar (1982); Roberts (1982); Wiest (1973); Wood (1981).

Page 194 **Migrants as diversifying risks**: Lauby and Stark (1988); Stark (1991); Stark and Bloom (1985); Stark and Levhari (1982); Taylor (1986).

Page 194 **"Fragmented" quote**: Massey et al. (1993, p. 432).

Page 194 **"test[ing] various theoretical explanations" quote**: Massey and Taylor (2004, p. 383).

Page 207 Performance of **scaling methods**: Milligan and Cooper (1988).

Page 207 **De-noise high variance variables**: Legendre and Legendre (1983); **tuning data reasonable**: Grimmer and King (2011).

Page 207 **Matlab implementation**: Matlab (2010).

Page 207 **K-means compared to alternative methods**: Hastie, Tibshirani, and Friedman (2009).

Page 208 **Distance measure more consequential**: Hastie et al. (2009).

Page 208–210 **clValid and fpc packages**: Brock et al. (2008); R Core Team (2010); **Goodman-Kruskal Gamma**: Everitt, Landau, and Leese (2001); **Pearson Gamma**: Halkidi, Batistakis, and Vazirgiannis (2001); **Dunn Index**: Dunn (1974).

Page 211 **Average distance**: Datta and Datta (2003); **figure of merit**: Yeung, Haynor, and Ruzzo (2001).

Page 213 **All individuals in the MMP data**: Life history information is available only for household heads, and spouses in select communities, in the MMP data (LIFE and SPOUSE files). My analysis included all household members to capture the full diversity in the population. I used the household rosters (PERS file), which record the timing of the first U.S. migration, to recreate the characteristics of individuals annually from age 15 onward. I back-projected attributes like age and education, assuming linear progression in the latter. I used information on asset purchases (HOUSE file) to reconstruct the economic status of the household over time, and retrospective community data (COMMUN file) to trace back community characteristics, like labor force composition or migration prevalence.

Page 217 I used a **linear probability model** instead of a logistic model. The latter involves a non-linear transformation of the outcome (migrate or not), which makes the comparison of estimates across samples difficult. See Karlson, Holm, and Breen (2012). The estimates in a linear probability model remain substantively similar to those based on a logistic model presented in table F.1 and figure F.1.

Page 218 **Neoclassical economic theory**: The 'neoclassical' label underlines this theory's focus on supply and demand. 'Classical' economists, like Adam Smith, David Ricardo, John Stuart Mill, and Karl Marx, saw value to be an inherent property of an object dependent only on the costs of production. In the late nineteenth century, this view began to give way to the "neoclassical" perspective, which based value on the relationship between the costs of production and "subjective elements," later called "supply" and "demand" (Weintraub 1993). For the application of this perspective to migration, see Harris and Todaro (1970); Todaro (1976); Todaro (1969). **Empirical evidence**: Many studies suggested Mexico-U.S. migration rates to be significantly associated with the wage and employment levels in the two countries. For example: Bean et al. (1990); Frisbie (1975); Jenkins (1977); White, Bean, and Espenshade (1990).

Page 218 **New economics theory**: Stark (1991), Stark and Bloom (1985), Stark and Taylor (1989), Katz and Stark (1986). **Empirical evidence**: Massey and Espinosa (1997) found that Mexicans are more likely to migrate when the Mexican interest rates—a measure for the availability of credit—are higher.

Page 218 **Segmented labor market theory**: Piore (1979). **Empirical evidence**: Studies found that migration rates from Mexico are higher when farm wages and productivity in the United States are higher (Frisbie 1975). Studies noted that wages and productivity in Mexico also matter—typically more than those in the United States (Bean et al. 1990; Jenkins 1977).

Page 218–219 **World systems theory**: Castells (1989); Portes and Walton (1981); Sassen (1988); Wallerstein (1974). **Empirical evidence**: Ricketts (1987) found the growth in foreign direct investment to predict migration from 18 Caribbean countries to the United States.

Page 219 **Connect migration flows to fertility rates**: Passel, Cohn, and Gonzalez-Barrera (2012) and **to the labor supply**: Bean et al. (1990); Hanson (2006).

Page 219 **Immigration policy**: Massey and Espinosa (1997) found that the odds of Mexican migration were higher for individuals with amnesty recipients in the household. White, Bean, and Espenshade (1990) observed that border apprehensions declined with increased line-watch hours and INS budget after the Immigration Reform and Control Act in 1986.

Page 219 **Crime rates as a determinant of migration**: Hernández-León (2008).

Page 219 **Indicators in our analysis**: The **average wages** for low-skill production workers in the United States come from the Bureau of Labor Statistics (BLS) data (series CES0500000008 for January of each year), adjusted to constant 2010 US$. The **GDP per capita in Mexico** is from the Penn World Tables in constant 2005 US$ (Feenstra, Inklaar, and Timmer 2013). The **unemployment rates** in Mexico and the United States, and the inflation rate in Mexico are from the NATLYEAR series of the Mexican Migration Project (MMP) data (available at http://mmp.opr.princeton.edu/). The **employment growth** in construction equals the annual rate of change in the BLS data series CES2000000001. The employment in agriculture is imputed by subtracting from the total civilian U.S. employment recorded in the NATLYEAR series of the MMP the BLS series for the total non-farm employment (series CES0000000001). The **value of U.S. exports to Mexico** comes from the NATLYEAR series of the MMP; it is adjusted to 2010 US$ and used in natural logarithm form. The **birth rate in Mexico** is measured with the number of births per 1,000 by the Instituto Nacional de Estadística y Geografía (INEGI) and lagged by 20 years to capture the labor supply in any given year. The **U.S. Border Patrol Enforcement budget** is from the NATLYEAR series in the MMP adjusted to 2010 US$. The **number of permanent residencies given to Mexicans** is obtained from the 1996, 1997, and 2012 Statistical Yearbooks on the Department of Homeland Security website (http://www.dhs.gov/immigration-statistics), accessed on June 2, 2014. For years 1986–2012, I have annual numbers of immigrants who were born in Mexico and who obtained permanent resident status (including new arrivals as well as individuals whose status was adjusted while in the United States). For years 1965–1986, I have decennial numbers of immigrants whose country of last residence was Mexico and who obtained permanent resident status. For the latter period, I obtain annual rates by dividing the decennial number by 10.

Page 219 **Other plausible measures**: I could use the minimum wage instead of the GDP per capita in Mexico as Bean et al. (1990) did; the two measures are expectedly correlated (+0.59) and lead to similar results. I could add the rate of change in the dollar value of peso or the interest rates as measures for economic volatility in Mexico like Massey and Espinosa (1997). But these measures would not bring any new information as both are highly correlated (+0.83 and +0.84, respectively) with the Mexican inflation rate included in the model. I could consider the foreign direct investment in Mexico as a measure of core-to-periphery capital flows, but that again is almost perfectly correlated (+0.90) with the value of U.S. exports to Mexico in the model. Instead of the number of permanent residencies granted to Mexicans, I could use the ratio of that number to the total entries (documented and undocumented) like Massey and Espinosa (1997). But, I have found that measure to be highly volatile prior to 1970 due to the declining reliability of the MMP data in estimating the undocumented entry rate, which the authors used to estimate the aggregate number of undocumented entries to the United States. To measure the labor supply in Mexico, I could choose the share of the population between ages 15 and 29 like Hanson (2006); the results remain similar as that indicator is highly correlated (+0.51) with the lagged birth rates in the model. Finally, I excluded indicators for crime rates in Mexico, as those indicators are not available prior to the 1990s. I do have regional variation in some measures (e.g., the number of homicides), which I use to disentangle the effect of crime on migration in chapter 5.

Page 219–220 **Dot plot** is based on Kastellec and Leoni (2007).

Page 220, 222–223 **Figure G.1** and **Table G.1**: I computed Variance Inflation Factors (VIF) to detect multi-collinearity in the models. Three variables attain values higher than 10, the commonly used threshold to determine serious multi-collinearity, which can lead to unstable parameter estimates, among other issues. But, this threshold should be considered in the context of other factors (e.g., R^2 of the model, sample size, t-value of the regression coefficient, etc.) that also affect the stability of estimates (O'brien 2007). In my case, the high R^2 (0.70 in the first model and 0.95 in the second) possibly reduces the variance of the regression coefficients far more than VIF inflates those estimates.

Page 221 It is hard to identify **causal effects** in migration. One reason is the interrelatedness—or endogeneity—of migration to the macro-level context. For example, higher wages in destination can attract migrants, and the presence of migrants in turn can depress the wages. Few studies to date have attempted to identify causal effects in migration using regional, environmental or economic shocks as sources of exogenous variation (e.g., Munshi 2003; Woodruff and Zenteno 2007; Yang 2008).

REFERENCES

Abbott, Andrew. 2001. *Time Matters: On Theory and Method.* Chicago: University of Chicago Press.

Abbott, Andrew, and Alexandra Hrycak. 1990. "Measuring resemblance in sequence data: an optimal matching analysis of musicians' careers." *American Journal of Sociology* 96:144–85.

Abraham, Katharine G., and John C. Haltiwanger. 1995. "Real wages and the business cycle." *Journal of Economic Literature* 33(3):1215–64.

Aguilar, Arturo, Georgia Hartman, David Keyes, Lisa Markman, and Mas Matus. 2010. "Coping with La Crisis." Pp. 15–46 in *Mexican Migration and the U.S. Economic Crisis: A Transnational Perspective*, edited by Wayne A. Cornelius, David FitzGerald, Pedro Lewin Fischer, and Leah Muse-Orlinoff. Boulder, CO: Lynne Rienner.

Alarcón, Rafael. 1992. "Norteñización: Self-perpetuating migration from a Mexican town." Pp. 302–18 in *U.S.-Mexico Relations: Labor Market Interdependence*, edited by Jorge A. Bustamente, Raul A. Hinojosa, and Clark W. Reynolds. Stanford, CA: Stanford University Press.

Alba, Richard, Tomás R. Jiménez, and Helen B. Marrow. 2014. "Mexican Americans as a paradigm for contemporary intra-group heterogeneity." *Ethnic and Racial Studies* 37(3): 446–66.

Alvarado, Steven Elías, and Douglas S. Massey. 2010. "Search of peace: Structural adjustment, violence, and international migration." *Annals of the American Academy of Political and Social Science* 630(1):137–61.

Amuedo-Dorantes, Catalina, and Francesca Mazzolari. 2010. "Remittances to Latin America from migrants in the United States: Assessing the impact of amnesty programs." *Journal of Development Economics* 91(2):323–35.

Anderson, Joan B., and James Gerber. 2009. *Fifty Years of Change on the US-Mexico Border: Growth, Development, and Quality Of Life.* Austin: University of Texas Press.

Andreas, Peter. 1998. "The Escalation of US Immigration Control in the Post-NAFTA Era." *Political Science Quarterly* 113(4):591–615.

———. 2012. *Border Games: Policing the US-Mexico Divide*. Ithaca, NY: Cornell University Press.

Arizpe, Lourdes. 1977. "Women in the informal labor sector: The case of Mexico City." *Signs* 3(1):25–37.

Aspe, Pedro. 1990. "Mexico: Foreign Debt and Economic Growth." Pp. 123–34 in *Mexico's Search for a New Development Strategy*, edited by Dwight Brothers and Adele Wick. Boulder, CO: Westview Press.

Audley, John, Demetrios G. Papademitriou, Sandra Polaski, and Scott Vaughan. 2003. "NAFTA's Promise and Reality: Lessons from Mexico for the Hemisphere." Carnegie Endowment for International Peace Report. http://carnegie endowment.org/files/nafta1.pdf

Bailey, Kenneth D. 1973. "Monothetic and polythetic typologies and their relation to conceptualization, measurement and scaling." *American Sociological Review* 38(1):18–33.

Baker, Bryan C. 2010. "Naturalization rates among IRCA immigrants: A 2009 update." U.S. Department of Homeland Security Fact Sheet. https://www.dhs .gov/sites/default/files/publications/irca-natz-fs-2009.pdf

Baker, Susan Gonzalez. 1990. *The Cautious Welcome: The Legalization Programs of the Immigration Reform and Control Act*. Washington, DC: Urban Insitute.

———. 1997. "The amnesty aftermath: Current policy issues stemming from the legalization programs of the 1986 immigration reform and control act." *International Migration Review* 31(1):5–27.

Battistella, Graziano. 1995. "Philippine overseas labour: From export to management." *ASEAN Economic Bulletin* 12(2):257–73.

Bean, Frank D., James D. Bachmeier, and Susan K. Brown. 2014. " A Crucial Piece of the Puzzle: Demographic Change and Why Immigrants Are Needed to Fill America's Less-Skilled Labor Gap." *Partnership for a New American Economy Research Report*. http://www.renewoureconomy.org/wp-content/uploads/2014/03/ less-skilled-final.pdf

Bean, Frank D., Susan K. Brown, and James D. Bachmeier. 2015. *Parents Without Papers: The Progress and Pitfalls of Mexican American Integration*. New York: Russell Sage.

Bean, Frank D., Rodolfo Corona, Rodolfo Tuiran, Karen A. Woodrow-Lafield, and Jennifer van Hook. 2001. "Circular, invisible, and ambiguous migrants: Components of difference in estimates of the number of unauthorized Mexican migrants in the United States." *Demography* 38(3):411–22.

Bean, Frank D., Barry Edmonston, and Jeffrey S. Passel. 1990. *Undocumented Migration to the United States: IRCA and the Experience of the 1980s*. Washington, DC: Urban Insitute Press.

Bean, Frank D., Thomas J. Espenshade, Michael J. White, and Robert F. Dymowski. 1990. "Post-IRCA Changes in the Volume and Composition of Undocumented Migration to the United States: An Assessment Based on Apprehensions Data." Pp. 111–58 in *Undocumented Migration to the United States:*

IRCA and the Experience of the 1980s, edited by Frank D. Bean, Barry Edmonston, and Jeffrey S. Passel. Washington, DC: Urban Institute Press.

Bean, Frank D., and Gillian Stevens. 2003. *America's Newcomers and the Dynamics of Diversity*. New York: Russell Sage.

Bean, Frank D., Edward E. Telles, and B. Lindsay Lowell. 1987. "Undocumented migration to the United States: Perceptions and evidence." *Population and Development Review* 13(4):671–90.

Bean, Frank D., Georges Vernez, and Charles B. Keely. 1989. *Opening and Closing the Doors: Evaluating Immigration Reform and Control*. Washington, DC: Urban Institute.

Becker, Gary S. 1962. "Investment in human capital: A theoretical analysis." *Journal of Political Economy* 70(5):9–49.

———. 1964. *Human Capital: A Theoretical and Empirical Analysis, with Special Reference to Education*. Chicago: University of Chicago Press.

———. 1993. "Nobel lecture: The economic way of looking at behavior." *Journal of Political Economy* 101(3):385–409.

Bonacich, Edna. 1993. "Asian and Latino Immigrants in the Los Angeles garment industry: An exploration of the relationship between capitalism and racial oppression." Pp. 51–73 in *Immigrant and Entrepreneurship: Culture, Capital, and Ethnic Networks*, edited by Ivan Light and Parminder Bhachu. New Brunswick, NJ: Transaction Publishers.

Borjas, George J. 1987. "Self-selection and the earnings of immigrants." *American Economic Review* 77(4):531–53.

———. 1991. "Immigration and self-selection." Pp. 29–76 in *Immigration, Trade, and the Labor Market*, edited by John M. Abowd and Richard B. Freeman. Chicago: University of Chicago Press.

———. 1996. "The earnings of Mexican immigrants in the United States." *Journal of Development Economics* 51(1):69–98.

———. 1999. "The economic analysis of immigration." Pp. 1697–1760 in *Handbook of Labor Economics*, edited by Orley C. Ashenfelter and David Card. Amsterdam: North-Holland.

Boyd, Monica. 1989. "Family and personal networks in international migration: Recent developments and new agendas." *International Migration Review* 23(3):638–70.

Boyd, Monica, and Elizabeth Grieco. 2003. "Women and migration: Incorporating gender into international migration theory." *Migration Information Source*. http://www.migrationpolicy.org/article/women-and-migration-incorporating -gender-international-migration-theory/

Bravo Aguilera, Luis. 1989. "La política comercial de México y el acuerdo general sobre aranceles aduaneros y comercio." Pp. 25–61 in *La adhesión de México al GATT: Repercusiones internas e impacto sobre las relaciones México-Estados Unidos*, edited by Pamela S. Falk and Blanca Torres. Mexico, DF: El Colegio de México.

Brock, Guy, Vasyl Pihur, Susmita Datta, and Somnath Datta. 2008. "clValid: An R Package for Cluster Validation." *Journal of Statistical Software* 25:1–22.

Burt, Ronald S. 1997. "A note on social capital and network content." *Social Networks* 19(4):355–73.

———. 1998. "The gender of social capital." *Rationality and Society* 10(1):5–46.

Bustamante, Jorge A. 1990. "Undocumented migration from Mexico to the United States: Preliminary findings of the Zapata Canyon Project." Pp. 211–26 in *Undocumented Migration to the United States: IRCA and the Experience of the 1980s*, edited by Frank D. Bean, Barry Edmonston, and Jeffrey Passel. Washington, DC: Urban Institute.

Calavita, Kitty. 1989. "The contradictions of immigration lawmaking: The Immigration Reform and Control Act of 1986." *Law & Policy* 11(1):17–47.

———. 1994. "US immigration and policy responses: The limits of legislation." Pp. 55–82 in *Controlling Immigration: A Global Perspective*, edited by Wayne Cornelius, Philip Martin, and James F. Hollifield. Stanford, CA: Stanford University Press.

———. 2010. *Inside the State: The Bracero Program, Immigration, and the INS*. New Orleans, LA: Quid Pro Books.

Camarillo, Albert. 1984. *Chicanos in California: A History of Mexican Americans in California*. San Francisco: Boyd & Fraser Publishing.

———. 2004. "Alambrista and the historical context of Mexican immigration to the United States in the twentieth century." Pp. 13–36 in *Alambrista and the US-Mexico Border: Film, Music, and Stories of Undocumented Immigrants*, edited by Nicholas Cull and David Carrasco. Albuquerque: University of New Mexico Press.

Camic, Charles, and Yu Xie. 1994. "The statistical turn in American social science: Columbia University, 1890 to 1915." *American Sociological Review* 59(5):773–805.

Cardoso, Lawrence A. 1980. *Mexican Emigration to the United States, 1897–1931: Socio-economic Patterns*. Tucson: University of Arizona Press.

Carrington, William J., Enrica Detragiache, and Tara Vishwanath. 1996. "Migration with endogenous moving costs." *American Economic Review* 86(4):909–30.

Carriquiry, Alicia, and Malay Majmundar (Eds.). 2012. *Options for Estimating Illegal Entries at the U.S.-Mexico Border*. Washington, DC: National Academies Press.

Castells, Manuel. 1989. *The Informational City: Information Technology, Economic Restructuring and the Urban-Regional Process*. Oxford: Blackwell Publishers.

Castles, Stephen. 2004. "The factors that make and unmake migration policies." *International Migration Review* 38(3):852–84.

———. 2010. "Understanding global migration: A social transformation perspective." *Journal of Ethnic and Migration Studies* 36(10):1565–86.

Castles, Stephen, Hein De Haas, and Mark J. Miller. 2014. *The Age of Migration: International Population Movements in the Modern World*. Basingstoke: Palgrave MacMillan.

Centeno, Miguel Angel. 2010. *Democracy within Reason: Technocratic Revolution in Mexico*. University Park: Pennslvania State University Press.

Cerrutti, Marcela, and Douglas S. Massey. 2001. "On the auspices of female migration from Mexico to the United States." *Demography* 38(2):187–200.

Chiquiar, Daniel. 2008. "Globalization, regional wage differentials and the Stolper–Samuelson theorem: Evidence from Mexico." *Journal of International Economics* 74(1):70–93.

Chiquiar, Daniel, and Gordon H. Hanson. 2005. "International migration, self-selection, and the distribution of wages: Evidence from Mexico and the United States." *Journal of Political Economy* 113(2):239–81.

Clemens, Michael A., Claudio E. Montenegro, and Lant Pritchett. 2008. "The place premium: Wage differences for identical workers across the U.S. border." World Bank Policy Research Working Paper No. 4671. http://elibrary.world bank.org/doi/abs/10.1596/1813-9450-4671

CNIE. 1998. *Informe estadístico sobre el comportamiento de la inversión extranjera directa en México*. Mexico, DF: Comisión nacional de inversiones extranjeras.

Cohen, Jeffrey H. 2004. *The Culture of Migration in Southern Mexico*. Austin: University of Texas Press.

Coleman, James S. 1986. "Social theory, social research, and a theory of action." *American Journal of Sociology* 91(6):1309–35.

Coleman, James Samuel. 1964. *Introduction to Mathematical Sociology*. New York: Free Press Glencoe.

———. 1994. *Foundations of Social Theory*. Cambridge, MA: Harvard University Press.

Cornelius, Wayne (Ed.). 1991. *Los migrantes de la crisis: The Changing Profile of Mexican Immigration to the United States*. San Diego: Center for U.S.-Mexican Studies, University of California.

Cornelius, Wayne A. 1978. *Mexican Migration to the United States: Causes, Consequences, and U.S. Responses*. Cambridge, MA: Center for International Studies, Massachusetts Institute of Technology.

———. 1989. "Impacts of the 1986 U.S. immigration law on emigration from rural Mexican sending communities." *Population and Development Review* 15(4):689–705.

Cornelius, Wayne A., and Philip L. Martin. 1993. "The uncertain connection: Free trade and rural Mexican migration to the United States." *International Migration Review* 27(3):484–512.

Cornelius, Wayne A., Philip L. Martin, and James Frank Hollifield. 1994. *Controlling Immigration: A Global Perspective*. Stanford, CA: Stanford University Press.

Cornelius, Wayne A. 1992. "From sojourners to settlers: The changing profile of Mexican immigration to the United States." Pp. 155–95 in *U.S.-Mexico Relations: Labor Market Interdependence*, edited by Jorge A. Bustamente, Clark W. Reynolds, and Raul A. Hinojosa. Stanford, CA: Stanford University Press.

———. 2001. "Death at the border: Efficacy and unintended consequences of U.S. immigration control policy." *Population and Development Review* 27(4):661–85.

Cowan, Nelson. 2001. "The magical number 4 in short-term memory: A reconsideration of mental storage capacity." *Behavioral and Brain Sciences* 24(1):87–114.

Craig, Richard B. 2015. *The Bracero Program: Interest Groups and Foreign Policy.* Austin: University of Texas Press.

Crane, Keith, Beth J. Asch, Joanna Zorn Heilbrunn, and Danielle C Cullinane. 1990. *The Effect of Employer Sanctions on the Flow of Undocumented Immigrants to the United States.* Lanham, MD: University Press of America.

Curran, Sara R., and Abigail C. Saguy. 2001. "Migration and cultural change: A role for gender and social networks." *Journal of International Women's Studies* 2(3):54–77.

Curran, Sara R., Filiz Garip, Chang Y. Chung, and Kanchana Tangchonlatip. 2005. "Gendered migrant social capital: Evidence from Thailand." *Social Forces* 84(1):225–55.

Curran, Sara R., and Estela Rivero-Fuentes. 2003. "Engendering migrant networks: The case of Mexican migration." *Demography* 40(2):289–307.

Czaika, Mathias, and Hein De Haas. 2013. "The effectiveness of immigration policies." *Population and Development Review* 39(3):487–508.

D'Unger, Amy V., Kenneth C. Land, Patricia L. McCall, and Daniel S. Nagin. 1998. "How many latent classes of delinquent/criminal careers? Results from mixed poisson regression analyses." *American Journal of Sociology* 103(6):1593–1630.

Darwin, Charles. 1859. *On the Origin of Species by Means of Natural Selection, or the Preservation of Favoured Races in the Struggle for Life.* New York: D. Appleton.

Datta, Susmita, and Somnath Datta. 2003. "Comparisons and validation of statistical clustering techniques for microarray gene expression data." *Bioinformatics* 19:459–66.

Dávila, Alberto, José A. Pagán, and Gökçe Soydemir. 2002. "The short-term and long-term deterrence effects of INS border and interior enforcement on undocumented immigration." *Journal of Economic Behavior & Organization* 49(4):459–72.

Davis, Benjamin, Guy Stecklov, and Paul Winters. 2002. "Domestic and international migration from rural Mexico: Disaggregating the effects of network structure and composition." *Population Studies* 56(3):291–309.

Davis, Brenda, and Paul Winters. 2003. "Gender, networks and Mexico-U.S. migration." *Journal of Development Studies* 38:1–26.

Dawes, Robyn M. 1998. "Behavioral decision making and judgment." Pp. 497–548 in *Handbook of Social Psychology*, edited by Susan T. Fiske, Daniel T. Gilbert, and Gardner Lindzey. New York: McGraw-Hill.

De Haas, Hein. 2005. "International migration, remittances and development: Myths and facts." *Third World Quarterly* 26(8):1269–84.

———. 2010a. "The internal dynamics of migration processes: A theoretical inquiry." *Journal of Ethnic and Migration Studies* 36(10):1587–1617.

————. 2010b. "Migration and development: A theoretical perspective." *International Migration Review* 44(1):227–64.

————. 2011. "The determinants of international migration: Conceptualizing policy, origin and destination effects." Oxford University International Migration Institute, Working Paper 32. http://www.devstud.org.uk/aqadmin/media/uploads/4dc3c9cac333a_WP32%20The%20Determinants%20of%20International%20Migration.pdf

de Janvry, Alain, Gustavo Gordillo, and Elisabeth Sadoulet. 1997. *Mexico's Second Agrarian Reform: Household and Community Responses, 1990–1994*. San Diego: Center for U.S.–Mexican Studies, University of California at San Diego.

de Janvry, Alain, and Elisabeth Sadoulet. 2001. "Income strategies among rural households in Mexico: The role of off-farm activities." *World Development* 29(3):467–80.

de la Rocha, Mercedes González. 1988. "Economic crisis, domestic reorganisation and women's work in Guadalajara, Mexico." *Bulletin of Latin American Research* 7(2):207–23.

————. 1994. *The Resources of Poverty. Women and Survival in a Mexican City*. Oxford, UK and Cambridge, MA: Blackwell.

————. 2007. "The construction of the myth of survival." *Development and Change* 38(1):45–66.

De la Peña, Guillermo. 1984. "Ideology and practice in Southern Jalisco: Peasants, rancheros, and urban entrepreneurs." Pp. 204–34 in *Kinship Ideology and Practice in Latin America*, edited by Raymond T. Smith. Chapel Hill: University of North Carolina Press.

Degg, Martin R. 1989. "Earthquake hazard assessment after Mexico (1985)." *Disasters* 13(3):237–46.

del Rey Poveda, Alberto. 2007. "Determinants and consequences of internal and international migration: The case of rural populations in the south of Veracruz, Mexico." *Demographic Research* 16(10):287–314.

Dell, Melissa. 2015. "Trafficking networks and the Mexican drug war." *American Economic Review* 105(6):1738–79.

Díaz-Cayeros, Alberto, Beatriz Magaloni, Aila M. Matanock, and Vidal Romero. 2011. "Living in fear: Mapping the social embeddedness of drug gangs and violence in Mexico." Working Paper. Stanford University. http://web.stanford.edu/~magaloni/dox/2011livinginfear.pdf

DiMaggio, Paul, and Filiz Garip. 2011. "How network externalities can exacerbate intergroup inequality." *American Journal of Sociology* 116(6):1887–1933.

————. 2012. "Network effects and social inequality." *Annual Review of Sociology* 38:93–118.

Dinerman, Ina R. 1978. "Patterns of adaptation among households of U.S.-bound migrants from Michoacán, Mexico." *International Migration Review* 12(4):485–501.

Divine, Robert A. 1957. *American Immigration Policy, 1924–1952*. New Haven, CT: Yale University Press.

Donato, Katharine M., and Shawn M. Kanaiaupuni. 1999. "Women's status and demographic change: The case of Mexico-U.S. migration." Pp. 217–42 in *Women, Poverty, and Demographic Change*, edited by Brígida Garcia and Karen Mason. Geneva: International Union for the Scientific Study in Population.

Donato, Katharine M. 1991. "Understanding U.S. immigration: Why some countries send women and others men." Pp. 159–84 in *Seeking Common Ground: Women Immigrants to the United States*, edited by Donna Gabaccia. Westport, CT: Greenwood.

——— 1993. "Current trends and patterns of female migration: Evidence from Mexico." *International Migration Review* 27(4):748–71.

Donato, Katharine M., Joseph T. Alexander, Donna R. Gabaccia, and Johanna Leinonen. 2011. "Variations in the gender composition of immigrant populations: How they matter." *International Migration Review* 45(3):495–526.

Donato, Katharine M., Jorge Durand, and Douglas S. Massey. 1992a. "Changing conditions in the US labor market." *Population Research and Policy Review* 11(2):93–115.

——— 1992b. "Stemming the tide? Assessing the deterrent effects of the Immigration Reform and Control Act." *Demography* 29(2):139–57.

Donato, Katharine M., and Donna Gabaccia. 2015. *Gender and International Migration: From the Slavery Era to the Global Age*. New York: Russell Sage.

Donato, Katharine M., Donna Gabaccia, Jennifer Holdaway, Martin Manalansan, and Patricia R. Pessar. 2006. "A glass half full? Gender in migration studies." *International Migration Review* 40(1):3–26.

Donato, Katharine M., and Douglas S. Massey. 1993. "Effect of the Immigration Reform and Control Act on the wages of Mexican migrants." *Social Science Quarterly* 74(3):523–41.

Donato, Katharine M., and Blake Sisk. 2015. "Children's migration to the United States from Mexico and Central America: Evidence from the Mexican and Latin American Migration Project." *Journal of Migration and Human Security* 3(1):58–79.

Donato, Katharine M., Charles M. Tolbert, Alfred Nucci, and Yukio Kawano. 2007. "Recent immigrant settlement in the nonmetropolitan United States: Evidence from internal census data." *Rural Sociology* 72(4):537–59.

Duncan, Otis Dudley. 1982. "Rasch measurement and sociological theory." Hollingshead Lecture, Yale University. http://scholar.princeton.edu/sites/default/files/yuxie/files/ducan1982rasch.pdf

Dunn, J. C. 1974. "Well-separated clusters and optimal fuzzy partitions." *Cybernetics and Systems* 4:95–104.

Durand, Jorge, and Douglas S. Massey. 1995. *Miracles on the Border: Retablos of Mexican Migrants to the United States*. Tucson, AZ and London, UK: University of Arizona Press.

Durand, Jorge, and Douglas S. Massey. 2003. *Clandestinos: migración México-Estados Unidos en los albores del siglo XXI*. México, DF: Editorial Porrua.

Durand, Jorge, Douglas S. Massey, and Chiara Capoferro. 2005. "The new geography of Mexican immigration." Pp. 1–20 in *New Destinations: Mexican Immigration in the United States*, edited by Victor Zúñiga and Rubén Hernández-León. New York: Russell Sage.

Durand, Jorge, Douglas S. Massey, and Emilio A. Parrado. 1999. "The new era of Mexican migration to the United States." *Journal of American History* 86(2):518–36.

Durand, Jorge, Douglas S. Massey, and Rene M. Zenteno. 2001. "Mexican immigration to the United States: Continuities and changes." *Latin American Research Review* 36(1):107–27.

Dutka, Anna. 1994. "Demographic trends in the labor force." Pp. 15–32 in *The Changing U.S. Labor Market*, edited by Eli Ginzberg. Boulder, CO: Westview Press.

Easterlin, Richard A. 1968. *Population, Labor Force, and Long Swings in Economic Growth: The American Experience*. New York: Columbia University Press.

England, Paula, and Nancy Folbre. 2005. "Gender and economic sociology." Pp. 627–49 in *The Handbook of Economic Sociology*, edited by Neil Smelser and Richard Swedberg. Princeton, NJ: Princeton University Press.

Epstein, Gil S. 2008. "Herd and network effects in migration decision-making." *Journal of Ethnic and Migration Studies* 34(4):567–83.

Eschbach, Karl, Jacqueline M. Hagan, Nestor Rodriguez, Rubén Hernández-León, and Stanley Bailey. 1999. "Death at the border." *International Migration Review* 33(2):430–54.

Espenshade, Thomas J. 1990. "Undocumented migration to the United States: Evidence from a repeated trials model." Pp. 159–81 in *Undocumented Migration to the United States: IRCA and the Experience of the 1980s*, edited by Frank D. Bean. Washington, DC: Urban Institute Press.

Espenshade, Thomas J., and Charles A. Calhoun. 1993. "An analysis of public opinion toward undocumented immigration." *Population Research and Policy Review* 12(3):189–224.

Espenshade, Thomas J., and Katherine Hempstead. 1996. "Contemporary American attitudes toward U.S. immigration." *International Migration Review* 30(2):535–70.

Espinosa, Kristin, and Douglas S. Massey. 1997. "Undocumented migration and the quantity and quality of social capital." *Soziale Welt. Sonderband* 12: 141–62.

Everitt, Brian S., Sabine Landau, and Morven Leese. 2001. *Cluster Analysis*. London: Arnold.

Ewick, Patricia, and Susan Silbey. 2003. "Narrating social structure: Stories of resistance to legal authority." *American Journal of Sociology* 108(6):1328–72.

Fairbrother, Malcolm. 2014. "Economists, capitalists, and the making of globalization: North American Free Trade in comparative-historical perspective." *American Journal of Sociology* 119(5):1324–79.

Fairris, David. 2003. "Unions and wage inequality in Mexico." *Industrial and Labor Relations Review* 56(3):481–97.

Feenstra, Robert C., Robert Inklaar, and Marcel Timmer. 2013. "The Next Generation of the Penn World Table." National Bureau of Economic Research Working Paper No.19255. http://www.nber.org/papers/w19255

Feliciano, Zadia M. 2001. "Workers and trade liberalization: The impact of trade reforms in Mexico on wages and employment." *Industrial and Labor Relations Review* 55(1):95–115.

Fennelly, Katherine. 2005. "Latinos, Africans and Asians in the north star state: Immigrant communities in Minnesota." Pp. 111–36 in *Beyond the Gateway: Immigrants in a Changing America*, edited by Elzbieta M. Gozdziak and Susan F. Martin. Lanham, MD: Lexington Books.

Fernandez-Kelly, M. Patricia 1983. *"For We Are Sold, I and My People": Women and Industry in Mexico's Frontier*. Albany: State University of New York Press.

Fernandez-Kelly, M. Patricia, and Anna M. Garcia. 1990. "Power surrendered, power restored: The politics of work and family among Hispanic garment workers in California and Florida." Pp. 130–49 in *Women, Politics, and Change*, edited by Louise A. Tilly and Patricia Gurin. New York: Russell Sage.

FitzGerald, David. 2008. *A Nation of Emigrants: How Mexico Manages Its Migration*. Berkeley: University of California Press.

Fix, Michael, and Paul T. Hill. 1990. *Enforcing Employer Sanctions: Challenges and Strategies*. Santa Monica: RAND Corporation.

Flores, Miguel, Mary Zey, Cinthya Caamal, and Nazrul Hoque. 2012. "NAFTA, industrial concentration, employment volatility, wages, and internal and international Mexican migration: 1990–2009." Pp. 155–72 in *Opportunities and Challenges for Applied Demography in the 21st Century*, edited by Nazrul Hoque and David A. Swanson. London: Springer.

Foerster, Robert. 1925. "The racial problems involved in immigration from Latin America and the West Indies to the United States." Report submitted to the Secretary of the U.S. Department of Labor. Washington, DC: U.S. Government Publishing Office.

Fox, Michael D., Abraham Z. Snyder, Justin L. Vincent, Maurizio Corbetta, David C. Van Essen, and Marcus E. Raichle. 2005. "The human brain is intrinsically organized into dynamic, anticorrelated functional networks." *Proceedings of the National Academy of Sciences of the United States of America* 102(27):9673–78.

Freeman, Richard B. 2007. *America Works: Thoughts on an Exceptional US Labor Market*. New York: Russell Sage.

Frisbie, Parker W. 1975. "Illegal migration from Mexico to the United States: a longitudinal analysis." *International Migration Review* 9(1):3–13.

Frye, Margaret. 2013. "Cultural Meanings and the Aggregation of Actions: The Case of Sex and Schooling in Malawi." Office of Population Research Working Paper, Princeton University.

Fussell, Elizabeth. 2004a. "Sources of Mexico's migration stream: Rural, urban, and border migrants to the United States." *Social Forces* 82(3):937–67.

———. 2004b. "Tijuana's Place in the Mexican migration stream: Destination for internal migrants or stepping stone to the United States." Pp. 147–70 in *Crossing the Border: Research from the Mexican Migration Project*, edited by Jorge Durand and Douglas Massey. New York: Russel Sage.

Fussell, Elizabeth, and Douglas S. Massey. 2004. "The limits to cumulative causation: International migration from Mexican urban areas." *Demography* 41(1):151–71.

Galton, Francis. 1889. *Natural Inheritance*. London and New York: Macmillan.

———. 1904. "Eugenics: Its definition, scope, and aims." *American Journal of Sociology* 10(1):1–25.

Garip, Filiz. 2008. "Social capital and migration: How do similar resources lead to divergent outcomes?" *Demography* 45(3):591–617.

Gathmann, Christina. 2008. "Effects of enforcement on illegal markets: Evidence from migrant smuggling along the southwestern border." *Journal of Public Economics* 92(10):1926–41.

Gibson, Campbell J., and Emily Lennon. 1999. "Historical census statistics on the foreign-born population of the United States: 1850–1990." *Population Division Working Paper No. 29*. Washington, DC: U.S. Census Bureau.

Ginzberg, Eli (Ed.). 1994. *The Changing U.S. Labor Market*. Boulder, CO: Westview Press.

Gladstein, Hannah, Annie Lai, Jennifer Wagner, and Michael Wishnie. 2005. "Blurring the lines." Migration Policy Institute Report. New York: NYU School of Law.

Goldring, Luin. 2004. "Family and collective remittances to Mexico: A Multidimensional typology." *Development and Change* 35(4):799–840.

Gonzalez-Barrera, Ana. 2015. "More Mexicans Leaving Than Coming to the US." Pew Research Center Report. http://www.pewhispanic.org/2015/11/19/more -mexicans-leaving-than-coming-to-the-u-s/

Gonzalez-Barrera, Ana, and Jens Manuel Krogstad. 2015. "With help from Mexico, number of child migrants crossing the border falls." Pew Research Center Report. http://www.pewresearch.org/fact-tank/2015/04/28/child-migrants -border/

Goodman, Leo A. 1974. "Exploratory latent structure analysis using both identifiable and unidentifiable models." *Biometrika* 61:215–31.

Grasmuck, Sherri, and Patricia R. Pessar. 1991. *Between Two Islands: Dominican International Migration*. Berkeley: University of California Press.

Greicius, Michael D., Benjamin H. Flores, Vinod Menon, Gary H. Glover, Hugh B. Solvason, Heather Kenna, Allan L. Reiss, and Alan F. Schatzberg. 2007. "Resting-state functional connectivity in major depression: Abnormally increased contributions from subgenual cingulate cortex and thalamus." *Biological Psychiatry* 62(5):429–37.

Griffith, David C. 2005. "Rural industry and Mexican immigration and settlement in North Carolina." Pp. 50–75 in *New Destinations: Mexican Immigration in the*

United States, edited by Victor Zúñiga and Rubén Hernández-León. New York: Russell Sage.

Grimmer, Justin, and Gary King. 2009. "Quantitative discovery from qualitative information: A general-purpose document clustering methodology." APSA 2009 Toronto Meeting Paper.

———. 2011. "General purpose computer-assisted clustering and conceptualization." *Proceedings of the National Academy of Sciences* 108(7):2643–50.

Grindle, Merilee Serrill. 1988. *Searching for Rural Development: Labor Migration and Employment in Mexico*. Ithaca, NY: Cornell University Press.

Gruben, William C. 2001. "Was NAFTA behind Mexico's high maquiladora growth?" Pp. 11–21 in *Economic and Financial Review*. Dallas, TX: Federal Reserve Bank of Dallas.

Guerrero Gutiérrez, Eduardo. 2011. "Security, drugs, and violence in Mexico: A survey." *7th North American Forum*, Washington, DC.

Gurak, Douglas T., and Fee Caces. 1992. "Migration networks and the shaping of migration systems." Pp.150–76 in *International Migration Systems: A Global Approach*, edited by Mary M. Kritz, Lin Lean Lim, and Hania Zlotnik. Oxford, UK: Clarendon Press.

Gutiérrez, David G. 1995. *Walls and Mirrors: Mexican Americans, Mexican Immigrants, and the Politics of Ethnicity*. Berkeley: University of California Press.

Hagan, Jacqueline M. 1994. *Deciding to Be Legal: A Maya Community in Houston*. Philadelphia: Temple University Press.

———. 1998. "Social networks, gender, and immigrant incorporation: Resources and constraints." *American Sociological Review* 63(1):55–67.

Hagan, Jacqueline M., and Susan Gonzalez Baker. 1993. "Implementing the US legalization program: The influence of immigrant communities and local agencies on immigration policy reform." *International Migration Review* 27(3):513–36.

Halkidi, Maria, Yannis Batistakis, and Michalis Vazirgiannis. 2001. "On clustering validation techniques." *Journal of Intelligent Information Systems* 17(2–3):107–45.

Hanson, Gordon H. 1996. "Economic integration, intraindustry trade, and frontier regions." *European Economic Review* 40(3):941–49.

———. 1998. "Regional adjustment to trade liberalization." *Regional Science and Urban Economics* 28(4):419–44.

———. 2003. "What has happened to wages in Mexico since NAFTA?": National Bureau of Economic Research Working Paper No. 9563. http://www.nber.org/papers/w9563

———. 2006. "Illegal migration from Mexico to the United States." National Bureau of Economic Research Working Paper No. 12141. http://www.nber.org/papers/w12141

———. 2007. "Globalization, labor income, and poverty in Mexico." Pp. 417–56 in *Globalization and Poverty*, edited by Ann Harrison. Chicago: University of Chicago Press.

Hanson, Gordon H., and Ann Harrison. 1999. "Trade liberalization and wage inequality in Mexico." *Industrial and Labor Relations Review* 52(2):271–88.

Hanson, Gordon H., and Craig McIntosh. 2009. "The demography of Mexican migration to the United States." *American Economic Review* 99(2):22–27.

———. 2010. "The great Mexican emigration." *Review of Economics and Statistics* 92(4):798–810.

Harbison, Sarah F. 1981. "Family structure and family strategy in migration decision making." Pp. 225–51 in *Migration Decision Making: Multidisciplinary Approaches to Microlevel Studies in Developed and Developing Countries*, edited by Gordon De Jong and Robert W. Gardner. New York: Pergamon Press.

Harris, John R., and Michael P. Todaro. 1970. "Migration, unemployment and development: a two-sector analysis." *American Economic Review* 60(1):126–42.

Hastie, Trevor, Robert Tibshirani, and Jerome Friedman. 2009. *The Elements of Statistical Learning: Data Mining, Inference, and Prediction*. New York: Springer.

Hatton, Timothy J., and Jeffrey G. Williamson. 1998. *The Age of Mass Migration: Causes and Economic Impact*. Oxford and New York: Oxford University Press.

———. 2005. *Global Migration and the World Economy: Two Centuries of Policy and Performance*. Cambridge, MA: MIT Press.

Heath, John. 1988. "An overview of the Mexican agricultural crisis." Pp. 129–63 in *The Mexican Economy*, edited by George Philip. London: Routledge.

Heckman, James J. 2001. "Micro data, heterogeneity, and the evaluation of public policy: Nobel lecture." *Journal of Political Economy* 109(4):673–748.

Hedström, Peter. 2005. *Dissecting the Social: On the Principles of Analytical Sociology*. Cambridge: Cambridge University Press.

Hedström, Peter, and Peter Bearman. 2009a. *The Oxford Handbook of Analytical Sociology*. Oxford and New York: Oxford University Press.

———. 2009b. "'What is analytical sociology all about?' An introductory essay." Pp. 3–24 in *The Oxford Handbook of Analytical Sociology*, edited by Peter Hedström and Peter Bearman. Oxford and New York: Oxford University Press.

Hedström, Peter, and Richard Swedberg. 1998. *Social Mechanisms: An Analytical Approach to Social Theory*. Cambridge: Cambridge University Press.

Hedström, Peter, and Petri Ylikoski. 2010. "Causal mechanisms in the social sciences." *Annual Review of Sociology* 36:49–67.

Henderson, Timothy J. 2011. *Beyond Borders: A History of Mexican Migration to the United States*. Chichester, West Sussex, UK, and Malden, MA: Wiley-Blackwell.

Hernández-León, Rubén. 2008. *Metropolitan Migrants: The Migration of Urban Mexicans to the United States*. Berkeley: University of California Press.

Hernández-León, Rubén. 1999. "'¡A la aventura!': Jóvenes, pandillas y migración en la conexión Monterrey-Houston." Pp. 115–43 in *Fronteras fragmentadas*, edited by Gail Mummert. Zamora: El Colegio de Michoacan.

Hernández-León, Rubén, and Víctor Zúñiga. 2000. "'Making carpet by the mile': the emergence of a Mexican immigrant community in an industrial region of the U.S. historic South." *Social Science Quarterly* 81(1):49–66.

Hilts, Victor. 1973. "Statistics and social science." Pp. 206–22 in *Foundations of Scientific Method: The Nineteenth Century*, edited by Ronald N. Giere and Richard S. Westfall. Bloomington: Indiana University Press.

Hinojosa-Ojeda, Raul, and Sherman Robinson. 1992. "Labor issues in a North American Free Trade Area." Pp. 69–98 in *North American Free Trade: Assessing the Impact*, edited by Nora Lustig, Barry P. Bosworth, and Robert Z. Lawrence. Washington, DC: Brookings Institute.

Hondagneu-Sotelo, Pierette. 1992. "Overcoming patriarchal constraints." *Gender & Society* 6(3):393.

———. 1994. *Gendered Transitions: Mexican Experiences of Immigration*. Berkeley: University of California Press.

Hossfeld, Karen J. 1990. "Their logic against them: Contradictions in sex, race, and class in Silicon Valley." Pp. 149–78 in *Women Workers and Global Restructuring*, edited by Kathryn Ward. Ithaca, NY: ILR Press, School of Industrial and Labor Relations, Cornell University.

Hufbauer, Gary Clyde, and Jeffrey J Schott. 1992. *North American Free Trade: Issues and Recommendations*. Washington, DC: Institute for International Economics.

Hugo, Graeme. 1997. "Asia and the Pacific on the move: Workers and refugees, a challenge to nation states." *Asia Pacific Viewpoint* 38(3):267–86.

———. 1981. "Village-community ties, village norms, and ethnic and social networks: A review of evidence from the third world." Pp. 186–224 in *Migration Decision Making: Multidisciplinary Approaches to Microlevel Studies in Developed and Developing Countries*, edited by Gordon De Jong and Robert W. Gardner. New York: Pergamon Press.

———. 2000. "Migration and women's empowerment." Pp. 287–317 in *Women's Empowerment and Demographic Processes: Moving Beyond Cairo*, edited by Harriet Presser and Gita Sen. Oxford: Oxford University Press.

INEGI. 1999. "Estadísticas históricas de México." Mexico City: Instituto Nacional de Estadística y Geografía e Informática.

Jasso, Guillermina, and Mark R. Rosenzweig. 2006. "Characteristics of immigrants to the United States: 1820–2003." Pp. 328–58 in *A Companion to American Immigration*. Oxford, UK: Blackwell Publishing Ltd.

Jasso, Guillermina, Mark R. Rosenzweig, and James P. Smith. 1998. "The changing skill of new immigrants to the United States: Recent trends and their determinants." National Bureau of Economic Research Working Paper No. 6764. http://www.nber.org/papers/w6764

Jenkins, J. Craig. 1977. "Push/pull in recent Mexican migration to the US." *International Migration Review* 11:178–89.

Jiménez, Tomás R. 2010. *Replenished Ethnicity: Mexican Americans, Immigration, and Identity*. Berkeley: University of California Press.

Johnson, Kevin R. 2005. "The forgotten 'repatriation' of persons of Mexican ancestry and lessons for the 'War on Terror.'" *Pace Law Review* 26(1):1–26.

Jones, Charles I. 2002. "Sources of U.S. economic growth in a world of ideas." *American Economic Review* 92(1):220–39.

Jones, Richard C. 1995. *Ambivalent Journey: US Migration and Economic Mobility in North-Central Mexico.* Tucson: University of Arizona Press.

Jorgenson, Dale W., and Kevin J. Stiroh. 2000. "U.S. economic growth at the industry level." *American Economic Review* 90(2): 161–67.

Kanaiaupuni, Shawn Malia. 2000. "Reframing the migration question: An analysis of men, women, and gender in Mexico." *Social Forces* 78(4):1311–47.

Kandel, William, and Grace Kao. 2001. "The impact of temporary labor migration on Mexican children's educational aspirations and performance." *International Migration Review* 35(4):1205–31.

Kandel, William, and Douglas S. Massey 2002. "The culture of Mexican migration: A theoretical and empirical analysis." *Social Forces* 80(3):981–1004.

Kandel, William, and Emilio A. Parrado. 2005. "Restructuring of the US meat processing industry and new Hispanic migrant destinations." *Population and Development Review* 31(3):447–71.

Karlson, Kristian Bernt, Anders Holm, and Richard Breen. 2012. "Comparing regression coefficients between same-sample nested models using logit and probit: A new method." *Sociological Methodology* 42(1):286–313.

Kasinitz, Philip, John H. Mollenkopf, Mary C. Waters, and Jennifer Holdaway. 2008. *Inheriting the City: The Children of Immigrants Come of Age.* New York: Russell Sage.

Kastellec, Jonathan P., and Eduardo L. Leoni. 2007. "Using graphs instead of tables in political science." *Perspectives on Politics* 5(4):755–71.

Katz, Eliakim, and Oded Stark. 1986a. "Labor migration and risk aversion in less developed countries." *Journal of Labor Economics* 4(1):134–49.

King, Russell. 1976. "The evolution of international labour migration movements concerning the EEC." *Tijdschrift voor Economische en Sociale Geografie* 67(2):66–82.

King, Russell, and Ronald Skeldon. 2010. "'Mind the Gap!' Integrating approaches to internal and international migration." *Journal of Ethnic and Migration Studies* 36(10):1619–46.

Kirk, David S., and Andrew V. Papachristos. 2011. "Cultural mechanisms and the persistence of neighborhood violence." *American Journal of Sociology* 116(4):1190–1233.

Korinek, Kim, Barbara Entwisle, and Aree Jampaklay. 2005. "Through thick and thin: Layers of social ties and urban settlement among Thai migrants." *American Sociological Review* 70(5):779.

Koslowski, Rey. 2002. "Information technology, migration and border control." in *Paper for presentation at the Institute for Government Studies,* University of California, Berkeley.

Kossoudji, Sherrie A. 1992. "Playing cat and mouse at the US-Mexican border." *Demography* 29(2):159–80.

Krugman, Paul. 1993. "The uncomfortable truth about NAFTA: It's foreign policy, stupid." *Foreign Affairs* 72(5):13–19.

Kuznets, Simon. 1958. "Long swings in the growth of population and in related economic variables." *Proceedings of the American Philosophical Society* 102(1):25–52.

Latapí, Augustín Escobar, and Bryan R. Roberts. 1991. "Urban stratification, the middle classes, and economic change in Mexico." Pp. 91–113 in *Social Responses to Mexico's Economic Crisis of the 1980s*, edited by Mercedes González de la Rocha and Agustín Escobar Latapí. San Diego: Center for U.S.-Mexican Studies.

Lauby, Jennifer, and Oded Stark. 1988. "Individual migration as a family strategy: young women in the Philippines." *Population Studies* 42(3):473–86.

Lazarsfeld, Paul F. 1937. "Some remarks on the typological procedures in social research." *Zeitschrift für Sozialforschung* 6(2):119–39.

———. 1962. "The sociology of empirical social research." *American Sociological Review* 27(6):757–67.

Lazarsfeld, Paul F., and Neil W. Henry. 1968. *Latent Structure Analysis*. Boston: Houghton Mifflin.

Leach, Mark A., and Frank D. Bean. 2008. "The structure and dynamics of Mexican migration to new destinations in the United States." Pp. 51–74 in *New Faces in New Places: The Changing Geography of American Immigration*, edited by Douglas Massey. New York: Russell Sage.

Legendre, Pierre, and Louis Legendre. 1983. *Numerical Ecology*. Amsterdam: Elsevier.

Levitt, Peggy. 1998. "Social remittances: Migration driven local-level forms of cultural diffusion." *International Migration Review* 32(4): 926–48.

Levitt, Peggy. 2001a. *The Transnational Villagers*. Berkeley: University of California Press.

———. 2001b. "Transnational migration: Taking stock and future directions." *Global Networks* 1(3):195–216.

Levitt, Peggy, and Nina Glick Schiller. 2004. "Conceptualizing simultaneity: A transnational social field perspective on society." *International Migration Review* 38(3):1002–39.

Lieberson, Stanley, and Freda B. Lynn. 2002. "Barking up the wrong branch: Scientific alternatives to the current model of sociological science." *Annual Review of Sociology* 28:1–19.

Light, Ivan, and Edna Bonacich. 1991. *Immigrant Entrepreneurs: Koreans in Los Angeles, 1965–1982*. Berkeley: University of California Press.

Lin, Nan. 2000. "Inequality in Social Capital." *Contemporary Sociology* 29(6):785–95.

Lindstrom, David P., and Nathaniel Lauster. 2001. "Local economic opportunity and the competing risks of internal and U.S. migration in Zacatecas, Mexico." *International Migration Review* 35(4):1232–56.

Long, James E. 1980. "The effect of Americanization on earnings: Some evidence for women." *Journal of Political Economy* 88(3):620–29.

López Malo, Ernesto. 1960. *Ensayo sobre localización de la industria en México*. Mexico: UNAM.

Lowell, B. Lindsay, Frank D. Bean, and Rodolfo O. De La Garza. 1986. "The dilemmas of undocumented immigration: An analysis of the 1984 Simpson-Mazzoli vote." *Social Science Quarterly* 67(1):118–27.

Lozano-Ascencio, Fernando. 2000. "Migration strategies in urban contexts: Labor migration from Mexico City to the United States." In *XXII International Congress of the Latin American Studies Association*. Miami, FL.

———. 2001. "Nuevos orígenes de la migración mexicana a los Estados Unidos: inmigrantes urbanos versus inmigrantes rurales." *Scripta Nova: Revista Electronica de Geografía y Ciencas Sociales* 94(5). http://www.ub.edu/geocrit/sn-94-14.htm

Lozano-Ascencio, Fernando, Bryan R. Roberts, and Frank D. Bean. 1999. "The interconnectedness of internal and international migration: The case of the United States and Mexico." Pp. 138–61 in *Migration and Transnational Social Spaces*, edited by Ludger Pries. Aldershot: Ashgate.

Lucassen, Leo, and Aniek X. Smit. 2015. "The repugnant other: Soldiers, missionaries and aid workers as organizational migrants." *Journal of World History* 26(1): 1–39.

Lustig, Nora. 1982. "Distribución del ingreso consumo del alimentos: estructura, tendencias y requerimentos redistribuidos a nivel regional." *Demografía y economía* 16(2):107–45.

———. 2000. *Mexico: The Remaking of an Economy*. Washington, DC: Brookings Institution Press.

MacDonald, John S., and Leatrice D. MacDonald. 1964. "Chain migration, ethnic neighborhood formation and social networks." *Millbank Memorial Fund Quarterly* 42(1):82–97.

Macrae, C. Neil, and Galen V. Bodenhausen. 2000. "Social cognition: Thinking categorically about others." *Annual Review of Psychology* 51(1): 93–120.

Mahler, Sarah J., and Patricia R. Pessar. 2005. "Gender matters: Ethnographers bring gender from the periphery toward the core of migration studies." *International Migration Review* 40(1):27–63.

Malone, Nolan, Kaari Baluja, Joseph Costanzo, and Cynthia Davis. 2003. "The Foreign-Born Population in the United States: 2000." In *Census 2000 Brief*. Washington, DC: U.S. Department of Commerce, Economics and Statistics Administration.

Manski, Charles F. 1993. "Identification of endogenous social effects: The reflection problem." *Review of Economic Studies* 60(3):531–42.

Marcelli, Enrico A., and Wayne A. Cornelius. 2001. "The changing profile of Mexican migrants to the United States: New evidence from California and Mexico." *Latin American Research Review* 36:105–31.

Markowitz, Harry. 1952. "Portfolio selection." *Journal of Finance* 7(1):77–91.

———. 1959. *Portfolio Selection: Efficient Diversification of Investments*. New Haven, CT: Yale University Press.

Markusen, James R., and Stephen Zahniser. 1997. "Liberalization and incentives for labor migration: Theory with applications to NAFTA." National Bureau of Economic Research Working Paper No. 6232. http://www.nber.org/papers/w6232

Marsden, Peter V. 1987. "Core discussion networks of Americans." *American Sociological Review* 52(1):122–31.

Martin, Philip L. 1993. *Trade and Migration: NAFTA and Agriculture.* Washington, DC: Institute for International Economics.

————. 1997. "Do Mexican Agricultural Policies Stimulate Emigration?" Pp. 79–116 in *At the Crossroads: Mexican Migration and U.S. Policy*, edited by Frank D. Bean, Rodolfo O. de la Garza, Bryan R. Roberts, and Sidney Weintraub. New York: Rowman & Littlefield.

————. 2003. *Economic Integration and Migration: The Mexico-U.S. Case.* Helsinki: World Institute for Development Economics Research.

Massey, Douglas S. 1986. "The settlement process among Mexican migrants to the United States." *American Sociological Review* 51(5):670–84.

————. 1990a. "Social structure, household strategies, and the cumulative causation of migration." *Population Index* 56(1):3–26.

————. 1990b. "The social and economic origins of migration." *Annals of the American Academy of Political and Social Science* 510:60–72.

————. 1999. "International migration at the dawn of the twenty-first century: The role of the state." *Population and Development Review* 25(2):303–22.

————. 2007. *Categorically Unequal: The American Stratification System.* New York: Russell Sage.

Massey, Douglas S., Rafael Alarcón, Jorge Durand, and Humberto González. 1987. *Return to Aztlan: The Social Process of International Migration from Western Mexico.* Berkeley: University of California Press.

Massey, Douglas S., Joaquín Arango, Graeme Hugo, Ali Kouaouci, Adela Pellegrino, and J. Edward Taylor. 1993. "Theories of international migration: A review and appraisal." *Population and Development Review* 19(3):431–66.

————. 1994. "An evaluation of international migration theory: The North American case." *Population and Development Review* 20(4):699–751.

————. 1998. *Worlds in Motion: Understanding International Migration at the End of the Millennium.* Oxford: Oxford University Press.

Massey, Douglas S., and Chiara Capoferro. 2008. "The geographic diversification of American immigration." Pp. 25–50 in *New Faces in New Places: The Changing Geography of American Immigration*, edited by Douglas S. Massey. New York: Russell Sage.

Massey, Douglas, Katharine M. Donato, and Zai Liang. 1990. "Effects of the Immigration Reform and Control Act of 1986: Preliminary data from Mexico." Pp. 182–210 in *Undocumented Migration to the United States: IRCA and the Experience of the 1980s*, edited by Frank D. Bean, Barry Edmonston, and Jeffrey Passel. Washington, DC: Urban Institute.

Massey, Douglas S., Jorge Durand, and Nolan J. Malone. 2003. *Beyond Smoke and Mirrors: Mexican Immigration in an Era of Economic Integration*. New York: Russell Sage.

Massey, Douglas S., Jorge Durand, and Karen Pren. 2015. "Border enforcement and return migration by documented and undocumented Mexicans." *Journal of Ethnic and Migration Studies* 41(7):1015–40.

———. 2016. "Why border enforcement backfired?" *American Journal of Sociology* 121(5):1557–1600.

Massey, Douglas S., and Kristin E. Espinosa. 1997. "What's driving Mexico-U.S. migration? A theoretical, empirical, and policy analysis." *American Journal of Sociology* 102(4):939–99.

Massey, Douglas S., and Felipe García-España. 1987. "The social process of international migration." *Science* 237:733–38.

Massey, Douglas S., Luin Goldring, and Jorge Durand. 1994. "Continuities in transnational migration: An analysis of nineteen Mexican communities." *American Journal of Sociology* 99(6):1492–1533.

Massey, Douglas S., and Fernando Riosmena. 2010. "Undocumented migration from Latin America in an era of rising U.S. enforcement." *Annals of the American Academy of Political and Social Science* 630(1):294–321.

Massey, Douglas S., and Audrey Singer. 1995. "New estimates of undocumented Mexican migration and the probability of apprehension." *Demography* 32(2):203–13.

Massey, Douglas S., and J. Edward Taylor. 2004. "Back to the future: Immigration research, immigration policy, and globalization in the twenty-first century." Pp. 373–88 in *International Migration: Prospects and Policies in a Global Market*, edited by Douglas Massey and Edward Taylor. Oxford: Oxford University Press.

Massey, Douglas S., and Rene M. Zenteno. 1999. "The dynamics of mass migration." *Proceedings of the National Academy of Sciences of the United States of America* 96(9):5328–35.

———. 2000. "A validation of the ethnosurvey: The case of Mexico-US migration." *International Migration Review* 34(131):766–93.

Matlab. 2010. "The Language of Technical Computing." *The Mathworks*.

Mayr, Ernst. 1982. *The Growth of Biological Thought: Diversity, Evolution and Inheritance*. Cambridge, MA: Harvard University Press.

McCall, Leslie. 2005. "The complexity of intersectionality." *Signs* 30(3):1771–1800.

McPherson, J. Miller., and Lynn Smith-Lovin. 1987. "Homophily in voluntary organizations: Status distance and the composition of face-to-face groups." *American Sociological Review* 52(3):370–79.

McPherson, J. Miller, Lynn Smith-Lovin, and James M. Cook. 2001. "Birds of a feather: Homophily in social networks." *Annual Review of Sociology* 27:415–44.

Mendoza, Jorge Eduardo. 2002. "Agglomeration economies and urban manufacturing growth in the northern border cities of Mexico." *Economia Mexicana NUEVA EPOCA* 11(1):163–90.

Meyers, Eytan. 2000. "Theories of international immigration policy—A comparative analysis." *International Migration Review* 34(4):1245–82.

Miller, George A. 1956. "The magical number seven, plus or minus two: Some limits on our capacity for processing information." *Psychological Review* 63(2):81.

Milligan, Glenn W., and Martha C. Cooper. 1988. "A study of standardization of variables in cluster analysis." *Journal of Classification* 5:181–204.

Mincer, Jacob A. 1974. "Schooling and earnings." Pp. 41–63 in *Schooling, Experience, and Earnings*. New York: Columbia University Press.

Mines, Richard. 1981. "Developing a community tradition of migration: A field study in rural Zacatecas, Mexico and California settlement areas." La Jolla: University of California at San Diego, Program in the United States-Mexican Studies.

Mines, Richard, and de Janvry, Alain. 1982. "Migration to the United States and Mexican rural development: A case study." *American Journal of Agricultural Economics* 64(3):444–54.

Moinester, Margot. 2015. "Beyond the border and into the heartland: Inequality in the spatial patterning of U.S. immigration enforcement." Unpublished manuscript. Cambridge, MA: Harvard University.

Molzahn, Cory, Viridiana Ríos, and David A. Shirk. 2012. "Drug violence in Mexico: Data and analysis through 2011." Trans-Border Institute, University of San Diego, San Diego.

Morales, Rebecca. 1983. "Transitional labor: Undocumented workers in the Los Angeles automobile industry." *International Migration Review* 17(4):570–96.

Moreno-Brid, Juan Carlos, and Jaime Ros. 2009. *Development and Growth in the Mexican Economy: A Historical Perspective*. Oxford and New York: Oxford University Press.

Moretti, Enrico. 1999. "Social networks and migrations: Italy 1876–1913." *International Migration Review* 33(3):640–57.

Morgan, Stephen L., and Christopher Winship. 2007. *Counterfactuals and Causal Inference: Methods and Principles for Social Research*. New York: Cambridge University Press.

Morton, Adam David. 2013. *Revolution and State in Modern Mexico: The Political Economy of Uneven Development*. Lanham, MD: Rowman & Littlefield.

Munshi, Kaivan. 2003. "Networks in the modern economy: Mexican migrants in the U.S. labor market." *Quarterly Journal of Economics* 118(2):549–99.

Muthén, Bengt, and Linda K. Muthén. 2000. "Integrating person-centered and variable-centered analyses: Growth mixture modeling with latent trajectory classes." *Alcoholism: Clinical and Experimental Research* 24:882–91.

Myrdal, Gunnar. 1957a. *Economic Theory and Under-developed Regions*. London: Methuen.

———. 1957b. *Rich Lands and Poor Lands*. New York: Harper & Row.

Neuman, Kristin E., and Marta Tienda. 1994. "The settlement and secondary migration patterns of legalized immigrants: Insights from administrative records." Pp. 187–226 in *Immigration and Ethnicity: The Integration of America's Newest Arrivals*, edited by Barry Edmonston and Jeffrey Passel. Washington, DC: Urban Institute Press.

Nevins, Joseph. 2007. "Dying for a cup of coffee? Migrant deaths in the U.S.-Mexico border region in a neoliberal age." *Geopolitics* 12(2):228–47.

Nuijten, Monique. 2003. "Family property and the limits of intervention: The Article 27 reforms and the PROCEDE programme in Mexico." *Development and Change* 34(3):475–97.

O'brien, Robert M. 2007. "A caution regarding rules of thumb for variance inflation factors." *Quality & Quantity* 41(5):673–90.

Orrenius, Pia M. 2001. "Illegal immigration and enforcement along the US-Mexico border: An overview." In *Economic and Financial Review–Federal Reserve Bank of Dallas*. Dallas, TX: Federal Reserve Bank of Dallas.

Ortiz, Vilma. 1996. "Migration and marriage among Puerto Rican women." *International Migration Review* 30(2):460–84.

Palloni, Alberto, Douglas S. Massey, Miguel Ceballos, Kristin Espinosa, and Michael Spittel. 2001. "Social capital and international migration: A test using information on family networks." *American Journal of Sociology* 106(5):1262–98.

Passel, Jeffrey S. 2005. "Unauthorized migrants: numbers and characteristics." Pew Research Center Report. http://www.pewhispanic.org/files/reports/46.pdf

Passel, Jeffrey S., D'Vera Cohn, and Ana Gonzalez-Barrera. 2012. "Net migration from Mexico falls to zero—and perhaps less." Pew Research Center Report. http://www.pewhispanic.org/2012/04/23/net-migration-from-mexico-falls-to-zero-and-perhaps-less/

Passel, Jeffrey S., and Jens Manuel Krogstad. 2014. "5 facts about illegal immigration in the U.S." Pew Research Center Report. http://pewrsr.ch/1LoS9Qr

Passel, Jeffrey S., and Karen A. Woodrow. 1984. "Geographic distribution of undocumented immigrants: Estimates of undocumented aliens counted in the 1980 census by state." *International Migration Review* 18(3):642–71.

Pastor, Manuel. 1998. "Pesos, policies, and predictions: Why the crisis, why the surprise, and why the recovery?" Pp. 119–47 in *The Post-NAFTA Political Economy: Mexico and the Western Hemisphere*, edited by Carol Wise. University Park: Pennsylvania State University Press.

Pastor, Manuel, and Carol Wise. 1998. "Mexican-style neoliberalism: State policy and distributional stress." Pp. 41–81 in *The Post-NAFTA Political Economy: Mexico and the Western Hemisphere*, edited by Carol Wise. University Park: Pennsylvania State University Press.

Paul, Anju Mary. 2011. "Stepwise international migration: A multistage migration pattern for the aspiring migrant." *American Journal of Sociology* 116(6):1842–86.

——. 2013. "Good help is hard to find: The differentiated mobilisation of migrant social capital among Filipino domestic workers." *Journal of Ethnic and Migration Studies* 39(5):719–39.

Pedraza, Silvia. 1991. "Women and migration: The social consequences of gender." *Annual Review of Sociology* 17:303–25.

Pérez, Ramón. 1991. *Diary of an Undocumented Migrant*. Houston, TX: Arte Publico Press.

Pessar, Patricia R. 1982. "The role of households in international migration and the case of US-bound migration from the Dominican Republic." *International Migration Review* 26(2):342–64.

Pessar, Patricia R., and Sarah J. Mahler. 2003. "Transnational migration: Bringing gender in." *International Migration Review* 37(3):812–46.

Piore, Michael J. 1979. *Birds of Passage: Migrant Labor and Industrial Societies*. Cambridge: Cambridge University Press.

Polaski, Sandra. 2004. "Mexican employment, productivity and income a decade after NAFTA." Carnegie Endowment for International Peace Report. http://carnegieendowment.org/2004/02/25/mexican-employment-productivity-and-income-decade-after-nafta.

Portes, Alejandro. 1997. "Immigration theory for a new century: Some problems and opportunities." *International Migration Review* 31(4):799–825.

Portes, Alejandro, and Robert L. Bach. 1985. *Latin Journey: Cuban and Mexican Immigrants in the United States*. Berkeley: University of California Press.

Portes, Alejandro, Luis E. Guarnizo, and Patricia Landolt. 1999. "The study of transnationalism: pitfalls and promise of an emergent research field." *Ethnic and Racial Studies* 22(2):217–37.

Portes, Alejandro, and Julia Sensenbrenner. 1993. "Embeddedness and immigration: Notes on the social determinants of economic action." *American Journal of Sociology* 98(6):1320–50.

Portes, Alejandro, and John Walton. 1981. *Labor, Class, and the International System*. New York: Academic Press.

Quételet, Adolphe. 1842. *A Treatise on Man and the Development of His Faculties*. Cambridge: Cambridge University Press.

R Core Team. 2010. *R: A Language and Environment for Statistical Computing*. R Foundation for Statistical Computing, Vienna, Austria. http://www.R-project.org/

Ragin, Charles C. 1987. *The Comparative Method: Moving Beyond Qualitative and Quantitative Strategies*. Berkeley and Los Angeles: University of California Press.

——— 2000. *Fuzzy-Set Social Science*. Chicago: University of Chicago Press.

———. 2008. *Redesigning Social Inquiry: Fuzzy Sets and Beyond*. Chicago: University of Chicago Press.

Randall, Laura. 2006. *Changing Structure of Mexico: Political, Social, and Economic Prospects*. New York: M.E. Sharpe.

Raudenbush, Stephen, and Anthony Bryk. 1986. "A hierarchical model for studying school effects." *Sociology of Education* 59:1–17.

Redburn, Steve, Peter Reuter, and Malay Majmundar. 2012. *Budgeting for Immigration Enforcement: A Path to Better Performance*. Washington, DC: National Academies Press.

Reich, Robert B. 2010. *Aftershock: The Next Economy and America's Future*. New York: Alfred A. Knopf.

Reichert, Joshua S. 1981. "The migrant syndrome: Seasonal U.S. wage labor and rural development in central Mexico." *Human Organization* 40(1):56–66.

Reichert, Joshua S., and Douglas S. Massey. 1979. "Patterns of US migration from a Mexican sending community: A comparison of legal and illegal migrants." *International Migration Review* 13(4):599–623.

Reisler, Mark. 1976. *By the Sweat of Their Brow: Mexican Immigrant Labor in the United States, 1900–1940*. Westport, CT: Greenwood Publishing Group.

Renzulli, Linda A., Howard Aldrich, and James Moody. 2000. "Family matters: Gender, networks, and entrepreneurial outcomes." *Social Forces* 79(2):523–46.

Richter, Susan M., J. Edward Taylor, and Antonio Yúnez-Naude. 2007. "Impacts of policy reforms on labor migration from rural Mexico to the United States." Pp. 269–88 in *Mexican Immigration to the United States*, edited by George J. Borjas. Chicago: University of Chicago Press.

Ricketts, Erol. 1987. "U.S. investment and immigration from the Caribbean." *Social Problems* 34(4):374–87.

Riley, Nancy E., and Robert W. Gardner. 1993. "Migration decisions: The role of gender." Pp. 195–206 in *Internal Migration of Women in Developing Countries*. New York: United Nations.

Ríos, Viridiana. 2013. "Why did Mexico become so violent? A self-reinforcing violent equilibrium caused by competition and enforcement." *Trends in Organized Crime* 16(2):138–55.

———. 2014. "The role of drug-related violence and extortion in promoting Mexican migration: Unexpected consequences of a drug war." *Latin American Research Review* 49(3):199–217.

Riosmena, Fernando, and Douglas S. Massey. 2012. "Pathways to El Norte: origins, destinations, and characteristics of Mexican migrants to the United States." *International Migration Review* 46(1):3–36.

Ritchey, P. Neal. 1976. "Explanations of migration." *Annual Review of Sociology* 2:363–404.

Rizzo, Socrates C. 1984. "Generation and allocation of oil economic surpluses." Pp. 99–128 in *The Political Economy of Income Distribution in Mexico*, edited by Pedro Aspe and Paul E. Sigmund. New York: Holmes & Meier.

Roberts, Bryan R., and Erin Hamilton. 2007. "La nueva geografía de la emigración: zonas emergentes de atracción y expulsión, continuidad y cambio." In *El país transnacional: migración mexicana y cambio social a través de la frontera*, edited by Marina Ariza and Alejandro Portes. Mexico City: Institute for Social Studies of the National Autonomous University of Mexico.

Roberts, Bryan R., and Agustín Escobar Latapí. 1997. "Mexican social and economic policy and emigration." Pp. 47–78 in *At the Crossroads: Mexican Migration and US Policy*, edited by Frank D. Bean, Rodolfo O. de la Garza, Bryan R. Roberts, and Sydney Weintraub. Lanham, MD: Rowman & Littlefield.

Roberts, Bryan R., Reanne Frank, and Fernando Lozano-Ascencio. 1999. "Transnational migrant communities and Mexican migration to the U.S." *Ethnic and Racial Studies* 22(2):238–66.

Roberts, Kenneth D. 1982. "Agrarian structure and labor mobility in rural Mexico." *Population and Development Review* 8(2):299–322.

Rodríguez Kuri, Ariel. 2011. "Challenges, political opposition, economic disaster, natural disaster and democratization, 1968 to 2000." Pp. 493–504 in *A Companion to Mexican History and Culture*, edited by William H. Beezley. Oxford, UK: Wiley-Blackwell.

Rosenblum, Marc R. 2003. "The intermestic politics of immigration policy: Lessons from the Bracero program." *Political Power and Social Theory* 16:139–84.

Rouse, Roger. 1991. "Mexican migration and the social space of postmodernism." *Diaspora: A Journal of Transnational Studies* 1(1):8–23.

Rytina, Nancy. 2002. "IRCA legalization effects: Lawful permanent residence and naturalization through 2001." Office of Policy and Planning, Statistics Division, US Immigration and Naturalization Service.

Sánchez Reaza, Javier, and Andrés Rodríguez Pose. 2002. "The impact of trade liberalization on regional disparities in Mexico." *Growth and Change* 33(1):72–90.

Sassen, Saskia. 1988. *The Mobility of Labor and Capital*. Cambridge: Cambridge University Press.

———. 1991. *The Global City: New York, London, Tokyo*. Princeton, NJ: Princeton University Press.

———. 1998. *Globalization and Its Discontents: Essays on the New Mobility of People and Money*. New York: New Press.

Schiller, Nina Glick, Linda Basch, and Cristina Szanton Blanc. 1995. "From immigrant to transmigrant: Theorizing transnational migration." *Anthropological Quarterly* 68(1):48–63.

Schultz, Theodore W. 1961. "Investment in human capital." *American Economic Review* 51(1):1–17.

Segura, Denise A. 1991. "Ambivalence or continuity?: Motherhood and employment among Chicanas and Mexican immigrant women workers." *Aztlan: A Journal of Chicano Studies* 20:119–50.

Sen, Amartya. 1980. "Description as choice." *Oxford Economic Papers* 32(3):353–69.

———. 1983. "Economics and the Family." *Asian Development Review* 1(2):14–26.

———. 1990. "Gender and cooperative conflicts." Pp. 123–49 in *Persistent Inequalities: Women and World Development*, edited by Irene Tinker. New York: Oxford University Press.

Sharpe, William. 1964. "Capital asset prices: A theory of market equilibrium under conditions of risk." *Journal of Finance* 19(3):425–42.

Singer, Audrey, and Douglas S. Massey. 1998. "The social process of undocumented border crossing among Mexican migrants." *International Migration Review* 32(3):561–92.

Sinke, Suzanne M. 2006. "Gender and immigration." Pp. 289–308 in *A Companion to American Immigration*. Malden, MA and Oxford: Blackwell.

Sjaastad, Larry A. 1962. "The costs and returns of human migration." *Journal of Political Economy* 70S:80–93.

Skeldon, Ronald. 2006. "Interlinkages between internal and international migration and development in the Asian region." *Population, Space and Place* 12(1):15–30.

Smith, James P., and Barry Edmonston. 1997. *The New Americans: Economic, Demographic, and Fiscal Effects of Immigration.* Washington, DC: National Academies Press.

Smith, Robert C. 2006. *Mexican New York: Transnational Lives of New Immigrants.* Berkeley: University of California Press.

Somers, Margaret R. 1992. "Narrativity, narrative identity, and social action: Rethinking English working-class formation." *Social Science History* 16(4):591–630.

Sorensen, Elaine, and Frank D. Bean. 1994. "The Immigration Reform and Control Act and the wages of Mexican origin workers: Evidence from Current Population Surveys." *Social Science Quarterly* 75(1):1–17.

Sorg, Christian, Valentin Riedl, Mark Mühlau, Vince D. Calhoun, Tom Eichele, Leonhard Läer, Alexander Drzezga, Hans Förstl, Alexander Kurz, and Claus Zimmer. 2007. "Selective changes of resting-state networks in individuals at risk for Alzheimer's disease." *Proceedings of the National Academy of Sciences* 104(47):18760–65.

Sørlie, Therese, Robert Tibshirani, Joel Parker, Trevor Hastie, J. S. Marron, Andrew Nobel, Shibing Deng, Hilde Johnsen, Robert Pesich, and Stephanie Geisler. 2003. "Repeated observation of breast tumor subtypes in independent gene expression data sets." *Proceedings of the National Academy of Sciences* 100(14):8418–23.

Stangor, Charles, Laure Lynch, Changming Duan, and Beth Glas. 1992. "Categorization of individuals on the basis of multiple social features." *Journal of Personality and Social Psychology* 62(2):207.

Stark, Oded. 1984. "Migration decision making: A review article." *Journal of Development Economics* 14:251–59.

———. 1991. *The Migration of Labor.* Oxford: Basil Blackwell.

Stark, Oded, and David E. Bloom. 1985. "The new economics of labor migration." *American Economic Review* 75(2):173–78.

Stark, Oded, and David Levhari. 1982. "On migration and risk in LDCs." *Economic Development and Cultural Change* 31:191–96.

Stark, Oded, and J. Edward Taylor. 1989. "Relative deprivation and international migration." *Demography* 26(1):1–14.

———. 1991. "Migration incentives, migration types: The role of relative deprivation." *Economic Journal* 101(408):1163–78.

Stark, Oded, J. Edward Taylor, and Shlomo Yitzhaki. 1986. "Remittances and inequality." *Economic Journal* 96(383):722–40.

———. 1988. "Migration, remittances and inequality: A sensitivity analysis using the extended Gini index." *Journal of Development Economics* 28:309–22.

Stark, Oded, and Shlomo Yitzhaki. 1988. "Labor migration as a response to relative deprivation." *Journal of Population Economics* 1:57–70.

Stier, Haya, and Marta Tienda. 1992. "Family, work and women: The labor supply of Hispanic immigrant wives." *International Migration Review* 26(4):1291–1313.

Stiglitz, Joseph E. 2012. *The Price of Inequality*. New York: W.W. Norton.

———. 2004. *The Roaring Nineties: A New History of the World's Most Prosperous Decade*. New York: W.W. Norton.

———. 2007. *Making Globalization Work*. New York: W.W. Norton.

———. 2010. *Freefall: America, Free Markets, and the Sinking of the World Economy*. New York: W.W. Norton.

Suárez-Orozco, Carola, and Marcelo M. Suárez-Orozco. 2009. *Children of Immigration*. Cambridge, MA: Harvard University Press.

Sullivan, Laura. 2009. "Enforcing nonenforcement: Countering the threat posed to sanctuary laws by the inclusion of immigration records in the national crime information center database." *California Law Review* 97(2):567–600.

Swedberg, Richard. 2014. *The Art of Social Theory*. Princeton, NJ: Princeton University Press.

Sykes, Christopher. 1995. *No Ordinary Genius: The Illustrated Richard Feynman*. New York: W.W. Norton.

Taylor, J. Edward. 1984. *Migration networks and risks in household labor decisions: A study of migration from two Mexican villages*. Ph.D. thesis, University of California, Berkeley.

———. 1986. "Differential migration, networks, information and risk." *Research in Human Capital and Development: Migration, Human Capital and Development* 4:147–71.

———. 1992. "Remittances and inequality reconsidered: Direct, indirect, and intertemporal effects." *Journal of Policy Modeling* 14(2):187–208.

Taylor, Paul, Mark Hugo Lopez, Jeffrey S. Passel, and Seth Motel. 2011. "Unauthorized immigrants: Length of residency, patterns of parenthood." Pew Research Center Report. http://www.pewhispanic.org/2011/12/01/unauthorized -immigrants-length-of-residency-patterns-of-parenthood/

Taylor, Paul S. 1935. "Songs of the Mexican migration." *Puro Mexicano (Publications of the Texas Folklore Society)* 12:221–45.

Telles, Edward E., and Vilma Ortiz. 2008. *Generations of Exclusion: Mexican Americans, Assimilation and Race*. New York: Russell Sage.

Thomas, Dorothy Swaine. 1941. "Social and economic aspects of Swedish population movements, 1750–1933." *Annals of the American Academy of Political and Social Science* 215(1):234–35.

Tiano, Susan. 1984. "Maquiladoras, women's work, and unemployment in Northern Mexico." *Aztlan: A Journal of Chicano Studies* 15:341–78.

Tibshirani, Robert, Trevor Hastie, Balasubramanian Narasimhan, and Gilbert Chu. 2002. "Diagnosis of multiple cancer types by shrunken centroids of gene expression." *Proceedings of the National Academy of Sciences* 99(10):6567–72.

Tienda, Marta, and Ronald Angel. 1982. "Headship and household composition among blacks, Hispanics, and other whites." *Social Forces* 61(2):508–31.

Tienda, Marta, and Jennifer Glass. 1985. "Household structure and labor force participation of black, Hispanic, and white mothers." *Demography* 22(3): 381–94.

Tilly, Charles. 2002. *Stories, Identities, and Political Change.* Lanham, MD: Rowman & Littlefield.

———. 2007. "Trust networks in transnational migration." *Sociological Forum* 22(1): 3–24.

Timmer, Ashley S., and Jeffrey G. Williams. 1998. "Immigration policy prior to the 1930s: Labor markets, policy interactions, and globalization backlash." *Population and Development Review* 24(4):739–71.

Todaro, Michael P. 1969. "A model of labor migration and urban unemployment in less developed countries." *American Economic Review* 59(1):138–48.

———. 1976. *Internal Migration in Developing Countries.* Geneva: International Labor Office.

———. 1980. "Internal migration in developing countries: A survey." Pp. 361–402 in *Population and Economic Change in Developing Countries.* Chicago: University of Chicago Press.

Todaro, Michael P., and Lydia Maruszko. 1987. "Illegal migration and U.S. immigration reform: A conceptual framework." *Population and Development Review* 13(1):101–14.

Unger, Kurt. 2005. "Regional economic development and Mexican out-migration." National Bureau of Economic Research Working Paper No. 11432. http://www.nber.org/papers/w11432

Van Hook, Jennifer, and Frank D. Bean. 1998. "Estimating unauthorized Mexican migration to the United States: Issues and results." Pp. 511–50 in *Migration between Mexico and the United States, Binational Study.* Mexico City and Washington, DC: Mexican Ministry of Foreign Affairs and U.S. Commission on Immigration Reform.

Vertovec, Steven. 2004. "Migrant transnationalism and modes of transformation." *International Migration Review* 38(3):970–1001.

Villarreal, Andrés, and Erin R. Hamilton. 2012. "Rush to the border? Market liberalization and urban- and rural-origin internal migration in Mexico." *Social Science Research* 41(5):1275–91.

Waldinger, Roger. 1989. "Immigration and urban change." *Annual Review of Sociology* 15:211–32.

Wallerstein, Immanuel. 1974. *The Modern World System, Capitalist Agriculture and the Origins of the European World Economy in the Sixteenth Century.* New York: Academic Press.

Warren, Robert. 2000. "Annual estimates of the unauthorized population residing in the United States and components of changes: 1987 to 1997." Washington, DC: U.S. Immigration and Naturalization Service.

Waters, Mary C. 1990. *Ethnic Options: Choosing Ethnic Identities in America.* Berkeley: University of California Press.

Watson, Tara. 2013. "Enforcement and immigrant location choice." National Bureau of Economic Research Working Paper. No 19626. http://www.nber.org/papers/w19626

Weber, Max. 1978 [1922]. *Economy and Society: An Outline of Interpretive Sociology*. Berkeley: University of California Press.

Weintraub, E. Roy. 1993. "Neoclassical economics." *The Concise Encyclopedia of Economics*. http://www.econlib.org/library/Enc1/NeoclassicalEconomics.html

White, Michael J., Frank D. Bean, and Thomas J. Espenshade. 1990. "The US 1986 Immigration Reform and Control Act and undocumented migration to the United States." *Population Research and Policy Review* 9:93–116.

Wiest, Raymond E. 1973. "Wage-labor migration and the household in a Mexican town." *Journal of Anthropological Research* 29:180–209.

———. 1984. "External dependency and the perpetuation of temporary migration to the United States." Pp. 110–35 in *Patterns of Undocumented Migration: Mexico and the United States*, edited by Richard C. Jones. Totowa, NJ: Rowman and Allanheld.

Wise, Carol. 1998. *The Post-NAFTA Political Economy: Mexico and the Western Hemisphere*. University Park: Pennsylvania State University Press.

Wishnie, Michael J. 2004. "State and local police enforcement of immigration laws." *University of Pennsylvania Journal of Constitutional Law* 4:1084.

Wong, Rebeca, and Ruth E. Levine. 1992. "The effect of household structure on women's economic activity and fertility: Evidence from recent mothers in urban Mexico." *Economic Development and Cultural Change* 41(1):89–102.

Wood, Charles H. 1981. "Structural changes and household strategies: A conceptual framework for the study of rural migration." *Human Organization* 40(4):338–44.

Woodrow, Karen, Jeffrey S. Passel, and Robert Warren. 1987. "Preliminary estimates of undocumented immigration to the United States, 1980–1986: Analysis of the June 1986 Current Population Survey." Paper presented at the annual meeting of the American Statistical Association, San Francisco, CA, 1987.

Woodrow-Lafield, Karen A. 1994. "Potential sponsorship by IRCA-legalized immigrants." Washington, DC: U.S. Commission on Immigration Reform.

Woodruff, Christopher, and Rene Zenteno. 2007. "Migration networks and microenterprises in Mexico." *Journal of Development Economics* 82(2):509–28.

World Bank. 1996. "Mexico, Rural Poverty." In *Report 15058-ME*. Washington, DC.

Xie, Yu. 2007. "Otis Dudley Duncan's legacy: The demographic approach to quantitative reasoning in social science." *Research in Social Stratification and Mobility* 25:141–56.

Yang, Dean. 2008. "International migration, remittances and household investment: Evidence from Phillipine migrants." *Economic Journal* 118:591–630.

Yeung, Ka Yee, David R. Haynor, and Walter L. Ruzzo. 2001. "Validating clustering for gene expression data." *Bioinformatics* 17:309–18.

Yùñez-Naude, Antonio. 2003. "The dismantling of CONASUPO, a Mexican state trader in agriculture." *World Economy* 26(1):97–122.

Yúñez-Naude, Antonio, and Fernando Barceinas. 2002. "Lessons from NAFTA: The case of NAFTA's agricultural sector." Office of the Chief Economist for Latin America and the Caribbean Report. Washington, DC: World Bank. http://web.worldbank.org/archive/website00955A/WEB/PDF/YUNEZ_TE.PDF

———. 2003. "The agriculture of Mexico after ten years of NAFTA implementation." Unpublished paper prepared for the Carnegie Endowment for International Peace.

Zabin, Carol, and Sallie Hughes. 1995. "Economic integration and labor flows: Stage migration in farm labor markets in Mexico and the United States." *International Migration Review* 29(2):395–422.

Zabin, Carol, Michael Kearney, David Runsten, and Anna Garcia. 1993. *A New Cycle of Poverty: Mixtec Migrants in California Agriculture*. Davis: California Institute for Rural Studies.

Zedillo, Ernesto 1986. "Mexico's recent balance-of-payments experience and prospects for growth." *World Development* 14(8):963–91.

Zelinsky, Wilbur. 1971. "The hypothesis of the mobility transition." *Geographical Review* 61(2):219–49.

Zepeda, Eduardo, Timothy A. Wise, and Kevin P. Gallagher. 2009. "Rethinking trade policy for development: Lessons from Mexico under NAFTA." Carnegie Endowment for International Peace Report. http://carnegieendowment.org/files/nafta_trade_development.pdf

Zhou, Min. 2010. *Chinatown: The Socioeconomic Potential of an Urban Enclave*. Philadelphia: Temple University Press.

Zolberg, Aristide R. 1989. "The next waves: Migration theory for a changing world." *International Migration Review* 23(3):403–30.

INDEX

Page numbers in italics refer to figures or tables.

CPSIA information can be obtained
at www.ICGtesting.com
Printed in the USA
JSHW081013070523
41357JS00002B/4